Cinematic Photoreal Environments in Unreal Engine 5

Create captivating worlds and unleash the power of cinematic tools without coding

Giovanni Visai

Cinematic Photoreal Environments in Unreal Engine 5

Group Product Manager: Rohit Rajkumar
Publishing Product Manager: Bhavya Rao
Book Project Manager: Shagun Saini
Senior Editor: Rakhi Patel
Technical Editor: Simran Ali
Copy Editor: Safis Editing
Indexer: Manju Arasan
Production Designer: Alishon Mendonca
DevRel Marketing Coordinators: Anamika Singh and Nivedita Pandey

First published: May 2024

Production reference: 1170424

Published by Packt Publishing Ltd.

Grosvenor House
11 St Paul's Square
Birmingham
B3 1RB, UK

ISBN 978-1-80324-411-2

www.packtpub.com

To the shimmer of Giulia's gaze, my beloved wife, who has whisked me away across the globe, unveiling the secrets of happiness.

And to Bianca, the mysterious muse I can't wait to meet.

- Giovanni

Contributors

About the author

Giovanni Visai is an Unreal Engine specialist, game designer, and teacher with extensive experience in real-time projects, both in gaming and virtual production. During the last five years, he has led a team in developing interactive solutions, software, and virtual production projects in Unreal Engine. In January 2023, he was selected by Epic Games to be part of the World building fellowship EMEA as TA. He is a passionate teacher. He teaches virtual production and gaming storytelling at some of the best universities in Italy, such as Politecnico di Milano and NABA. He has an MA in screenplay and directing at Scuole Civiche Milano and a BA in computer-generated animation at IED Milan. He has worked in the game industry as an environment artist and lead artist and now works as an Unreal Engine supervisor and mentor.

I want to thank all the people who have been close to me and supported me on this extraordinary journey. Thanks to everyone involved in the development process of this book, especially the Packt team. Thanks to Marco Secchi, who gave me the opportunity to write a book. Thanks to Emanuele Lomello and Leonardo Villa for their friendly support, and last, but not least, thanks to metal music.

About the reviewer

Francesca Simoni is a 3D artist with extensive experience in Unreal Engine. Having graduated in new technologies for applied arts from the NABA Academy of Fine Arts in Milan, she has worked in the world of agencies and advertising, as well as video games. Her skills do not only stop at the 3D world but are enhanced by her 2D drawing and illustration abilities.

Table of Contents

3

Exploring Unreal Engine 5 Project Structure   63

4

Importing and Working with Assets   85

5

Mastering Materials and Shading   117

Part 3: Cinematic Fundamentals and Rendering

11

12

13

Preface

Unreal Engine 5 is conquering all industries thanks to its real-time technology and quality. Being able to use Unreal Engine 5 to represent environments in a realistic way can improve any kind of pipeline, from marketing to high-end movie production, and make previsualization faster than ever. Last but not least, Unreal Engine 5 skills are some of the most searched job descriptions on the web.

Starting from Unreal Engine 5 fundamentals to achieving epic photorealistic environments, this book takes you on a learning journey through the creation of a personal cinematic shot in a great new world.

The book is divided into three parts that cover all the processes behind the creation of an environment in Unreal Engine 5. Starting from the very beginning with installing the Engine and learning about its potential, the book scales up the process with every page in a way that is easy to follow. You will generate a variety of different outputs that will be bigger (in terms of quantity and quality) every time than the previous one. After completing the first part and achieving some realistic shots of a single object, you will dive into the world of landscapes, procedural material and foliage, the Landmass plugin, and water tools by working on a first attempt at creating an environment using Megascans assets. At this point, you will know everything you need to create a great and realistic environment. The third and last part is fully dedicated to improving the visual aspect of the environment by crafting cinematic shots and enhancing the final quality with postprocessing effects and Niagara.

By the end of this book, you will be able to create outstanding and realistic environments by using the powerful tools that Unreal Engine 5 provides. You will also have understood the importance of filming and composition in world-building and have gained the ability to export a high-resolution video. Finally, you will be able to add a creative and personal touch to your worlds.

Everything you learn in this book will give you a strong knowledge of the Unreal Engine 5 environment creation fundamentals as a starting point to improve your skills in real-time technologies.

Who this book is for

If you are a creative director, a designer, or a creator with a passion for technology and CGI, this book is for you. World-building and storytelling are changing thanks to all the new tools that Epic Games and Unreal Engine are coming out with. With this book, you will learn how simple it is to create outstanding environments and visuals. After reading this book, you will be able to implement Unreal Engine 5 in your pipeline or creative process. If you are a game developer or a tech artist, this book can help you to understand what the environment artist workflow is and how to optimize performance on the art side.

What this book covers

Chapter 1, Creating Your First Project in Unreal Engine 5, teaches you how to download and install Unreal Engine 5. You will discover the importance of the learning portal and how to use the marketplace. By the end of the chapter, you will be able to create a project based on a temple, as well as a blank one.

Chapter 2, Navigating through the Unreal Engine 5 Interface, explores the Unreal Engine user interface. Throughout the chapter, you will be introduced to all the features that are going to be explored in depth throughout the book. By the end of this chapter, you will know a bunch of essential shortcuts; you will also be able to navigate the main Viewport and manipulate objects with the Gizmo.

Chapter 3, Exploring the Unreal Engine 5 Project Structure, teaches you how Unreal Engine works and where to find folders and files. By the end of this chapter, you will be confident with carrying out the saving process.

Chapter 4, Importing and Working with Assets, teaches you how to import a 3D model and all the characteristics that a 3D asset must have to be correctly imported. By the end of this chapter, you will be able to import and save any kind of assets.

Chapter 5, Mastering Materials and Shading, teaches you the fundamentals of PBR shading in Unreal Engine 5. Starting with very simple examples, by the end of the chapter, you will be able to create a complex master material with material functions.

Chapter 6, Illuminating Your World with Lighting, teaches you how to use the lighting system in Unreal Engine 5 to create stunning lighting for your objects and environments. By the end of this chapter, you will be able to create a variety of different types of lighting for single and multiple objects and massive environments.

Chapter 7, Exploring Nanite, RVTs, and the World Partition Tool, teaches you what ray tracing means, how lumen is revolutionizing real-time rendering, and the difference between these two systems. You will also learn what Nanite is and why it is revolutionizing the industry, as well as how the World Partition tool works.

Chapter 8, Utilizing the Megascans Library, teaches you how to use the Megascans assets library with the Quixel Bridge plugin. By the end of this chapter, you will be able to create a simple environment by using Megascans assets.

Chapter 9, Mastering Landscape and Terrain, teaches you how to create and manage a landscape, create a landscape material, and use foliage tools. At the end of this chapter, you will be able to manage a landscape in all its aspects, including landscape auto-material and procedural foliage.

Chapter 10, Creating Diverse Environments with Plugins, teaches you how to activate and use the Landmass plugin to modify the landscape shape. You will also learn how to activate and use the Water Tools plugin to add a water system to your environment. By the end of this chapter, you will be able to create a landscape scenario from the draft by using the Landmass tool and will be able to modify the morphology of the landscape to add rivers, lakes, and oceans.

Chapter 11, Crafting Cinematic Shots with Cameras and Sequencer, teaches you how to create and set up a cine camera actor and how to create and use a sequencer inside Unreal Engine 5. By the end of this chapter, you will be able to use a cine camera actor, compose a frame, animate a camera inside a Sequencer and edit complex cinematic shots directly inside Unreal Engine.

Chapter 12, Enhancing Scenes with Post-Processing and Niagara, teaches you what a PPV is and how to use it. You will understand how exposure control works and learn how to modify the visual appearance of the frame with PPV. You will also learn the fundamentals of Niagara. By the end of this chapter, you will be able to create a Color Lookup Table, carry out colour grading inside Unreal Engine, and create a night light setup. You will also be able to create a simple smoke system and add dust to your scene.

Chapter 13, Rendering and Exporting Cinematic Shots, teaches you how to set up a render with a movie render queue. By the end of this chapter, you will be able to render images and videos to the best quality possible by modifying settings and adding some variables in the rendering process.

To get the most out of this book

There are no prerequisites to start the learning journey of this book. We will start from the very beginning with a detailed step-by-step guide on how to install Unreal Engine 5.

Software/hardware covered in the book	Operating system requirements
Unreal Engine 5.3	Windows (the examples in this book use Windows workstations) or macOS (works with some restrictions)
Adobe Photoshop 2022 or any other 2D graphics software	Windows or macOS

If you are using the digital version of this book, we advise you to type the code yourself or access the code from the book's GitHub repository (a link is available in the next section). Doing so will help you avoid any potential errors related to the copying and pasting of code.

One of the greatest parts of Unreal Engine 5 is its resources ecosystem, which allows you to obtain incredible results without ever going outside the Engine. For this reason, you can follow this book and achieve something beautiful even if you don't have strong experience in the CGI world. But there are some prerequisites if you want to use your own assets: you need to know the fundamentals of 3D modeling, such as UVs and topology, as well as some knowledge about texturing and how it works in general. But thanks to the Unreal Engine resources ecosystem, you can easily follow along with the book without experience in CGI.

Conventions used

There are a number of text conventions used throughout this book.

`Code in text`: Indicates code words in text, database table names, folder names, filenames, file extensions, pathnames, dummy URLs, user input, and Twitter handles. Here is an example: "The most common are `.fbx` and `.obj` files."

Bold: Indicates a new term, an important word, or words that you see onscreen. For instance, words in menus or dialog boxes appear in **bold**. Here is an example: "You can save your assets by clicking on the **Save All** button."

> **Tips or important notes**
> Appear like this.

Get in touch

Feedback from our readers is always welcome.

General feedback: If you have questions about any aspect of this book, email us at `customercare@ packtpub.com` and mention the book title in the subject of your message.

Errata: Although we have taken every care to ensure the accuracy of our content, mistakes do happen. If you have found a mistake in this book, we would be grateful if you would report this to us. Please visit `www.packtpub.com/support/errata` and fill in the form.

Piracy: If you come across any illegal copies of our works in any form on the internet, we would be grateful if you would provide us with the location address or website name. Please contact us at `copyright@packt.com` with a link to the material.

If you are interested in becoming an author: If there is a topic that you have expertise in and you are interested in either writing or contributing to a book, please visit `authors.packtpub.com`.

Share Your Thoughts

Once you've read *Cinematic Photoreal Environments in Unreal Engine 5*, we'd love to hear your thoughts!
Scan the QR code below to go straight to the Amazon review page for this book and share your feedback.

https://packt.link/r/1803244119

Your review is important to us and the tech community and will help us make sure we're delivering
excellent quality content.

Download a free PDF copy of this book

Thanks for purchasing this book!

Do you like to read on the go but are unable to carry your print books everywhere?

Is your eBook purchase not compatible with the device of your choice?

Don't worry, now with every Packt book you get a DRM-free PDF version of that book at no cost.

Read anywhere, any place, on any device. Search, copy, and paste code from your favorite technical books directly into your application.

The perks don't stop there, you can get exclusive access to discounts, newsletters, and great free content in your inbox daily

Follow these simple steps to get the benefits:

1. Scan the QR code or visit the link below

https://packt.link/free-ebook/9781803244112

2. Submit your proof of purchase
3. That's it! We'll send your free PDF and other benefits to your email directly

Part 1:
Getting Started
with Unreal Engine 5

In this part, you will take your first steps inside Unreal Engine 5. Starting at the very beginning by installing the Engine on your workstation, you will learn how to create your first project inside Unreal Engine 5. After exploring its interface and gaining confidence with the Engine's project structure, you will learn how to import 3D models and textures inside Unreal Engine 5. At this point, you will be confident enough to jump into the materials and shading world and, after that, you will learn several lighting techniques to be used inside Unreal Engine 5. This fundamental part ends with a chapter about the newest features in which you will explore Nanite, Virtual Textures, and the World Partition tool. At the end of this part, you will be able to import your own 3D model, create a Master Material to modify its aspect in real time, and create a perfect lighting setup.

This part has the following chapters:

- *Chapter 1, Creating Your First Project in Unreal Engine 5*

- *Chapter 2, Navigating through the Unreal Engine 5 Interface*

- *Chapter 3, Exploring Unreal Engine 5 Project Structure*

- *Chapter 4, Importing and Working with Assets*

- *Chapter 5, Mastering Materials and Shading*

- *Chapter 6, Illuminating Your World with Lighting*

- *Chapter 7, Exploring Nanite, RVTs, and World Partition Tool*

1
Creating Your First Project in Unreal Engine 5

Welcome to this fantastic journey that will allow you to discover how to create photorealistic environments for cinematics in **Unreal Engine 5**. In this chapter, we will start from the very beginning of the process by installing the **Epic Games Launcher** and Unreal Engine 5. We will learn the potential of the Epics Game Launcher and how to use its features such as **Marketplace** and **Samples**.

We will cover the following topics:

- Downloading and installing the Engine
- Epic Games Launcher – not just a launcher
- Creating your first project
- Choosing the perfect template

By the end of this chapter, you will be able to create a new project and know how to use project templates.

Technical requirements

In this chapter, you will take your first steps into the Unreal Engine world. To do that, you only need a workstation that achieves the Engine system requirement. You can check Unreal Engine system requirements for Windows, Mac, and Linux at the following link: `https://docs.unrealengine.com/5.0/en-US/hardware-and-software-specifications-for-unreal-engine/`.

Downloading and installing the Engine

In this section, we will see how to download and install Unreal Engine 5. But first, we will need to install the Epics Game Launcher:

1. Go to www.unrealengine.com.

2. Create an Epic Games account by clicking on the **SIGN IN** option at the top right of the page:

Figure 1.1 – Unreal Engine 5's official web page with the SIGN IN link in the top-right corner

3. Once you create an Epic Games account, click on the **DOWNLOAD** option at the top right of the page.

Figure 1.2 – Unreal Engine 5's official web page with the DOWNLOAD link in the top-right corner

4.   Click on **DOWNLOAD LAUNCHER** and install it.

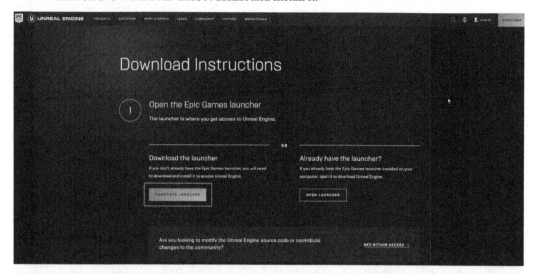

Figure 1.3 – The Epic Games Launcher download page

At the end of this page, you can also find **System requirements** for Windows, macOS, and Linux:

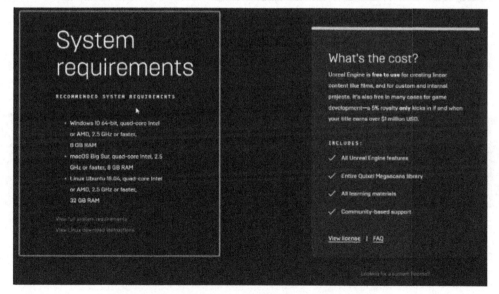

Figure 1.4 – Unreal Engine 5 System requirements – click on
View Full system requirements to see the full list

Once you have installed Epic Game Launcher, you can launch it and log in with your Epic Games account.

Next, it's time to install the Engine with the following steps:

1. Open Epic Games Launcher and click on the **Unreal Engine** tab on the left-hand side.

2. Click on **Library** at the top of the screen.

3. To install the Engine, click on the plus (+) icon.

    A rectangular thumbnail with a number and an **Install** button will appear. If you click on the number inside the thumbnail, you can choose the version of the Engine you want to install. In this book, we will use version 5.3.1. You can use later versions of the Engine as well.

Figure 1.5 – This is how you will find the Library tab for the first time

4. Click on **Install**. Alternatively, you can also click on the **Install Engine** button on the top right of the windows. This button will install the latest version of the Engine. It will take a while to end the process.

Figure 1.6 – The Library tab will be shown in this way if you don't have any version of the Engine installed

5. Once you have installed the Engine, the install button becomes the **Launch** button. Click on the **Launch** button, and the Engine will be launched.

Figure 1.7 – This is how the Library tab will look when you've installed the Engine for the first time

If you click on the row near the **Launch** button, you can choose from different options:

Figure 1.8 – Engine versions scroll-down menu

Let's understand what these options are:

- **Options**: Here, you can change the installation options. You can save a lot of space on your local hard drive by deselecting some components that will be useless for our work such as Android, iOS, and Linux. This will take several minutes.

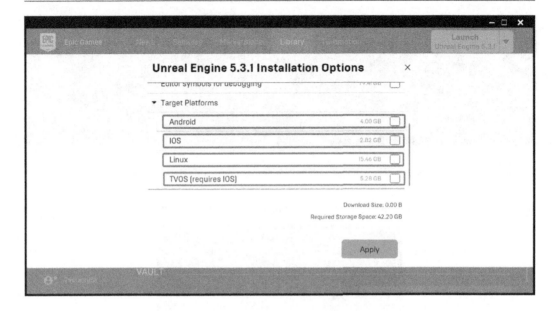

Figure 1.9 – Engine version installation options menu

- **Set Current**: Set this Engine version as the current version. This means that any time you launch the Engine from the Epic Games Launcher, it will be in the version selected by you. This also changes the version in the general **Launch** button on the top-right corner of the Epic Games Launcher.

- **Create Shortcut**: A shortcut of this specific Engine version will be automatically created on your desktop.

- **Remove**: This will delete a specific Engine version.

- **Verify**: This option will repeat the verifying process of the Engine installation. It can correct some Engine errors. This can help in case of some malfunction of the Engine. This process takes several minutes but can be lifesaving during projects.

Now that we have downloaded and installed the Epic Games Launcher and Engine, let's move on to the next section, where we will learn more about the Epic Games launcher.

Epic Games Launcher – not just a launcher

The Epic Games Launcher isn't only the tool with which you can download and install the Engine. It's a powerful tool where you can find any kind of resources you will need to create your projects.

In this section, we will discover how to manage projects with the Epic Games Launcher, how to get content from the Marketplace, and where to find learning content inside the Epic Games Launcher.

Library

This is the place where you can install the Engine and manage all your projects and contents. The **Library** tab is divided into three different parts, which are described in the following subsections.

ENGINE VERSIONS

As we saw before, we can choose which Engine version we want to install by clicking on the + icon. We can delete a specific Engine version by clicking on the **X** icon in the top-left corner of the Engine version thumbnail. (**X** appears by leaving the mouse over the Engine version thumbnail.)

The version name of the Engine is composed of three numbers.

Figure 1.10 – Engine version thumbnail – the Engine version name is composed of three different values

Let's see what these numbers represent:

- The first is the **main version** of the Engine, which, in our case, is 5.

- The second is the **major update** version, which, in our case, is 2. A major update usually apports significant updates such as new features or bug fixes.

- The last one is the **minor update** version. A minor update usually fixes bugs.

The Epic Games Launcher will let you know when a new version, a new major update, or a new minor update will be available to download. When a new version or update is available, an orange circle will appear on the **Library** tab and near the **Unreal Engine** link on the left side of the Epic Games Launcher. An orange circle with **i** inside will appear near **ENGINE VERSIONS**. If you are working with multiple versions, the version that receives an update will have the **Update** button instead of the **Launch** button:

Figure 1.11 – New update or version notifications

What should you do when a new update is coming? Well, it depends. A minor update is usually safe, and you can update the Engine. A major update can be more problematic. It usually adds some new features or replaces old features with a new one. This can change important Engine files that could compromise your ongoing projects. So, be careful! In general, if you are working on a project, it is safer that you finish working on your project first and then update the Engine and the project to the new version. Usually, a major update is preceded by a preview version of the update. A preview version is a testing version that allows you to test all the new features coming to the new major update. As a preview version, it is usually unstable and full of bugs. Finally, a version update is a totally new version of the Engine. Your project probably doesn't work seamlessly with this new version. Just to be clear, to see a new Engine version update, we have to wait for Unreal Engine 6.

Figure 1.12 – The Preview version thumbnail

> **Note**
>
> You can install multiple versions of the Engine for several reasons; for example, if you're working on various projects that are compatible with specific Engine versions. Additionally, certain plugins you've installed (we'll cover plugin installation in *Chapter 2*) may exclusively function with older Engine versions. Lastly, even when in the midst of a project, you might want to explore the new features of the latest Engine version.

Coming back to the **Library** tab, finally, on the right we have the following:

- **GitHub source**: Unreal Engine is an open-source code software. This means that you can find the source code for free on GitHub to compile the Engine by yourself.

- **Release notes**: By clicking on this option, you can browse the documentation page for the notes about the current release.

- **The last number** is the quantity of memory that all the Engine versions you have installed are taking on your local drive.

Figure 1.13 – On the right side of the ENGINE VERSIONS section,
there are some useful links and information

> **Note:**
>
> When you install the Engine from the Epic Games Launcher, you are installing a pre-compiled version of the Engine. That means that you can't modify the source code of the Engine *but* you can "only" use the features that Epic Games developers give to you with the Engine. If you want to learn more about Engine source code and compiling the Engine, you can browse here: `https://docs.unrealengine.com/5.1/en-US/building-unreal-engine-from-source/`. (Note that this is an *advanced option*.)

MY PROJECTS

If you scroll down, you will find all the projects you have created in the default folder:

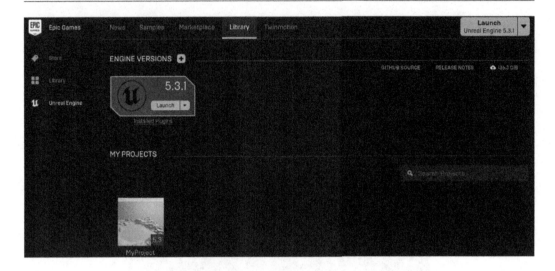

Figure 1.14 – When you create a project, you can find it in MY PROJECTS

We will go deep into Engine folders later in *Chapter 3*. You can open a project by double-clicking on a project thumbnail. If you right-click on a project thumbnail, you get the following options:

- **Open the project**: The Epic Games Launcher will be closed, and a new instance of the Engine will be launched with your project.

- **Show in folder**: Navigate to the project folder in your local drive.

- **Create a shortcut**: A shortcut to the project will be automatically created on your desktop.

- **Clone**: Create a copy of the project by choosing a new name and destination path.

Note that you can also create a copy of the project directly in a folder by copying and pasting the project folder *but* be sure to have the project saved and closed. You can delete a project by deleting the project folder.

VAULT

The last section of the library is **VAULT**. **VAULT** shows all the contents you have acquired from the Marketplace. For each piece of content, you can do the following:

- Create a project with the selected content (if it is a project content)

- Add selected content to an existing project (if it is an assets content)

- Install content to a specific Engine version (if it is a code content or a plugin)

You can also sort content by category or search for specific content. Besides the **Filter by** menu, there is the amount of memory that **Vault Cache** is taking on your local drive.

Figure 1.15 – The Unreal Engine vault is filled with hundreds of assets acquired on the Marketplace

Note: **Vault Cache** is heavy on local hard drives, so you can change the location of the `Vault Cache` folder in Epic Games Launcher settings on the bottom-left of the window.

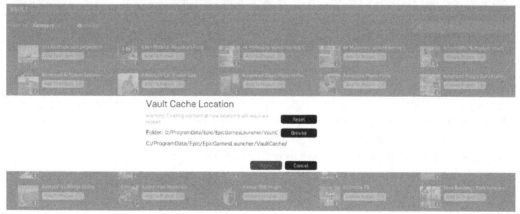

Figure 1.16 – If you browse to Settings | Vault Cache Location, you can change the Vault Cache folder

Marketplace

One of the greatest things about Unreal Engine 5 is its resources ecosystem that allows you to obtain incredible results without ever going outside the Engine. **Marketplace** is the place where you can find thousands of contents for your project. There are 3D assets, animations, plugins, code plugins, and **Blueprints** but also entire projects to explore, use, and study. You can find free content or pay to buy some. Every month, hundreds of contents go on sale, and you can obtain very expensive assets for free. **Marketplace** is linked to your Epic Games account. You will find each content that you've bought in **VAULT** inside the **Library** tab. When you log in with the Epic Games account on a new workstation, you will find all the content that you have bought with that specific account *but* you will need to download it again.

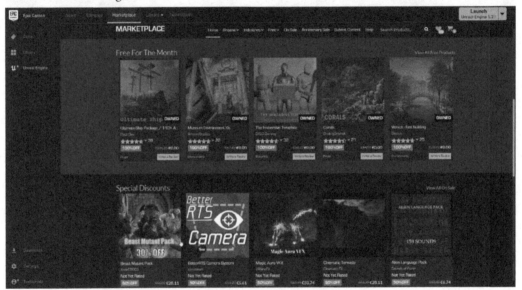

Figure 1.17 – Unreal Engine Marketplace

If you click on an asset in the Unreal Engine Marketplace, you will find several useful pieces of information about that item. You can buy it or, if you already have it in the vault or if that item is free, you can add it to a project or create a new project with it. Near the **Add To Project** or **Create Project** button (if it's full-project content), you can find the item's compatibility information.

Figure 1.18 – This asset pack is compatible with Engine versions until 5.1.

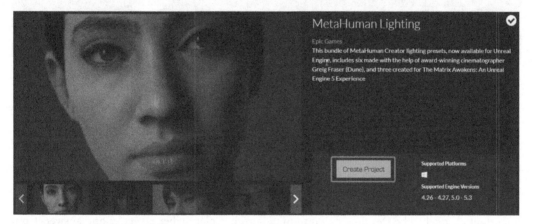

Figure 1.19 – This is a full project content – it will create a new project with its content inside

Samples

This is the portal for every learning resource that Epic Games gives to us to learn how the Engine works. In the **Samples** tab, you will find several projects for any level of skills divided into themes. These projects involve one or more specific topics. It looks like a marketplace, but everything is free. For each sample, you can download the project, read the documentation, or follow a video tutorial if available.

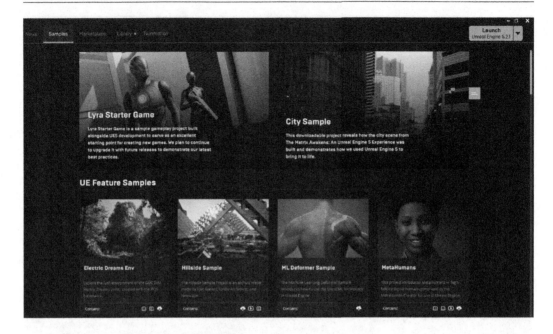

Figure 1.20 – The Epic Games Launcher Samples tab

This is a powerful resource for both beginners to learn the fundamentals of the Engine in a practical way and for experts to be updated on the newest Engine features.

News

In this tab, you can find all the news about Unreal Engine and access all its social channels. The most important channel is the Developer Community Forum, a place where you can find answers from Unreal Engine developers all around the world.

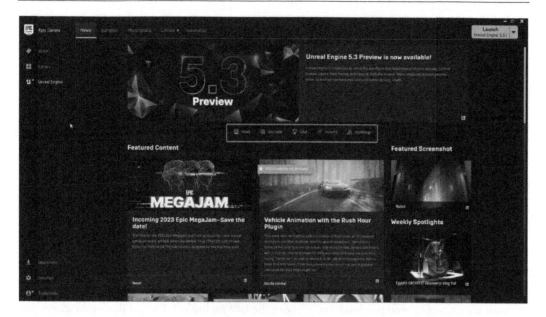

Figure 1.21 – The Epic Games Launcher News tab

Now that we have learned how to use the Epic Games Launcher and discovered all of its features, we can move on to the next section and discover how to create our first project in Unreal Engine 5.

Creating a new project

It's time to create your first project. To do that, you have two options:

- Click on the **Launch** button on a specific Engine version inside the **Library** tab. This will create a project running with this specific Engine version.

- Click on the **Launch** button on the top right of the Epic Games Launcher window. This will create a new project running with the version set as current.

If you have installed the Engine for the first time, you probably have only one version of the Engine. In this case, both options are identical.

When you click on the **Launch** button, the Epic Games Launcher will be closed. It will take a while and then the **Unreal Project Browser** window will appear.

Figure 1.22 – The Unreal Project Browser window will open, showing the RECENT PROJECTS tab

You can open a project that was created in your library and if you don't have any projects yet, this tab will be empty.

To create a new project, you need to browse one of the tabs on the left. Each of these tabs allows you to either create a blank project or create a project starting from a template.

Let's start with creating a blank game project:

1. Click on the **GAMES** tab.

2. Select the **Blank** project preset.

3. Once you click on the **GAMES** tab, take a look at the **Project Defaults** section on the right.

Figure 1.23 – The Unreal Project Browser's Games preset tab

Let's go over the various options in this menu:

- **Blueprint/C++**: Here, you can choose whether you want to create a project based on Blueprint or a C++ project. For all the things we are going to create in this book, you will always need a Blueprint project.

> **Note:**
> Blueprints are a visual scripting system with a node-based interface. As with many common scripting languages, it is used to define object-oriented classes or objects in the Engine. It's a very intuitive way to add complex code lines to your project as gameplay mechanics without the need to write code *but* it still is a code language that has to be learned. C++ is the most common scripting language in the game industry. To create a C++-based project, you need to compile the Engine from the source.

- **Target platform**: Here, you can choose the target platform for your project. You can choose between **Desktop** and **Mobile**. **Desktop** creates a project suitable for desktop platforms and consoles. **Mobile** creates a project that is already set to be playable on a mobile device. This means that the project will be created with different project settings according to your choice. You can choose **Desktop**.

- **Quality preset**: This is the quality setting of your project. You can choose between **Maximum** and **Scalable**. **Maximum** will set any options at the maximum value available for the target platform. **Scalable** will disable some complex features in favor of performances. You can choose **Maximum**. You can change these settings at any time directly inside the Engine.

- **Starter content**: If this option is checked, you will find a lot of interesting assets loaded inside your projects. This can be very useful at the beginning for study and test purposes and time saving for specific types of assets such as Niagara samples and shaders. You can use a project with starter content to follow the book's first section.

- **Raytracing**: If this option is checked, the project will be set for using real-time Raytracing. We will learn how to use Raytracing and Lumen in *Chapter 7*. If you have the recommended system requirement, you can check this box.

> **Note**
> Real-time Raytracing has an impact on performance *but* also on final quality. You can also follow this book with a project without real-time Raytracing *but* you can't use some explained features.

1. Choose the location of your project from the **Project Location** option and name your project in the **Project Name** box. These options can be found at the bottom of the window:

Figure 1.24 – Here, you can choose the project location and name

> **Note**
> Unreal Engine projects are very heavy on local drive, in terms of both heaviness and loading time. Creating your project on a fast SSD disk is the best solution. Speaking about the name, spaces aren't allowed. Unreal Engine also doesn't like very long names (the maximum limit is 20 characters).

2.   When you've set everything, click on **Create**.

When you create a project or open a project for the first time, Unreal Engine will take some time to create everything it needs and compile all the shaders. If the loading seems to be stuck at 45%, don't worry – it's normal! You can check this in the Task Manager. Search for the **UnrealEditor** process and click on the left arrow near the process name to expand the **UnrealEditor** process. Here, you will find the shader compiler. It can take several minutes.

⌄ ⓤ UnrealEditor (9)	70.4%	1,785.8 MB	0.8 MB/s	0 Mbps
ⓤ ShaderCompileWorker	8.6%	49.5 MB	0 MB/s	0 Mbps
ⓤ ShaderCompileWorker	9.8%	144.3 MB	0.1 MB/s	0 Mbps
ⓤ ShaderCompileWorker	8.6%	33.1 MB	0.1 MB/s	0 Mbps
ⓤ ShaderCompileWorker	8.6%	140.2 MB	0.1 MB/s	0 Mbps
ⓤ ShaderCompileWorker	7.7%	88.3 MB	0.1 MB/s	0 Mbps
ⓤ ShaderCompileWorker	8.7%	109.2 MB	0.1 MB/s	0 Mbps
ⓤ ShaderCompileWorker	10.0%	119.3 MB	0 MB/s	0 Mbps
ⓤ ShaderCompileWorker	8.2%	110.2 MB	0.1 MB/s	0 Mbps
ⓤ UnrealEditor	0.2%	991.7 MB	0.8 MB/s	0 Mbps

Figure 1.25 – You can check the Unreal Engine's loading status inside Windows Task Manager

Now that we know how to create a new project from a draft, in the next section, we will learn how new project templates work and how to use them to create a new project.

Choosing the perfect template

Now that you know how to create a blank project, we can look at the available samples that you can use as a starting point for your projects. They are divided into five main categories: **Games**, **Film/Video & Live Events**, **Architecture**, **Automotive Product Design and Manufacturing**, and **Simulation**.

Note that the blank project of each category has different settings in terms of quality, plugins, and target platform. Blueprint samples are different from C++ samples. In this section, we will go only through blueprint samples.

In the **GAMES** category, you can find several presets that help you build your game:

- **First Person**: This preset gives you the perfect starting point to create a first-person shooter, featuring a character represented with a pair of arms, which is viewed from the first-person perspective. The character is already set up to be played with keyboard and mouse controls. This is also great for navigating your environment in a "more gaming way." If you are planning to create something similar to *Call of Duty*, *Doom*, or *Quake*, then this is the preset for you.

- **Third Person**: This preset is very similar to the first person preset but it gives you a complete character with a full set of movements. The camera is positioned behind and slightly above the character. This is great for exploring your new environment like a player. If you are planning to create something similar to *Dark Souls*, *Uncharted*, or *Gears of War*, this is the preset for you.

- **Top Down**: More of the same – this preset gives you a fully animated character viewed with a top-down camera. If you are planning to create something similar to *Diablo* or *Hades*, then this is the preset for you.

- **Vehicle**: This preset gives you a fully rigged vehicle that can be modified and used for your racing sequence or game. "Fully rigged" means that you can control the vehicle with a keyboard and mouse or a gamepad with car wheels and suspensions that work propriety. If you are planning to create a racing game or a racing sequence, then this is the preset for you.

- **Handler AR** and **Virtual Reality** are presets that are a great starting point for developing AR/VR applications for desktop, console, android, or iOS, providing interactive objects, plane detection, and spatialized audio.

- In **FILM/VIDEO & LIVE EVENTS**, you can find several presets that will help you in virtual production/cinematic projects and live events:

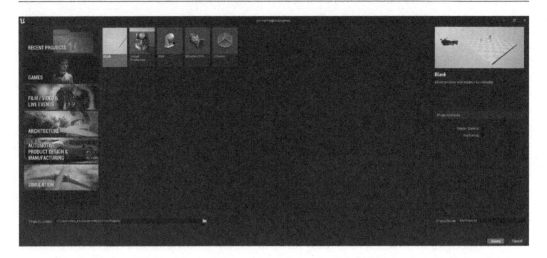

Figure 1.26 – The Unreal Project Browser's FILM/VIDEO & LIVE EVENTS preset tab

- **Virtual Production**: This preset is a great starting point for everyone who wants to jump into virtual production with Unreal Engine 5; it contains functionality for a virtual camera, VR scouting, and live compositing.

- **Dmx**, **InCameraV.FX**, and **nDisplay** are presets that are an in-depth demonstration of every single possibility you have with Unreal Engine 5 and virtual production. This is an advanced level. Just to be clear, some of the features included in these presets were part of the workflow during *The Mandalorian* production.

- **Blank Project**: This is a great preset because it's a blank project set up with high values in quality settings. This could also be great for us.

- **ARCHITECTURE**, **AUTOMOTIVE PRODUCT DESIGN & MANUFACTURING**, and **SIMULATION** are far from our interest *but* every sample has something new to teach you. Exploring them is useful and helps you to understand the potential of Unreal Engine. The presets inside the **AUTOMOTIVE PRODUCT DESIGN & MANUFACTURING** category give you the possibility to create a product configurator or an automotive shot in a very short time.

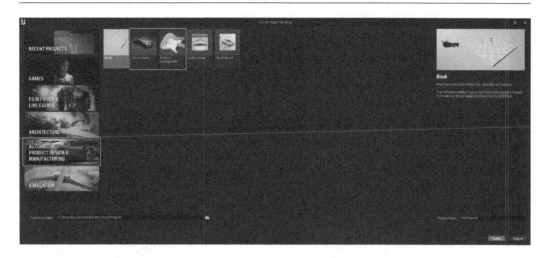

Figure 1.27 – Unreal Project Browser's AUTOMOTIVE PRODUCT DESIGN & MANUFACTURING preset tab

Note that any preset or sample can be recreated directly inside the Engine starting from a blank project.

In the end, which is the best preset to create a cinematic photorealistic environment? **First Person** and **Third Person** are great presets because they give you the possibility to "play" your environment and simulate what the player will see. However, if you are creating an environment that you will only use for cinematic purposes, maybe a blank project is the better choice. If you want a project already set to achieve high quality in the Viewport, the **FILM/VIDEO & LIVE EVENTS** blank project is a good choice. Remember that you can always change settings inside the project or create the exact same preset starting from a blank project.

Summary

In this chapter, you learned how to install the Engine and how to take advantage of the Epic Games Launcher. Now, you know how to create a project in Unreal Engine 5 with different settings and how to use presets, Marketplace assets, and projects to speed up your workflow.

In the next chapter, we will learn how the Unreal Engine 5 interface works, how to move inside the Viewport, and how to transform objects in the 3D space.

2

Navigating through the Unreal Engine 5 Interface

In this chapter, we will explore the Unreal Engine **user interface** (**UI**) and we will meet all the features that are going to be explored in depth throughout the book. Starting with an overview of the UI, we will learn how the **Outliner** and the **Details** panels work. We will also learn about the importance of **Content Drawer** and how to use it properly. Overall, we will be covering the following topics:

- Interface overview and project settings
- Exploring **Outliner**
- Exploring the **Details** panel
- Discovering **Content Drawer**

At the end of this chapter, you will know some essential shortcuts and you will also be able to navigate the Level Viewport and manipulate objects with a **Gizmo**.

Technical requirements

In this chapter, we will work inside Unreal Engine. You need to have Unreal Engine installed on your workstation to follow this chapter.

Interface overview and project settings

In this section, we will give you an overview of all the menus and panels inside Unreal Engine 5's UI. Please note that we will not go deep into every command. We will learn specific commands that are useful to us and how they work during the learning process in this book. Don't worry if you don't understand some words or concepts because we will cover everything later.

When Unreal Engine is open, you will find the following UI:

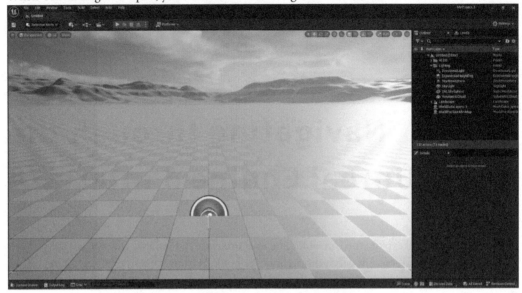

Figure 2.1 – Unreal Engine 5 starting UI

The UI is fully customizable. All the panels are floating panels and you can move them by dragging them with the **left mouse button** (**LMB**). You can leave them floating on the screen or dock them in the Viewport. As we will see in a minute, you can save your own Viewport layout.

Figure 2.2 – Floating panels

The UI is divided into the following key panels:

- The Menu Bar
- The Main Toolbar
- The Level Viewport
- The Bottom Toolbar

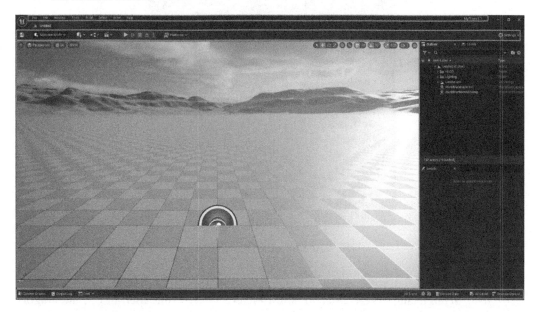

Figure 2.3 – The main UI is divided into the Menu Bar, Main Toolbar, Level Viewport, and Bottom Toolbar

Let's go over all these panels, starting with the Menu Bar.

The Menu Bar

This is the standard Menu Bar that most Unreal Engine software has. Here, you can find the following:

- **File**: In this menu, you can find options that allow you to open levels and projects, save options, which allow you to save your project, levels, and other single assets, import/export options, which allow you to import/export one or multiple assets, and project options, which you to manage your projects directly inside the Engine.

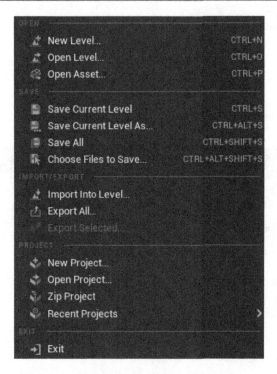

Figure 2.4 – The File menu

- **Edit**: In this menu, you can find common operations such as **Copy**, **Cut**, **Paste**, and undo/redo. In this menu, you can also find **Editor Preferences…**, **Project Settings…**, and **Plugins**.

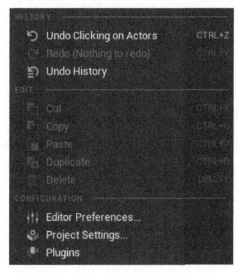

Figure 2.5 – The Menu Bar's Edit menu

In **Editor Preferences**, you can set general preferences for the editor, such as appearance and shortcuts:

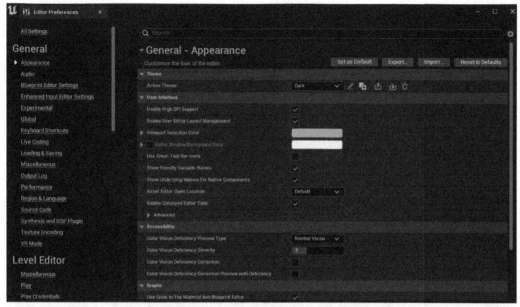

Figure 2.6 – The Unreal Engine 5 Editor Preferences window

In **Project Settings**, you can set your preferences for the current project you are working on such as rendering features and quality settings:

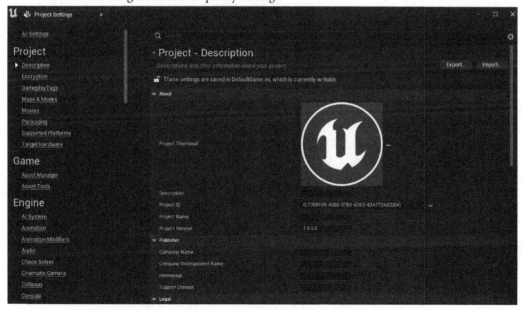

Figure 2.7 – The Unreal Engine 5 Project Settings window

In **Plugins**, you can manage the installed plugins by activating or deactivating them. When you install a new plugin from the marketplace, you will have to activate it from inside this window. You find the plugin you are looking for and flag the box to activate the plugin. Most of the time, Unreal Engine 5 must be restarted.

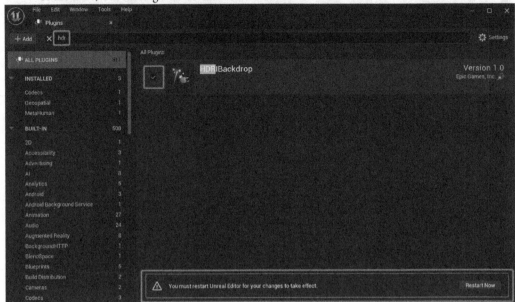

Figure 2.8 – An example of how to install a new plugin

- **Window**: This menu allows you to add or remove tabs and other menus to/from the Viewport. Here, you can also save and load your UI layout and recall Quixel Bridge (the Megascans Library, which we will learn how to use in *Chapter 8*) and Marketplace directly inside the Engine.

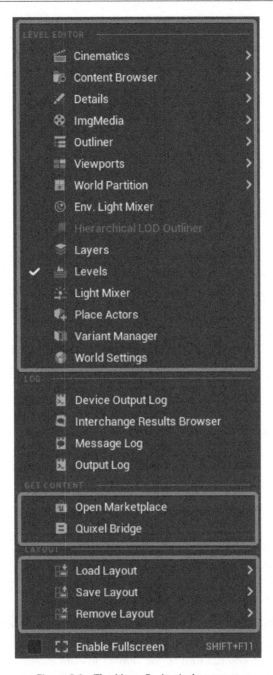

Figure 2.9 – The Menu Bar's window menu

- **Tools**: In this menu, you can find useful performance tools, debugging tools, and actor tools such as nanite tools, revision control tools, and word partition tools.

Figure 2.10 – The Unreal Engine 5 Menu Bar's Tools menu

- **Build**: In this menu, you can find all the commands and tools that you need to build your projects. Building something means rendering some or all components of the projects offline to save performance costs during real-time rendering. For example, you can render the lights into a lightmap texture that is applied to all your assets. You can build all of your assets inside the level in a single process or any single part of the project one by one.

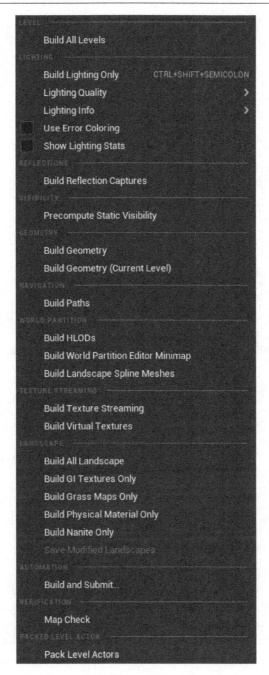

Figure 2.11 – The Unreal Engine 5 Menu Bar's Build menu

- **Select**: This menu includes some useful options and shortcuts to select assets in a faster and more organized way.

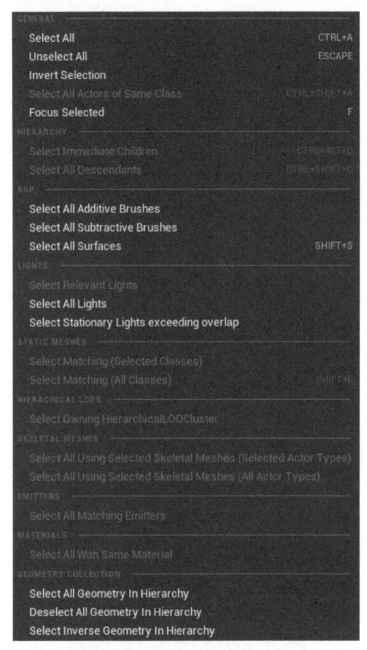

Figure 2.12 – The Unreal Engine 5 Menu Bar's Select menu

- **Actor**: In this menu, you can find useful options to manage actors inside your project, such as copy, cut, and paste, transform options, and visibility options. This menu will show you its content only if you have something selected in the Viewport.

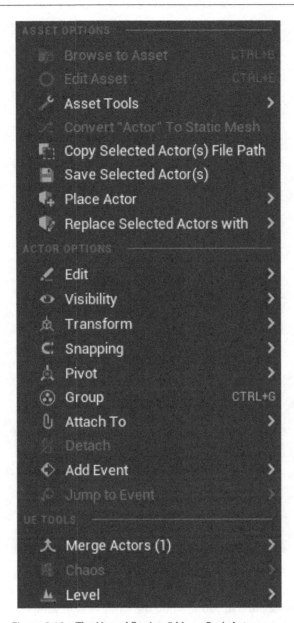

Figure 2.13 – The Unreal Engine 5 Menu Bar's Actor menu

- **Help**: This menu contains links to documentation, forums, and shortcuts that can help you resolve troubles or learn something new about the Engine.

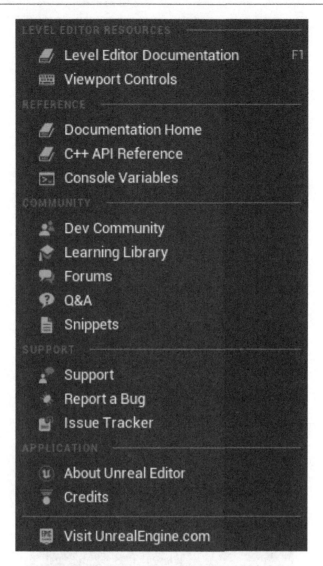

Figure 2.14 – The Unreal Engine 5 Menu Bar's Help menu

On the right side of the Menu Bar, you will find the name of your project. If you hover the mouse cursor above the project name, the Engine will show you the general project information such as the Engine version you used to create it and some technical information.

Figure 2.15 – The name of the project and general project information

Now, let's go over the Main Toolbar.

Main Toolbar

This toolbar contains buttons with commonly used operations. It's divided into five groups:

Figure 2.16 – Unreal Engine 5's Main Toolbar

- The first group allows you to easily save the current level. We will learn more about the saving process in *Chapter 3*.

- The second group allows you to change the Viewport mode. If you open the drop-down menu and try to zap into various modes, you will see the Viewport change, new commands will appear, and some commands will be disabled. Inside this drop-down menu, you find some of the most important features for creating an environment:

  - The **Selection** mode is the default mode. When this mode is activated, you can freely navigate through the Viewport, manage assets, and use all the commands that the toolbar gives to you. It depends on your work, but you will probably spend 85% of your time in this mode.

  - **Landscape**: This mode allows you to create, manage, and modify a landscape that is a special actor, which allows you to create a massive environment ground. We will be mastering **Landscape** in *Chapter 9*.

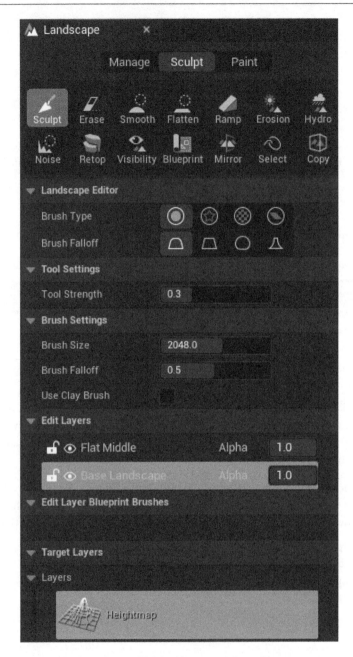

Figure 2.17 – The Landscape mode options

- **Foliage**: This mode allows you to paint assets on a landscape (or a static mesh) such as grass, bushes, trees, and stones. This is very useful in environmental creation. We will learn how to use this feature in *Chapter 9*.

Figure 2.18 – The Foliage mode options

- **Mesh Paint**: This mode allows you to directly paint your textures on assets. This requires specific shading, but it isn't so complex to use. We will not go deep into this feature but if you want to learn more about it, you can browse this link: https://docs.unrealengine.com/5.0/en-US/mesh-paint-mode-in-unreal-engine/.

Figure 2.19 – The Mesh Paint mode options

- **Modeling**: This is one of the biggest additions to Unreal Engine that came in Unreal Engine 5. This mode gives you a complete suite of modeling tools with which you can modify geometry or create a new one. Many of the modeling features are still in beta state but the future is shining. If you want to know more about this feature, you can browse this link: `https://docs.unrealengine.com/5.0/en-US/modeling-mode/`.

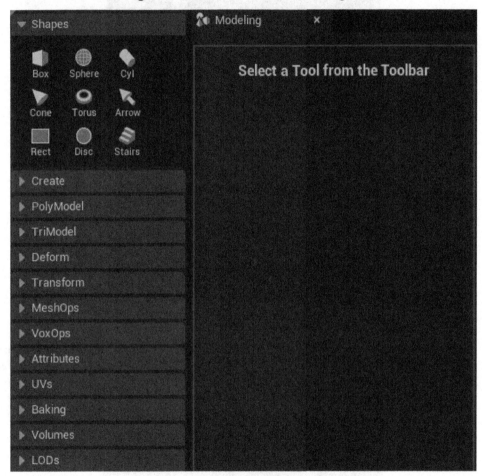

Figure 2.20 – The Modeling mode options

- **Fracture**: This is one of the newest features introduced in Unreal Engine. Thanks to Chaos technology, this mode gives you the possibility to simulate destruction in real-time with a realistic physics system. This is a very advanced feature. If you want to learn more about this feature, you can browse this link: `https://docs.unrealengine.com/5.0/en-US/chaos-destruction-in-unreal-engine/`.

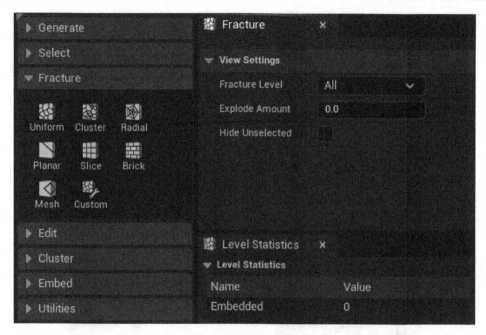

Figure 2.21 – The Fracture mode options

- **Brush Editing**: This mode gives you access to some tools that allow you to modify basic brush meshes. This is quite an old feature.

Figure 2.22 – The Brush Editing mode options

- **Animation**: This mode gives you access to all the animation features inside Unreal Engine 5 such as **Control Rig**, **Animation Settings**, and **Anim Outliner**. If you want to learn more about animation inside Unreal Engine, you can browse this link: https://docs.unrealengine.com/5.0/en-US/animation-editor-mode-in-unreal-engine/.

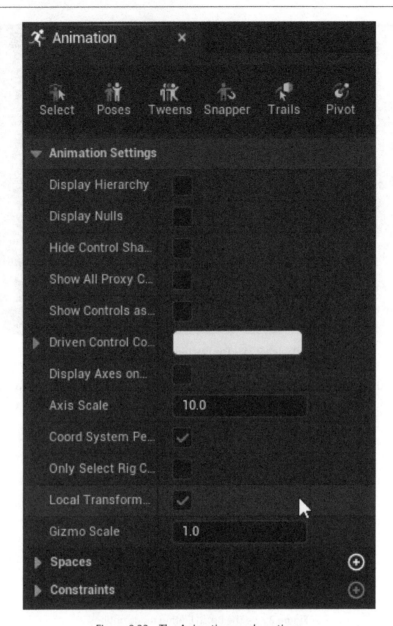

Figure 2.23 – The Animation mode options

- The third group allows you to add various types of actors and code to your project. The first icon, a cube with a green plus on it, gives you access to content options that allow you to import assets from outside Unreal Engine such as from your local drive, from the Marketplace, and from Quixel Bridge (we will learn how to use this in *Chapter 8*).

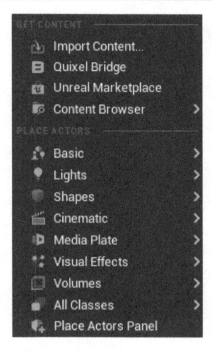

Figure 2.24 – The Place Actors menu

Otherwise, the **PLACE ACTORS** options allow you to use actors provided by Unreal Engine. There are different kinds of actors that you can use. They are divided into the following categories:

- **Basic**: This contains a selection of the most common assets of each category.

- **Lights**: This contains all the different light types that you can use inside Unreal Engine.

- **Shapes**: This contains basic primitives such as cubes and spheres.

- **Cinematic**: This contains cameras and all cinematic utilities.

- **Media Plate**: This contains only one asset, which allows you to place a media file on a plane.

- **Visual Effects**: This is intended to be used as a post-production utility, including post-process volume, but also as a tool to generate skies, fog, and clouds.

- **Volumes**: This contains actors that allow you to trigger something (it can be an audio effect, a visual effect, or something else) when the camera is inside them. We will learn how to use some of them in the third part of this book.

- **All Classes**: This is a category with all the categories inside.

The **Place Actors** panel allows you to dock the **Place Actors** options panel to the Viewport. This action will make the Viewport more like the Unreal Engine 4 Viewport, but it steals space from the Viewport. You can place these objects in the Level Viewport by dragging and dropping them.

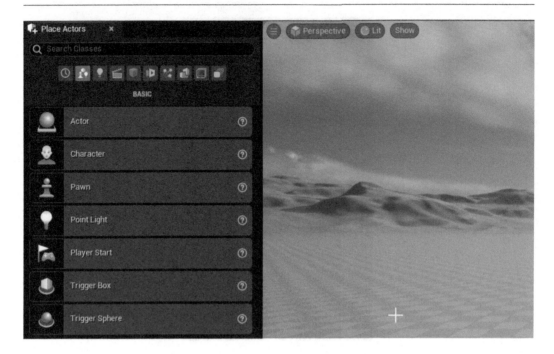

Figure 2.25 – The Place Actors panel docked into the UI

In the same group, you can find the blueprint menu, which is one of the ways you can create and manage blueprints. Here, you can also edit **Level Blueprint** and **Game Modes** – these two options allow us to modify how the game will be played by Unreal Engine in terms of coding to be executed at launch, inputs, and, more generally, everything regarding game mechanics. Finally, in this group, there is the Level Sequence menu, which allows you to create a **Level Sequence**. This will be one of the topics of *Chapter 11*.

- The fourth group allows you to play at the current level, which means trying your game or simply your environment as a player will do. This allows you to check whether everything is OK in terms of performance, input, and everything concerned with the game and the destination platform.

- The fifth group allows you to manage platforms to launch our game. If you have modified the installation of the Engine, as we saw in *Chapter 1*, we might not find mobile platforms or Linux. We will not go through this specific topic but you can learn more about platforms by browsing this link: `https://docs.unrealengine.com/5.0/en-US/sharing-and-releasing-projects-for-unreal-engine/`.

Finally, the **Settings** menu, at the right end of the Main Toolbar, gives you access to some important Engine and project settings with a specific focus on quality settings. This menu allows you to personalize your experience inside Unreal Engine 5 according to your hardware and performance limitations. With **Engine Scalability Settings**, you can easily change several options to optimize the work experience. Obviously, this will affect the image quality, so, remember that if you want/need to work at medium quality preset, some effects, shaders, shadows, or the general image quality may not be shown at its maximum quality. This doesn't affect the final rendering quality. We will learn about rendering and scalability options in the last part of this book.

Now that we've explored the Menu Bar, the Main Toolbar, and all their options, we can move on and learn how the Level Viewport works.

Level Viewport

The Level Viewport is the core of the environmental creation experience. It is a 3D Viewport that represents the level you are working on. You can drag and drop objects in the Level Viewport and move around in the 3D space.

In this section, we will learn how to move inside the Level Viewport by discovering its options and we will learn how to transform objects inside the Level Viewport.

Moving inside the Viewport

When you move inside the Viewport, you are moving a virtual camera. So, you can make every movement that a camera can. You can use the mouse or mouse and keyboard to move around. By pressing and holding the **right mouse button** (**RMB**) while moving the mouse around, you can orbit the camera. By pressing and holding the LMB while moving the mouse, you can move the camera on the X and Y axis. By pressing and holding the RMB + LMB while moving the mouse, you can pan the camera.

You can make all the same movements by pressing and holding the RMB + W, A, S, or D to move around the world (if you have some experience in gaming, this would be familiar). The RMB + Q moves the camera up on the Z axis and the RMB + E moves it down. Although the "only mouse" solution may seem easier, I suggest you get used to the mouse + keyboard solution. You can manage the camera speed movement with the mouse wheel or with the **Camera Speed** icon, the second icon from the right:

Figure 2.26 – Camera speed options

Here's a recap of the shortcut keys:

- Pressing the RMB + moving the mouse orbits the camera
- Pressing the LMB + moving the mouse moves the camera forward
- Pressing the RMB + LMB + moving the mouse pans the camera
- Pressing the RMB + *W* moves the camera forward
- Pressing the RMB + *S* moves the camera backward
- Pressing the RMB + *D* moves the camera to the right
- Pressing the RMB + *A* moves the camera to the left
- Pressing the RMB + *Q* moves the camera down
- Pressing the RMB + *E* moves the camera up
- The Mouse Wheel adjusts the camera speed

Now, let's look at the menus under the Level Viewport.

Exploring Level Viewport options

Let's take a look at the menus at the top left of the Level Viewport:

Figure 2.27 – Viewport menus

- **Hamburger menu**: This is a general Level Viewport options menu. Inside this menu, you can find some useful commands to check performance stats, such as **Show FPS**, which shows FPS in the Level Viewport, and **Show Stats**, which allows you to choose several details to be shown in the Level Viewport. You can also modify some camera options such as **Field Of View**, **Far View Plane**, and **Screen Percentage** (this last one can help you manage some performance issues by reducing the Viewport rendering area); **Game View** (can be accessed by pressing *G*) allows you to enter/exit the game mode (in terms of visual that means to show/hide assets interface inside the Viewport); **Immersive Mode** (can be accessed by pressing *F11*) sets the Level Viewport to full screen. If you press *F10*, you can activate another mode that maximizes the Level Viewport scale without totally excluding the UI.

Figure 2.28 – Maximized Viewport

- Finally, you can find some camera and rendering options such as **Create Camera Here** and **High Resolution Screenshot…**, which we will learn about in *Chapter 13*; **Layouts** allows you to load different Level Viewport layouts such as two, three, or four Viewports presets with orthographic cameras; **Advanced Settings…** move you directly to some Level Viewport options inside the editor preferences.

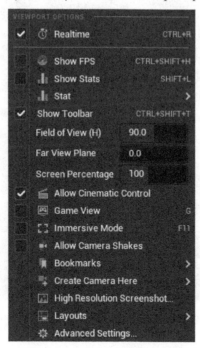

Figure 2.29 – Viewport menu options

- **VIEW MODE**: This is a very useful menu because it allows you to change the way you want to see your assets inside the Level Viewport, in terms of rendering features and image components. There are many options that help you see what is going on in your scene. This menu is shown with the name of the view options you are using. By default, it is **Lit**, which means Unreal Engine is showing you the Level Viewport with everything activated and rendered in real-time. The other options can show you, for example, only the lights (**Lighting Only**), the lights and reflections (**Detail Lighting**), or no lights at all (**Unlit**); there is almost anything you can think of. This is useful both for creating and debugging. Changing the view mode in **Lighting Only** can help you adjust some light spots or light artifacts; using the **Buffer Visualization** option can help you find errors on textures or something else. Try them!

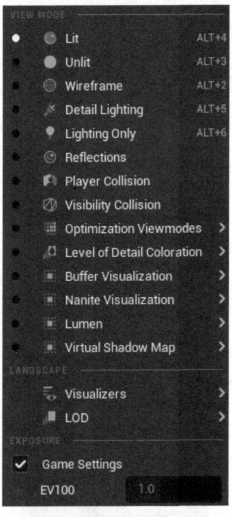

Figure 2.30 – The VIEW MODE menu options

- **Show**: This menu allows you to choose what you want to see in the Level Viewport in terms of assets but also rendering features. So, you can decide to see only the Spot Light actor and disable the **Anti-Aliasing** feature in the Viewport or tell the Engine that you don't want to see **Landscape** but want to see all the available rendering features working in the Viewport. This is very useful for both performance purposes and better workflow during projects.

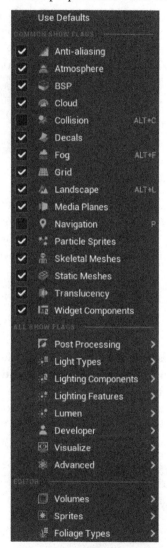

Figure 2.31 – The Show menu options

We can now go on and learn how to transform assets inside the Level Viewport. We will learn how to move, rotate, and scale an object.

Transforming assets inside the Level Viewport

On the top right of the Viewport, we have a series of commands that help us manage objects in the Level Viewport. To easily understand them, you should drag and drop one actor from the **Place Actors** panel to the Level Viewport. You can pick a cube.

When you drag and drop an asset in the Level Viewport, it goes to the exact position in the world that you chose. You can easily check the exact position in the **Details** panel on the right. In the **Transform** panel, you can manually change the position, rotation, and scale of your assets (we will learn more about the **Details** panel in the *Exploring the Details panel* section).

Figure 2.32 – The Transform panel inside the Details panel

When you select an object in the Level Viewport or select a new one, a yellow outline appears on the selected objects. When your object is selected, you are in the **Selection** mode. You can enter or exit the **Selection** mode by pressing Q. The following screenshot shows different commands (on the top left of the Viewport) that help you manipulate objects in the Viewport:

Figure 2.33 – These commands allow you to manipulate objects in the Viewport

The first group of commands suggest in which object transformation mode you are. Next to **Selection** mode, we have **Translation** mode (accessed by pressing *W*), **Rotation** mode (accessed by pressing *E*), and **Scale** mode (accessed by pressing *R*). When you enable one of these modes, a Gizmo appears at the center of your object. It's different for each transformation mode. It's interactive and you can use it to modify the position, rotation, and scale of your object in the three dimensions. You can move to the next transformation mode by pressing the SPACE bar.

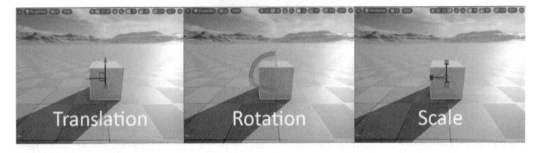

Figure 2.34 – Three different types of Gizmo according to three different transformation modes

The Gizmo is the center point of all the transformations of your object. If you try to rotate your object, you will see that the object will rotate around the center of the Gizmo.

The globe icon allows you to change the transformation space of your objects. You can use **world** or **local** transformation space. World means that the Gizmo is always aligned with the World transformation axis. Local means that the Gizmo is always aligned with the object. In other words, when you modify your object in World, the Z axis will always point to the top; otherwise, when you modify your object in Local, the z axis will always be aligned to the top of the object.

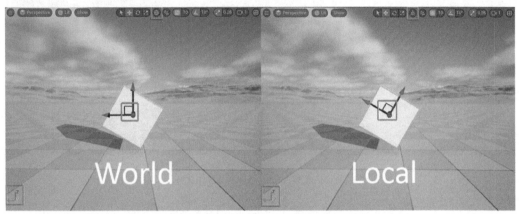

Figure 2.35 – The difference between world and local transformation

Next, you can find **snapping tools**. The first allows you to enable or disable grid snapping. Then, you can find translation snap, rotation snap, and scale snap. Any command has two icons. The first with the grid symbol allows you to enable or disable snaps. If these are disabled, you can transform your objects with a Gizmo without any constraints. If these snaps are enabled, the transformations will increase by steps. You can set the value of each step for each transformation with the second command.

Figure 2.36 – Snapping Viewport options

The next one is the camera option that we've already seen.

The last one isn't an object transformation option. It allows you to pass from one Viewport setup to four Viewport setups and show orthographic cameras. When the four-Viewport mode is activated, you just need to click on the Viewport you want to use to work inside it. Every single Viewport has the same command and menu you have when the single Viewport mode is activated. To come back to one Viewport mode, you need to click on the same command on one of the four Viewports.

Figure 2.37 – Four Viewports mode

We can now go on and learn more about the Bottom Toolbar and how to use menus under it.

Bottom Toolbar

Under the Level Viewport, you can find the Bottom Toolbar and it looks like this:

Figure 2.38 – Bottom Toolbar main options

On the left, we have the following:

- **Content Drawer**: This is one of the most important panels inside Unreal Engine. You can also recall it with *Ctrl* + SPACE. We will learn how to use it in the *Discovering Content Drawer* section of this chapter.

- **Output Log**: This panel records every action you have done during your section inside the Engine. If there is an error, **Output Log** will tell you that. Sentences inside **Output Log** have different colors, and different colors mean different levels of alert. White sentences are actions you have done, or commands executed correctly; yellow sentences are warnings; and red sentences are errors. Usually, errors are blocking issues, and warnings are not.

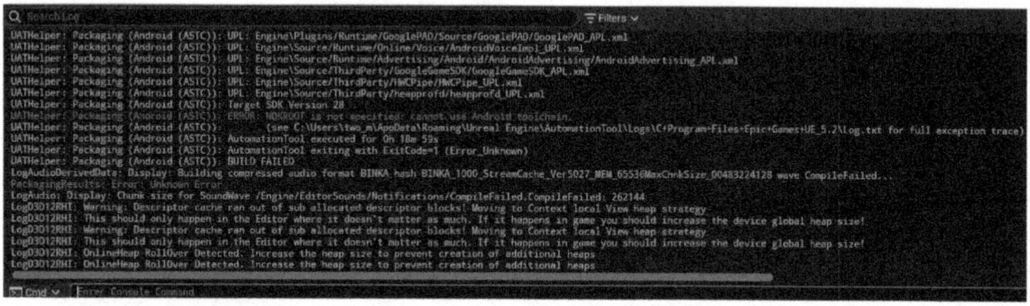

Figure 2.39 – An example of different messages in the Output Log window

- **Cmd**: This allows you to launch scripts inside the Engine. If you try to write something, a lot of possibilities will be shown to help you with typing. This is helpful, for example, for setting rendering features and optimizing the workflow in the Viewport. This is an advanced feature *but* it can also be useful for beginners. For example, try to write stat fps and press *Enter*. This command will show you the FPS in the Viewport. With the scroll-up menu, you can change the script language.

Figure 2.40 – You can show the FPS on Viewport by typing a simple command

In the right part, there are a couple of important panels but we are interested only in the following:

- **Derived Data**: This is a link to some editor preferences settings. This allows you to change the delivery data cache folder. We will learn more about this in *Chapter 3*.

- **All Saved**: This button comes together with Unreal Engine 5 and it's a huge improvement because it notifies us if there is something that hasn't been saved. We will learn everything about the saving process in *Chapter 3*.

- **Revision Control**: This is the menu where you can configure and manage your revision control system.

> **Note**
>
> **Revision Control** is the system responsible for managing changes in your project by tracking and saving every version of your work. This allows you to work in a safer way and gives you the option to come back at any time on a previous version of a single asset or of your entire project. You can easily set up Unreal Engine 5 to work with **Revision Control**, *but* you need a third-party application to do so. If you want to know more about **Revision Control**, you can browse this link: `https://docs.unrealengine.com/4.27/en-US/Basics/SourceControl/`.

Now that we have learned the basics about Unreal Engine 5's UI, we can go on and learn about what **Outliner** is and how it works.

Exploring Outliner

On the right of your screen, you can find the **Outliner** panel. Everything you can see in the Level Viewport is sorted in this panel. To be clear, when you drag and drop an actor from the **Place Actors** panel or **Content Drawer** (we will talk about it in a couple of pages) to the Level Viewport, that actor will appear in **Outliner**. Any actor is presented with a name preceded by an icon, which defines its type. With the eye icon, you can toggle the asset visibility in the Level Viewport. You can order assets by name or by type by clicking on the top labels. When you select an asset in **Outliner** with a left-click, you are selecting the same assets in the Level Viewport. If you right-click on one label, you can change the label.

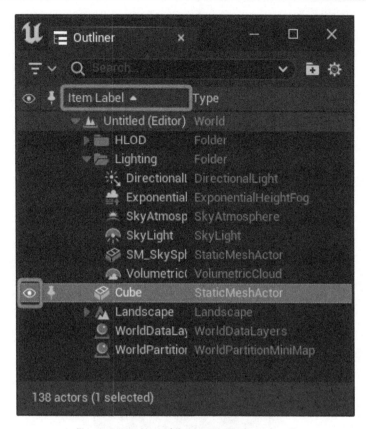

Figure 2.41 – Unreal Engine 5's Outliner panel

If you right-click on an actor name, you can choose from different options:

Figure 2.42 – The ACTOR OPTIONS menu inside the Outline panel

Let's go over these options:

- **ASSET OPTIONS**: You can select **Browse to Asset** in **Content Drawer** – this will automatically select the asset in **Content Drawer**; edit the asset by opening the dedicated editor, which will open a specific editor according to the type of asset (we will explore some of them in *Chapter 4*); and substitute the asset with another one already loaded.

- **VIEW OPTIONS**: You can use the **Snap View to Object** option in the Viewport, which will move the camera to center its view with the object position. **Snap Object to View** allows us to move the object in the same position as our camera view. **Pilot the asset** means placing the camera in the same position as the asset and moving the asset with the same commands of the camera.

- **ACTOR OPTIONS**: Here, you have a lot of options that allow you to work with your actor. You can edit it, work with its visibility, or transform it. The **Snapping** category helps you with several snapping tools and **Pivot** allows you to work with the actor pivot. If you have selected more than one actor, you can group them by selecting **Group** (you can also use the *Ctrl + G* shortcut); **Attach** allows you to parent the selected object to another; and **Level** allows you to create a level instance with the selected object inside. We will talk about levels in *Chapter 3*. Finally, the **Move To** option allows you to move the selected object inside an **Outliner** folder or to a new one.

Finally, we have some options in the **Outliner** tab:

- **Filter assets**: You can filter assets in **Outliner** to find what you are looking for faster.

- **Search**: You can search for a specific asset by typing the name in the search type field. Naming is very important. We will talk about naming conventions in *Chapter 3*.

- **Create a new folder**: You can create a new folder and rename it to keep **Outliner** organized. For example, you can create a `Lighting` folder for all light assets or a `Static Mesh` folder for all static meshes in the scene.

> **Note**
>
> **Outliner** will be very crowded! Keeping it organized is very important. Create all the folders you need to make finding assets faster.

- **Settings**: You can decide what to show in **Outliner** and expand or collapse all the actors.

If you press and hold the LMB on an asset, you can move it onto another asset. This action allows you to attach the selected object to another. This is the same command as the **Attach** command.

> **Note**
>
> A folder in Unreal Engine is equal to a Windows folder. You can move assets inside it, rename it, or move it inside another folder. You can't apply transformation to a folder. The **Group** action creates a new actor in **Outliner** that allows you to select all the actors inside it in a faster way. You can apply some basic transformations to the group; the **Attach** action allows you to parent one or more actors to other actors. This means that all the transformations applied to the father actor are transferred to all children actors.

Now that we have learned how the **Outliner** panel works, we can go on and learn about how the **Details** panel works.

Exploring the Details panel

Under the **Outliner** panel, you can find the **Details** panel tab. This panel is where you can modify your assets with their specific options. The **Details** panel is "sensitive," which means that it changes according to the asset's type.

Say you do the following:

1. Add **Sphere** from the **Place Actors** menu to the Level Viewport.
2. Add **Point Light** from the **Place Actors** menu to the Level Viewport.

If you've done it right, you will have a new sphere and a new Point Light in the Level Viewport and **Outliner**. Now, if you select the sphere, the **Details** panel will be set up for the Static Mesh actor, with specific options such as its material.

Figure 2.43 – This is the Details panel when you select a Static Mesh actor; in this case, a cube

If you select the Point Light actor, the **Details** panel will change to allow you to modify a light actor. In this case, you will find light options such as **Light Color** and **Intensity**.

Figure 2.44 – This is the Details panel when you select a Light actor; in this case, a Point Light

In the **Details** panel, you can search for a specific command by using the **Search** typing field. You can filter all the commands by using the preset filter. As we saw in the *Transforming assets inside the Level Viewport* part, in the **Details** panel, you will always find the **Transformation** tab, which allows you to transform your assets by typing values. In the **Scale** row, you can find a lock. If this is locked, you can proportionally scale your object. If it's unlocked, you can type different values in each scale axes.

Now that we have learned more about all the panels that compose Unreal Engine 5's UI, we can finally explore the **Content Drawer** panel.

Discovering Content Drawer

Content Drawer is the place where you can manage all the assets inside your projects. When you import an asset, whether it is a 3D model, a texture, or an animation, or when you create a new actor directly inside the Engine, you will find it in **Content Drawer**. We will learn how the **Content Drawer** folder works and how to work with assets in the next two chapters.

By default, **Content Drawer** is hidden in the Bottom Toolbar. You can open it by clicking on the dedicated button (as we saw before in the Bottom Toolbar section), or you can press *Ctrl* + SPACE. **Content Drawer** is a special instance of the **Content Browser** tab. They are the same thing but have slightly different behavior. Indeed, **Content Browser** is locked to the Viewport. If you want to lock **Content Drawer** to the layout, you can use the **Dock in Layout** command on the top right of the panel.

Figure 2.45 – The Dock in Layout option in the Content Drawer panel

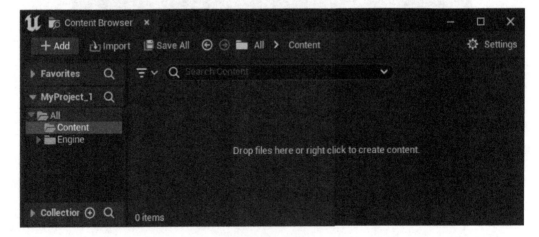

Figure 2.46 – The Content Drawer Dock in Layout is a Content Browser panel

As you can see, when you dock the **Content Drawer** in layout, it automatically opens a **Content Browser** tab. From now on, I will always use **Content Browser**. Every time you read **Content Browser** or see **Content Browser** in an image, you can use **Content Drawer**.

Now, we can look at all the options inside **Content Browser**.

Starting on the top right, you can see the following:

- **Settings**: Here, you can choose what you want to see and how to see it inside the **Content Browser**. I suggest you tick **Show Source Panel**, which allows you to browse folders in a faster way. **Show Engine Content** shows **Content Folder**, which includes some interesting and helpful assets, and **Show Plugin Content**, which shows the content folder of the installed plugins.

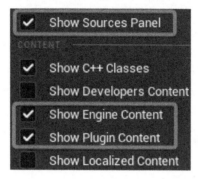

Figure 2.47 – Enabling Show Engine Content and Show Plugin Content helps you find useful actors

- **Save All**: This command allows you to save all the assets in the project. We will learn more about the saving process in the next chapter.

- **Import**: This command allows you to import assets from your local drive to the project. We will learn about assets and how to manage them in *Chapter 4*.

- **+Add**: Through this menu, you can import an asset from your local drive or add actors to your project by browsing all the different types of assets that Unreal Engine 5 provides to you. One very interesting feature is **Add feature or content pack**, which allows you to add all the actors (including mechanics and logic) from one or more presets to the project that you can choose during the process of creating a new project. This allows you to add, for example, the third-person sample feature in your current project without creating a new one.

You can drag and drop actors from **Content Browser** to the Level Viewport to add an actor to the level. Any time you add something from the **Content Browser** to the Level Viewport, you will find this asset in **Outliner**. You can have more than one panel of the same type in your UI layout such as more than one **Content Browser**.

Summary

In this chapter, we learned how the Unreal Engine UI works and how to move inside the Level Viewport. We discovered how the **Outliner** tab works, we have learned how the **Details** panel changes according to different assets, and we also now know what **Content Browser** is. You can now create and save your personal UI Layout, keep your project organized with folders and groups, and add content samples to your project. You have also learned how to add objects to the Viewport and how to transform them using a Gizmo and other transformation tools.

In the next chapter, we will discover how the Engine works and how the Engine's folders are organized. We will also learn how to save the project correctly and how to work with levels. We will also discuss naming conventions.

3
Exploring Unreal Engine 5 Project Structure

In this chapter, we will learn how **Unreal Engine** works, where to find folders and files, and how **levels** work. You will also learn about the saving process. We will first look at how the folders are organized in the Engine and look at some important ones that will be useful for us. Next, we will learn about how to work with levels and how working with levels helps us to keep our project organized. We will then move on to understanding the saving process of the assets, and, in the end, we will know how to properly name our files so that it is easier for us to work on a particular project without getting lost.

We will cover the following topics in this chapter:

- Discovering project folders and files
- Working with levels
- Understanding the saving process
- Using a clear naming convention

By the end of this chapter, you will feel confident about the saving process, and you will know how to organize your project by dividing it into levels and using a property naming convention.

Technical requirements

In this chapter, we will work inside the Engine. You need to have the Engine installed on your workstation to follow this chapter.

Discovering project folders and files

In this section, we will learn how the Engine folders are organized and how some files in them are very useful for our work.

When you create a new project, Unreal Engine 5 creates a set of folders in the destination path you've chosen in the **Unreal Project browser** window. The default path is /documents/Unreal Projects. The main folder has the name of the project you've chosen. Inside it, you will always find the following folders: Config, Content, DerivedDataCache, Intermediate, and Saved:

Figure 3.1 – Default project folder structure

Let's learn about these folders in detail:

- Config: In this folder, you can find some Engine files that define the options that the Engine uses by default at the first launch. You can open these files with a text editor. By modifying them, you can manually change several options without opening the Engine. The most useful for you is the DefaultEngine.ini file. Inside this file, you can easily and quickly change rendering settings. You can activate some expensive (in terms of hardware resources) rendering features, and your project won't be opened again. One solution to this is that you can disable that rendering feature directly inside this file. An example of this is **Raytracing** (we will talk more about it in *Chapter 6*). If you activate this feature on a poor workstation, your project will probably crash every time you try to open it. In this case, you can disable it in the DefaultEngine.ini file.

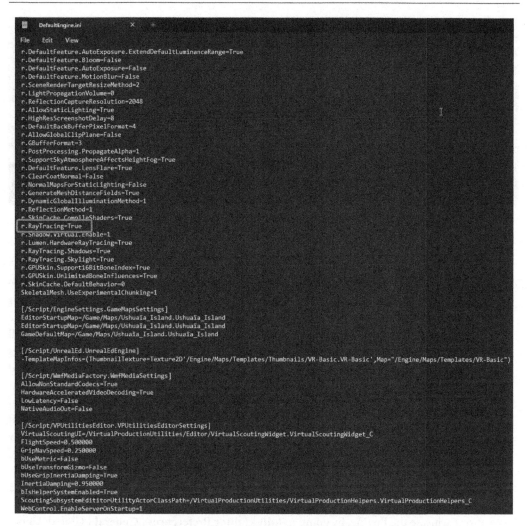

Figure 3.2 – You can change True to False to disable a specific rendering feature

- Content: This is the folder where Unreal Engine stores any actors you have imported to the Engine, or you have created inside it. Everything you create inside the **Content Browser**, you will find it inside the Content folder. If you create a folder in the **Content Browser**, you will find the same folder inside the Content folder. If you create an actor inside the **Content Browser**, you will not find it in the Content folder until you save it inside the Engine. For the same reason, if you copy and paste a file into the Content folder, those assets will not appear in the **Content Browser**. It's the same for deleting operations. Although you can create and delete folders directly in the Content folder, it's always better to do this operation inside the Engine because, especially for deleting operations, the Engine takes care of instanced objects and dependencies, avoiding some tedious errors.

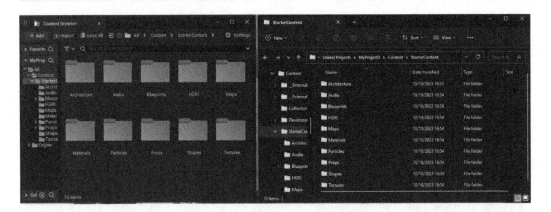

Figure 3.3 – You can find the same folder you have inside Content Browser in the Content folder

- `DeliveredDataCache`: Many Unreal Engine assets require additional "derived data" before they can be used. For example, materials need shaders to be compiled before they can be rendered. This data is stored as a cache in the `DeliveredDataCache` folder. This folder is large and could be a problem in a bigger project. The first time you open a project, the Engine will take several minutes (according to the number of assets that need to be compiled) to fill this folder. The next time you open the same project, Unreal Engine 5 will read all the things it needs from this folder, and it will be opened in a faster way. If Unreal Engine 5 doesn't find the folder, it needs to compile all the assets again. By default, the `DeliveredDataCache` folder is inside the project folder. That means that at the cost of a larger project folder, you need to compile your project only the first time even if you are changing the workstation. If you don't need to change your workstation or share your project with others, the delivery data cache position is only a hard drive space problem. One good habit to get into could be placing the `DeliveredDataCache` folder on a large hard drive usually dedicated to file storage. You can delete this folder to free some space on the hard drive, but Unreal Engine 5 will create it on the next start. You can change the `DeliveredDataCache` folder position directly inside the Engine, by going to **Edit** | **Editor Preferences** | **General** | **Global**. Under the **Global** settings, go to the **Derived Data Cache** option, where you can change the location of the `DeliveredDataCache` folder.

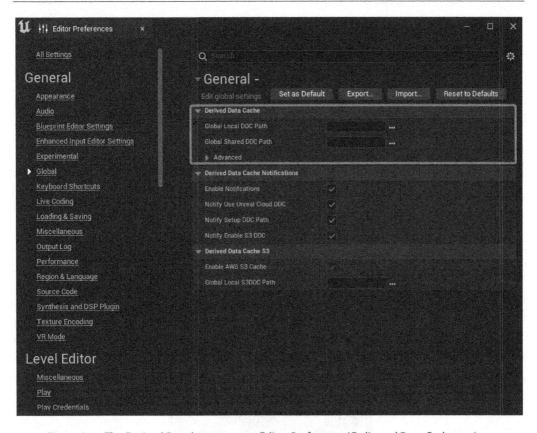

Figure 3.4 – The Derived Data button opens Editor Preferences' Delivered Data Cache options

- `Intermediate`: The `Intermediate` folder is where "intermediary" files go, which means that this folder is full of files that the Engine creates during the work session. We are not talking about generic assets but files useful for the Engine and specific processes. Nothing in the intermediate folder should be permanent. You can delete this folder to free up space on the hard drive but Unreal Engine 5 will create it on the next start.

- `Saved`: This folder contains files that are generated by the Engine such as configuration files and logs. Here, you can also find `Autosaves`. These files allow you to recover your work in case of problems or errors. To use them, you need to copy and substitute the file you need to recover in the `Content` folder. The `Saved` folder also contains a few subfolders where the Engine saves the screenshots created inside it. You can delete the `Saved` folder *but* remember to backup the `Screenshots` folder if you need it. When you delete this folder, you also lose `Autosaves`. If you delete this folder, Unreal Engine 5 will create it on the next start.

Figure 3.5 – The Saved folder's subfolder structure

Finally, in the project folder, you can find the project file. The project file has the project name set as name and *.uproject as the extension. You can open the project by double-clicking on it without opening the Epic Game Launcher. When you create a project shortcut on the desktop, using the **Create Shortcut** option in **My Projects** inside the Epic Game Launcher, you are creating a shortcut to this file. When you double-click on this file, the project will be opened with the version in which that project was created. If you right-click on the project file and select **Switch Unreal Engine Version...**, you can change the Engine version you want to use to open this specific project from the ones installed on your workstation.

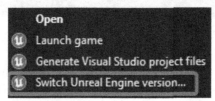

Figure 3.6 – Right-click menu on Unreal Engine project file

If your workstation runs Windows 11, right-click on the project file and click on **Show more options**. This action will show all the options, including the one about Unreal Engine.

> **Note**
>
> As we saw, you can delete some folders to free up space on your hard drive but be sure to do that with the Unreal Engine project closed. If you need to share your project with someone else, they will be able to create a compressed (*.zip) file of the project including only the Config and Content folders and the Uproject file, and the rest will be excluded. You can perform the same action directly inside the Engine by selecting **Zip Project** inside the **File** menu.

Now that we have learned how an Unreal Engine project works and how we can manage its folders, we can start to talk about levels and how to use them.

Working with levels

In this section, we will learn how to create a level, how to save it, and understand how working with multiple levels is the best workflow to achieve massive environments.

A level is all or a part of your world. A game is usually divided into multiple levels with various kinds of transitions between them. Sometimes, there are no transitions at all, and levels are loaded seamlessly during the game or during a cinematic. Levels contain everything we can see in our game. In your case, everything you can see in your cinematic environment. A level can contain static mesh actors (3D models) such as trees, buildings, or a vehicle; lighting actors; landscapes; skeletal mesh actors (animated assets) such as characters; sounds; visual effects such as a particle system; volumes and any kind of utilities that improve the visual quality of your project; and cameras and level sequences. It also includes blueprints and code assets. A level is like a snowball where you can see inside your world and modify it.

Creating a new level

You can create a level directly inside the Engine. You can do that in a couple of different ways. We will look at these methods in this section.

From the File menu

In the **File** menu, click on **New Level…**. From the **File** menu, you can also open an existing level or save the current one. To create a new level, you can also use *Ctrl + N* shortcut.

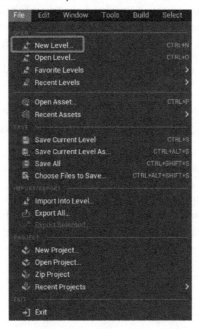

Figure 3.7 – The first part of the File menu is dedicated to levels

When you click on **New Level…**, the **New Level** window will open up:

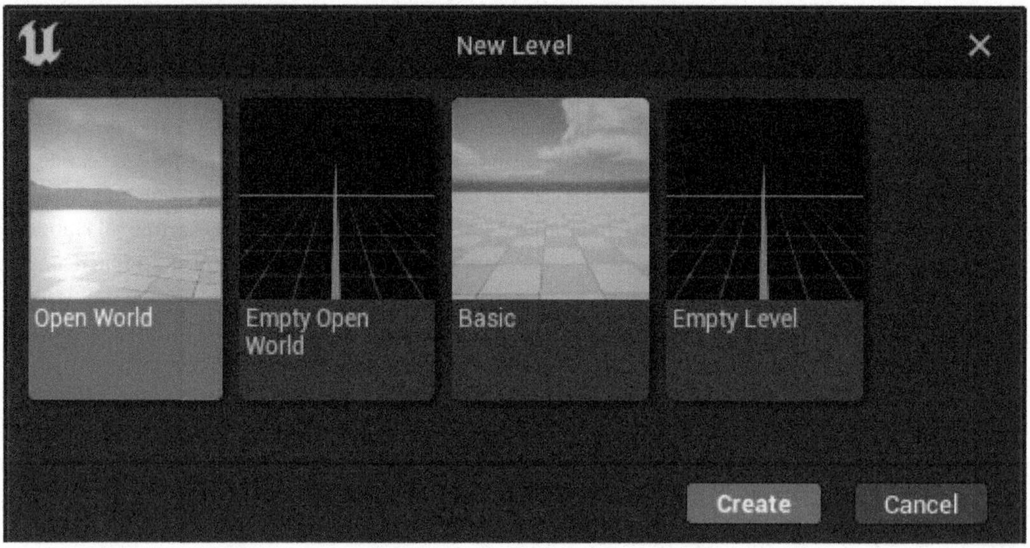

Figure 3.8 – The New Level window with different options to create a new level

Inside it, you can choose which kind of level you want to create. There are four different options:

- **Open World**: This option creates a new level already set with the new world partition tool, which allows you to manage massive worlds in a new and easier way. You can find an overview of this feature in *Chapter 7*. This level already comes filled with a landscape and a light system.

- **Empty Open World**: This option creates a level set as a world partition level but without any actors inside.

- **Basic**: This option creates a level with a floor plan, a lighting system, an atmosphere, and exponential fog. This is a perfect starting point to test assets, study, or try some content acquired on the marketplace.

- **Empty Level**: This option creates a level with nothing in it.

Select the preset you want to use and click on **Create**. You can use the basic options listed in the preceding bullet points. This automatically opens the new level. When you create a new level from the **File** menu, that level isn't already saved in the Content folder. In fact, you can't find it in the **Content Browser**, either.

You can save the level using the **File** menu by clicking on **Save Current Level…**. You can also use the *Ctrl + S* shortcut. The first time you save the level (and every time you use the **Save Current Level as…** command), the **Save Level As** window opens. In this window, you can choose the level name and where to save it in the Content folder.

Figure 3.9 – The Save Level As window

Click on **Save** to save the level in the selected location with the chosen name. Now, you should find your level in the **Content Browser**. You should also see it in the Content folder.

Level assets are saved in the Content folder as a file that has the name of the level and the .umap extension.

We can summarize the process in these steps:

1. In the **File** menu, click on **New Level…**.
2. Select the **Basic level** preset and click on **Create**.
3. In the **File** menu, click on **Save Level**.
4. Choose a name, select a location, and click on **Save**.

Next, we will learn how to create a new level directly inside the **Content Browser**.

Inside the Content Browser

You can also create a level directly inside the **Content Browser**. To do that, right-click in the **Content Browser** and select **Level** from the **CREATE BASIC ASSET** category:

Figure 3.10 – Create a new level option inside the Content Browser right-click menu

This option creates a level asset in the path you have launched the command in. The new level is ready to be renamed when you create it. The level asset that you have created is represented with a yellow underlined thumbnail. When you create a level directly inside the **Content Browser**, Unreal Engine will not open it automatically. The level has to be saved.

Now that we know how to create and save new levels, we can go on and learn how to work with multiple levels inside Unreal Engine 5.

Working with multiple levels

You can have more than one level asset for each project. You can create another level asset in the same way you have created the first one. You can jump into a new level by double-clicking on it in the **Content Browser** or by selecting the **Open Level** command in the **File** menu. You can also use *Ctrl + O* shortcut. When you try to open a new level, the Engine asks you if you want to save unsaved assets, if there are any. You can also duplicate the level to create a copy of it.

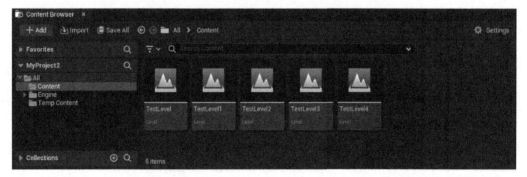

Figure 3.11 – Multiple levels in the same project look like this in the Content Browser

Having more level assets allows you to create different worlds inside the same projects. The perfect example is the *Super Mario* games. The game is your project, any level is a different world, with different assets and textures.

Working with sublevels

When you work with multiple levels, you can use them as a single entity or transform them into **sublevels**. A sublevel is a level asset that contains all assets or part of another level assets. You can use them to organize your projects in a more optimized way and decide which level has to be loaded and which not. You can manage sublevels with the **Levels** panel. You can find it in the **Windows** menu.

Figure 3.12 – Find the Levels panel in the Windows menu

You will always have a persistent level and you can have one or more sublevels that are always loaded or not loaded. Each time a new level is opened, it becomes the persistent level. Right-clicking on the **Persistent Level** within the **Levels** panel reveals various options for organizing the panel with folders, designating **Persistent Level** as the current level (this means that everything you will add to the Viewport will be added to this level), adjusting the levels' **Visibility** settings (meaning which levels we want to see and which not – this option will be useful next when we will add sublevels), some level **Selection** options, which allow us to select or deselect multiple levels inside the **Levels** panel, and some **Actors** options, which allow us to perform actor's selections inside the selected level.

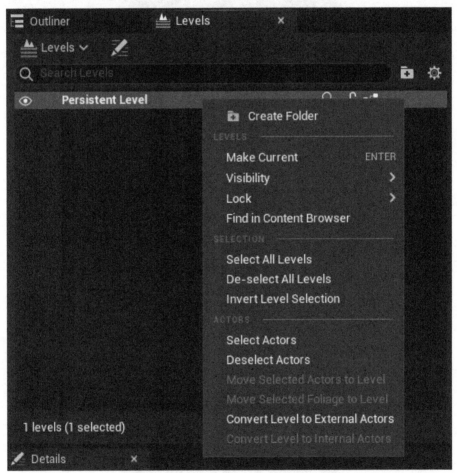

Figure 3.13 – The Persistent Level options in the Levels panel

Next, we will learn how to add sublevels to our project.

Adding sublevels

You can add a sublevel by creating a new level, including the assets that you have created in the persistent level, or create a new empty level and add assets to it later. When you create a new sublevel, it will be automatically transformed into the current level. After creating new sublevels, make sure to select the **Make Current** option to work in the level you were using before. You can also press *Enter* to make the selected sublevel the current level.

Creating a sublevel from an existing level

Follow these steps to create a sublevel from an existing level:

1. Click on the **Levels** drop-down menu and select **Add Existing…**:

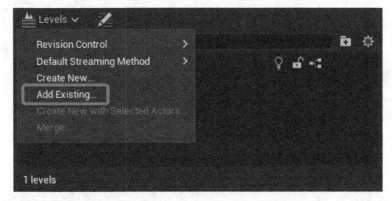

Figure 3.14 – The Levels drop-down menu – create a sublevel from an existing level

2. Select the level you want to add as a sublevel and click on **Open**.

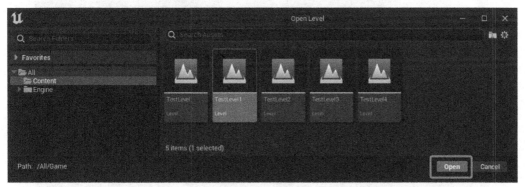

Figure 3.15 – The Open Level panel to add an existing level as a sublevel

You can also drag and drop the level from the **Content Browser** to the Levels panel.

Creating a new empty sublevel

To create a new empty sublevel, follow these steps:

1.   Click on the **Levels** drop-down menu and select **Create New...**:

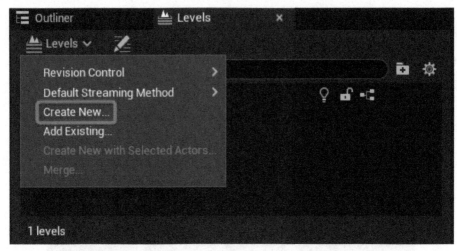

Figure 3.16 – The Levels drop-down menu – create a sublevel from an existing level

2.   Select the level type you want to create and click on **Create**:

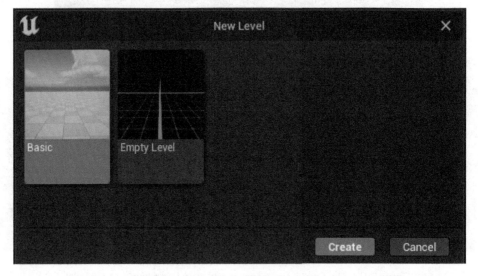

Figure 3.17 – The New Level window allows you to choose which kind of sublevel you want to create

3. Choose a name and select where to save the new level.

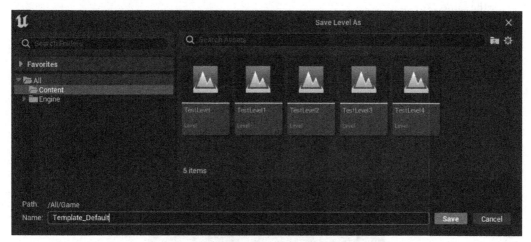

Figure 3.18 – This is the same Save Level As window you use when you create a new level

The new level is automatically added as a sublevel and marked as the current level. Creating a new empty level in the **Content Browser** and performing the drag and drop action in the **Levels** panel gives the same result.

Creating a level from existing assets

You can also create a new sublevel from one or more selected assets by following these steps:

1. Select all the actors you want to include in the new sublevel; select them inside the Outliner or Level Viewport.

2. Select **Create New with Selected Actors…** from the **Levels** drop-down menu.

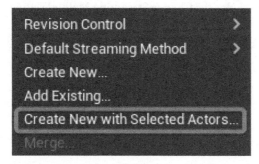

Figure 3.19 – The Levels drop-down menu – create a sublevel with selected actors

3. Choose a name and select where to save the new level. (The **Save Level As** window is always the same.)

4. All the selected actors will be removed from the original level, and they will be added to the new one.

Moving actors between sublevels

You can move actors from a sublevel to another with the following steps:

1. Select all the actors you want to move from one sublevel to another.

2. Right-click on the destination level (the level in which you want to move assets) inside the **Levels** panel. Select **Move Selected Actors to Level**.

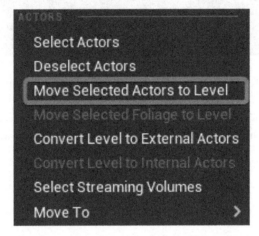

Figure 3.20 – The Levels right-click options menu – Move Selected Actors to Level

When you add a sublevel, you can right-click on it. The menu shows the same options you have on the persistent level plus the **Change Streaming Method** setting.

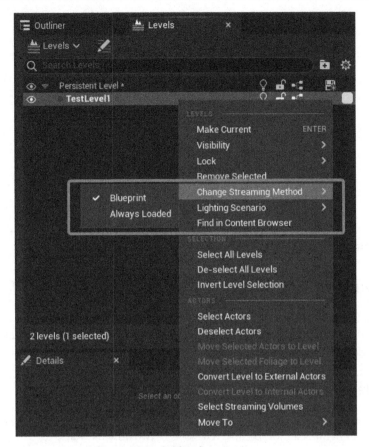

Figure 3.21 – Sublevels options menu

Here, you can change the way sublevels will be loaded. **Blueprint** allows you to control via script when this sublevel will be loaded. **Always Loaded** keeps the sublevel always loaded in the project.

Using sublevels is a great way to keep your projects organized and optimized. Dividing assets into different sublevels allows you to work in a non-disruptive mode on any assets inside any single sublevel. When projects become bigger, working with a sublevel helps to work in a better and faster way.

A good starting point to divide your project into sublevels is the following:

- An empty **Persistent Level**. This level will include all sublevels.

- The **Assets** sublevel with all the 3D assets inside.

- **Foliage** with procedural foliage assets.

- **Landscape** with landscape assets and painted foliage assets.

- The **Lighting** sublevel with all the lighting assets. You can have more than one lighting sublevel to create different lighting setups and switch between them.

Figure 3.22 – An example of how to organize projects using sublevels

Now that we have learned how to create and manage multiple levels inside our project, we can finally understand how the saving process works inside Unreal Engine 5.

Understanding the Saving process

In this section, we will learn how to properly save our assets inside Unreal Engine's project. This is a very important part of the learning process. Understanding it prevents you from losing part of the projects and working with the correct workflow.

Saving a level asset

As we already saw, when you create a level asset directly inside the **Content Browser**, it hasn't been saved yet. Unreal Engine 5 shows you unsaved assets in two different ways.

Figure 3.23 – You can see unsaved actors in different ways

On the modified and not yet saved asset's icon in the **Content Browser**, you will always see a little star. This star is telling you that this asset has been modified after the last save. Starting from Unreal Engine 5, on the bottom-right of the screen, the Engine notifies us if there are some assets unsaved. If you click on this button, the **Save Content** panel will show up. You can also click on the **Save All** button in the top-left of the **Content Browser**.

Figure 3.24 – Open the Save Content panel by clicking on the Save All button or the Unsaved button

The **Save Content** panel shows you all the actors you've modified from the last save. The actors are filtered by name, location, and type. You can check or uncheck any single actor. Click on the **Save Selected** button to save. The Engine will save only the checked files. The unchecked files are still in unsaved status inside your project. You will lose unsaved files only when you close the Engine without saving them.

What does a level save?

When you save a level asset, you are saving exactly what you can see in the Level Viewport and in the Outliner.

These are things that you are saving in a level:

- The actors that are placed in the level – any type, including lights, volumes, and blueprints

- The position, rotation, and scale of each actor that are placed in the level

- The materials that are assigned to each asset that are placed in the level

- Any values set in the **Details** panel for each asset that are placed in the level

The following aren't saved in a level:

- Actors in **Content Browser**

- Materials in **Content Browser**

- Any actors imported and placed in the level but not saved yet.

Unreal Engine 5's saving process works in three different steps. Levels are in the middle. At the lowest part, there is **Content Browser**/the `Content` folder, where all your assets imported from outside or created directly inside the Engine are stored. Between these assets, you also find level assets. So, when you save all the actors in the **Content Browser**, you are also saving level assets.

Going up a step, when you save a level asset, you are saving which actors from the **Content Browser** are used in this level with their specific settings. These settings will be valid only for the level in which they are saved.

At the top of the saving process, there is the `.uproject` file. This file launches the Engine and loads the project with all the assets contained in the `Content` folder.

This means that you can use a single actor in the **Content Browser** infinite times in infinite levels with infinite different settings, but in the `Content` folder, you will always have only one actor. Its different versions for each level will be saved in the level assets.

To be clear – if you have imported a chair model into your project, you can have it simultaneously in different levels with different materials without the need to have multiple assets in the **Content Browser**.

Now that we learn how the saving process works, we can explore some naming convention templates to use in our projects.

Using a clear naming convention

Unreal Engine projects grow in size quickly. Creating a massive environment or a game with a lot of different environments inside it requires a lot of actors of all kinds. In *Chapter 5*, we will learn, for example, that a basic material has at least three textures and that you can have hundreds of material instances, lights, and volumes. All of them are on the same projects or on the same level.

The only way to work in a faster and more relaxed way is to adopt a strong and clear naming convention starting from the beginning of the projects.

First, you need to create some folders and name them in a proper way. To create a folder, right-click in the **Content Browser**, select **New Folder**, and create the following folders:

- `Assets`: Populate this folder with 3D models

- `Textures`: Populate this folder with textures (any kind)

- `Material`: Populate this folder with materials.

- `Maps`: Populate this folder with levels.

- `Cinematics`: Populate this folder with level sequences.

You can also assign a different color to each folder to make it easier to find them. To do that, right-click on the folder and select **Set Color**:

Figure 3.25 – Set color options in the FOLDER OPTIONS menu

You can rename different types of actors in this way:

- **3D models**: `SM_Name_V01` (SM stands for static mesh).

- **Textures**: `T_name_textureType`. Texture types are as follows: B (base color), R (roughness), N (normal), AO (ambient occlusion), M (metalness), and D (displacement).

- **Materials**: We will learn about materials in a couple of chapters. For now, you need to know that we will have a master material (`M_name`) and (material instances (`MI_name`).

- **Levels**: You can name them with the name of the level. Be sure to use a simple and easily recognizable name.

- **Level sequences**: We will learn cinematics in the last part of the book. For now, you need to know that you can create a Level Sequence per scene or per shot. For per scene, you will use `SC_name` and for per shot, you will use `SH_name`.

We are now able to work with levels and sublevels, and we have understood the importance of a clear naming convention. Keeping the project organized will always speed up your workflow and prevent the loss of work.

Summary

In this chapter, you have learned about how project folders are organized and how to work with Engine files to modify settings without launching the project. You are now able to work with multiple levels and organize your project with sublevels. You have learned how to save a single asset, a level, or save all the actors in projects, and how the saving process works. Finally, you have understood how to use and the importance of using a simple and clear naming convention to keep your project organized.

In the next chapter, we will learn how to import 3D models, textures, and animated objects and how to work with them.

4
Importing and Working with Assets

In this chapter, we will learn how to import a **3D model** and all the characteristics that a 3D asset must have to be correctly imported. We will also learn how to import a **texture** and an **animated object**. At the end of this chapter, you will be able to import and save any kind of asset. This is a very important chapter for understanding how the Engine works with assets and how we can use any kind of 3D model or texture to build our environment. Knowing the fundamentals of asset importing is very useful to better understand the next chapters.

In this chapter, we will cover the following main topics:

- Importing a new 3D model
- Importing a new texture
- Importing an animated object
- Exercise: Creating a new project

Technical requirements

In this chapter, we will work inside **Unreal Engine 5**. You need to have the Engine installed on your workstation to follow this chapter.

You should also have a 3D model, an image, and an animated object. These are not mandatory but if you have them, you can try all the import processes we will learn in this chapter by yourself.

You can find thousands of free-to-use assets on Sketchfab: `https://sketchfab.com/`. You can log in with an Epic Games account. **CCO**-licensed (**Creative Common license**) assets are free to use even for commercial purposes.

Importing a new 3D model

In this section, you will learn how to import a 3D model into Unreal Engine 5. You can import different types of 3D assets, the most common being `.fbx` and `.obj` files.

3D assets need to have three prerequisites to be correctly imported into Unreal Engine and ensure the best visual quality and usability. These are as follows:

- **UV map**: Your model needs to have clear and non-overlapping UV maps to avoid textures and lighting issues. We can't go through UV mapping techniques in this book, but you can read about creating UVs inside Blender at the following link: `https://www.youtube.com/watch?v=Y7M-B6xnaEM`. UV mapping is generally a 3D modeler's task. Today, most of the 3D models you can download from an online library have good UVs. All the assets coming from Unreal Engine Marketplace have no UV issues, and it is the same for the Megascans Library (we will talk about that in *Chapter 8*).

- **Smoothing groups**: You need to assign smoothing groups to your geometry to let the light properly diffuse on your model's surface. A smoothing group is a group of polygons that share the same **normal** (the line that defines the way the light hits the polygon) to create a smoother surface, which is the same thing we said about UVs.

- **Material-based geometry**: This is not mandatory but highly suggested. It involves having a complex object divided considering its different materials. In other words, if you have a car model, you can merge all the chassis parts (that have the same material) to make it easier to assign materials in Unreal Engine. This will result in a single mesh with multiple materials. We will talk more about that in *Chapter 5*.

To import a new 3D model into Unreal Engine 5, you have two different methods: you can use the **Content Browser's Add** or **Import** option or drag and drop your files directly into the Content Browser.

Importing using the Content Browser options

To import a new file using the **Add** option from **Content Browser**, follow these steps:

1. In the source panel on the left, select the folder destination of your new file. If you don't have any folders yet, the file will be imported into the main content folder.

Figure 4.1 – Source panel on the left side of Content Browser

2. Click on the **Add** button in the top left of **Content Browser**.

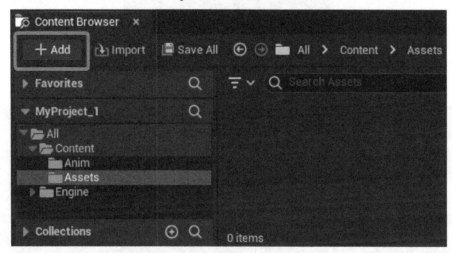

Figure 4.2 – The Add button in Content Browser

3. Select **Import to** [your Folder path].

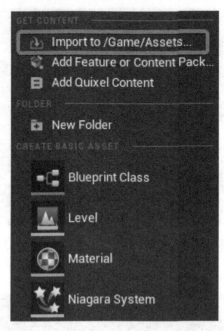

Figure 4.3 – The Import to options inside the Add menu in Content Browser

4.   Browse to the file you want to import to and click on **Open**.

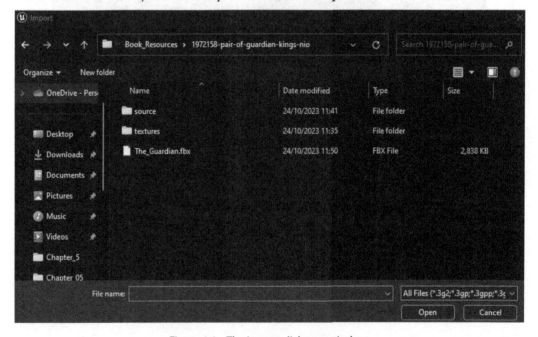

Figure 4.4 – The Import dialogue window

5. You can perform the same import action by clicking on the **Import** button instead of the **Add** button.

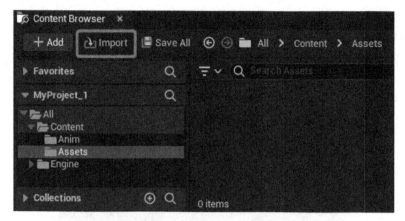

Figure 4.5 – The Import button in Content Browser

Independent of the method you decide to use, Unreal Engine 5 will display the **Import Options** window. We will learn more about it in the *Importing the assets* section of this chapter.

We can now explore the second import method that we can use to import 3D models inside Unreal Engine 5.

Importing using drag and drop

To import a new asset with the drag and drop method, you need to follow these steps:

1. In the source panel on the left, select the folder destination of your new file or files. If you don't have any folders yet, the file will be imported into the main Content folder.

2. Browse to your asset in your local drive, select your files, and drag and drop them into **Content Browser**.

3. Unreal Engine 5 will display the **Import Options** window.

> **Note**
>
> You can import assets only in the Content folder or in a Content folder's subfolder. If you try to import an asset into a folder that is not allowed to be an import destination folder, then Unreal Engine will not execute the import operation.

> **Note**
>
> **Asset** refers to any type of file. A 3D model is an asset; a texture is an asset; and an audio file is an asset. **Actors** are to be considered as containers of assets. Everything you import inside the Engine is an asset that Unreal Engine converts into an actor when you add it to a level.

Now that we know all how to import a new asset inside the Engine, we can go on and explore all the options the Engine gives us.

Importing the assets

Regardless of the method you use to import a new asset, Unreal Engine will display the **Import Options** window. This window allows you to modify importing options that will affect your assets inside the Engine.

When you import **Static Mesh Actor** (3D model), the **Import Options** window looks like this:

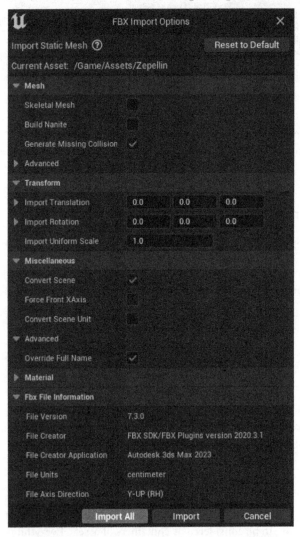

Figure 4.6 – The Static Mesh Import Options menu

Its content is divided into categories and some options are enabled by default. Let's take a look at what you can do inside this window:

- **Mesh**: Here, you can manage some mesh options. In this category, you can choose which part of the file you want to import or if you want to convert the mesh in some way. Here are further details:

  - **Skeletal Mesh**: This is about animated objects. If you are importing an animated object, this box will be checked by default. We will learn about it in the *Importing an animated object* section of this chapter.

  - **Build Nanite**: This allows you to import an asset already converted into a Nanite asset. We will learn more about Nanite in *Chapter 7*.

  - **Generate Missing Collision**: This is enabled by default and allows the Engine to generate collisions for your asset it doesn't have yet. This is a useful option for game projects. You can't pass through an object with collisions.

  - **Advanced**: In this panel (as you can see in *Figure 4.7*), there are a lot of different options to manipulate your mesh before importing it inside the Engine. The most relevant are **Combine Meshes**, which allows you to combine your assets into a single mesh, and **Import Mesh LODs**, which allows you to import **level of detail** (**LOD**) meshes if you have one or more.

  - LODs allow you to scale the complexity of your 3D model according to the distance of it from the camera. This feature is very useful in game production when there is a need to create a massive environment with a large field of view that is always loaded.

  - With LODs, you can tell the Engine to use the high-resolution version of the asset (in terms of polycount and texture resolution) when this asset is in front of the camera, and the lowest-resolution version when it is far away.

  - You can learn more about LODs by reading the official documentation of Unreal Engine: `https://docs.unrealengine.com/4.26/en-US/WorkingWith-Content/Types/StaticMeshes/HowTo/LODs/`.

  - You can leave the default values for the other options.

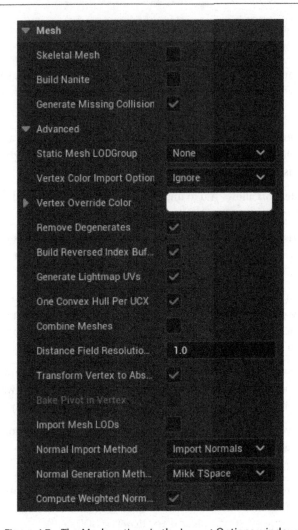

Figure 4.7 – The Mesh options in the Import Options window

- **Transform**: Here, you can set a starting offset value for both translation and rotation to apply to the asset you are importing. You can also set a starting scale.

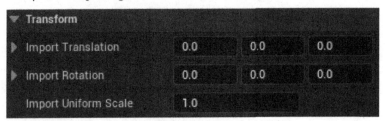

Figure 4.8 – The Transform options in the Import Options window

- **Miscellaneous**: Here, there are a couple of interesting options that can't fit into other categories but could be useful to speed up your workflow:

  - **Convert Scene**: This is enabled by default and allows the Engine to convert FBX coordinates to the Unreal Engine coordinate system.

  - **Convert Scene Unit**: This allows the Engine to convert whatever units you used to create the assets into Unreal Engine units (centimeters). Creating your assets in centimeters is a good habit.

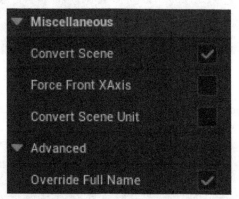

Figure 4.9 – The Miscellaneous options in the Import Options window

- **Material**: Here, you can change some material options:

  - **Search Location** means where the Engine can search for matching materials; in other words, where the Engine will search in the Content Browser for similar materials to assign to your 3D model. You can leave the default value: **Local**.

  - **Material Import Method**: This allows you to choose which kind of material Unreal Engine has to create for your new asset. If you choose the **Create New Material** option inside the drop-down menu, it will create a new master material; if you select **Create New Instanced Material**, the Engine will create a new material instance from an existing master material (you need to select the master material); and **Do not create material** will assign a default material to the new assets. If you choose this option, you can also choose whether you want to import a texture (if the asset file has one or more inside it). We will learn everything about material and shading in *Chapter 5*.

  - In the **Advanced** panel, you have two more options. **Invert Normal Maps** tells the Engine to invert the normal map texture values; **Reorder Material to FBX** is enabled by default and allows you to import an asset that will maintain the same material structure in terms of ID material (we will learn about that in *Chapter 5*). You can leave the default value.

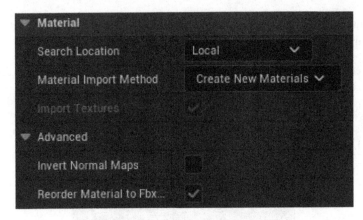

Figure 4.10 – The Material options in the Import Options window

- **FBX File Information**: In this panel, you can check information about FBX file format, such as version and owner.

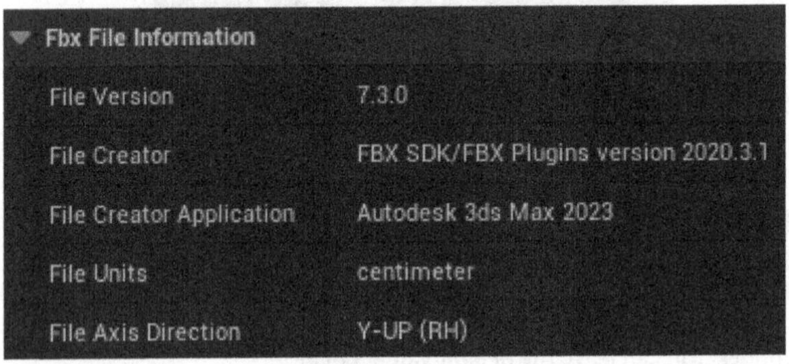

Figure 4.11 –FBX File Information in the Import Options window

When you have set all the options for your new asset, you have two options to finally import your new 3D model:

- **Import**: The Engine will import your asset with all the settings you have enabled or disabled in the **Import Options** window. In case you are importing a file with multiple objects inside, a new import window will appear to allow you to set import settings for each object inside the file.

- **Import All**: The Engine will import all the objects inside the file with the same options you have set in the import window.

If you have a single asset file, these buttons will perform the same command.

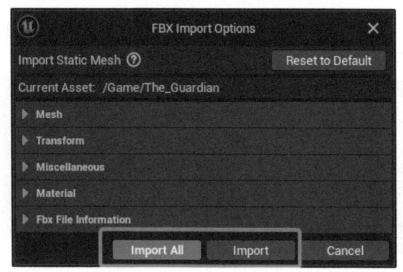

Figure 4.12 – The Import All and Import commands

Once you have imported your new 3D model, you will find it in **Content Browser** inside the destination folder you chose before. Importing a Static Mesh Actor always creates at least two different assets in **Content Browser**: the **Static Mesh** actor file and the **Material** actor file (except if you have selected the **Do Not Create Material** option).

Assets in **Content Browser** have different colors so you recognize them faster. The Static Mesh Actor's thumbnail is underlined with a *light blue* line. The material's thumbnail is underlined with a *green* line. If your file includes textures, you will also find texture assets in **Content Browser**. The texture's thumbnail is always underlined with a *red* line. We will talk more about how to import textures in the *Importing a new texture* section of this chapter.

Figure 4.13 – Different types of assets in Content Browser

Once you have imported your new asset, you will find that it hasn't been saved. You can check this in the same way we learned to with Level Actors in *Chapter 3*. A little star on the Static Mesh thumbnail tells you that the asset hasn't been saved. For this reason, if you open your Content folder in your local drive, you can't find your new asset. You can save your assets by clicking on the **Save All** button. Once you have saved it, you will find it in the Content folder.

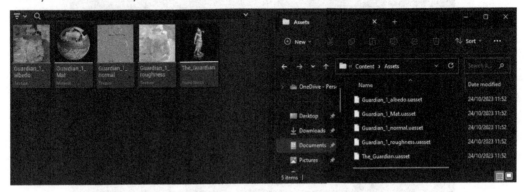

Figure 4.14 – Your asset is saved as a *.uasset file in the Content folder

Every time you import a new 3D model or, in general, a new asset from outside the Engine, Unreal Engine 5 will convert it into a proprietary file type. All the 3D models are converted into *.uasset files. This allows the Engine to work with optimized assets and allows you to use all the assets inside the Engine for different purposes including coding and mechanics.

> **Note**
>
> The fact that Unreal Engine converts any imported assets into a new file means that your project will work properly even without your source files. But this doesn't mean that you don't need an organized Reference folder. Understanding the difference between the Content folder and your Reference folder is very important. The content folder is full of converted files that you have imported and saved into the Engine. You will find all these files inside the Engine every time you open the project. The Reference folder isn't a folder created by the Engine; you can create it anywhere in your local drive. In this folder, you have to collect all your source files, such as your fbx files, your png files, and everything you have created to be imported into the Unreal Engine project. This allows you to keep your local library organized and reimport files in a faster way.

In **Content Browser**, you can perform some actions with your new asset. First, you can move, copy, and paste your asset through your folder structure. To do that, press and hold the LMB on your asset and drag and drop it on the folder destination.

Unreal Engine 5 will ask you if you want to copy or move your asset. Selecting **Copy** will create a copy of your asset in the destination folder. All the actors in the level referenced to the origin asset will not be modified. Selecting **Move** will cut and paste your asset to the destination folder. This action will take a while because the Engine will redirect all the instanced actors to the new asset position.

Advanced Copy Here opens a window that allows you to also copy the referenced actors. For example, you can also copy the assigned material.

Figure 4.15 – The Move or Copy options

> **Note**
>
> It's very important to perform copying or moving actions directly inside the Engine and not in the Content folder on your local drive. The reason for this is that the Engine will check for you all the dependencies linked to the assets you are copying or moving. This avoids reference problems or losing assets.

Now that we know how to import a new 3D model and how to save it in the Content folder, we can explore the Static Mesh Editor. If you left-click twice on your asset, the Static Mesh Editor will be opened.

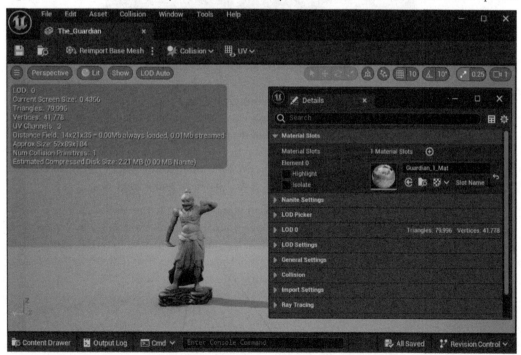

Figure 4.16 – The Static Mesh Editor window

The Static Mesh Editor is a window where you can manage the default status of your 3D asset. It's built like the main user interface and allows you to work with some important 3D asset settings. On the left, you have the Viewport (with the same options as the Level Viewport), which shows you the asset in its default status. On the right, you have a bigger version of the **Details** panel, which has a lot of options. Going through them now could be a little bit confusing because we need to learn some more things to understand these advanced options. Throughout the book, we will open the Static Mesh Editor to understand some of these settings and help us work on our project.

If you right-click on your asset in **Content Browser**, you can perform several commands:

- **STATIC MESH ACTIONS**: Here, you can open **UV Editor**, which allows us to manage UV mapping directly inside the Engine; remove vertex color if the asset has it (vertex color means assigning different colors to different mesh's vertices); convert the asset into a **Nanite** asset (we will learn more about Nanite in *Chapter 7*); and manage **Level of Detail** (here, you can change options regarding LODs. We learned what LOD is in the *Importing the assets* section earlier in this chapter).

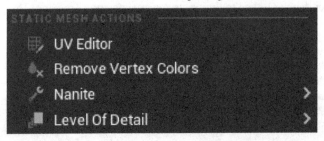

Figure 4.17 – The STATIC MESH ACTIONS options

- **IMPORTED ASSET**: In this panel, the **Reimport** option allows you to reimport your asset. This command only works if the source asset is in the original folder (the same folder you use to import it in the Engine). This is one of the reasons why is very important to organize a Reference folder. The **Reimport** action can be very useful because it allows you to start by blocking and updating your assets during the project without losing work. If the Engine doesn't find the asset in the original folder, it will ask you to choose a new asset.

The **Reimport With New File** option allows you to substitute the asset with a new one or reimport it from a different file. With the **Open Source Location** command, you can open the source folder location in your local drive. Last but not least, **Open in External Editor** allows you to open the file with software different from Unreal Engine. This only works if the Engine finds the source file. This is useful for updating a file in a faster way.

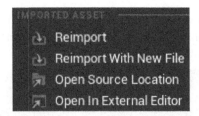

Figure 4.18 – The IMPORTED ASSET options

- **COMMON**: The **Edit** option opens the Static Mesh Editor that we saw before; you can duplicate, save, and delete your asset. When you decide to delete an asset, the Engine will show you all the dependencies of the asset before deleting it.

  In **Asset Action**, you have a couple of very important commands. **Select Actor Using This Asset** selects all the actors in the level that are using this asset. This is very useful for knowing, for example, which actors will be affected after a **Reimport** action. **Export** allows you to export the asset as FBX (the asset will be triangulated). **Migrate** is the safest way to move assets between projects. When you click on **Migrate**, the Engine will ask you to save all unsaved files. Then, it will open the **Asset Report** window.

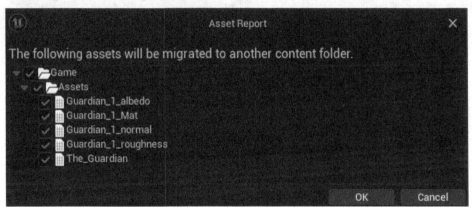

Figure 4.19 – The Asset Report window

In the **Asset Report** window, the Engine shows all the actors instanced to the asset you want to migrate. In other words, the Engine shows what It is going to migrate together with the selected asset to make it work properly. You can choose whether you want to migrate all the actors or part of them. The Engine will also migrate the folder's structure. If the destination project has the same folder structure, the asset will be migrated to the correct path. If not, the Engine will create all the new folders.

Lastly, you need to choose the destination project. To perform a correct migration action, you need to select a `Content` folder. If you select a different folder, Unreal Engine will ask you to select a `Content` folder.

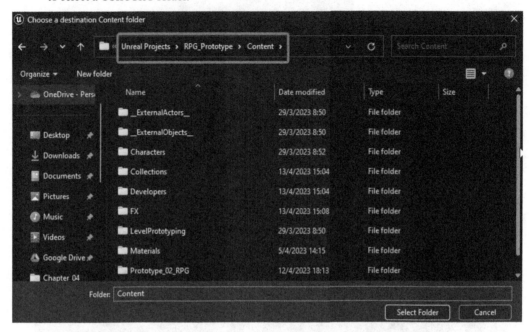

Figure 4.20 – Selecting a Content folder inside a project folder to perform a migration action

---

Note

Migration actions are complex, and you need to perform them with attention. However, they are sometimes very useful for cleaning up your project or starting a new project with a solid starting point. Migrating a level actor to an empty project will migrate all the actors inside the level and populate **Content Browser**.

- **EXPLORE: Show in Folder View** selects the asset in **Content Browser**. **Show in Explorer** opens the `Content` folder on your hard drive (so, outside of the Engine) and it automatically selects the `*.uasset` file referenced to the asset you have performed the command on.

Figure 4.21 – The EXPLORE options

- **References**: In this last section, you can perform some actions regarding references. The most useful option is **Reference Viewer**, which opens the **Reference Viewer** window. This window allows you to see all the references and dependencies of the assets in a clear node layout.

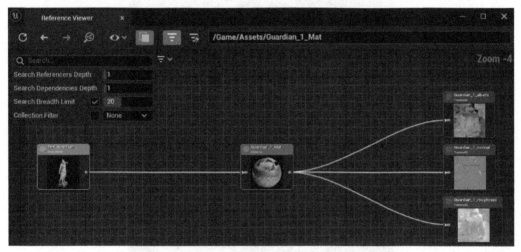

Figure 4.22 – The Reference Viewer window

Lastly, you can add your asset to your current level by dragging and dropping it into the Level Viewport. This action will render the current level unsaved.

When you drop the asset in the Viewport, you will find it in the Outliner. As we already saw in *Chapter 2*, you can transform the asset in the Viewport using the different transformation's Gizmo.

If you right-click on the object in the Level Viewport, you can see several commands to perform.

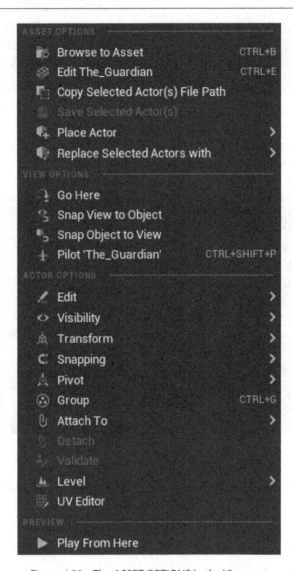

Figure 4.23 – The ASSET OPTIONS in the Viewport

Let's take a look at the most relevant ones:

- **ASSET OPTIONS**: Here, you have some options to manage your assets. You can select **Browse to asset** to navigate to the asset in **Content Browser**; edit and save your asset; and place an actor in the same position as the asset or replace the selected actor with another.

- **VIEW OPTIONS**: Here, you can find the same options we saw in the **Actor** options menu in the **Outliner** tab in *Chapter 2*. In addition, it has the **Go here** option, which centers the camera view on the object's position. You can perform the same command by pressing *F*.

- **ACTOR OPTIONS**: Here, you can find the same options we saw in the **Actor** options menu in the **Outliner** tab in *Chapter 2*. The most relevant in this case is **Pivot**. Inside it, you can find options to modify your asset's **Pivot** (Gizmo) position. This can be very useful if you need to perform transformations such as rotating the object around a point different from its center.

> **Note**
>
> When you import a 3D model, the Engine will always move the Gizmo to the center of the world. This means that if the model in your file isn't at the 0 , 0 , 0 position in the world, it will maintain its position also in Unreal Engine. *However*, its Gizmo will be moved to the center of the world. The reason why the Gizmo has been moved needs to be sought in the needs of the gaming industry. Sometimes you need to create a blocking map outside Unreal Engine. Moving the Gizmo to the origin during an import action allows you to import a file with an entire map, maintaining the position of all assets.
>
> If you want to import an object with the Gizmo at its center, you need to create a file in which you have the Gizmo at the center of the object and the object at the 0 , 0 , 0 position.

Figure 4.24 – Asset at the 0,0,0 position with Pivot not set on 3D model center

Exploring the Static Mesh Details panel

We can now explore the Static Mesh **Details** panel. As we learned in *Chapter 2*, the **Details** panel is "sensitive" and changes its content according to the selected actor type. Let's take a look at the **Details** panel options for Static Mesh Actors.

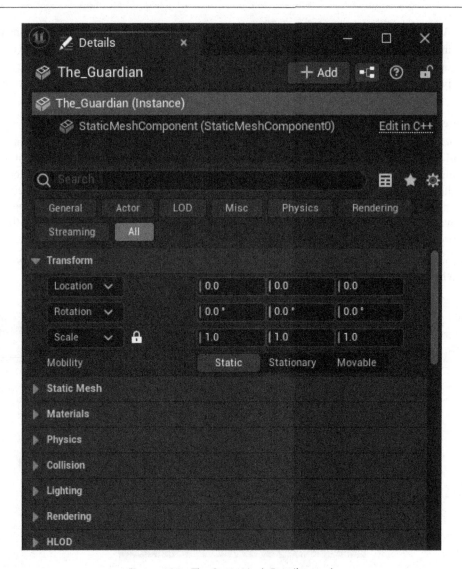

Figure 4.25 – The Static Mesh Details panel

The first part of the **Details** panel is the component panel. Here, you can find your Static Mesh Actor name and all the components included in this actor. Components aren't so relevant in Static Mesh Actors but, for example, a blueprint actor can have several components in it.

If you select a different component, the options in the **Details** panel will change. You can add a component to a single actor by pressing the **Add** button at the top right of the **Details** panel or by dropping assets directly into the component panel. For example, you can add a Rotator component, which allows your object to rotate on a specific axis.

Figure 4.26 – Component panel in the Details panel

Under the component panel, the **Search** box allows you to search for a specific option in the **Details** panel. Under this, filters can help you navigate through the options.

The **Details** panel options are divided into categories. There are a lot of options, so we are only going to learn the ones we need:

- **Transform**: We have already seen this in *Chapter 2*. Here, you can move, rotate, or scale your actor. If you click on the **Location**, **Rotation**, or **Scale** drop-down menus, you can change the type of transformation. **Relative** means that any transformation you apply considers the actual transformation of the object. In other words, if you are changing the location values, that value is relative to the position of the object in the world. The other option is **World**, which means that the transformation is always referred to as the world coordinates. The lock icon near the scale allows you to enable or disable proportional scale.

  Under the transformation values, we can find the **Static**, **Stationary**, and **Movable** options, which define the type of movability of the actor. A Static Actor can't be animated and can't be affected by dynamic lights. A stationary actor can be animated but it can't be affected by dynamic lights. A movable actor is a totally dynamic actor that can be moved and lighted by dynamic lights.

Figure 4.27 – The Transform options in the Details panel

- **Static Mesh**: Here, you can check the instanced asset to this actor. In other words, you can see to which asset this actor is referred. Under the asset thumbnail, there are two icons. The first with the arrow allows you to apply to this field an asset selected in **Content Browser**. This is very useful if you need to add the same asset to more actors. The second one with the folder allows you to browse to the asset in **Content Browser**.

Figure 4.28 – The Static Mesh options in the Details panel

- **Materials**: Here, you can see and change the material assigned to the assets. If the asset has only one material, you will find here only one element. An asset with multiple materials will have multiple elements. Elements are equal to material IDs. Material IDs are the different information that you can assign to a group of polygons to have multiple materials on a single mesh. Under the material's thumbnail, you can find the same commands we just saw for the Static Mesh asset plus the possibility to browse to the base color texture assigned to the material. The scroll menu next to the material thumbnail allows you to change material by selecting from a list of the materials loaded in the project. We will learn more about materials in *Chapter 5*.

Figure 4.29 – The Materials options in the Details panel

- **Other categories**: In the other categories, you can change rendering features and optimization settings that are, for now, useless to us.

Figure 4.30 – The Details panel's all option categories

In this section, we learned how to import and work with 3D assets. Now, we can move on and see how you can import an image to be used as textures.

Importing a new texture

In this section, we will learn how to import a new texture into Unreal Engine. The process is quite simple and similar to what we saw for 3D assets.

You can use the **Add** or **Import** option or drag and drop them directly into **Content Browser** (exactly as we saw for 3D assets).

When you import an image file, the process doesn't require a dedicated window. You will find your new image asset in the destination folder inside **Content Browser**.

The image asset has a preview of the image as a thumbnail, and the thumbnail is always underlined with a *red* line.

You can drag and drop your image asset in the Level Viewport on a specific actor. This will create and assign to the actor a new material with the image asset as a base color. You can perform this only with Static Mesh Actors. If you have an empty level or you are dragging your image asset on an empty part of the level, the command doesn't work. We will learn more about materials and shading in *Chapter 5*.

If you left-click twice on your image asset, the image editor window opens. This is the same as the Static Mesh Editor that we saw before but for the image.

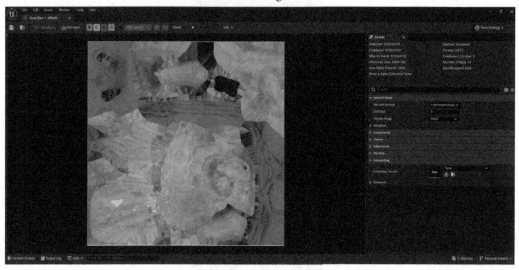

Figure 4.31 – The image editor window

In the main toolbar, you can save the asset in the Content folder by pressing the floppy disk icon; reimport the asset; enable or disable (this affects only visualization inside the image editor) the RGB image channel and Alpha channel by clicking on the **R**, **G**, **B**, or **A** icons; and zoom in/out the image in the Viewport (you can perform the same with the mouse wheel).

Figure 4.32 – Image Editor's main toolbar

On the right, you can find the **Details** panel. Here, you can find several options to manage how your image is interpreted by the Engine, especially in terms of quality and type.

The first part of the **Details** panel is dedicated to general information about the image file. Here, you can check the native resolution of your image; the resolution that the Engine is currently using to display the image; the image size; whether the image has or does not have the alpha channel; and information about the rendering method.

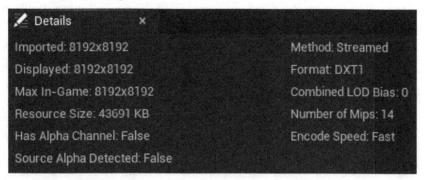

Figure 4.33 – The general information tab in the texture's Details panel

Under the **Search** text field, which allows you to search for a specific option, options are divided into categories as usual.

Let's take a look at the most relevant commands:

- **Level of detail**: This is the same thing as Static Mesh LODs but for image assets. It works with "presets" that are called **Mipmaps**. Mipmaps are a sort of chain of multiple levels of the sample image, each half the resolution of the level before. If enabled, it allows the Engine to scale the resolution of the texture according to the LODs of the Static Meshes. This is an optimization feature that affects the texture quality.

  In **Mip Gen Settings**, you can choose which type of Mipmap you want to apply to the image assets. **NoMipmaps** disables this feature and ensures that the Engine will always load the image at its maximum quality. You can also use Mipmaps to apply a calibration effect to the texture. **Sharpen4**, for example, makes the image sharper.

Figure 4.34 – The Level of Detail tab in the texture's Details panel

- **Compression**: In this category, the most important option is **Compression Settings**. This drop-down menu allows you to change the compression settings of the image. In other words, you can tell the Engine the function that the image will have. In some cases, the Engine will automatically change the compression settings. For example, if you are importing a normal map (we will learn more about that in *Chapter 5*), the Engine will automatically change the compression setting to **Normal Map (DXT 1/5, BC1/3 on DX11)**.

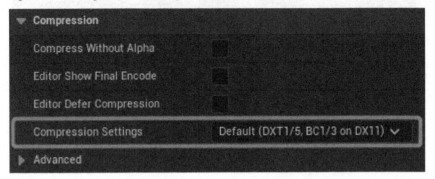

Figure 4.35 – Compression Settings in the texture's Details panel

- **Texture**: If you are using the image assets as a texture, you can change some settings to create material effects in this category. We will explore them in *Chapter 5*.

Figure 4.36 – The Advanced options in the Texture category

- **Adjustments**: In this category, you can apply some color correction adjustments to your image asset.

Figure 4.37 – The Adjustments options in the texture's Details panel

We can now check which actor options we have in the Content Browser. If you right-click on the image assets in **Content Browser**, you can perform the same commands that we already saw for the Static Mesh Actor, except for the **TEXTURE ACTIONS** category.

The **Create Material** option allows you to create a new material using this image as a base color texture. Additionally, the **Convert to Virtual Texture** option converts the image asset to a virtual texture. Virtual textures are a new feature that allows the Engine to manage very high-resolution textures.

If you want to learn more about **Runtime Virtual Textures**, you can check the official documentation of Unreal Engine: https://docs.unrealengine.com/4.26/en-US/ RenderingAndGraphics/VirtualTexturing/.

Lastly, the **Find Materials Using This** option will show you all the materials that are using this image asset. We are not interested in other options.

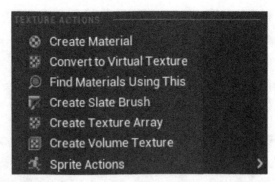

Figure 4.38 – The TEXTURE ACTIONS options in the image asset options menu

Now that we know how to import and manage 3D assets and textures, we can take a look at how to import animated objects.

Importing an animated object

In this section, we will understand how to import an animated object. Every file with a keyframe animation (on both simple transformations or rig) or a backed simulation has to be considered an animated object.

In our journey in environment creation, we probably don't need to import complex animated objects and we will learn how to create simple animations directly inside the Engine. But maybe you have experience in animation and have a lot of animated objects to import inside the Engine and use to populate your environment. For this reason, it is important to know the basics of how to manage an animated object.

The import process is the same as importing a Static Mesh asset. The **Add** or **Import** button or dragging and dropping will work also for animated objects.

When you import an animated object, the same **Import Options** window that we saw for Static Mesh Actors will be opened with some different options. All of the same options will work in the same way.

Let's take a look at the differences:

- **Mesh**: If you are importing an animated object, Unreal Engine recognizes it and enables **Skeletal Mesh** by default. The Skeletal Mesh is a mesh that can be deformed by an animation. As a result, when you import an animated object, you will always have a Skeletal Mesh asset. However, if you disable **Import Mesh**, the Engine will import only the Skeletal Mesh. Why? Sometimes, you need to update an animation or a rig and you want to reimport only that. In such cases, the **Skeleton** option allows you to choose a different Skeletal Mesh for this animated object.

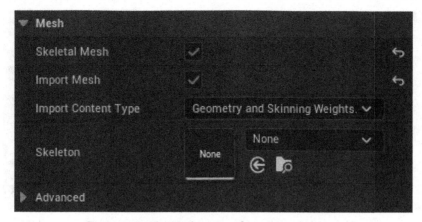

Figure 4.39 – The Mesh options for animated objects

- **Animation**: If **Skeletal Mesh** is enabled, you can explore the animation category. If you have any kind of animations in your file, you need to enable **Import Animations** to import them. When you enable the **Import Animations** option, you have access to the **Animation** options. **Animation Length** allows you to modify the animation range to import. We are not interested in the **Advanced** options.

Figure 4.40 – The Animation settings for animated objects

Every time you import an animated object, you will find at least three assets in **Content Browser**. The first is **Skeletal Mesh**, which has the name of the asset and the thumbnail underlined in *pink*.

The second one is the **Skeleton** asset. This is equal to a rig made in Maya, Blender, or any 3D manipulation software. This file always has a *light blue* underlined thumbnail. Its name is [asset name]_skeleton.

The third one is the **Physics** asset that, in an extremely simple way, helps to manage bones and collisions. This file always has a *yellow* underlined thumbnail. Its name is [asset name]_PhysicsAsset.

If you have enabled the **Import Animation** options, you will also find the animation asset. This animation works only with the Skeletal Mesh you have imported along with it. Animation assets always have a *green* underlined thumbnail.

Figure 4.41 – Different types of assets generated when you import an animated object

We need to explore how to use a sequencer to play animations in the Level Viewport. Animation will not be covered in this book because it does not align with the book's objectives. However, Chapter 11 will explore the art of crafting cinematic shots through camera animation. For further insights into playing animations within the Engine, refer to the guide provided at the following link: `https://dev.epicgames.com/documentation/en-us/unreal-engine/animating-characters-and-objects-in-unreal-engine`

At this point in the book, you should be able to move confidently inside the Engine, manage your asset library, folders, and Engine files, and import all you need inside the Engine. After this chapter, your level will grow. We are going to explore materials, lighting, and some more advanced features that will allow us to create something nice inside the Engine at the end of *Chapter 7*.

Before that, we need to be sure that we have understood everything clearly.

Let's do an easy exercise to consolidate what we have learned in these four chapters.

Exercise: Creating a new project

In this section, you need to create a new project with specific settings and perform some actions to verify all the notions that we learned before that point.

Follow these steps:

1. Create a new **film blank** project and set it to reach the best visual quality. You don't need starter content. Enable/disable Raytracing according to your hardware specs.

2. Import a 3D asset.

3. Create a new level and add the asset to the level.

4.   Now, create another two levels and add two copies of the same asset to them. Move any single assets into different positions, rotate them, and scale one of them in proportional mode.

5.   Transform one or more levels into a sublevel.

6.   Save, close the Engine, and reopen it to verify your work.

If you do everything well, you will have the first level with an asset inside, and the second level with four assets inside and at least one sublevel.

Summary

In this chapter, we learned how to import and work with different types of assets. You should be able to import 3D models, images, and animated objects, and work with assets inside the Engine.

You can modify basic texture settings and manage options in different **Details** panels, including Static Mesh Actor's **Details** panel and animated object's **Import** options. With the final exercise, you should have covered all the processes to start working on a new project with custom assets.

Now, we are ready to level up and introduce **material fundamentals** in the next chapter.

5

Mastering Materials and Shading

In this chapter, we will learn the fundamentals of PBR shading in Unreal Engine 5. Starting from very simple examples, we will be able to create a complex Master Material with Material Functions by the end of the chapter. We will learn how to create Material Instances and how to organize parameters. We will also be able to start creating Master Materials and Material Functions for use in future projects.

The following topics will be covered:

- Understanding PBR fundamentals
- Creating your first material
- Understanding Material Instances
- Creating a Master Material
- Using Material Functions

Technical requirements

In this chapter, we will create materials with textures. To easily follow the learning process, you will need a texture set composed of a Base Color texture, Roughness texture, Ambient Occlusion texture, and Normal Texture. You can also use Unreal Engine 5's Starter Content.

Understanding PBR fundamentals

In this section, we will learn how Unreal Engine interprets materials and what PBR means. Every rendering software adopts specific rendering rules to achieve the most accurate final frame. These software use Materials to show how objects look when they are hit by a light.

What does PBR mean?

First, we need to understand what a material is. A **material** is an asset applied to a mesh to control its final visual look. In simple terms, it is like a "paint" with several properties, such as color or reflectivity. When the rendering process starts, materials define how light interacts with the surface it is applied to.

Unreal Engine 5 is a real-time rendering software based on PBR.

PBR (Physically based rendering) *"means that surfaces approximate the way light behaves in the real world, as opposed to the way we intuitively think it should. Materials that adhere to PBR principles are more accurate and typically more natural looking than a shading workflow that relies fully on artist intuition to set parameters."*

This is how the Unreal Engine 5 documentation defines PBR. In other words, working with the PBR model means working with a system that simulates real light physics, ensuring a more realistic result. It's an intuitive and consistent system; it's physically accurate and uses real-world measurements. PBR is a combination of **Materials**, **Lighting**, and **Exposure** and works well for both photorealistic and non-photorealistic renderings.

The main rule to follow when you start to create a physically based material is to create the material you will see and not the material in which the asset is made. In other words, if you are creating a colored metal container, you need to create a varnish material instead of a metal material.

To understand this simple but extremely important concept, look around you and try to understand which material you need to create to reproduce objects in your room. A fabric with an all-over stamp needs the stamp material; painted plastic needs the painting material; a brick wall with graffiti on it needs a material made of concrete and painting.

We are now ready to discover the PBR model's primary inputs.

Primary PBR inputs

Material creation in Unreal Engine 5 passes through a specific value (which can also be textures) that will define the physical attributes of your surfaces.

There are four primary PBR values:

- **Base Color**: This defines the color your material will show. It's a linear RGB value between 0 and 1. Avoid pure black (0) and pure white (1), as they don't really exist in nature. It can also be a texture. A Base Color texture has flat color without specularity or shading.

Figure 5.1 – Good/bad Base Colors

- **Metallic**: This defines the **metalness** of your material. In other words, this defines whether your material is a metal or not. For this reason, its most common usage is on (value 1) or off (value 0). It can also be grayscale textures, with values ranging from 0 (a pure black color) to 1 (a pure white color).

Figure 5.2 – Metallic values from 0 to 1

- **Roughness**: This defines how rough your surface is. Its values are a range of smoothness that goes from 0 (a mirror-like surface) to 1 (a rougher matte surface). It can also be defined by a grayscale textures, with values ranging from 0 (a pure black color) to 1 (a pure white color). Unlike with Metallic, fine-tuning the roughness value between 0 and 1 allows you to create infinite material variations.

Figure 5.3 – Roughness values from 0 to 1

- **Specular**: This defines the specular value of your material. It's a grayscale value that ranges from 0 to 1. It's a good habit to leave this value at 0.5 and work with a roughness value to obtain the desired effect.

> **Note**
> Working with the specular value can help to create very stylized effects or generate an over-the-top glossiness effect. Textures should always be powers of two. This means a resolution starting from 16x16 pixels to 8192x8192. Textures do not have to be square, as long as they are powers of two. This means that 16x128 pixels or 2x4096 pixels are all acceptable examples.

In this section, we have learned the fundamentals of the PBR rendering model. We are now ready to create our first material.

Creating your first material

In this section, we will learn how to create a new material, and we will take our first steps in creating different kinds of surfaces using the **Material Editor**.

You can create a new material directly in the **Content Browser** by clicking the right-mouse button inside it and selecting **Material**. The command will create a new asset in the **Content Browser**, ready to be renamed. Remember to rename it properly (you can check naming convention tips in *Chapter 2*). As we saw in the previous chapter, Material thumbnails are always **green underlined**.

Figure 5.4 – Creating basic assets in the right-mouse button content browser options menu

To take our first steps in material creation, we can add a simple sphere to the Viewport and assign to it our new material.

You can assign a material in three different ways:

- Drag and drop the material asset directly on an object placed in the Level Viewport.

- Drag and drop the material asset in the material slot inside the details panel.

- With the material selected in the **Content Browser**, you can assign the material by clicking on the arrow icon under the material thumbnail in the asset's details panel

Figure 5.5 – Assign the selected material icon

Perfect! We are now able to assign a material to an actor placed inside the Level Viewport.

> **Note**
>
> 3D models can have more than one material slot. Any material slot is referred to a mesh or a part of the mesh inside the asset. The material slots are equal to the number of materials IDs that the source file has saved for the 3D model. To change material elements in terms of the portion of the asset they are referred to, you need to modify the source file.
>
>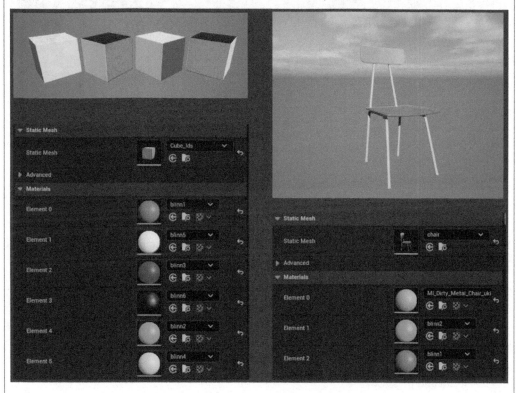
>
> Figure 5.6 – Assets with multiple material slots

Note

You can also assign a material in the **static mesh editor** (you can open it by double-clicking on the asset in the **Content Browser**). The first part of the details panel is dedicated to Materials. Here, you can isolate any single material element (this affects only the visualization inside the static mesh editor viewport) or highlight one or more material element. Materials assigned in the static mesh editor are default material assigned to that 3d model. This means that these will be the materials that the object will have available any time you add it to a new level. Otherwise, materials assigned in the static mesh details panel work only in the level you are working on.

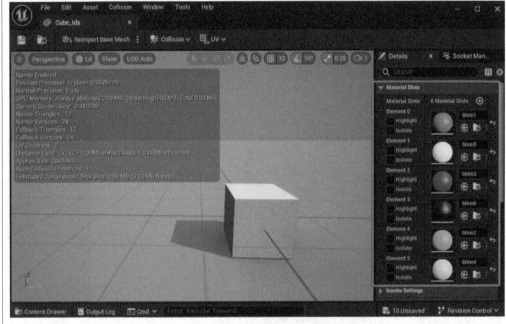

Figure 5.7 – Material slots inside the static mesh editor

The three different material assigning methods that we have just discussed will achieve the same result – the material will be assigned and visualized in the Viewport.

A Material is an asset exactly in the same way a 3D model or a texture is. For this reason, when you create a new one, it is not automatically saved. You can save it in different ways:

- Click the **Save all** command
- Right-click in it and select the **Save** command
- Select it and press *Ctrl + S*

Now that you have assigned your new material to a sphere in the Level Viewport, you should see this:

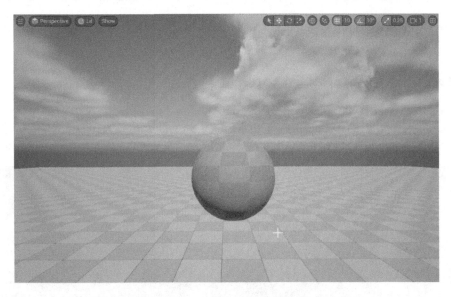

Figure 5.8 – A new material on a sphere looks like this

Note

The first time you assign your new material without applying any settings, it could be totally black instead of having the default squared texture. It depends on the Engine version you are using.

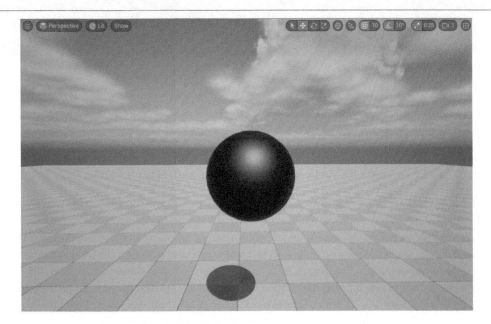

Figure 5.9 – A new material on a sphere could look like this

We have just created our first material. But how we can modify it? We are now ready to learn how to use the **Material Editor**.

Exploring the Material Editor

Once you have created your material, you need to modify it in order to create exactly the surface type you want for your asset. The only way to do that is through the Material Editor. You can open it by double-clicking with the left-mouse button on the material thumbnail in the **Content Browser**.

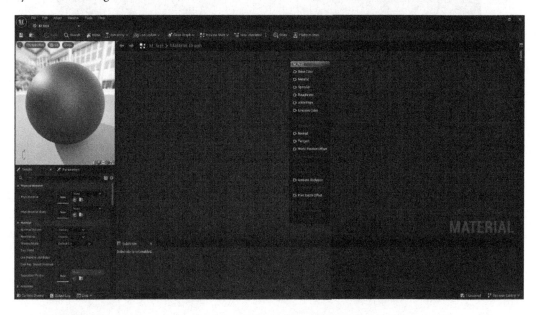

Figure 5.10 – Unreal Engine 5 Material Editor

The Material Editor is a very intuitive node-based editor that allows you to create any kind of surfaces you need for your project.

The Material Editor's user interface is like Unreal Engine's asset editor, which we saw in previous chapters. Let's take a look at the commands we can find inside the Material Editor:

- **Main toolbar**: Here, you can save your material and browse it into the **Content Browser**. There are also some utilities to make the material creation workflow easier. The most relevant are **Apply**, which allows you to update your material, affecting the material preview; **Home**, which recenters the camera to the material main node and performs the same command that *F* performs in the Level Viewport(centering the camera view to the object position) but on the material main node; **Live update** with its default value, updates the material preview in real-time; and **Clean Graph**, which allows you to clean unused expressions or hide them.

Figure 5.11 – The Material Editor's main toolbar

- **Preview viewport**: This works exactly the same way as the Level Viewport, *but* it shows a preview of the material. In the top left of the viewport, you have the same options that you have in the Level Viewport(which we saw in *Chapter 2*), such as changing the viewport type, changing the visualization mode, and deciding what to show in terms of rendering features. In the down-right side, you can change the preview mesh to use to preview your material. You can choose between different basic meshes or use an asset from the **Content Browser**. To do that, you have to select **Static Mesh Asset** in the **Content Browser** and click on the last mesh preview options.

Figure 5.12 – With this command, you can use a static mesh imported
in the Engine as a preview mesh for your new material

- **Viewport**: Here is where you can build your material from scratch. If you click the right-mouse button, you can search for and add new nodes to your graph. On the right side, you can open the **palette** to see all the available nodes. The main node at the center of the viewport represents your material output with all the inputs you need to link. You do not need to fill in all the available inputs. You can use one or all of them. The available input can change according to the **Material Domain**you are using. You can change the Material Domainin the details panel on the left side.

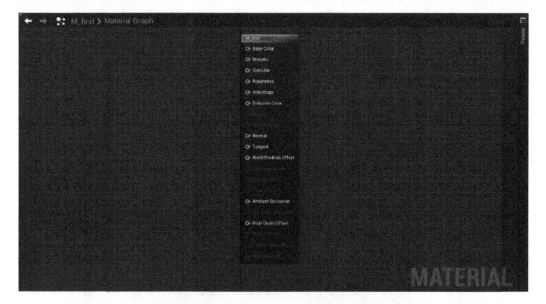

Figure 5.13 – The Material Editor's viewport

- **Detail panel**: This is the details panel dedicated to the material you are creating. The are several options inside it. The most relevant are in the **Material** category. **Material Domain**allows us to change the type of material we want to create, in terms of physical characteristics. The physical characteristics result in different inputs inside the material main node. The default option is **Surface**, which allows you to create any kind of surfaces that exist in the real world, **Deferred Decal** sets the main material node to create a decal material. We will learn more about Decal assets in *Chapter 8*. **Light Function** allows you to create a material to modify light assets. For example, you can create a material that allows you to make a light flicker, which we will learn about in *Chapter 6*. **Volume** and **Post Process** allow you to create materials that can be assigned to volume actors. This is useful to create effects in your scene such as color correction effects or atmospheric effects. **User Interface** allows you to create material for use in your user interfaces. The next option is **Blend Mode**. This allows you to choose the consistency of your material. In other words, you can choose the level of visibility of your material. **Opaque** is a solid surface, and **Masked** means that your material can be totally visible (pure white) or totally invisible (pure black value). The **Masked** option enables **Opacity Mask** input to the material main node. **Translucent** means that your material can be transparent. These options will enable an opacity value in the material main node, and it will also disable a lot of inputs that can work only on opaque surfaces. The last option is **Shading Model**, which determines how light interacts with your material. We don't need to know all the options inside this menu. The most relevant are **Default Lit**, which will light your material in the standard physical way, and **Unlit**, with which your material will ignore the lighting, showing you only the Base Color; the other options are types of presets to create not standard surfaces or different material types.

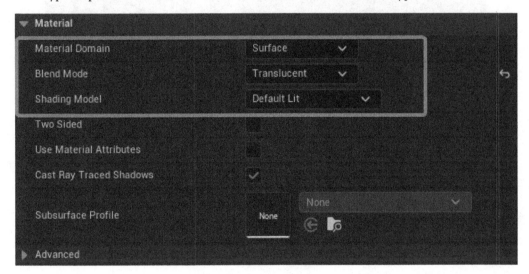

Figure 5.14 – The Material Editor's detail panels

In this chapter, we will create a surface opaque material. You can leave the Material Domain option as default.

Before we start to add some basic nodes, we need to learn how we can move inside the Material Editor's viewport. It works like the Level Viewport without the *WASD* movement. You can pan the viewport by moving the mouse while clicking and keeping the right-mouse button pressed. A hand icon will appear inside the viewport. With the mouse wheel, we can zoom in and zoom out of the viewport.

Figure 5.15 – The pan icon inside the Material Editor's viewport

Now that we know how to move inside the Material Editor's viewport, we can now start to add some basic nodes to our material.

Adding basic nodes

We are now ready to create our first material. We can start by adding values to the **primary PBR inputs** that we saw before. To add a new node, click the *right-mouse button* in the Material Editor viewport and type the name of the node you are looking for. You can also browse manually through all the categories. Follow these steps:

1. Add a **Constant3Vector**. You can search for it or click and keep *3* pressed on the keyboard, and then press the left-mouse button.

2. Add a **Constant**. You can search for it or click and keep *1* pressed on the keyboard, and then press the left-mouse button.

Figure 5.16 – Constant3Vector and Constant nodes.

A **Constant3Vector** is a constant RGB value. Inside this node, you can change red, green, and blue values to obtain a specific RGB value. In other words, you can obtain a plain color. To change values inside a Constant3Vector, double-click the left-mouse button on the node. The color wheel will appear. With the node selected, you can also change the color inside the details panel. This will be the color of your material.

3. To connect a node output to a material domain's input, you can simply drag the node's output into the Material Domaininput. We can connect the Constant3Vector node to the **Base Color** input.

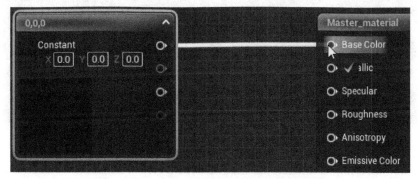

Figure 5.17 – Adding color to your material

A **Constant** node is a constant value that ranges from minus infinite to plus infinite. You can change the value directly inside the node or in the details panels, with the **Constant** node selected. As we saw before, we can change a physical material's properties by adding different values to the **Metallic**, **Specular**, and **Roughness** inputs. The **Constant** node is the easiest way to change these values. You can now create three different **Constant** nodes and link them to the **Metallic**, **Specular**, and **Roughness** inputs.

4. You can set **Metallic** to 0.0, **Specular** to 0.5, and **Roughness** to 1.0 and choose a **gray color**.

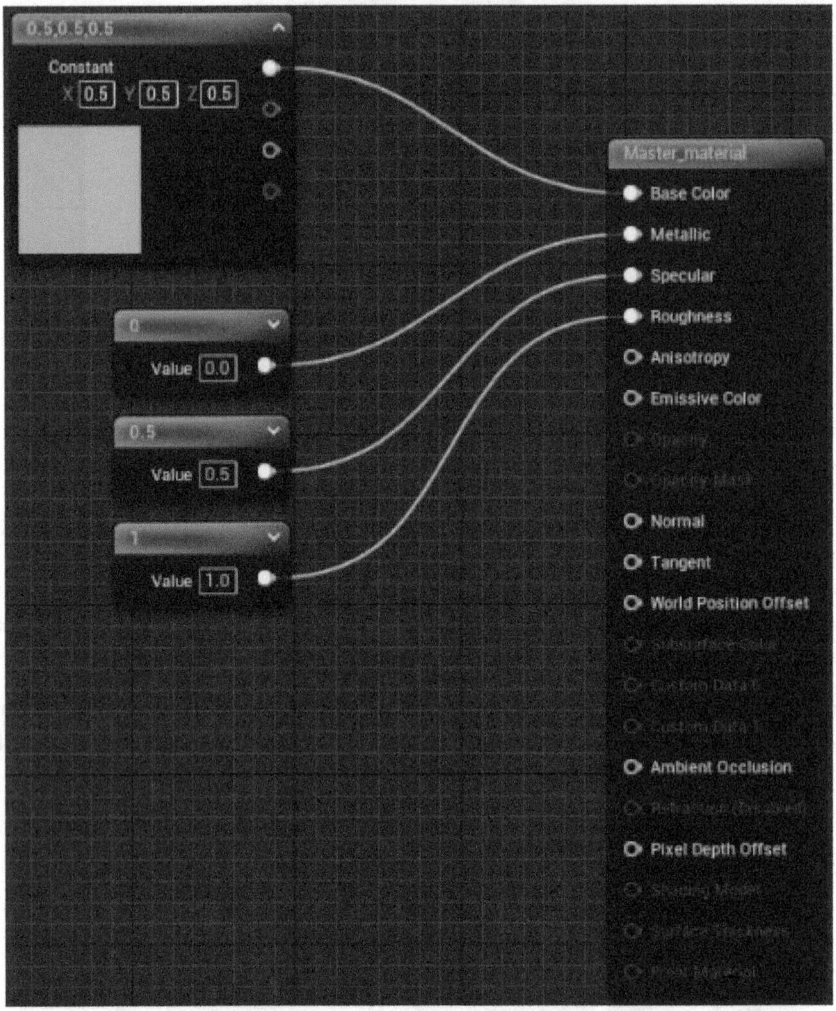

Figure 5.18 – A base material with simple vector nodes

We have just created a **concrete** material. Concrete is gray (a Constant3Vector set to 0.5, 0.5, and 0.5); It is one of the roughest materials in the world (with **Roughness** set to 1.0) and is not a metallic material (with **Metallic** set to 0.0). Finally, we leave **Specular** at 0.5. By modifying these values, you can create the base of any opaque surfaces that exist in the real world.

5. To be able to see how your material looks assigned to an object in viewport, click on the **Apply** button in the main toolbar. This will apply all the work you made inside the Material Editor to the Level Viewport. The **Apply** command will not save your material asset. To do that, you can click on the floppy disk icon in the main toolbar. The **Save** button will also perform the **Apply** command.

> **Note**
>
> To unplug a node, you need to press and hold the *Ctrl* key on the input/output pin you want to unplug. A closed-hand icon should appear. By holding down *Ctrl*, you can now left-click and move the connection away from the input/output pin. You can also use this technique to move a connection from an input/output pin to another input/output pin.

You can now try to create some basic materials. This will help you become confident with Unreal Engine 5's Material Editor and its node system. You should be able to create **Matte Plastic**, **Shiny Plastic**, **Leather**, **Rubber**, **Wood**, and **Chrome**.

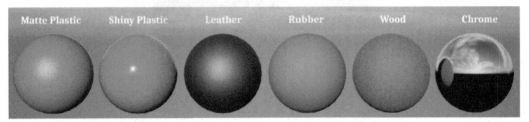

Figure 5.19 – Basic materials created with basic nodes

We are now able to create basic materials by changing values to only two different nodes. We can now move on to learn how to use textures.

Adding basic textures

The next step is adding textures to your material. Using textures allows you to create realistic materials with variations and different effects. You can create textures from scratch with external software, such as Substance 3D Painter or Photoshop, or download textures from online libraries, such as Quixel Megascans (we will learn more about that in *Chapter 8*).

To create a realistic material, you will need at least two textures, **Base Color** (**D**) and **Roughness** (**R**). If you are creating a metallic material, you will also need a **Metallic** (**M**) texture. I am going to create a brick wall. Let's start by adding **Base Color** and **Roughness**.

> **Note**
>
> You can find thousands of *free-to-use* textures online. One of the best websites is www.polyhaven.com. You can also use the Megascans Library for free with your Epic Games account.

To add a texture to your material, follow these steps:

1. Import an image file into Unreal Engine 5.

2. Drag and drop the image file from the **Content Browser** into the Material Editor viewport. This action will create a new **Texture Sample** node.

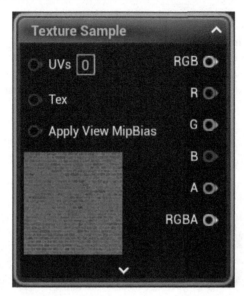

Figure 5.20 – The Base Color texture in the Texture Sample node

You can also create a **Texture Sample** node by pressing *T* and keeping it pressed on the keyboard, and then clicking the left-mouse button in the Material Editor viewport. Alternatively, you can click the right-mouse button in the Material Editor viewport and search for it. When you create a **Texture Sample** node directly inside the Material Editor viewport, it doesn't already have a texture assigned. You can add a texture to an empty **Texture Sample** node in the details panel when the node is selected.

Figure 5.21 – The Texture Sample details panel – add a texture here

A **Texture Sample** node is very similar to a Constant3Vector node. Why? Because an image is a sum of RGB values. Just think about Photoshop – to color-correct your image, you need to change RGB channels. In the Texture Sample node, we also have an **Alpha (A)** output and a **Texture + Alpha (RGBA)** output. You can decide which output to link to the material domain. For now, we will link the RGB output.

3. Link the **Base Color** texture output to the **Base Color** input and the **Roughness** texture output to the **Roughness** input.

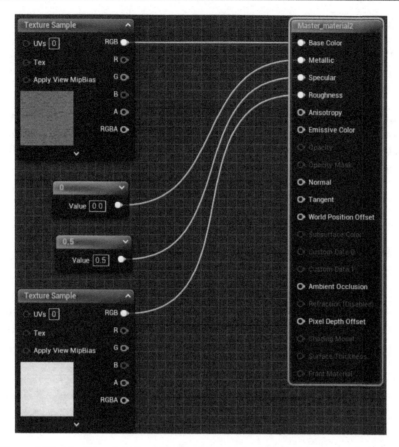

Figure 5.22 – The Base Color and Roughness textures linked to the material domain

4. We can set metallic to zero by using a **Constant**. We can also set specular to 0.5.

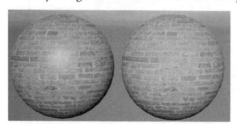

Figure 5.23 – On the left, a material with only a Base Color texture, and on
the right, a material with Base Color and Roughness textures

As you can see in *Figure 5.23*, the material without roughness reacts to light in the wrong way and loses a lot of detail. We can improve the realism of the brick material by adding some more textures. We are now ready to learn how Normal Map and ambient occlusion work.

Adding Normal Map and Ambient Occlusion

To achieve the highest quality, we need to add another two textures that help us to simulate tridimensionality on our surface. The textures that can do this job are the Normal Map texture and the Ambient Occlusion texture:

- **Normal Map**: This is a texture used to fake the lighting incidence on the object and create the illusion of a 3D extrusion. It is used to add details without using more polygons on the 3D model. Normal Maps are commonly stored as regular RGB images, where the RGB components correspond to the *X*, *Y*, and *Z* coordinates of the surface normal.

Figure 5.24 – A brick Normal Map texture

- **Ambient Occlusion**: This texture is used to manage the darkest part of your object and increase or decrease the black value. It is a grayscale texture that is usually multiplied on the Base Color.

Figure 5.25 – A brick ambient occlusion texture

You can add the **Normal Map (N)** to your material by linking it to your material domain's **Normal** input.

You can add the **ambient occlusion** (**AO**) map to your material by linking it to your material domain's Ambient occlusion input. You can also multiply your Ambient occlusion texture on your Base Color textures. The results will be essentially the same. To multiply a Texture Sample to another, follow these steps:

1. Add the AO texture to your material.

2. Add a **Multiply** node by pressing and holding *M* and left-clicking in the Material Editor viewport. You can also use the right-mouse button in the Material Editor viewport and search for it.

3. Link the AO texture's **RGB** output to the **Multiply A** input and the **D** texture's **RGB** output to the **Multiply | B** input.

4. Link the **Multiply** output to the **Base Color** material domain's input.

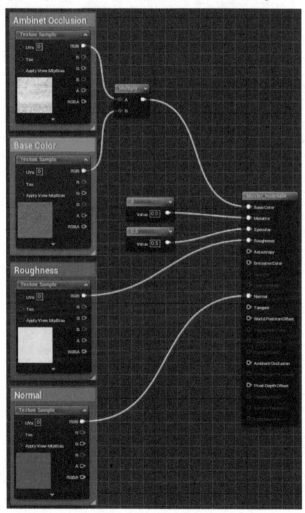

Figure 5.26 – A material with a full set of textures

The preceding steps results in a **Base Color** output that is the result of the multiplication between the AO textures and the D textures. The D texture is now darker when AO is black and brighter when AO is white.

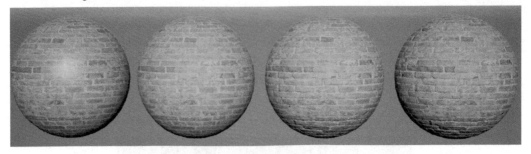

Figure 5.27 – The first material has only the D texture. The second one has D and R textures. The third one has D, R and N textures. The last one also has AO textures

Note

Some texture libraries, including the Megascans Library, use to merge AO, R, and Displacement textures (a greyscale texture that allows you to add details by adding geometry) in a single image file. How? The single textures are stored in the single RGB channel of the image. Usually, the red channel is dedicated to AO, the green channel to Roughness, and the blue channel to Displacement texture. But this depends on the texture's creator. To use these textures, you need to link the RGB output of the Texture Sample to the correct input in the material domain. This is a very optimized way to create a set of textures, as you need to import one file instead of three and leave the Texture Sample's RGB output free.

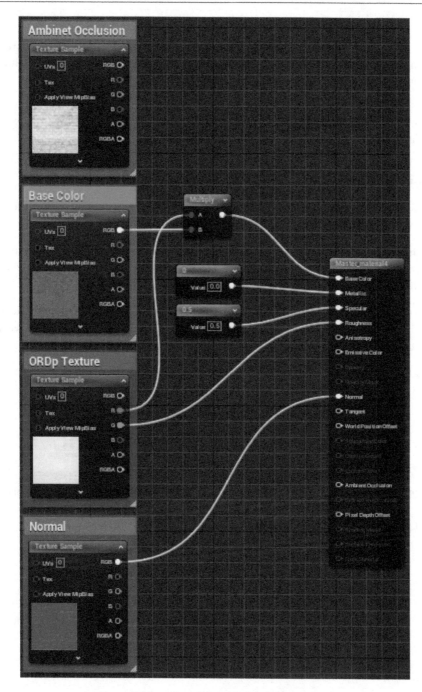

Figure 5.28 – A base material with ORDp Texture

> **Note**
>
> The colored squares around the Texture Sample you can see in *Figure 5.28* are **comments**. You can create them by pressing *C* on the keyboard. Everything selected will be included in the comment.

Now that we can create a material from a set of textures, we are ready to understand how to modify our material in the viewport and how to manage texture values.

Understanding Material Instances

In this section we will learn what a **Material Instance** is and why it is so important to use a material creation workflow based on them.

Material instancing is a method to create a material that you can use as a base to generate infinite variations of it. This process creates a parent material (**Master Material**) and allows you to create infinitely different looking children (**Material Instances**) for use in your project.

To do that, the proprieties (**parameters**) of the Master Material are passed to all the Material Instances generated from it. This concept process is called **inheritance**. The parameters that are created as a node in the Master Material are exposed as values inside the **Material Instance Editor** (as we will see shortly).

To create a Material Instance, click the *right-mouse button* on the material you want to use as a parent and select **Create Material Instance**.

Figure 5.29 – The Create Material Instance command in the material's right-mouse button option menu

A Material Instance looks exactly like a material in the **Content Browser**. If you double-click with the *left-mouse button* on the Material Instance, the **Material Instance Editor** will open.

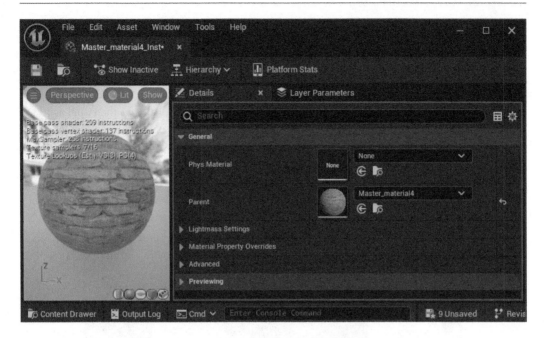

Figure 5.30 – The Material Instance Editor

The Material Instance editor is a simplified version of the Material Editor in which you can't add nodes or modify existing ones; you can only change the values of the parameters you decided to expose in the Master Material (the parent material).

In *Figure 5.30*, you can see the Material Instance Editor showing a Material Instance created from our brick material. We don't have any parameters to modify yet.

We are now ready to learn how to add parameters to our Material Instance.

Converting constants to parameters

We can now return to our concrete material (*Figure 5.18*). In this material, we have a Constant3Vector to manage the color and three Constants to change physical values.

We saw that we can create all the basic materials from this Master Material by simply changing constant values and color. To do that, we created a copy of the material for each variation, applied and saved the new materials, and, only at this point, saw the results in the Level Viewport. In addition to being tedious, this method forces us to create a Master Material for each variation, which is not exactly an optimized workflow.

The best way to create all the material variations is by using Material Instances. To do that, we need to convert, in **parameters**, a Constant3Vector to manage the color and three Constants to change physical values:

1. To convert a constant into a parameter, click the *right-mouse button* on the node that you want to convert and select **Convert to Parameter**. This command will change the visual aspect of the node. You need to rename a parameter. You can rename the parameter directly inside the node or inside the node's details panel.

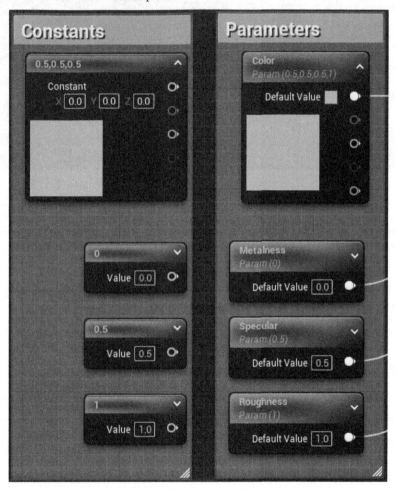

Figure 5.31 – Constants and parameters have different node types

2. Now, you can apply and save your material. Create a new Material Instance in the **Content Browser** and open it. The Material Instance Editor should look like this:

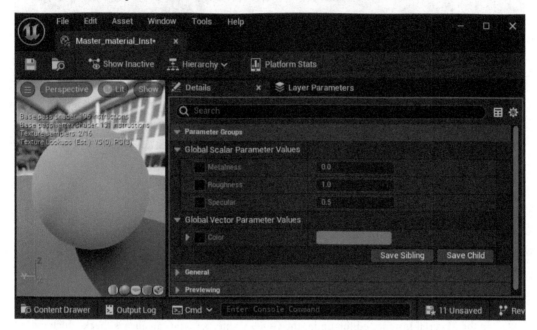

Figure 5.32 – The Material Instance editor with exposed parameters

3. You can now activate parameters by flagging them and changing their values. The default value is the value you have set in the Master Material. If you change a parameter value in the Material Instance editor, this parameter will not be modified in the Master Material. If you change a parameter value in the Master Material, this value will become the default one of that parameter in any Material Instance. If you have assigned the Material Instance to your object in the scene, you can see the material change in real time in the Level Viewport any time you will modify a parameter in the Material Instance editor.

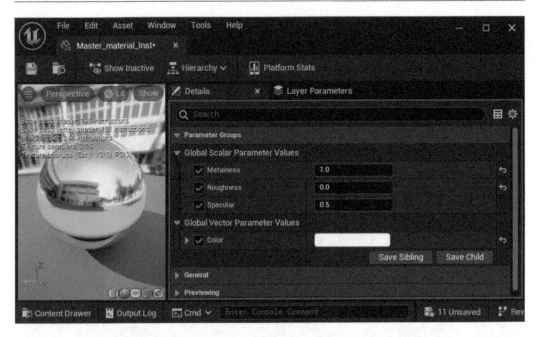

Figure 5.33 – Material Instance values to create a chrome material

4. In the Material Instance editor, under the **General** category, you can always check which parent material is referenced to this instance. You can open the Material Editor to edit the Master Material by double-clicking the *left-mouse button* on the parent material thumbnail.

> **Note**
>
> Assigning a Material Instance instead of a Master Material to your asset is a good habit. Remember that any change on the Master Material will affect all the Material Instance children.
>
> You can create a Material Instance from an existing Material Instance. Why? A master material can be very big and full of different parameters. Using a Material Instance as parent allows you to set a starting point for the creation of new Material Instances, without changing default Master Material parameters.
>
> Inside the parameter's details panel, we can change the value range that the user can use inside the Material Instance by changing the **Slider Min** and **Slider Max** values. By default, these two values are set to 0 (zero means that we can use infinite values inside the Material Instance).

Now that we know what a Material Instance is and how to create and use it, we can start to create a Master Material that will allow you to generate hundreds of different surfaces, by creating different Material Instances.

Creating a Master Material

In this section, we will learn how to create a complex **Master Material** (parent material) to generate Material Instances, allowing you to create hundreds of different solid surfaces. This Master Material will be useful for all your future projects. This will be a practical section in which we will learn step by step how to create our Master Material.

We can start with the material we created with the ORDp texture (*Figure 5.28*). We should use this because all the Megascans Library surfaces have this type of texture set, which we will use in this book.

Let's start creating a Material Instance of this material and assign it to the assets you want to use to preview the material in the Level Viewport.

Step 1 – adding texture parameters

First, we need to convert our **Texture Sample** nodes into parameters that can be modified in the Material Instance. You can do that in the same way you converted the other nodes. Click the *right-mouse button* on the node, and then click on **Convert to Parameter**.

A Texture Sample parameter node looks the same as a Texture Sample constant except for the name.

> **Note**
>
> Assigning a clear and easy understandable name to your parameters is very important. The name you choose in the Master Material is the name that will be shown in the Material Instance. Everyone needs to be able to understand what any parameter does.

Apply and save your material. Now, you can change the textures inside the Material Instance editor by dragging new texture into the dedicated slot.

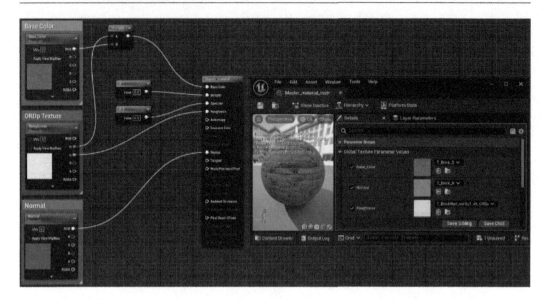

Figure 5.34 – Texture parameters in the Material Instance editor

As you saw in *Figure 5.34*, for now we can leave specular and metallic as constant nodes.

We are now ready to add parameters that allow us to modify any single texture in terms of color and intensity. We can start with the Base Color.

Step 2 – adding Base Color parameters

The first thing we want to be able to do is to make some color correction tweaks to our Base Color texture. To do that, we need to blend a color with our Base Color texture:

1. Add a **Blend_Overlay** node. This node allows us to blend two 3-vector nodes, emulating the Photoshop overlay blend mode.

2. Link the D texture's **RGB output** to **Blend_Overlay**'s **Base** input. This represents the lower layer of our blending action.

3. Create a Constant3Vector and link it to the Blend Overlay's **Blend** input. Then, convert the Constant3Vector to a parameter and name it `Color Overlay`.

4. Set a color different to black in the Constant3Vector.

You can verify these steps by clicking the *right-mouse button* on the **Blend_Overlay** node and selecting **Start Previewing node**. This command sets the final output of the material graph on the node you performed the command. So, in this case, the material preview viewport will show you the result of the blending node. You should see your Base Color tinted with the color set in the Constant3Vector node.

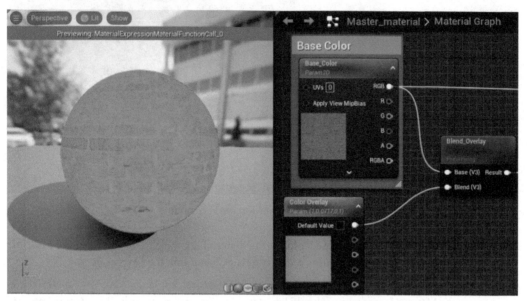

Figure 5.35 – Previewing the Blend_Overlay node

Now, we want to be able to modify the power of the color overlay. The best way to do that is to use a **Linear Interpolate** node. This node allows us to blend two different input values based on a third input value used as mask, which is exactly what we need.

5. Create a Linear Interpolate (**Lerp**) node. You can search for it or press *L* and keep it pressed on the keyboard, and then press the *left-mouse button*.

6. Create a parameter and call it `Color Power`. You can create a Constant and convert it to a parameter, or you can press *S* and keep it pressed on the keyboard, and then press the *left-mouse button* to directly create a parameter.

7. Link the **RGB** output of the D texture to the **A** input of the **Lerp** node. Link **Blend_Overlay**'s output to the **B** input of the **Lerp** node. Link the **Color_Power** parameter to the **Lerp** node's **Alpha** input.

You can verify the result by previewing the **Lerp** node. Now, you can change the intensity of the color blended on your **Base Color** texture.

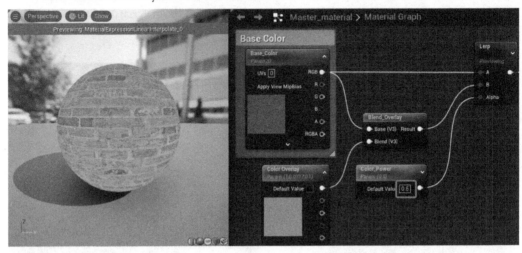

Figure 5.36 – Previewing the Lerp node

8. Last, we need to re-link our Base Color to the material domain. To do that, find the **Multiply** node linked to the **ORDp** texture's red channel (AO) and link the **Lerp** node to it.

9. Now, you can change the color of your Base Color texture. Apply and save your material and open the Material Instance. You should have two new parameters to work with – **Color Power** to control how much color you want to be overlaid to your Base Color texture and **Color Overlay** to choose which color you want to add.

> **Note**
>
> Changing color with a blend overlay node means blending two layers with an overlay function. The Base Color is not replaced but mixed with the blend color to reflect the lightness or darkness of the original color. Preserving the Base Color allows you to not lose details, *but* the resulting color will be a mix between the two layers. If you want full control of your Base Color texture's color, you can use a grayscale version of your Base Color textures.
>
> Parameters have 0 (zero) as a default value. When you create a Material Instance, all the parameters have as a value what you set in the Master Material.

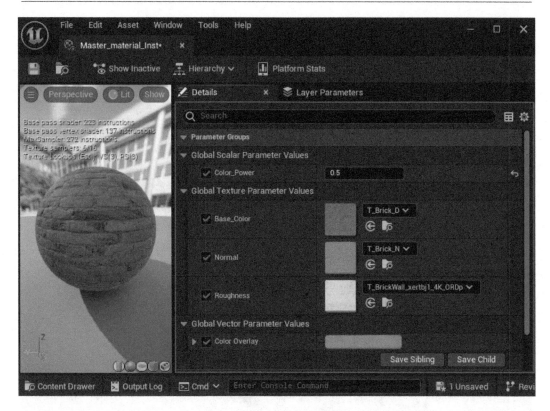

Figure 5.37 – A material instance at the end of step 2 of creating a Master Material

We are now ready for the next step. We will learn how to modify textures such as **Roughness** or **Metallic**.

Step 3 – modifying texture values

When you use a texture as parameter, you are using a fixed value for each pixel of the image. Changing the color values of the textures (which means opening them in an external editor such as Photoshop) every time you need to modify the final effect of your material can be tedious and time-consuming. To avoid that, we can manipulate a color value directly inside the Material Editor using a simple multiply operation.

We will start with the roughness texture. Follow these steps:

1. Create a **Mutiply** node. As we saw before, you can use the *M* shortcut.

2. Create a parameter and name it Roughness. As we saw before, you can use the *S* shortcut.

3. Link the **ORDp** texture's **G** output (**Roughness** is stored in the green channel) to the **Multiply** node's **A** input, and link the **parameter output** to the **Multiply** node's **B** input.

4. Connect the **Multiply** node's output to the **Roughness** material domain's input.

You should have something like this:

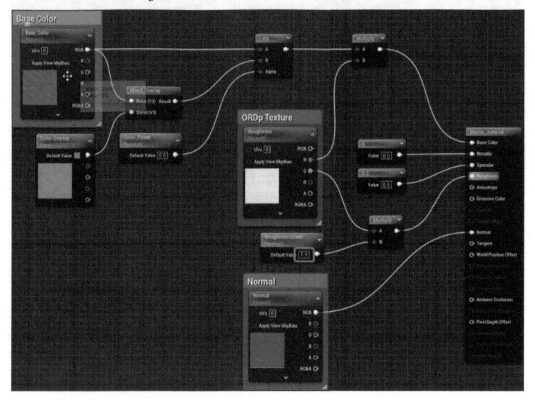

Figure 5.38 – The Material Editor view after adding the Roughness power parameter

Remember that parameters have 0 as a default value. This means that, by default, your roughness will be multiplied by 0. Everything multiplied by 0 is equal to 0. In terms of colors, 0 is equal to black. So, if you set your parameter value to 0, your default roughness will be totally black, which means fully reflective. A value of 1 results in the same values as the textures.

You can now repeat the same process for the AO texture. The only thing you have to change is the **Multiply** node with an **Add** node. An **Add** node is simply a sum operation. To manage AO power, try by yourself to add a parameter named AO Power. Remember that we are using an **ORDp** texture, so the AO texture is stored in the red channel.

The result should be like this:

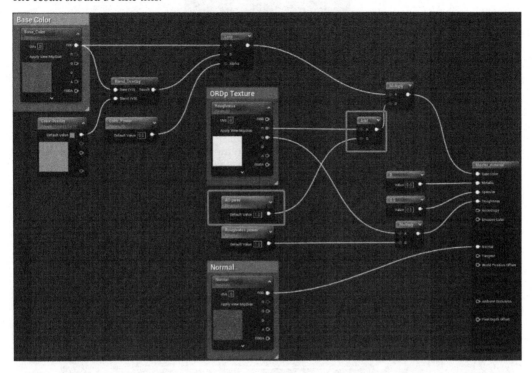

Figure 5.39 – The Material Editor view with parameters to modify Roughness and AO

> **Note**
>
> In *Figure 5.34* we used a **Multiply** node instead of an **Add** node to link the AO texture. **Multiply** and **Add** are two different operations that have different results. AO is usually multiplied by the Base Color, but sometimes, adding it is convenient. You can use both.

We can now move on and learn how to modify the Normal Map intensity.

Step 4 – modifying the Normal Map intensity

As we have already learned, Normal Map is a particular red and blue scale texture that allows us to add detail to our material without adding geometry to our 3D model. To do so, it works with lighting and tangents to simulate a tridimensional effect on surfaces. For these reasons, we can't simply multiply or add a parameter to change its values. To manage the intensity of a Normal Map, we need a specific node.

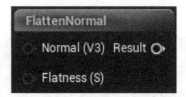

Figure 5.40 – A FlattenNormal node

Follow these steps:

1. Create a **FlattenNormal** node. This node has two inputs and one output. We can understand which kind of input it needs to work properly by checking the input names. **Normal (V3)** means a normal Texture Sample node. **Flatness (S)** means a parameter to manage the flatness value.

2. Connect the **Normal** texture's **RGB** output to **FlattenNormal**'s **normal** input.

3. Create a parameter and call it `Normal Flatness`.

4. Connect the parameter's output to **FlattenNormal**'s **Flatness** input.

5. Connect **FlattenNormal**'s **Result** output to the Material Domain's **Normal** input.

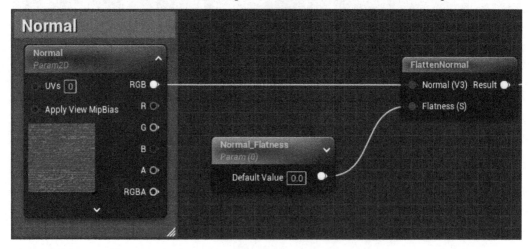

Figure 5.41 – The Normal texture's Flatness value

Be careful about the parameter name. A high flatness value means a flat surface. So, the **Normal_Flatness** parameter set to 1 will disable the normal texture effect. **Normal_Flatness** set to 0 will use the normal texture's values.

We are now able to change the color of our material and modify the intensity of all the texture we use in our Master Material.

We are now ready to learn how to manipulate the texture placement.

Step 5 – adding UV manipulation

In this section, we will learn how to add texture Tiling and Panning options to our Master Material.

Tiling is the repetition of a texture inside the UV space. **Panning** allows you to move a texture inside UV space. UVs are the coordinates used to place a texture on an object. We can call these operations **texture placements**.

We can control the texture placement by creating some new nodes inside the Material Editor. We can start with Tiling. Try to follow these steps:

1. Create a **TextureCoordinate** node. You need to search for it with the *right-mouse button* menu. This node helps us to declare that after that node, we will work on a texture coordinate (UVs).

2. To tile our textures, we need to multiply by the number of time we want to see it in UV space. So, we need a **Multiply** node. Connect the **TexturesCoordinate** node's output to the **Multiply** node's **A** input.

3. Now, we need to split the **multiply B** value to be able to modify U and V Tiling (U represents vertical repetition, V the horizontal one). To do that, create an **AppendVector** node and connect its output to the **Multiply** node's **B** input.

4. Create two parameters, one for **Tiling U** and one for **Tiling V**. Connect them to the **AppendVector** node's **A** and **B** inputs.

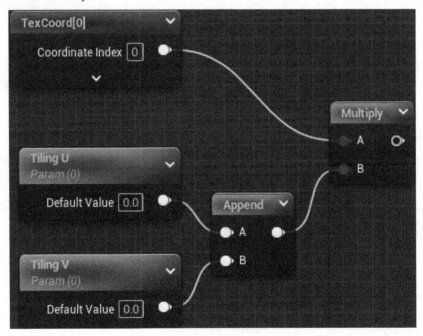

Figure 5.42 – The Tiling node graph

We can now add Panning values. Follow these steps:

1. Create an **AppendVector** node with two parameters connected. Name one `Pan U` and the other `Pan V`.

2. Now, we need to add the Panning nodes to our Tiling nodes to be able to make both transformations. Create an **Add** node and connect the Tiling **Multiply**'s output to the **Add** node's **A** input and the **AppendVector** node's output to the **Add** node's **B** input.

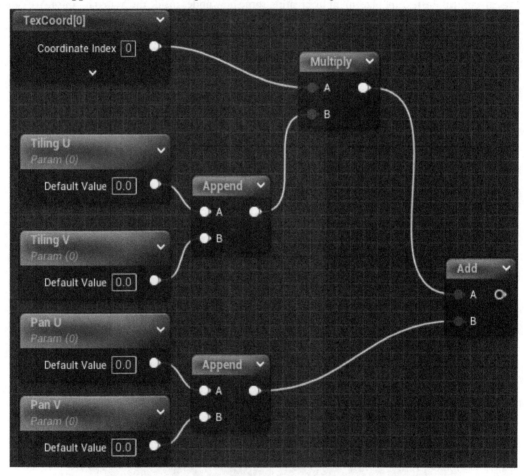

Figure 5.43 – The Tiling and Panning UVs' complete node graph

3. Finally, we need to connect out Tiling and Panning node graphs to our textures. To do that, connect the **Add** node's output to the Texture Sample **UV** input of any of the textures you want to modify with these Tiling and Panning parameters.

> **Note**
>
> Remember that the Base Color, Roughness, AO, and Normal textures work together. It's very important to connect the UV nodes to all the textures in the graph.
>
> You can decide how textures will be multiplied on UVs with the **Advanced Texture** options inside the **image editor** (refer to *Figure 4.36* in *Chapter 4*). There are two different options to know about. The default option is **Warp** and allows you to repeat textures in UV spaces. This is the most common setting for tile textures. **Clamp** stretches the texture's edge pixels when you set a Tiling value bigger then 1. This is useful if you are trying to manipulate something such as an alphed logo or patch. The result will be a bigger/smaller logo/patch.

Our Master Material should look like this:

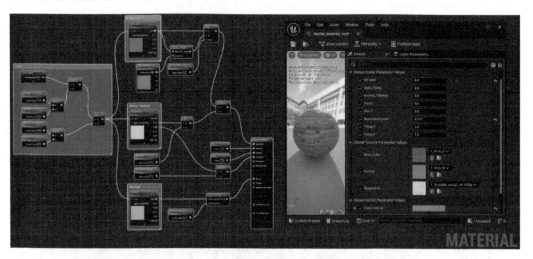

Figure 5.44 – The Master Material node graph at the end of step 5

At this point, we need to find out a way to organize parameters inside the Material Instance. We will do that in the next step.

Step 6 – organizing parameters into groups

It's time to make our parameters clearly understandable by everyone who will use our Material Instances. The Material Editor allows us to organize them into groups to be shown in the Material Instance.

To do that, select a node and create a new parameter group by typing the name of the group in the details panel.

We can start from the textures by adding them to a group named **01_Textures**.

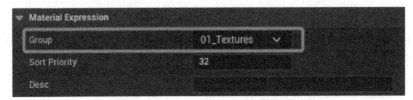

Figure 5.45 – Creating a group for instance parameters

The groups will be organized in alphabetical order. For this reason, it is a good habit to name groups with increasing numbers.

We can create four different groups – one for textures, one for color variations, one for UVs, and one for physical parameters. The final result should look like *Figure 5.46*.

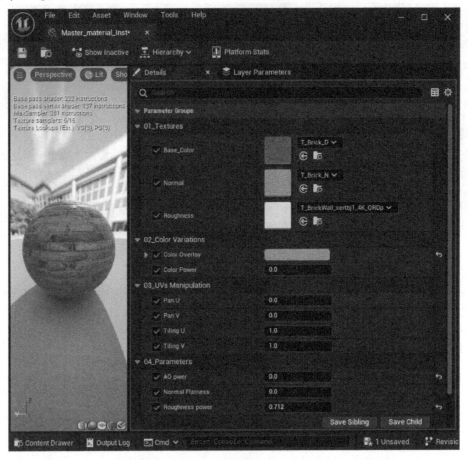

Figure 5.46 – A material instance with parameters organized into custom groups

Now, we are ready to introduce static switch parameters in the next section.

Step 7 – adding Switch parameters

The last thing we need to add to our Master Material is the possibility to create choices inside the Material Instance, allowing the user able to decide which kind of material (in terms of parameters) they want to create.

In our Master Material, we have decided that it can't generate a metallic material by connecting a constant set to 0, instead of a parameter, to the metallic input. However, the best approach is to create a parameter that allows us to choose whether we want to create a metallic material or not.

To do that, we can use a **StaticSwitchParameter** node.

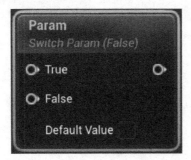

Figure 5.47 – A static Switch parameter

StaticSwitchParameter works as an on/off switcher. When the switcher is on, everything connected to the **True** input will happen; when the switcher is off, everything connected to the **False** input will happen. If the **Default Value** box is enabled, the default switcher status will be **True**. If the **Default Value** box is disabled, the default switcher status will be **False**.

The **StaticSwitchParameter** name is very important. I used to add a question mark to make clearer what the switcher does. We can use something such as `Metallic?`.

We will start with the **False** input. When **StaticSwitchParameter** is set to **False**, we don't want to use **Metallic**. This means that the **Metallic** value will be 0, and we will not modify it. So, we can create and connect a Constant and set it to 0 (this isn't a parameter and will not appear in the Material Instance).

Conversely, when **StaticSwitchParameter** is set to **True**, we want to be able to use a metallic texture and have the possibility to modify the **Metallic** value with a dedicated parameter. To do that, follow these steps:

1. Create a **Texture Sample** node. Convert it to a parameter and rename it `Metallic`. You can assign a plain white texture as default. You can find it by searching for `white` in the **Material Expression Texture Base** tab in the details panel.

2. Create a new parameter and call it `Metallic power`.

3. Multiply the Texture Sample parameter with the **Metallic Power** parameter.

4. Connect the **Multiply** output to the **StaticSwitchParameter**'s **True** input.

You are now ready to connect the switcher to the **Metallic** input in the material domain. The result should look like *Figure 5.48*.

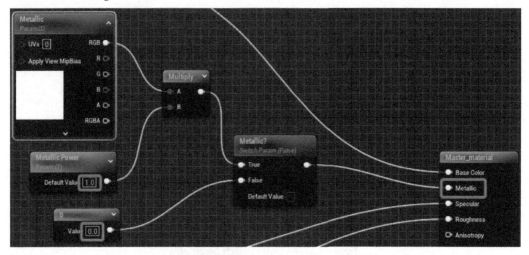

Figure 5.48 – The Metallic switcher in the Master Material node graph

Remember to assign the correct group to any new parameter you've created. We can also create a new group for switchers. The Material Instance should look like *Figure 5.49*.

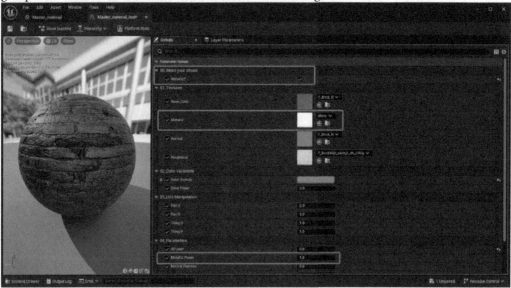

Figure 5.49 – The material instance with the Metallic switcher set to True

We can add another simple but very useful switcher to our material. We want to allow Material Instances to use a plain color instead of a Base Color texture.

To do that, you need to create a switcher with a **Color** parameter set to **True** and all the **Base Color** graph nodes we previously created set to **False**. It should look like *Figure 5.50*.

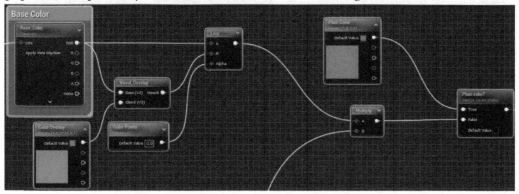

Figure 5.50 – The Base Color switcher for plain color diffuse

We have almost done it. In the next (and last) step, we will learn some "quality of life" tricks to make our material more readable and organized.

Step 8 – organizing the graph node

Everything is set and ready to be used to create hundreds of different Material Instances and solid surfaces. The last thing we need to do is to make our Master Material more organized. We want to free up space and nodes to be able to add more parameters in the future.

There is a very useful node that allows us to create a connection between groups of nodes without a "wired" connection. This node is called the **Named Reroute Declaration** node. It works like a box that stores inside everything that is connected to its input. Once you have created it, you can reuse it everywhere in the graph node to use all the nodes inside it.

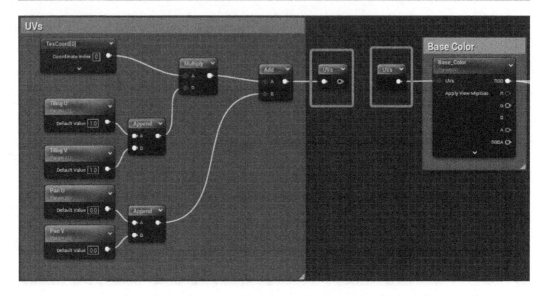

Figure 5.51 – The Named Reroute Declaration node used to create
a reroute node with UV manipulation nodes inside

To use the new node, you need to search its name by clicking on the *right-mouse button* menu inside the Material Editor (the menu you can open by clicking right-mouse button inside the Material Editor viewport). For this reason, it has to be given a clear and memorable name.

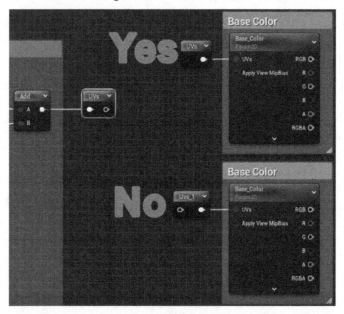

Figure 5.52 – Make sure to reuse the node and not to copy and paste the Named Reroute Declaration node

You can use **Named Reroute Declaration** nodes to better organize the nodes inside the Material Editor. You can try to apply this technique to the Master Material to make it lighter and more readable.

The result will look like *Figure 5.53*.

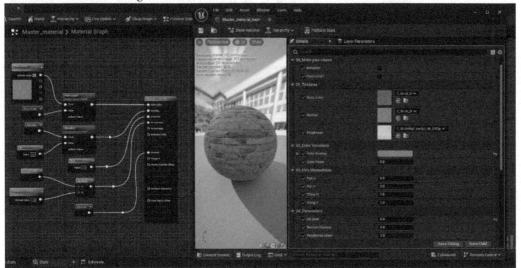

Figure 5.53 – A final look of our Master Material and Material Instance

This was the final step of our Master Material creation process. You should now be able to create it from scratch or modify it according to your needs. We are now ready for the last part of this intense chapter – **Material Functions**.

Using Material Functions

In this section, we will learn what a Material Function is and how using it allows you to create more complex material, speeding up the material creation process. This will be a quick overview of Material Function usage. To learn more about Material Functions, you can browse this link: `https://docs.unrealengine.com/4.26/en-US/RenderingAndGraphics/Materials/Functions/#:~:text=Material%20Functions%20allow%20complex%20Material,material%20creation%20easier%20for%20artists`.

A Material Function is like a box, inside of which you can create complex material graphs abstracted in a single node. You can also create **custom inputs** and **custom outputs** for this node. Material Functions can be reused in multiple materials to make material creation easier and faster. In the next section, we will discover the most common functions you can find inside the Engine.

Exploring the most common functions

You can create a new Material Function or use a pre-created one. In this chapter, we have already used a couple of Material Functions. The **Blend_Overlay** and **FlattenNormal** nodes are two Material Functions. If you click on one of them, the **Material Function editor** will open, showing you what there is inside the Material Function. The Material Function editor looks like the Material Editor and works in the same way.

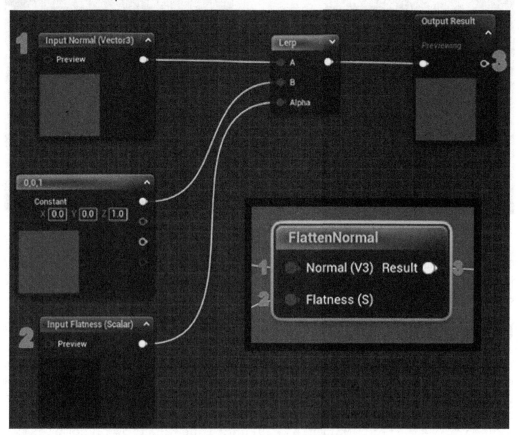

Figure 5.54 – The FlattenNormal function opened in the Material Function editor

As you can see in *Figure 5.54*, elements **1** and **2** are the final Material Function's input. Element 3 is the output. **Blend_Overlay** is a little bit more complex, but the concept is the same. The function's graph node looks like this:

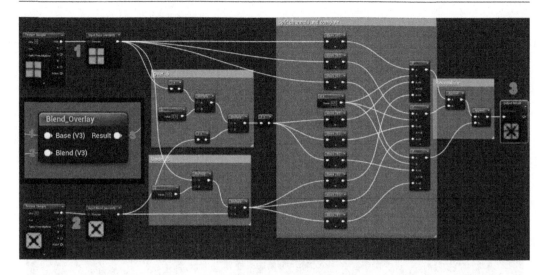

Figure 5.55 – The Blend_Overlay function opened in the Material Function editor

Blend_Overlay and **FlattenNormal** are very simple Material Functions. You can find hundreds of pre-created Material Functions inside the Engine to help you in the material creation process.

In the next section, we will learn how to create a new Material Function.

Creating a new Material Function

In this practical section, we will learn how to create a Material Function to manipulate UVs. You will be able to use this Material Function in all your following Master Materials or new projects (you can migrate a function to a different project; we discussed the migration process in *Chapter 4*):

1. To create a new Material Function, press the *right-mouse button* in the **Content Browser**, browse to **Material**, and select **Material Function**. Rename the function MF_UVs, and then open the Material Function editor by double-clicking on the new Material Function.

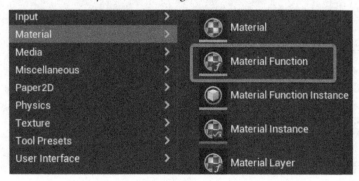

Figure 5.56 – The Material Function creation option

2. Next, open your Master Material, copy all the nodes we created to manage UVs, and paste them into the Material Function editor. You should have something like this:

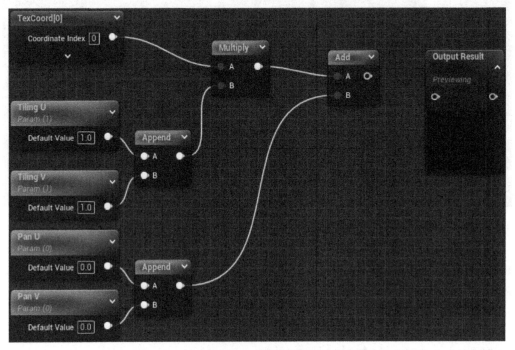

Figure 5.57 – The UV manipulation nodes inside the Material Function editor

3. We can now connect the **Add** node's output to the output node's input. This will make our new Material Function work. Before using it, we need to expose our Material Function to the node library in order to be able to find it in the Material Editor. To do that, we need to enable the **Expose to Library** option. You can find it in the details panel inside the Material Function editor. Make sure no nodes are selected.

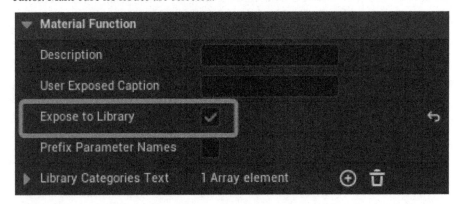

Figure 5.58 – The Expose to Library option in the Material Function editor's details panel

4. Apply and save the Material Function, and then go back to the Master Material. To use the Material Function we have just created, you can do the following:

- Drag and drop the Material Function from the **Content Browser** into the Material Editor.

- Search for it in the right-mouse button Material Editor's menu (if the **Expose to Library** option is enabled).

- Create the **Material Function Call** node in the Material Editor and select the Material Function inside the details panel. If you have a Material Function selected in the **Content Browser**, it will be directly assigned.

Your new Material Function should look like *Figure 5.59* inside the Material Editor:

Figure 5.59 – The new Material Function node

Now, you can use this function in the same way we use the **Named Reroute Declaration node**. The main difference is that a Material Function can work in multiple Master Materials and projects. It maintains all the parameters you have set inside it.

The last thing you need to know is how to create custom input inside your Material Function. In the next section, we will learn how to substitute parameters with inputs.

Adding custom inputs

Creating a Material Function with all the parameters inside can be binding. In some cases, leaving the possibility to add a custom parameter in the Material Editor is a better choice to create a versatile and reusable Material Function.

To make it possible to link a custom parameter to our Material Function, follow these steps:

1. Delete all the parameters in the Material Function editor. To be clear, you need to delete the **Tiling U** and **Tiling U V** parameters and **Panning U** and **Panning V** parameters.

2. Press the right-mouse button and search for FunctionInput.

3. By default, The new node is named **Input In (Vector3)**. **In** is the default name for input nodes; **(Vector 3)** is the type of input the node needs to work. As we saw before in this chapter (in the *Adding basic nodes* and *Adding basic textures* sections), a 3-vector node can be a color or an image. However, we need a **scalar** parameter to manage Tiling and Panning.

4. With the input node selected, in the details panel, change the input type from **Function Input Vector 3** to **Function Input Scalar** (it's the first option).

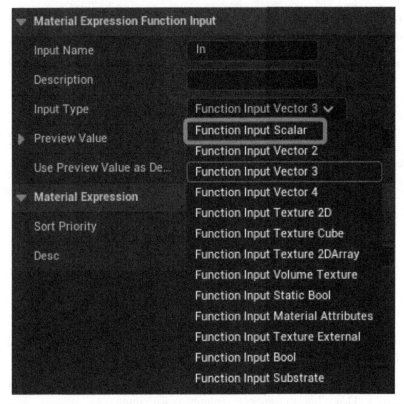

Figure 5.60 – The Input Type option in the Material Function editor's details panel

5. Rename it `Tiling U` and connect its output to the first **Append** node's **A** input.

6. Do the same for the **Tiling V**, **Pan U**, and **Pan V** parameters.

7. Save and apply.

    Your updated Material Function should now look like *Figure 5.61*.

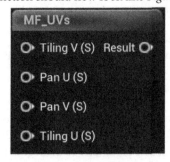

Figure 5.61 – The updated Material Function node

Finally, you can change the order of parameters by changing the **Sort Priority** value in the details panel. You can assign 0 to **Tiling U** and **Tiling V** and 1 to **Pan U** and **Pan V**. The order follows an incremental criterion.

Figure 5.62 – The Sort Priority value in the Material Function's details panel

You can now add parameters to your function directly in the Material Editor. This is very useful, for example, if you want different Tiling values for different textures. With the possibility to add custom parameters, you can duplicate your function and create different parameters with different names.

Material Functions are very useful and will help you to improve your material creation workflow. Using Material Functions can also improve the complexity you can achieve with a Master Material.

A good exercise to explore the potentiality of Material Function is to try to create a Material Function that includes a complete material inside it.

A good habit is saving in a "work in progress" project all the Material Functions that you will create for any project. This will allow you to migrate them to a new project any time you need to. This will work also for Master Materials and everything you create inside the Engine that can be reused.

Summary

In this chapter, we have raised the level. After learning what PBR means and which primary inputs this rendering model uses, we created our first material by adding constant values and textures. The next step was to convert our constants to parameters to be able to modify values in real time inside our Material Instances. We covered all the steps to create a complex Master Material that allows you to create solid surfaces with Material Instance. Finally, we learned the Material Function basics. You are now able to experiment with Master Materials and Material Functions, and you can reproduce a Master Material from scratch and modify it with your own parameters and functions.

Material creation is a huge and very complex topic. The goal of this chapter was to give you the fundamental techniques so that you can use an existing material or create a simple one from scratch. Everything we learned in this chapter is mandatory if you want to explore more complex material creation techniques.

We are now ready for the next chapter, in which we will talk about lighting in Unreal Engine 5.

6
Illuminating Your World with Lighting

In this chapter, we will learn how to use the lighting system in Unreal Engine 5 to create stunning lighting for objects and environments. We will learn what Lumen is and how it works. We will explore all the different lighting assets inside Unreal Engine 5 and we will discover some useful tricks to make your light more realistic. Lighting is a very important thing inside the environment creation workflow. Knowing all the different lighting techniques will allow you to improve the final quality of your work.

By the end of this chapter, we will be able to create a variety of different types of lighting for single and multiple objects and for massive environments, both interior and exterior.

In this chapter, we will cover the following main topics:

- Understanding lighting in Unreal Engine 5
- Lighting system in Unreal Engine 5
- Tips and tricks to improve lighting
- Exercise: Import a new asset and try to light it
- Illuminating your first environment

Technical requirements

In this chapter, we will use some assets that you can find in the Unreal Engine Marketplace.

To easily follow the chapter, you can add the **Posed Humans 1** asset pack to your project (`https://www.unrealengine.com/marketplace/en-US/product/twinmotion-posed-humans`).

You can also download the **Megascans Abandoned Apartment** project (`https://www.unrealengine.com/marketplace/en-US/product/c26355353df843289701d632508d4fb0`).

Note that this chapter can also be followed without these assets.

Understanding lighting in Unreal Engine 5

In this section, we will learn how lighting works in Unreal Engine 5 and how to set up your project to use Lumen to illuminate your scene.

What is Lumen?

To understand the lighting process in Unreal Engine 5 we first need to understand what Lumen is and why it is so important.

Lumen is Unreal Engine 5's fully dynamic global illumination and reflection system, which allows us to reproduce raytraced lighting via software. This is a game-changer feature not only for game projects that need to illuminate massive dynamic environments but also for everyone who wants to achieve high-quality images and videos without an extremely powerful graphics card.

In other words, Lumen allows us to simulate what raytraced global illumination does.

In the real world, when you switch on the light in your room, the light coming from the ceiling lamp hits the ground and then bounces infinitely onto other surfaces in the room. Thanks to this process, your room will be brighter or darker according to the intensity of the source light. In the 3D world, **global illumination (GI)**, or **indirect lighting**, is lighting coming from light rays bouncing. Without GI, the rays coming from light will illuminate only the surface hit.

The number of bounces defines the realism of the lighting in the scene. More bounces mean more processes on your graphics card to be done in real time.

Lumen simulates all additional bounces and uses hardware to improve the quality only if available and if you allow it to do that.

Lumen is the lighting system Unreal Engine 5 uses to generate lighting by default. It is optimized and works very well with all the new features that have been introduced with Unreal Engine 5, such as **Nanite**, **Virtual textures**, and the **World Partition** tool. We will overview all these new features in *Chapter 7*.

Everything we learn in this chapter will consider Lumen as the enabled lighting method. So, we are now ready to learn how to activate it and set your project up to use it.

Setting projects up to use Lumen

All the new projects you create in Unreal Engine 5 will have the Lumen system enabled. You can check all the Lumen settings directly inside the Engine in **Project Settings**.

Open the **Project Settings** window, browse to the **Rendering** category on the left, and search for **Global Illumination** by scrolling down. Be sure to set or enable the following options:

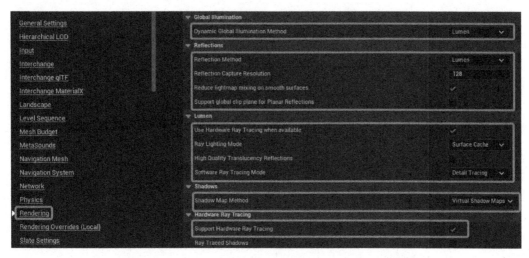

Figure 6.1 – Lumen settings in the Project Settings window

Use Hardware Ray Tracing when available allows you to use an RTX graphics card to improve the final quality of the scene by using features such as **Ray Traced Shadows** instead of **Virtual Shadow Maps**. We will learn more about these features later in this chapter, in the *Improving shadow quality* section.

Support Hardware Ray Tracing allows you to use hardware Ray Tracing. These two options need an RTX graphics card to work properly.

Lumen works only with **DirectX 12**. You need to check whether your project has the DirectX version correctly set. To do that, type `directx` in the search field in the **Project Settings** window.

Figure 6.2 – DirectX setting in the Project Settings window

Now that we have set our project to work with Lumen, we are ready to explore all the different types of light assets that Unreal Engine 5 provides and how to use them.

Lighting system in Unreal Engine 5

In this section, we will learn how to create and use light assets in Unreal Engine 5. We will explore all the different settings that you can change to create realistic lighting in your scene.

Before starting to explore the different types of lights we can use, we need to understand the difference between baked lights and dynamic lights. To do that, we need to talk about lighting movability.

Lighting movability

As we have already learned in *Chapter 4*, any kind of asset (including lighting assets) can be **Static**, **Stationary**, or **Movable**. These movability states define whether your asset is static or dynamic. You can change the movability settings under the **Transformation** options at the top of the **Details** panel.

According to these states, in Unreal Engine 5, you can have two different lighting systems: a baked lighting system or a full dynamic lighting system.

A **baked lighting system** means setting the lights in your scene as **Static** or **Stationary** and pre-calculating everything regarding lights (including shadows and GI) in an offline process. In this way, you can take advantage in terms of performance because everything has already been calculated and written on textures called **lightmaps**.

Every time you modify a light, you need to repeat the process. When you set a light to be baked (so you are setting the light as static or stationary), the Level Viewport will show you only a preview of the result in terms of quality and accuracy. The process that calculates static lights to be shown with the final quality is called **Build Lights** and you can perform it inside the **Build** menu in the menu bar. This process is very common in the gaming industry.

A **full dynamic lighting system** is a system composed only of movable lights. These types of light are calculated in real time and will always be shown inside the level viewport equal to the final result. A fully dynamic system is heavy in terms of performance but allows you to change in real time any aspects of the light without rendering time. Dynamic lights can be animated, and they influence movable objects in the scene.

In this book, we will not go into the baking light process in depth because it is an advanced option and because our final purpose is to create a cinematic shot to be rendered. We will try to take advantage of the most recent features, such as Lumen, that allow us to obtain amazing lighting results in real time with both a fully dynamic and optimized lighting system. Otherwise, you can find more information about baking light at this link: `https://docs.unrealengine.com/5.3/en-US/gpu-lightmass-global-illumination-in-unreal-engine/`.

We are now ready to explore light assets that you can use in Unreal Engine 5.

Exploring light assets

As we already saw in *Chapter 2*, you can find all the lighting assets in the **Place Actor** menu, under the **Lighting** category.

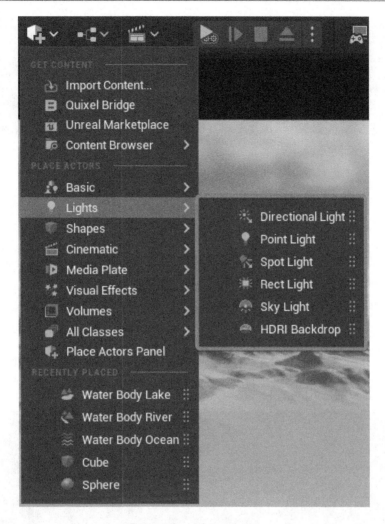

Figure 6.3 – Lighting assets

To add a new light to your level, you can simply click on it or *drag and drop* it onto the level to place it in a specific position. We have five different types of lights and a blueprint light system called **HDRi Backdrop**. In the following pages, we will go through these light assets by exploring their specific features and usage and their different options.

Directional Light

Directional light is infinite light that illuminates in one direction. *Infinite light* means that it has the same intensity everywhere in the scene. *One direction* means that it will always generate shadows in the same direction everywhere in the scene. For all these reasons, **Directional Light** is the perfect light asset to simulate a *Sun effect*.

Figure 6.4 – A scene illuminated by directional light

You can move or rotate directional light in the same way we learned for 3D models and assets in general. You can also rotate directional light by pressing and holding *ALT GR + L* and *moving the mouse*. A special *gizmo* will be shown:

Figure 6.5 – Directional light rotation gizmo

In *Figure 6.4* and *Figure 6.5*, you can see four spheres and one asset with colored squares. The four spheres have been assigned four different materials that can help us understand how the light is working in our scene. We can call them Lighting Helper Assets. I placed a totally black sphere, a gray sphere, a totally white sphere, and a chrome sphere. The cube with colored squares is a **Color Calibrator** and can help us have a preview of how different colors will be rendered in our scene. You can find this asset in the **Engine Content** folder.

Figure 6.6 – Color calibrator asset

> **Note**
>
> In nature, pure black and pure white doesn't exist. For this reason, you need to avoid pure white and pure black colors in your scene. My totally black material has a 0.04 color value. My totally white material has a value of 0.85 (the whitest material in nature is fresh snow, which has a color value of 0.8/0.9).
>
> The gray material value is not set at 0.5. Its value is 0.18 because of exposure. When you are working with lighting, you need to think about exposure exactly as you do working with cameras and lighting in the real world. Exposure is measured with *stops*. Any stop doubles the preview exposure value. Our eyes don't perceive exposure in a linear way. This is the reason why 0.18 results in the middle point between black and white.

You can check what we have just learned and how exposure works in *Figure 6.6*:

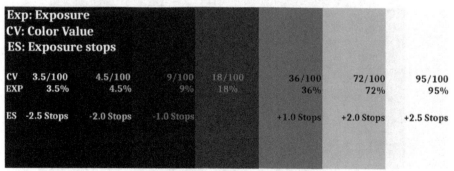

Figure 6.7 – Exposure explanation scheme

We are now ready to explore directional light settings. As always, you can find all the directional light options and settings inside the **Details** panel when the light is selected. For educational reasons, in the next section, we are going to cover only the fundamental settings. We will learn more in later parts of this chapter.

Exploring the Directional Light Details panel

With **Directional Light** selected, we can now explore the basic light settings in the **Details** panel. Directional light, and light assets in general, are assets exactly like a 3D model or a material. For this reason, some of the options in the **Details** panel we already know about – they are the same and they work in the same way. The **Transform** options allow you to move your directional light.

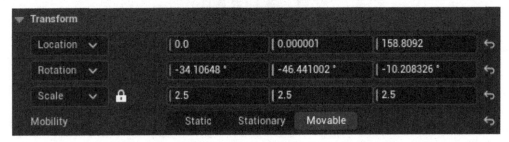

Figure 6.8 – The Transform panel in the Details panel always works in the same way

In the **Light** category, you can find all the options that allow you to change the basic proprieties of the directional light:

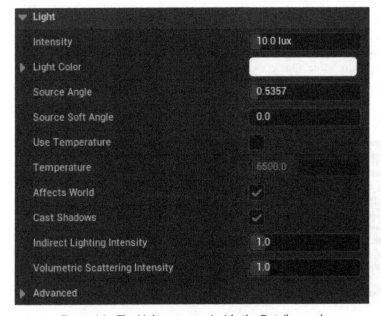

Figure 6.9 – The Light category inside the Details panel

- **Intensity**: Here, you can change the intensity of the light. The higher the value, the more powerful the light. **lux** is the unit that Unreal Engine 5 uses by default to set light intensity. If you try to change the intensity of the directional light, you will notice that the intensity does not change very much, even at a very high intensity level. The reason is the project has **Exposure Control** enabled. We will learn how to manage exposure next. For now, you can disable exposure control in the **Project Settings** window.

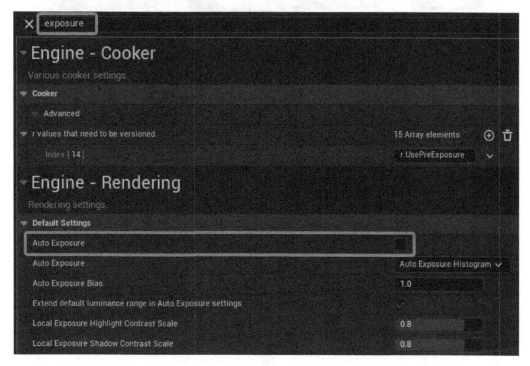

Figure 6.10 – Exposure control options inside the Project Settings window

- **Light Color**: Here, you can change the color of your directional light. It works like translucent colored paper that you could put in front of the light.

- **Source Angle**: This value allows you to increase the softness of the shadow. The higher the value, the smoother the shadow. By default, the value is set to 0.53 to simulate the source angle of the Sun. Take a look at the shadow in the following screenshot:

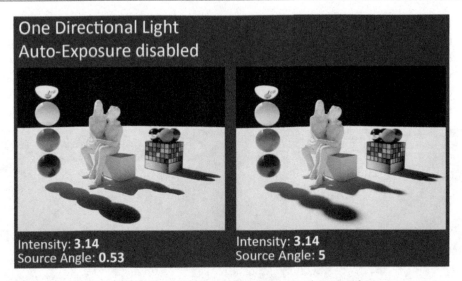

Figure 6.11 – Source Angle explanation example screenshot

- **Source Soft Angle:** This value allows you to smooth the specular point on reflective surfaces.

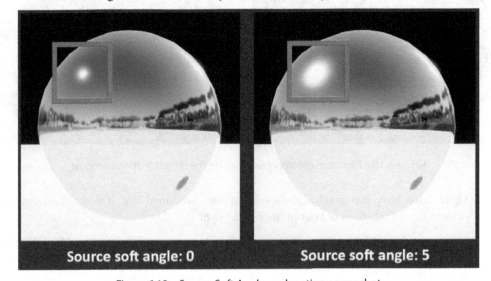

Figure 6.12 – Source Soft Angle explanation screenshot

- **Use Temperature:** If this option is enabled, you can change the temperature of your light. This will affect the light color. You can change the temperature value with the *temperature slide* (this is active only if the **Use Temperature** option is enabled). The lower the value, the warmer the light. The higher the value, the colder the light. The temperature unit is Kelvin. By default, the value is 6500, which is equal to white light.

Figure 6.13 – Light temperature explanation screenshot

- **Affects World**: If this option is disabled, the light will not contribute in any way to the scene's lighting. This is equal to deleting the light. This option is useful for non-destructive experiments.

- **Cast Shadow**: This option allows you to enable or disable shadows being cast by the light.

Figure 6.14 – A scene illuminated by a single directional light with Cast Shadow disabled

- **Indirect Lighting Intensity**: This option allows you to increase or decrease the contribution of this light to GI. This is a very useful option to make your lighting more realistic (or simply brighten/darken an interior scene).

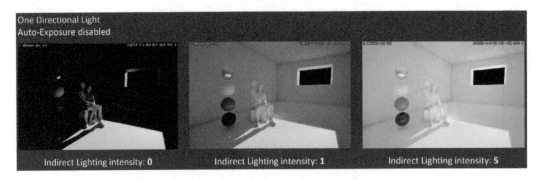

Figure 6.15 – Indirect Lighting Intensity explanation screenshot

You can also improve the intensity of indirect lighting by improving the intensity of the light or by changing the albedo color of the surfaces where the light will bounce.

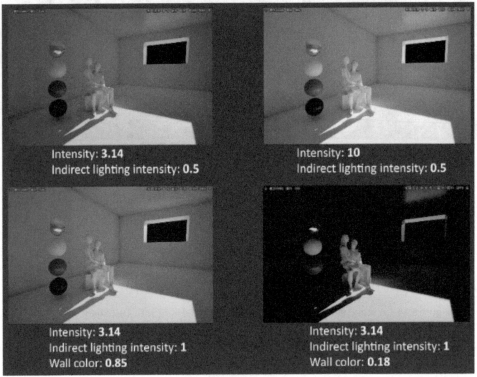

Figure 6.16 – Indirect lighting methods overview image

- **Volumetric Scattering intensity**: This value allows you to increase the volumetric scattering effect of your light. This is very useful to create a *God rays* effect or a foggy mood. It works along with **Exponential Height Fog**. We will learn more about it in the *Step 3: Adding God rays* section later in this chapter.

Figure 6.17 – Volumetric Scattering Intensity set to 100 in a scene with one directional light and Exponential Height Fog set to be volumetric

We can now go on and learn more about **Point Light**.

Point Light

A **point light** is a light that illuminates in all directions starting from a point. Unlike directional light, a point light is not infinite and its intensity linearly decays. That means that its intensity decreases as it gets further from the light source.

Figure 6.18 – A scene illuminated by a point light without changing any light settings

Most of the settings we have already seen for direction light work in the same way for point light. We don't need to explain them again.

However, if you have selected a point light, there are a couple of different options in the **Details** panel that we need to learn about to use the point light in the best way. Let's check them out:

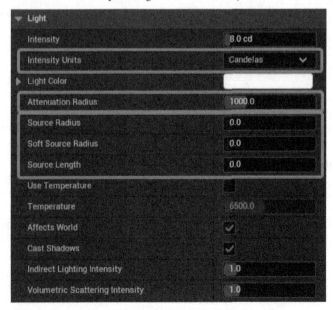

Figure 6.19 – Point light's specific settings in the Details panel

- **Intensity Units**: Here, you can change the unit type to use to define the intensity of the light. By default, it is **Candelas**. You can also use **Lumens**, **EV**, or **Unitless**. Changing the intensity unit can be useful for architectural or interior design projects to reproduce real-life light.

- **Attenuation Radius**: Point light intensity decays in space. That means that its intensity decreases as it gets further from the light source. The attenuation radius defines the area where the intensity decays. It looks like a sphere whose center is the center of the light (that is, the source of the light). At this point, the intensity has its max value (the value we set in the intensity field). On the border of the sphere drawn by the attenuation radius, the intensity of the light is zero. From the center to the border, the intensity of the light decreases linearly.

Figure 6.20 – Point light's Attenuation Radius set to 100

- **Source Radius**, **Soft Source Radius**, **Source Length**: The options **Source Radius** and **Soft Source Radius** work in the same way we saw for directional light, with the difference that we can see the shape of the source in the viewport. **Source Length** allows you to modify the source shape with a vertical transformation. The combination of these three values can help to create particular light effects in Reflection.

Figure 6.21 – Point light with Source Radius set to 24, Soft Source
Radius set to 24, and Source Length set to 272

Other values work in the same way as we saw for directional light. So, we can go on and learn more about **Spot Light**.

Spot Light

A **spot light** emits light in one direction from a single point in a cone shape. It works like a point light and its intensity linearly decays. That means that its intensity decreases as it gets further from the light source.

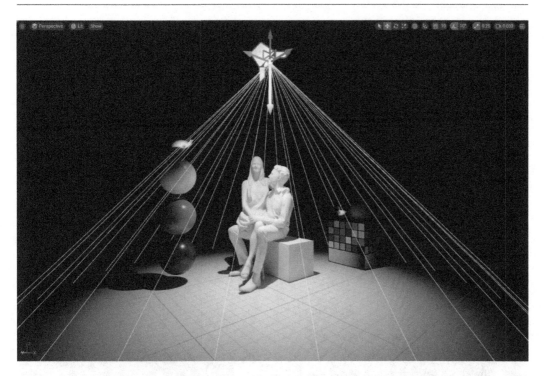

Figure 6.22 – A scene illuminated by a single spot light with default values

We have already learned about all the settings we need, except for the options that allow us to modify the cone shape used by the spot light to emit light:

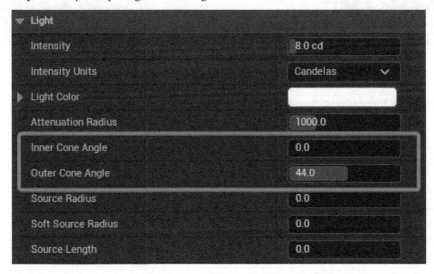

Figure 6.23 – Spot light's cone shape option inside the Details panel

- **Inner Cone Angle**: This option allows you to increase the area where your light maintains its max intensity (the value we set in the **Intensity** field). It looks like a smaller cone inside the spot light's cone shape. After the inner cone's border, the light starts to decay. By default, it is set to **0**, meaning that the light has its maximum intensity only at the source point.

- **Outer Cone Angle**: This option allows you to define the size of the spot light's cone shape. At the outer cone's border, the light's intensity is zero.

Figure 6.24 – An example of how Inner Cone Angle and Outer Cone Angle work

There is another interesting option that can improve the usage of a spot light. You can find it in the **Details** panel under the **Light Profile** category. It is called **IES Texture**.

IES Texture works like a tri-dimensional alpha applied to the light source. The result is a particular source shape that simulates real-life light assets to create specific effects.

You can find some samples directly inside Unreal Engine 5 or find them in various online libraries such as at https://ieslibrary.com/. This is a very useful option for interior design projects but also for specific creative effects, as you can see in *Figure 6.24*.

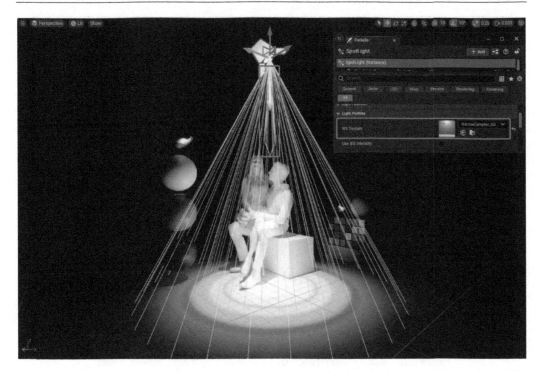

Figure 6.25 – Spot light with IES Texture assigned

> **Note**
>
> A point light and a spot light are very similar lights. A spot light is a point light with the attenuation radius sphere "cut" with a cone. A point light is perfect to simulate a bulb light effect. A spot light can be used to simulate a street light or theatrical spotlight.

We are now ready to learn more about **Rect Light**.

Rect Light

A **rect light** is a light that emits light in one direction from a rectangular shape. The main characteristic of a rect light is that we can change the size of the rectangular shape to create various light effects.

Figure 6.26 – A scene illuminated by a single rect light with default values

You can change the size of the rectangular shape with some values in the **Details** panel:

Figure 6.27 – Source shape options inside the Details panel

- **Source Width, Source Height**: These two values allow you to change the shape size. A bigger shape generates smoother light and shadows. The intensity of a rect light is averaged over the surface area of the light. As you increase the **Source Width** and **Source Height** values, you will need to increase **Intensity** in order to maintain the same apparent brightness.

- **Barn Door Angle, Barn Door Length**: These values simulate the barn door you can find in real-life light bodies. They work like lateral panels that occlude the emission of the light.

- **Source Texture**: This option works in the same way as **IED Textures** works but it uses a 2D alpha texture to change the source shape.

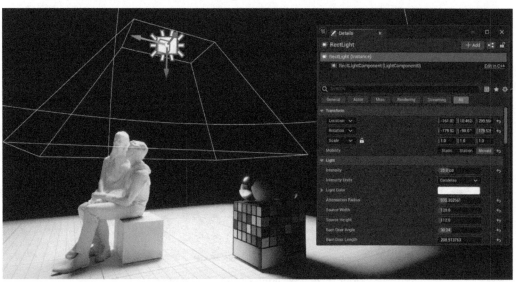

Figure 6.28 – A scene illuminated with a single rect light with specific values

Rect Light is very useful and allows you to create a very realistic set of lights for your objects; the ability to change the size of a rectangular shape makes it the perfect light for automotive projects. Thanks to its rectangular shape, it is also useful to improve lighting coming from windows or doors.

We can now go on and explore the power of **Sky Light**.

Sky Light

Sky Light is one of the most important light assets inside Unreal Engine 5. It is also one of the most difficult to understand, but mastering its usage can consistently improve the quality of the lighting in your scene.

Sky Light captures distant parts of your scene and uses them to create light and reflection in your scene. Thanks to this process, lighting and reflection will perfectly match.

Sky Light can't work in an empty scene. To work, it needs something to capture. The best way to check how **Sky Light** is working is to place a sphere with a totally reflective material (a chrome ball) at the center of the scene.

According to its different nature, the **Sky Light Details** panel has different options. To understand how **Sky Light** works, we can't check all the settings one by one as we have done for other light assets. To make it as clear as possible, we need to start from the most important value: **Sky Distance Threshold**. This value sets the point (in terms of distance from the **Sky Light** asset) where the sky light starts to capture the world to reproduce the light inside your scene.

If we place a sky light in the scene that we are using in this chapter, near our assets, without any other light assets, our scene will remain totally dark, even if we set the sky light's intensity to 10 or 100. The reason is that the **Sky Distance Threshold** value is set to **150000** by default. This means that the sky light is capturing 150,000 units away from its place in the scene. If we change the **Sky Distance Threshold** value to 1, our assets will appear illuminated by the sky light.

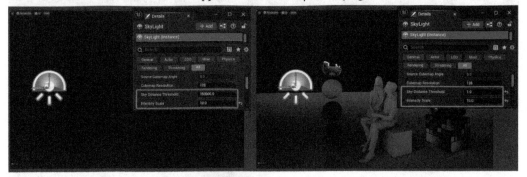

Figure 6.29 – Sky light explanation example

Sky Distance Threshold works like a sphere that has its center as the position of the skylight and its diameter as the value you set in the sky distance threshold. Everything inside this sphere is ignored by the sky light.

You can change the intensity of the sky light and its color in the same way we learned for the other light types.

Another exclusive feature of **Sky Light** is the possibility to use an HDRi instead of the scene environment to generate lighting. To do that, you need to change the **Source Type** option. By default, it is set to **SLS Captured Scene**. With this option selected, the sky light works as we just saw. If you want to use an HDRi, you need to change this option to **SLS Specified Cube Map** and add an HDRi in the cube map slot.

With an HDRi assigned, the skylight uses the HDR image to reproduce light and reflection. You can find some HDRis directly inside the Engine or search for them in several online libraries. One of the best online libraries is *Poly Haven* (https://polyhaven.com/hdris). Here, you can find hundreds of high-resolution HDRis for free.

Be careful to download the HDR version of the file instead of the EXR version. Unreal Engine 5 can import both file extensions, but to use an HDRi with the sky light, you need an *.HDR file.

Using an HDRi instead of a captured scene sky light can help you to create several lighting scenarios and improve the realism of the scene. Remember that a sky light also influences reflection, so if you use an HDRi, any reflective object will reflect the HDRi.

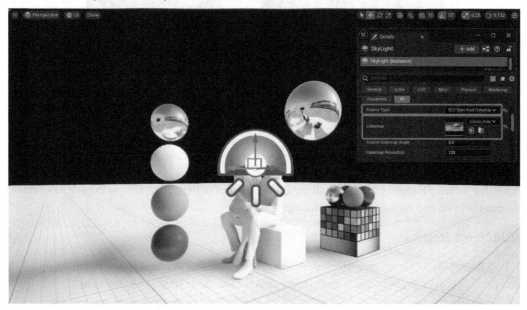

Figure 6.30 – A scene illuminated with a skylight and HDRi

With **Source Cubemap Angle**, you can change the rotation of the HDRi. This allows you to decide what to see in reflective objects and the position (direction) of the main light in the HDRi.

Cubemap resolution allows you to change the maximum resolution that can be used to render the HDRi. The higher the value, the better the quality of the light will be in terms of diffusion and smoothness.

A good habit is to align the directional light rotation to what we can see in the HDRi. The directional light should have the same direction as the main light source in the HDRi.

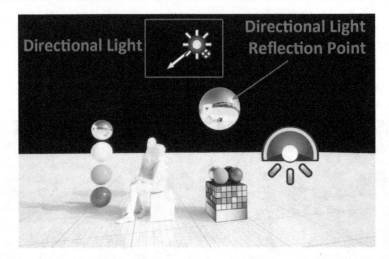

Figure 6.31 – Skylight and directional light aligned

Now that we have learned how to use all the different types of lights that Unreal Engine 5 provides, we can move on and explore **HDRi Backdrop**.

HDRi Backdrop

HDRi Backdrop is a pre-compiled blueprint that simulates an exterior light system. Inside this blueprint, there is a sky light and a mesh dome with the selected HDRi projected onto it.

Figure 6.32 – A scene illuminated only by HDRi Backdrop

> **Note**
>
> **HDRi Backdrop** is a plugin, and it is not enabled by default. To be able to use it, you need to enable it in the Plugin panel (we have already seen how to enable/disable plugins in *Chapter 2*).

In the **Details** panel, you can change the HDRi assigned to **HDRi Backdrop** to simulate different environments. You can also change the overall intensity of the light.

Figure 6.33 – HDRi options in the Details panel

By moving the *diamond* icon, you can change the projection center of the HDRi. In other words, you can change the placement of the HDRi on the dome mesh.

Figure 6.34 – HDRi Backdrop's projection center

HDRi Backdrop is very useful for quick visualization or as a starting point for your lighting system.

You are now ready to illuminate any kind of object inside Unreal Engine. By using all the light assets, we have discovered in this chapter, you can easily create a lighting set to shoot an object or a composition of different assets.

Rect lights are perfect to create a three-light system; with spot and point lights, you can bring to life lighting props; directional light can be used to create very hard shadows; and a sky light can improve indirect lighting and reflection.

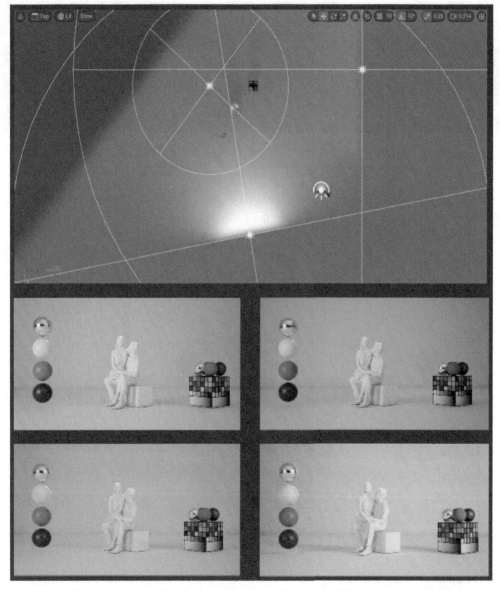

Figure 6.35 – Some examples of a scene illuminated by a three-light system and a sky light

Before going on and learning how to illuminate environments, we need to learn about a couple of techniques that can be very useful to improve the final quality of the lighting.

Tips and tricks to improve lighting quality

In this section, we will explore some options that can be very useful to improve the final quality of the light or to create some specific light effects.

Using lighting channels

Inside the light actors' **Details** panel (except for **Sky Light** and **HDRi Backdrop**), there is a very useful option that allows us to create links between objects and lights –links in terms of what the single light can illuminate inside the Level.

Lighting channels allow us to control how different lights interact with specific objects in your scene. Think of lighting channels as a way to selectively illuminate or exclude certain elements from the influence of specific lights. This helps achieve more control over the lighting in your scenes and create visually appealing effects.

We can find the **Lighting Channels** options in the **Details** panel under the **Light** category.

Figure 6.36 – Lighting Channels options

We can find the same options we can see in *Figure 6.35* inside any Static Mesh actor's **Details** panel. To create a link between one or more lights and one or more objects in the scene, the lights and the objects must have the same lighting channel.

Any object and any light could have one, two, or three lighting channels.

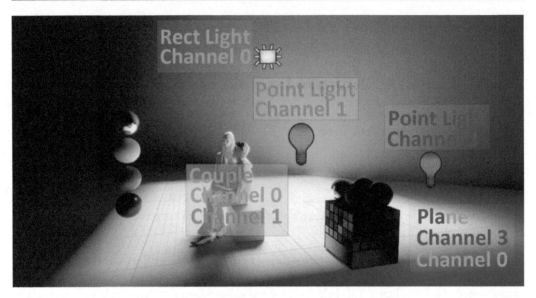

Figure 6.37 – Lighting channels example screenshot

Lighting channels in Unreal Engine 5 provide a way to control and customize how lights affect different parts of your scene. This feature is particularly useful for achieving specific lighting effects and enhancing the overall visual appeal of our Level.

Now that we have learned how to use lighting channels, we can move on and learn more about shadow quality.

Improving shadow quality

One of the most important realism aspects to consider in your scene is shadows. A well-rendered shadow allows you to create a much more realistic scene. If you try to disable **Cast Shadow** options for all of your lights, the entire scene will seem fake. In the same way, low-resolution shadows will compromise the realism of the scene.

As we saw at the beginning of this chapter, Lumen uses **Virtual Shadow Map** to generate realistic shadows. This system works very well, especially because it is very optimized. But if you need a very smooth shadow on the ground or something like that, the result can be unsatisfying. For this reason, when we set the project to use Lumen, we also enabled the **Support Hardware Raytracing** option. This option allows us to change the type of shadow any single light will cast in the scene.

To do that, you can search for `ray` in the **Details** panel's search field and browse to **Cast Ray Traced Shadows**. By default, this option is set to **Use Project Settings**, which means, in our case, using **Virtual Shadow Map**. If we change that setting to **Enabled**, that light will cast ray traced shadows.

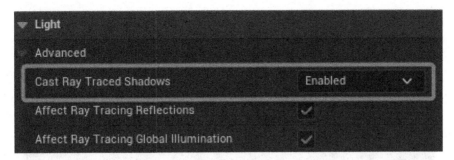

Figure 6.38 – Cast Ray Traced Shadows enabled

With **Cast Ray Traced Shadows** enabled, the shadows should now look more realistic and smooth:

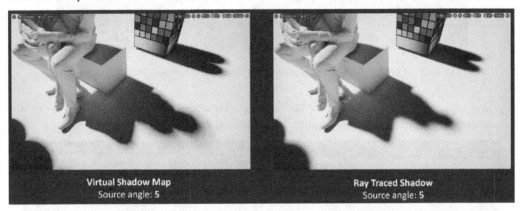

Figure 6.39 – Virtual Shadow Map versus Ray Traced Shadow

Now that we have learned how to improve shadow quality, we can move on and learn more about emissive materials.

Illuminating with emissive materials

Thanks to Lumen technology, assets with emissive materials can be used to illuminate your scene in Unreal Engine 5.

Being **emissive** is a material property that allows a surface to emit light.

Figure 6.40 – A scene illuminated by a simple sphere with an emissive material assigned

To add an emissive property to your material, you can create a color parameter, multiply it for a scalar parameter, and connect the Multiply output to the material domain's emissive input.

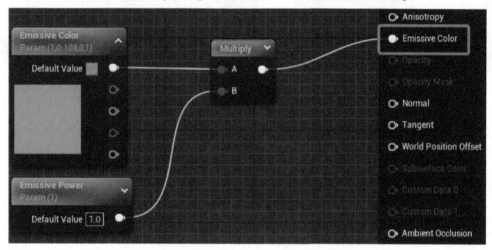

Figure 6.41 – Emissive node graph

Using emissive material's propriety to illuminate your scene is very useful because it can help you to create specific light assets such as neon or emissive objects and obtain a realistic effect.

Emissive material's propriety is also very useful to create effects with light by creating Light Material Functions.

Creating a flickering light with a Light Function Material

In *Chapter 5*, we saw that we can change the Material Domain to create different types of material. One of those types is **Light Function**.

A **light function** is a particular material domain with only emissive input that allows us to create materials to be assigned to our light assets. Through this special material, we can create special light effects.

For example, we can tell the light to flicker without animating its intensity.

To do that, we need to create a new material and change **Material Domain** to **Light Function**. For length reasons, we cannot create it step by step, but you can find the result in the following screenshot:

Figure 6.42 – Light Function Material's node graph

Now that we have learned how to use all the light assets in Unreal Engine and how to improve the quality of our light system with some tricks inside the Engine, we can go on and try to illuminate our first environment. But before that, you can do an exercise to verify all the stuff we have learned so far.

Exercise: Importing a new asset and lighting it

In this section, you need to import a new asset and try to illuminate it by applying all the notions we have learned in this chapter. The result should look like a product photo shoot. Take time to do some research, find some references, and try to reproduce it in the Engine.

Illuminating your first environment

In this section, we will learn how easy it is to illuminate an environment with Lumen and all the light assets we have seen in this chapter. To do that, we will use Epic Games' free content. The project is called **Megascans Abandoned Apartment**. You can download it from the marketplace (`https://www.unrealengine.com/marketplace/en-US/product/c26355353df843289701d632508d4fb0?sessionInvalidated=true`) to easily follow this section.

Figure 6.43 – Megascans Abandoned Apartment project on the marketplace

This project has been created to use hardware Ray Tracing. Before we start, we need to set it to use **Lumen** and all the features we have seen in this chapter. To do that, once you have opened the project (it could take a while the first time because it's huge!), go to **Project Settings** and be sure that all the following settings are enabled:

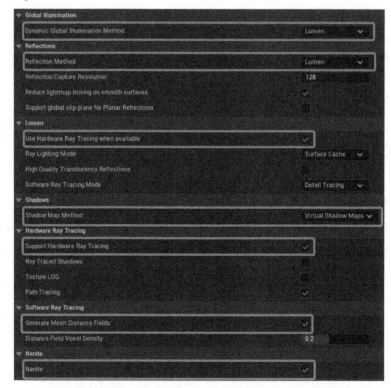

Figure 6.44 – Settings to change to run the project with Lumen

Make sure to have **DirectX12** set and **SM6** as the shader format (don't worry about this setting – you need to enable it to make all the shaders in this project work properly with Lumen).

Figure 6.45 – DirectX 12 and SM6 settings inside the Project Settings window

The project could ask you to restart the Engine. This is normal because it needs to recompile the shaders.

Once you have reopened the project, if you get some warnings don't worry. You can fix them automatically by clicking on the **Fix** command at the end of the description of any warning.

The last thing we need to do is set **Nanite**, the newest virtualized geometry system in Unreal Engine 5. For now, what you need to know is that Lumen is built to work very well together with Nanite. So, to achieve the best results, we need to convert all the assets of the scene into Nanite meshes. To do that, you can select all the assets you want to convert in the **Content Browser**, *right-click* on them, search for the **Nanite** category, and check the **Nanite** *checkbox*.

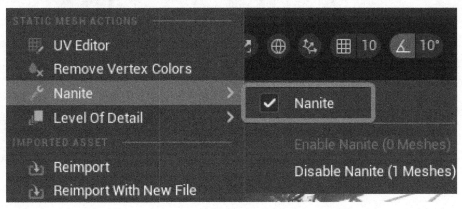

Figure 6.46 – Nanite command to convert meshes

The conversion process could take a while. When the Engine is done, we don't have to replace any assets in the scene. To check whether everything has worked, you can enable the **Nanite Visualization** option in the viewport option menu. It should look like this:

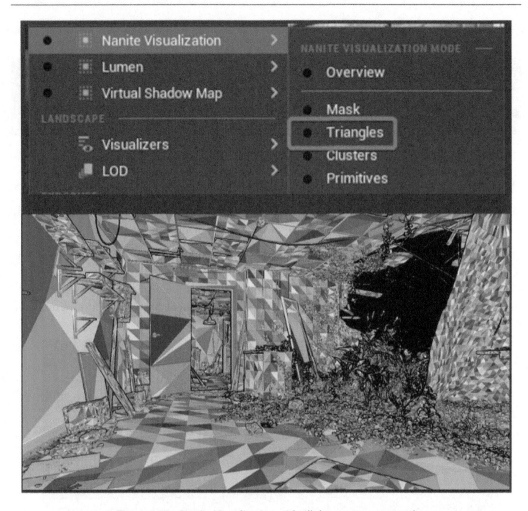

Figure 6.47 – Nanite Visualization with all the assets converted

Now, we have to set the Level we have inside the `Megascans Abandoned Apartment` project to create our light setup. To do that, we need to create a copy of the Level. Go to the **File** menu and click on **Save Current Level As…**. This command will create a copy of the main Level of the project. We can name it `Relight`.

There are two more things we need to do before start to work on our lighting setup. First, we want to reorder the Outliner a little bit to make it more comfortable to work on the project. We can create a new folder in the Outliner (we can call it `Env`) and move all the folders and all the assets inside this new one, except for the folders called `Cameras` and `Lighting_Post_Atmosphere` and the file called `Trailer_00`. You can delete them. The result should be a totally black viewport with only the `Env` folder in the Outliner.

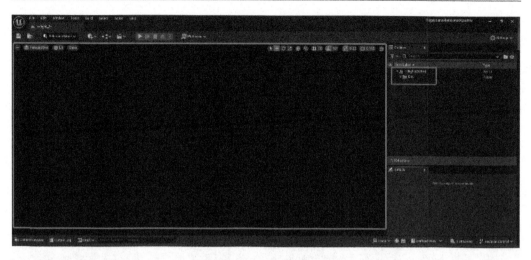

Figure 6.48 – This is how the level should look before we start to create the new lighting setup

We are now ready to illuminate our scene. I have illuminated the environment in the project by myself. We want to achieve the same result together. At the end of this section, you should have something like this:

Figure 6.49 – Re-lighting result

This will be a practical section. Try to follow all the steps to achieve the same result.

Step 1: Creating base lighting

The first thing we need to do is understand which kind of environment we are going to illuminate. Is it an interior environment or an external one? Maybe both? What kind of lighting we are trying to create? Day or night? There are infinite types of environmental light you can create. Having the final goal clear is very important to decide which workflow is better to apply for your lighting setup.

In our case, we have an interior environment with a huge hole in the wall, an opened window, and an opened door. We want to create a daylight setup. All these factors mean a lot of light coming inside from the outside.

Unreal Engine 5 has a tool that is perfect for creating a starting point for the kind of lighting we are trying to create. The tool is **Env. Light Mixer**. You can search for it inside the **Windows** menu.

Figure 6.50 – The Env. Light Mixer tool

Env. Light Mixer, or the Environmental Light Mixer, allows us to create atmospheric lighting with time-of-day system simply by adding a couple of assets in the scene. By clicking on the buttons with the name of the light asset, the tool will create that light asset in the Level. If you try to add all the assets that you can find in **Env. Light Mixer**, a complete atmospheric system will be created in the Level.

The result should be like this:

Figure 6.51 – A scene illuminated with Env. Light Mixer

If you check the **Outliner**, you can find all the light assets that **Env. Light Mixer** has created for you. There are some assets that we already know (a sky light and directional light) but also some new assets, such as **Sky Atmosphere**, **Exponential Height Fog**, and **Volumetric Cloud**. The way they have been automatically set allows you to manage the time-of-day system by simply rotating the directional light.

If you try to use the *ALTGR + L* shortcut, you can see that by rotating the directional light, the time of day will change together with the light in the scene.

Figure 6.52 – Different directional light rotation generates different atmospheric lighting

Env. Light Mixer is an incredible tool and the way it allows us to create a consistent light setup is ridiculously easy. I always use it to start my lighting setup independently if I am creating an interior or exterior environment. Obviously, if you are trying to create a deep dark cave, you can't use it, but most of the time it is the perfect starting point.

Don't worry about the assets you don't know. We are going to learn how to use them in the next steps of this section.

The next step is related to exposure. If you try to move up the viewport camera and go outside the apartment, over the roof, and then go down again inside the apartment, you can see the intensity of the light increase and decrease like a dimmer light. This is because of Unreal Engine 5's **Auto Exposure** control.

In the next step, we will learn how to manage exposure in our Level.

Step 2: Managing exposure in your Level

The **Auto Exposure** control is a great feature, but we don't want to let the Engine do the work for us. We can disable the exposure control inside **Project Settings**.

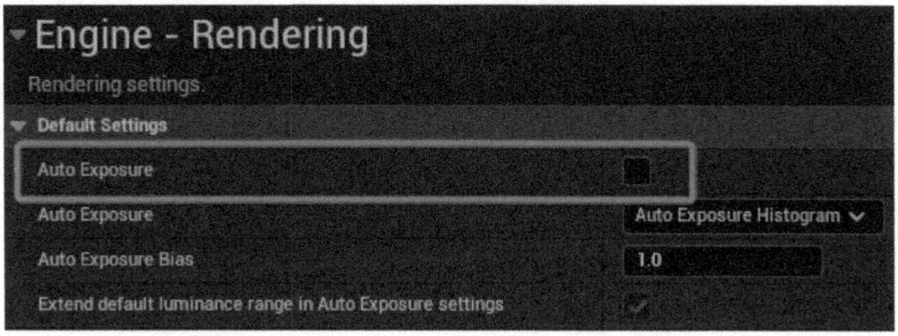

Figure 6.53 – Exposure control options in Project Settings

Without automatic exposure control, our scene is now darker, but the lighting maintains its intensity everywhere. Now, the exposure of our scene has a fixed value.

Figure 6.54 – A scene with the Auto Exposure control disabled

To change this value and be able to make our scene brighter or darker, we need to place a **Post Process Volume (PPV)** inside our Level. You can find this in the **Place Actor** menu under the **Visual Effects** category. A PPV is an actor that allows you to change the overall look and feel of the scene in terms of both effects such as bloom and vignetting and rendering features such as Lumen and motion blur, but also color grading, camera features, and, of course, exposure.

PPV has hundreds of options. In this section, we will go through a few of them. We will learn more about **PPV** in *Chapter 12*.

Any options we set inside the PPV will work only when the camera is inside the PPV. This is very useful if you want to create diverse effects in different rooms or different sites in your environment. In our case, it would be more convenient to have a PPV that affects the entire level. To do that, select **PPV** and search for infinite in the **Details** panel's search field. You should find the **Infinite Extent (Unbound)** option, which allows you to make the PPV infinite.

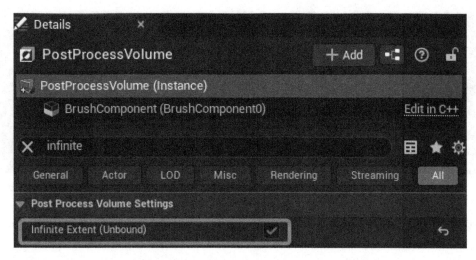

Figure 6.55 – Infinite PPV option inside the Details panel

Now, we can finally modify the **Exposure** value inside the PPV. In the **Details** panel, search for the **Exposure** category. We want to manually modify the exposure level in the scene. So, be sure that **Metering Mode** is set to **Manual** and that **Apply Physical Camera Exposure** is disabled (you need to *flag* the *box on the left* and *de-flag* the *box on the right*), which means that we won't use a physical camera option.

Figure 6.56 – Exposure control options inside the Details panel

You can change the exposure level of the scene by modifying the **Exposure Compensation** value. If you try to slowly increase this value, the brightness in your scene will increase. With this single value, you can change the overall look of your scene in terms of brightness without modifying the intensity of each light asset in the Level.

Figure 6.57 – Exposure Compensation examples

Working with exposure together with all the lighting settings we have learned about in this chapter is a fundamental technique to achieve realistic lighting with Lumen.

We are now ready to bring some atmospheric density or fog to our scene. We want to make the light rays coming from the huge hole in the wall we have in this environment visible to create a dreamier effect.

Step 3: Adding God rays

First, we need to learn more about the actor called **Exponential Height Fog** that we have already added with **Env. Light Mixer**. **Exponential Height Fog** brings a fog effect to our scene. To see what it does, we can set a high value in the **Fog Density** setting inside the **Details** panel. By default, it is set to **0.02**. We can try something such as 1 to stretch it and make the effect very visible.

Figure 6.58 – Exponential Height Fog's density set to 1

As you can see in *Figure 6.57*, the result is a fog with the same density visible everywhere in the Level. It also has a prominent bluish effect that affects the final overall look of the scene. What we want to achieve is different. We want to see the fog only through the light rays, something like we saw in *Figure 6.16*.

If you scroll down in the **Details** panel, you can find the **Volumetric Fog** option. You can enable it by simply checking the box.

Figure 6.59 – Volumetric Fog setting inside the Details panel

Volumetric Fog computes the fog density on any pixel of the scene to allow different density levels. The density changes according to the intensity of all the light assets in the scene and by considering objects that stop light rays. In other words, the higher the intensity of the light, the more visible the fog. If an object stops the propagation of the light rays, the fog will not be visible.

Figure 6.60 – Volumetric Fog enabled with fog density set to 1

We have God rays! If you try to rotate your directional light, you will see the rays moving around in the scene.

Figure 6.61 – Rotating light affects God rays' direction

The effect is now too strong because, before, we stretched the fog density value. We can set it to its default value: 0.02. Now the fog is barely visible.

To improve the visibility of the God rays effect, we can modify **Volumetric Scattering Intensity** of the directional light (we learned about it in the *Directional Light* section of this chapter). By default, it is set to **1**. If you try to slowly increase the value, you will see the God rays appear again. A value between 5 and 10 could work well for us.

Figure 6.62 – Fog density set to 0.02; directional light intensity
set to 1; Volumetric Scattering Intensity set to 7

We now have an acceptable God rays effect coming through the big hole in the wall. If we take a look around our scene, we can see that the light hasn't enough variation. We want to create variation near the door at the end of the corridor and around the window on the left side of the apartment. To do that, we need to add some more light assets.

Step 4: Adding rect lights

Rect Light is the perfect asset to improve light coming from the outside through a window or a door. Thanks to the ability to modify the size of the light source, we can create a light that perfectly fits with our window to help increase the quantity of light that is coming inside.

We can start with the window. We can create a rect light and scale its source to the size of the windows.

Figure 6.63 – The light improved by a rect light behind the window

As you can see, adding a rect light behind the window allows us to have more realistic lighting coming from outside. The reflection on the ground makes a difference in terms of realism.

To obtain this result, I set the rect light's **Intensity** to 5 and **Volumetric Scattering Intensity** to 25. The light is rotated by 90° and its location is **X** = 612.099892, **Y** = -291.210873, **Z** = 1250.568481. You can modify these values to obtain a different effect.

We can do the same thing for the door at the end of the corridor. The result should look like this:

Figure 6.64 – Adding a rect light outside the corridor's door

To obtain this result, I set the rect light's **Intensity** to 5 and **Volumetric Scattering Intensity** to 50. The light is rotated by 90° and its location is **X** = -226.866605, **Y** = 160.643306, **Z** = 1218.675876. You can modify these values to obtain different effects.

We are almost done. Before going on to the next step, we need to add the helper assets we used before, in the *Directional Light* section.

Figure 6.65 – Helper assets added to the scene

Thanks to our helper assets, we can see that the light burns the white sphere a little bit and the shadows are too dark. We can adjust the brightness of the scene by changing the **Exposure Compensation** value inside **PPV**. We can decrease it from 3 to 2. The scene now should be darker, but the shadows also. We can easily fix shadows by increasing the **Indirect Lighting Intensity** value of our directional light. We can set it to 2. The scene should now look like this:

Figure 6.66 – The scene at the end of Step 4

We are now ready to color-correct our scene a little bit. To do that, we can use the PPV in our scene.

Step 5: Changing the lighting scene's temperature

Our light setup is almost done but, if we look at our reference images (see *Figure 6.48*), our scene looks too warm. We have a dominant yellow tint instead of a colder blue overall look of the reference images. To obtain a different scene mood, we can simply change the temperature of our scene. To do that, search for **Temperature** in the PPV's **Details** panel.

Figure 6.67 – The PPV's Temperature settings inside the Details panel

The **Temp** value allows us to change the overall temperature of the scene. The value unit is kelvin. By default, it is set to **6500.0** kelvins, the temperature of white light. If we increase the value, the scene will become warmer; if we decrease the value the scene will become colder. We can try a value between 4000 and 5000. Let's set 4500 kelvins.

Figure 6.68 – The scene with the temperature value set to 4500

Temperature is one of the most powerful options inside the PPV. With only one value, you can obtain hundreds of different moods for your scene. Temperature setting is part of the color correction toolset that the PPV gives you to color-correct your scene. We will learn more about PPVs in *Chapter 12*.

We are now ready for the last step. We want to see something outside to increase the realism of the scene.

Step 6: Adding the HDRi backdrop

In this last, very short step, we want to add something to see outside the apartment. This will increase the realism of the scene. To do that, we can add an HDRi backdrop to our Level.

Figure 6.68 – The scene with the HDRi backdrop added to the Level

You can change the HDRi according to the effect you want to obtain. By changing the HDRi backdrop's **Size** value, you can make the image more visible. In the preceding screenshot, we have set 75 as the **Size** value, and we have loaded the HDRI_forest image in the HDRi backdrop **Cube map** option.

Finished! You have just illuminated your first environment in Unreal Engine 5! We used only three light assets but the result is still impressive. Thanks to Lumen and **Post-Process Colume** (PPV), obtaining good lighting in Unreal Engine 5 is quite simple. Once you have a solid starting point like the one that we have created together, creating variations is very fast and fun.

Practicing is very important to improve lighting skills. Trying to relight a project like **Megascan Abandoned Apartment** is a very good exercise to try out various lighting techniques or try to reproduce something you saw in a movie or video game.

Summary

In this rich chapter, we have learned a lot of things about lighting in Unreal Engine 5. We started by understanding what Lumen is and how it works. We learned how to use all the different light assets that the Engine provides, and we now understand the difference between static and movable lights. We discovered how **Ray Traced Shadows** can improve shadows' quality; we learned that **Lumen** allows us to illuminate scenes with emissive objects, and we understand how to create a Light Function that makes our light asset flicker. Finally, we illuminated an environment from scratch.

We are coming to the end of the first part of this book. In the next chapter, we will overview the newest Unreal Engine 5 features before starting to learn all the techniques needed to create an environment from scratch.

7
Exploring Nanite, RVTs, and the World Partition Tool

In this theoretical chapter, we will cover the newest features that Epic Games has introduced with **Unreal Engine 5**. We will learn what **Nanite** is and how it can improve your workflow, and we will also learn what a virtual texture is and how the world partition tool can help us create a massive world.

We will cover the following topics in this chapter:

- Understanding Nanite

- Understanding **Runtime Virtual Textures** (**RVTs**)

- Understanding the new World Partition tool

By the end of this chapter, you will know what Nanite is and how it works; you will understand what an RVT is and how to merge an asset with the terrain's material in a more realistic way; and you will have a clearer idea of what the World Partition tool is used for.

Technical requirements

This will be a demonstrative chapter. You need to have the Engine installed on your workstation to follow this chapter.

Discovering Nanite

In this section, we will learn what Nanite is and how it works. This will be an overview of the Nanite technology to let you know what we can and cannot do with Nanite.

Nanite is the new virtualized geometry system in Unreal Engine 5. In other words, Nanite is a new, smarter, and faster way to render triangles (polygons) on screen, which allows you to populate your scene with highly detailed assets in terms of **polycount** (number of polygons per asset) without stressing graphics cards and performances.

To allow us to do that, Nanite uses a new technique to generate **level of detail** (**LOD**) meshes (LOD allows the Engine to scale the quality of the asset according to its distance from the camera), which considers **clusters** instead of the entire mesh.

Nanite divides geometry into clusters. You can see them by entering the **Nanite Visualization** mode and selecting **Clusters**. To do that, click on **Lit** in the top-left corner of the Level Viewport, and from the **Nanite Visualization** category, select **Clusters**.

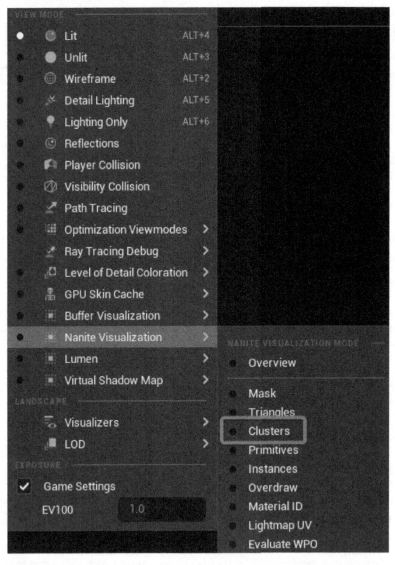

Figure 7.1 – The Clusters option inside the Nanite Visualization category

Once we have activated the cluster visualization mode, the Level Viewport should look like this:

Figure 7.2 – The Nanite Visualization | Clusters mode

Clusters change on the screen according to the asset size, asset distance from the camera, and screen resolution. LODs usually work by asset, meaning that, according to the distance from the camera, the asset changes its resolution in terms of the number of polygons and textures resolution.

By dividing all the level geometries into clusters, Nanite allows us to have a LOD system that considers any single cluster instead of an entire mesh. Nanite will simply delete any cluster that will be outside of the screen. In other words, the Engine will render only the clusters that we can see in our frame, and it will ignore the ones that we can't see.

This allows us to have an almost-per-pixel LOD system. In other words, Nanite doesn't change the resolution of an entire geometry, but it works on any single cluster that composes a geometry.

This genius LOD system allows us to have millions and millions of polygons inside the level without stressing our graphics card.

To understand how Nanite can do that in a better way, we need to talk about draw calls. In a very simplified way, any different asset Unreal Engine 5 needs to load in the level from the **Content Browser** is a **draw call**. The higher the number of draw calls, the heavier is the project in terms of performance. Thanks to the cluster technology, Nanite can massively reduce the number of draw calls that Unreal Engine 5 needs to load to render the level because Nanite considers all the Nanite meshes as a single draw call split up into multiple clusters. For this reason, Nanite can allow you to achieve extremely realistic results without a huge impact on performance.

Finally, Nanite meshes are very well compressed. One million polygons mesh is around 15 MB on a hard drive. A 4K resolution texture is barely the same weight.

Now that we have understood the fundamentals of Nanite technology, we can learn how to enable Nanite in our project.

Activating Nanite

Unreal Engine 5 comes with Nanite technology pre-compiled inside it. We don't need to enable it from project settings. Converting a Static Mesh into a Nanite mesh is extremely easy and it's a non-destructive process. This means that you can convert a Static Mesh into a Nanite mesh and come back to a Static Mesh again any time you need to without losing your work.

To convert a Static Mesh into a Nanite mesh, follow these simple steps:

1. Inside the **Content Browser**, right-click on the Static Mesh you want to convert to a Nanite mesh.

2. Select **Nanite** and click on **Enable Nanite**. Then, you can flag the **Nanite** checkbox.

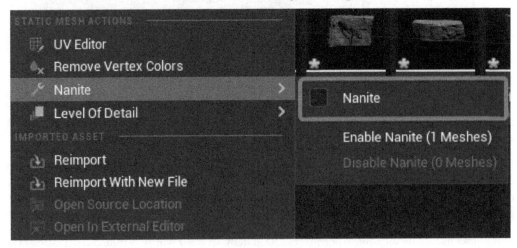

Figure 7.3 – Converting a Static Mesh into a Nanite mesh with the RMB menu in the Content Browser

You can perform the preceding step (*Step 2*) on a multiple selection.

You can also convert a Static Mesh into a Nanite mesh directly inside the Static Mesh Editor by checking the **Enable Nanite Support** option:

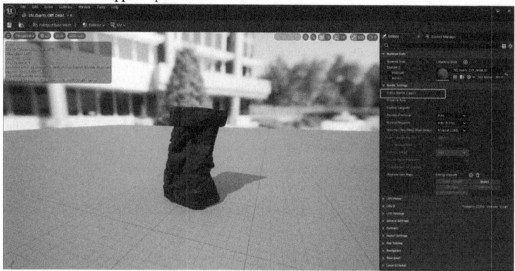

Figure 7.4 – Enable the Nanite option inside the Static Mesh Editor

Using the *right-click* method or the Static Mesh Editor option will perform the same result, but with the Static Mesh Editor, you can convert only one Static Mesh per time.

If you are importing a new Static Mesh, you can tell the Engine to convert the new asset into a Nanite mesh. To do that, you need to check the **Build Nanite** option in the **Import Options** window:

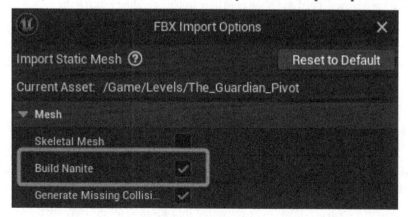

Figure 7.5 – Nanite conversion option inside the Import Options panel

Now that we know how to convert a Static Mesh into a Nanite mesh, we can go on and explore the pros and cons of using Nanite.

Nanite pros and cons

As for any new technology, Nanite gives us a lot of advantages but also some limitations. We will start with the pros:

- **Polycount and draw calls**: The number of triangles (polygons) in the scene that we can achieve with Nanite meshes is huge. The way Nanite meshes interpret LODs with clusters allows us to place a very high number of assets in the scene.

- **Kitbashing**: The possibility to place a huge number of assets in the scene, with no impact on draw calls, allows us to combine different high-resolution assets to create new ones (kitbashing) and populate our scene in a realistic way.

- **Non-destructive workflow**: All the Nanite features can be activated or deactivated on any single asset. This action will not force you to change anything in the scene.

- **Compression**: As we already said before, Nanite meshes are incredibly well optimized and very light on your hard drive.

However, there are some limitations in using Nanite that we need to know about to make the most of the advantages if we decide to enable Nanite:

- **High resolution**: Nanite becomes expensive when you start working with a higher resolution. The higher the resolution is, the higher the number of clusters Nanite needs to create a high-quality level of detail.

- **Overdrawing**: **Overdraw** refers to the number of times Nanite needs to process a single pixel of the scene. In a very complex scene with a lot of different assets overlapped, there are a lot of different pixels overlapped and Nanite can have trouble deciding which is the correct pixel to render.

- **Foliage**: At this moment, Nanite doesn't work perfectly with foliage assets. Foliage assets are leaves, trees, and grass. (We will learn more about foliage in *Chapter 9*.) You can enable Nanite on foliage meshes but it could generate some visualization problems, such as flickering.

- **Two-sided faces**: At this moment, Nanite doesn't support two-sided faces. We have talked about the two-sided material option in *Chapter 5*.

- **Skeletal Meshes**: At this moment, Nanite doesn't support Skeletal Meshes (animated objects). We discussed Skeletal Meshes in *Chapter 4*.

- **Translucent and masked materials**: At this moment, Nanite doesn't support translucent and masked materials. We discussed these features in *Chapter 5*.

So, when is a mesh a good candidate to be converted into a Nanite mesh? Here are the instances when it is a good candidate for conversion:

- When it contains a lot of triangles (polygons)

- When it is an asset that you plan to replicate a lot of time inside your level

- When it contains very small modeling details

Nanite is a great new feature that represents a huge improvement for artists in the environment creation workflow. We are now ready to introduce another new feature, this time regarding texturing.

Discovering RVTs

RVTs represent a way to manage huge textures and with the newest Engine's version, they became much faster and more optimized.

The primary use of RVTs is to reduce the texture's overdraw. As we will see in *Chapter 9*, we can paint textures on our terrain (**Landscape**) with multiple layers. The Engine keeps calculating all these layers to show you the correct results. All this information is stored in the GPU and processed in real time. When the number of textured layers on a single pixel on the screen is too much to be calculated in real time by our GPU, we have performance issues.

An RVT takes all this layer information and baked them on a single texture that is stored on the GPU, but it has been already calculated. It is something very similar to the concepts of Static Lights that we saw in *Chapter 6*, but RVTs work in real time.

This solution allows us to create huge and very complex terrain with a high number of high-resolution textures without impacting performance too much.

In using an RVT, we are storing material information inside a backed texture, which allows us to use this information on top of all the assets in the level. In other words, we can apply RVT information on an asset to blend this asset with the terrain in a more realistic way.

In the following image, we can see the differences between using an RVT and not using one:

Figure 7.6 – The same asset with (left trunk) and without (right trunk) the RVT blending mode

In the next section, we will learn how to use an RVT to blend assets on terrain. The RVT blending technique works only with Landscape. We will learn everything about it in *Chapter 9*. This will just be a demonstrative section on how an RVT can be used.

Blending assets with RVTs

In this demonstrative section, I will show you how to blend assets with terrain by using RVTs. This will be a very simple example of how we can use RVTs in our project to push up the realism of our environment.

First, we need to enable RVT support in our project. To do that, we need to open the project settings windows and search for `virtual texture`. We need to check the **Enable virtual texture support** option.

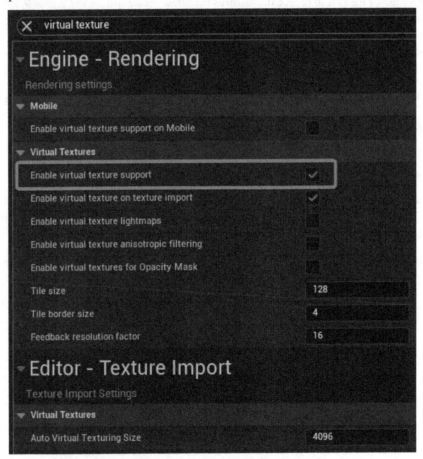

Figure 7.7 – The Enable virtual texture option inside project settings

This command allows us to create RVT assets and utilities inside our project.

Here, we are trying to blend the terrain's material with an asset placed on it. To do that, we need to define which attributes of the terrain material we want to blend and how to place them on the asset. For these reasons, we need to create two different RVTs.

Creating an RVT

To create an RVT, right-click inside the **Content Browser** and select **Runtime Virtual Texture** inside the **Texture** category:

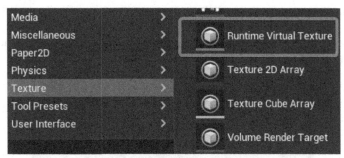

Figure 7.8 – The Runtime Virtual Texture creation menu

This asset is the virtual texture that the Engine will fill with the material's information. We can rename it RVT_Env. If we double-click on it, we can change some virtual texture options. We are interested in the **Virtual texture content** setting:

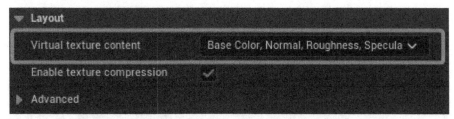

Figure 7.9 – The Virtual texture content option inside the RVT options window

This drop-down menu allows us to decide which information we want to be stored inside our virtual texture. Our goal is to merge our assets with our terrain material. So, we need to store all of the terrain's material information that determines the final aspect of the terrain. By default, **Virtual Texture Content** is set to store **Base Color, Normal, Roughness, Specula**. We don't need to change it.

Then, we want the terrain's material to be added to our assets according to its height in the world. This will allow us to manage the amount of terrain material we want to see on our assets. To do that, we need to create a second RVT and set its **Virtual texture content** option to **World Height**:

Figure 7.10 – The Virtual texture content option set to World Height

Inside this RVT, the Engine will store the asset's height information. We can rename it RVT_Height. Now that we have created all the RVTs we need, we can go on and create **RVT volumes** to set the RVT work area.

Creating an RVT volume

You can find **Runtime Virtual Texture Volume** inside the **Place Actor** menu, under the **Volumes** category. Or, you can search for it by using the search type field:

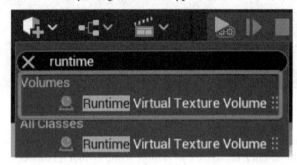

Figure 7.11 – You can find Runtime Virtual Texture Volume inside
the Place Actor menu under the Volumes category

We need two volumes, one for each RVT we have created. Inside each volume's **Details** panel, you need to set **Bound Align Actor** as **Landscape**:

Figure 7.12 – The Runtime Virtual Texture Volume options inside the Details panel

In the first RVT volume, you need to assign RVT_Env to the **Virtual Texture** option. In the second RVT volume, you need to assign RVT_Height. Remember to click on **Set Bounds** inside both volumes. This command will rescale the RVT volume to the Landscape scale.

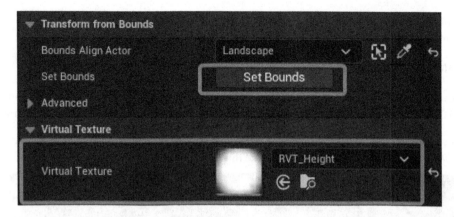

Figure 7.13 – The second RVT volume should look like this

The last thing we need to do is tell our Landscape that we are going to work with an RVT. To do that, we need to assign RVT_Env and RVT_Height to our Landscape. Inside the Landscape's **Details** panel, search for the **Virtual Texture** category. We are looking for the **Draw in Virtual Texture** option.

Figure 7.14 – The Draw in Virtual Texture option inside the Landscape's Details panel

This option allows us to set the Landscape to use RVTs. To add our RVTs to the Landscape, we need to add two different arrays by clicking on the + icon (*(Figure 7.14)* and assign RVT_Env to the first array and RVT_Height to the second.

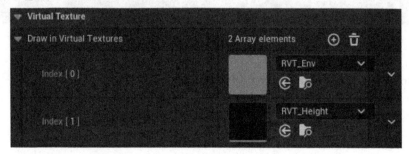

Figure 7.15 – Adding RVT arrays to the Landscape

Now that we have created and set all the assets that we need to work with RVTs, we can go on and add some nodes to our materials.

Updating Landscape material

To see the result of the RVTs and RVT volumes that we just created, we need to tell our Landscape material that it has to use an RVT. To do that, we need to add some nodes to our material graph.

For this demonstration, I'm using material from Megascans Library (we will learn everything about it in *Chapter 8*). The master material looks like this:

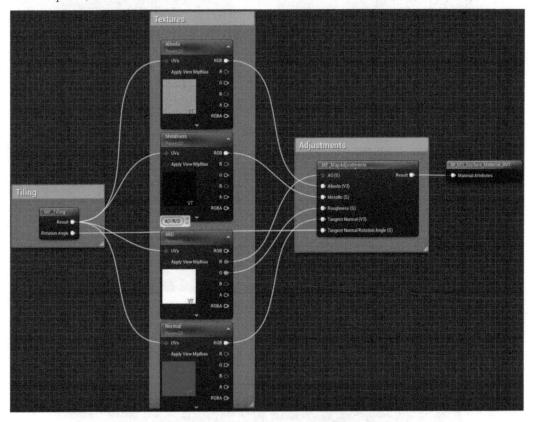

Figure 7.16 – The master material I'm using for my terrain

We need to add some nodes after the MF_MapAdjustments node. I'm not going deep into any nodes. The final graph should look like this:

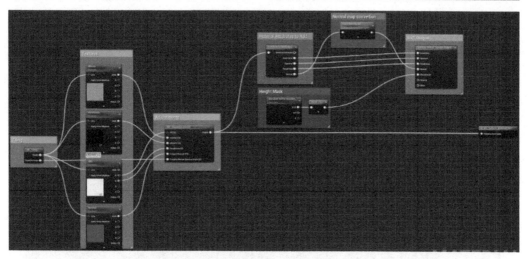

Figure 7.17 – Terrain material with RVT nodes

You can see the nodes we need to add in *Figure 7.18*:

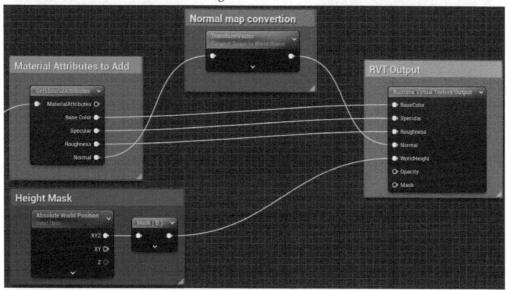

Figure 7.18 – RVT nodes to add to the terrain material

What we have just done is tell the new **RVT Output** (the node inside the yellow comment) which material attributes we want to store inside the virtual texture (the node inside the green comment in *Figure 7.18*). We have also converted the normal map from its default **Tangent Space** to **World Space** (the node inside the pink comment). Nodes inside the blue comment are telling to use **B channel** of the world position (**Y**) to calculate **World Height** (the terrain height in the world).

Perfect! The last thing we need to do is modify the material assigned to the asset we want to blend with the terrain.

Modifying asset material

As for the terrain's material, I'm using material from Megascans Library (we will learn everything about it in *Chapter 8*). The master material looks like this:

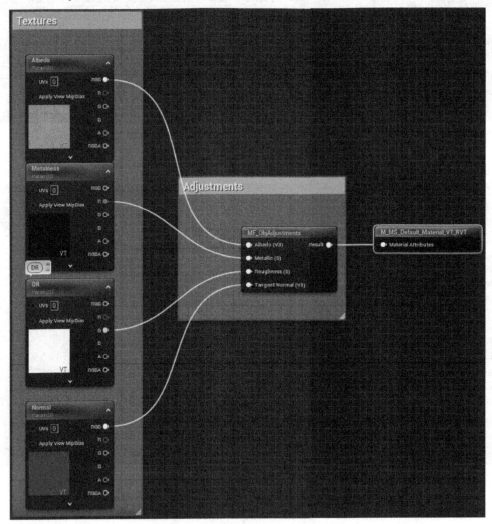

Figure 7.19 – Asset's master material's graph node

The master material is very similar to the one we used for the terrain instead of the fact that the asset material does not have the Tiling function.

We need to add some nodes after the `MF_MapAdjustement` node. The final graph should look like this:

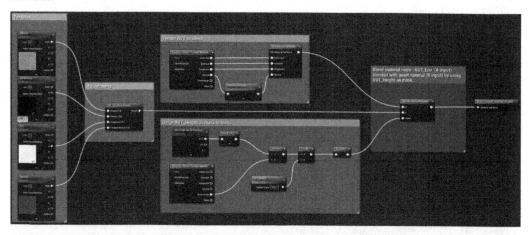

Figure 7.20 – Asset material with RVT nodes

You can see the nodes we have to add in *Figure 7.21*:

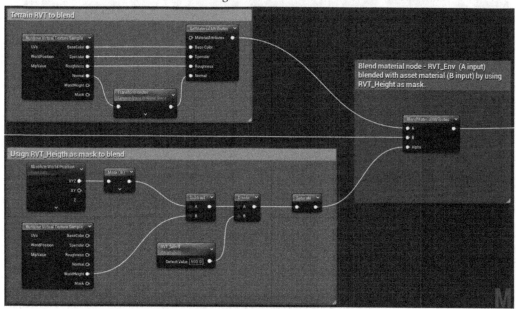

Figure 7.21 – RVT nodes to add to the asset material

What we have just done is blend our terrain virtual texture (`RVT_Env`) with the material asset (**B input** of the **Blend Material Attributes** node) by using our `RVT_Height` virtual texture as alpha.

Our two RVTs have been added to the asset material with the **Runtime Virtual Texture Sample** node and you can see them in the yellow and green comments. By selecting this node, you can add an RVT in the **Details** panel:

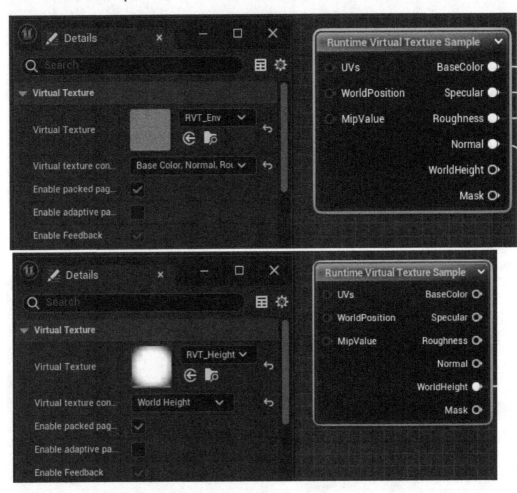

Figure 7.22 – RVT_Height and RVT_Env added to the Runtime Virtual Texture Sample node

The result allows you to blend an asset on the terrain by using RVTs. The RVT_Falloff parameter allows you to change the amount of terrain material you want to see on the blended asset. The higher the value is, the higher the portion of the asset covered by the terrain's material, according to its height.

Figure 7.23 – Different levels of RVT falloff mean different RVT blending effect

RVTs are very useful for both optimizing huge textures and helping us to place our assets in our world in a more realistic way. Using RVTs together with Nanite can consistently improve the LOD of your world and help you to create a massive world in a more optimized way.

We are now ready to discover more about World Partition.

Discovering the World Partition tool

Unreal Engine 4 had a problem with the workflow to create a massive environment. The level-based structure that we learned in *Chapter 3* works very well with projects that have multiple levels that live as a single entity inside the whole project.

As we already saw, the perfect examples are the *Super Mario* games or any kind of game that has a multiple-level structure. A racing game with different tracks is another good example. Also, a cinematic project can fit very well with the level structure that allows us, for example, to divide the project into several levels equal to the number of scenes we need to shoot. This workflow allows developers to work simultaneously on different levels and speed up production. But what happens if we need to work together in a single, huge world, like the one you can find in a modern open-world game such as *Elden Ring* or *Red Dead Redemption 2*? In these cases, the level structure became a limitation for developers who can't work together in an easy way because the source control system (which we talked about in *Chapter 2*) considers the entire world a single level.

To avoid this problem, Unreal Engine 5 has introduced the World Partition tool, which divides the world into multiple single portions that can be streamed as a single entity.

The World Partition tool has been created to be used in a huge level. Giant levels can cause performance problems. Dividing it into multiple smaller portions can help us improve performance and avoid frame drops.

The fastest way to test the World Partition tool is to create a new open-world level. As we already saw in *Chapter 3*, you can create a new level using the **New level…** command inside the **File** menu or by pressing *Ctrl + N* on the keyboard.

In the **New Level** window, you can find the **Open World** option:

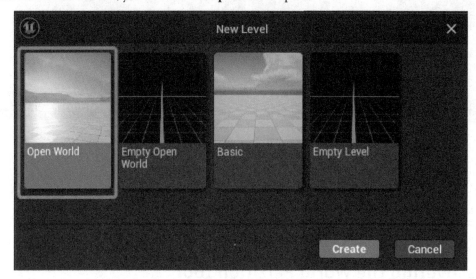

Figure 7.24 – The Open World level option inside the New Level window

The level we have just created should look like this:

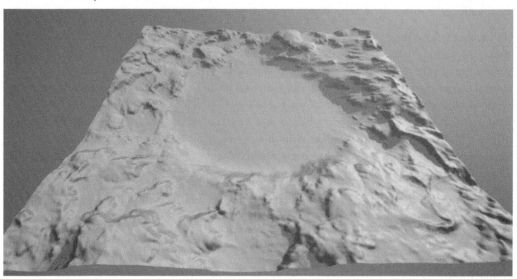

Figure 7.25 – This is what a new Open World level looks like

You can check whether the World Partition tool is working inside the **World Settings** panel (if you can't see it, you can enable it from the **Windows** menu). The **Enable Streaming** checkbox should be checked.

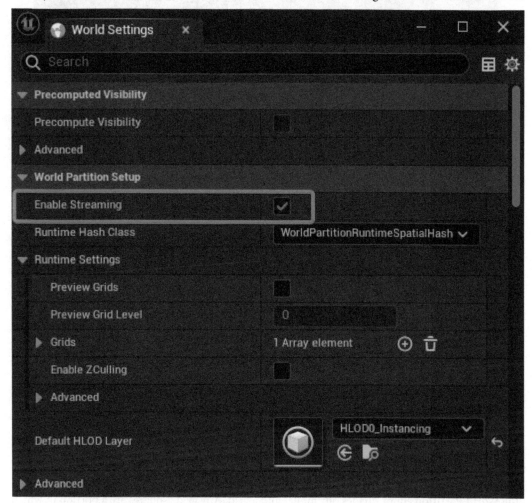

Figure 7.26 – The Enable Streaming option inside the World Settings panel

Creating an open-world level should automatically open the **World Partition** editor panel.

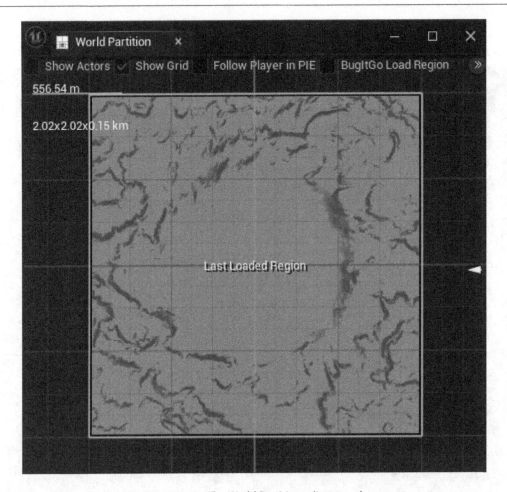

Figure 7.27 – The World Partition editor panel

If you can't see it, you can find it inside the **Windows** menu under the **World Partition** category.

The **World Partition** editor divides our model into a grid. Any grid's squares are a portion in which our level is divided. We can see the grid in the Viewport by checking the **Preview Grid** option inside the **World Settings** panel:

Figure 7.28 – The World Partition tool grid preview in the Viewport

Each cell of the grid represents a part of the map that can be loaded. White cells are the number of cells inside **Loading Range**. We can change the size of the cells inside the **World Settings** panel by changing the **Cell Size** value. We can change the number of cells that we want to be loaded together by changing the **Loading Range** value inside the **World Settings** panel:

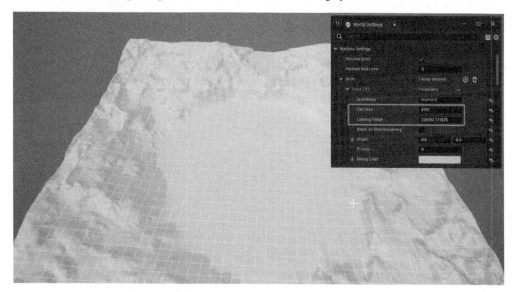

Figure 7.29 – Decreasing Cell Size together with increasing Loading Range
allows you to manage how the World Partition tool works

Loading Range is the range that the World Partition tool uses to decide which cells load and which do not. The range looks like a circle in which the center is the **streaming source**. The streaming source could be the player position or the camera position (by default and when we work inside the Level Viewport, the streaming source is the camera).

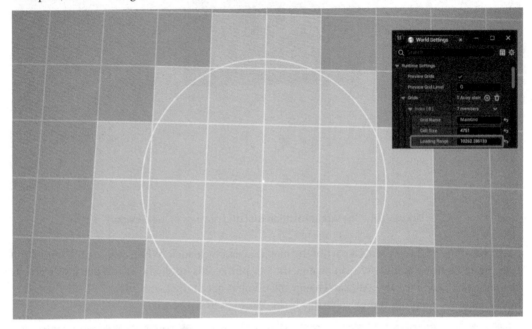

Figure 7.30 – Loading Range set to load a low number of cells

Inside the **World Partition** editor, an arrow always tells us the position of our streaming source. By pressing and holding the *LMB*, you can create an area selection on the **World Partition** editor map. If you *right-click* inside the selection, you can decide whether to load or unload all the cells inside the selection.

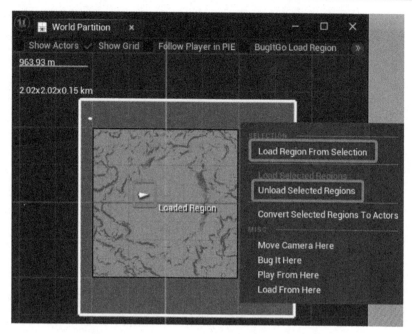

Figure 7.31 – The World Partition editor options

The **World Partition** tool is a very useful feature if you are creating a massive environment that has to be explored seamlessly. By using the **World Partition** tool, Unreal Engine 5 allows your team members to work together on a single level by dividing it into different cells that can be loaded and unloaded like a single and separated entity.

Otherwise, if you are creating a smaller environment or a project with different levels, the level structure workflow is still the best way to approach project organization.

Summary

In this chapter, we have covered the most relevant new features that Epic Games has introduced with Unreal Engine 5. We understood what Nanite is and how it works. We are now able to convert a Static Mesh into a Nanite mesh and take advantage of the cluster geometry virtualization system. We have also learned what an RVT is and how its usage can consistently improve performance and realism. We are now able to merge assets with terrain material using an RVT. Finally, we understood what the World Partition tool does and when you need to use it and when not.

At the end of this chapter, we close the first part of this book. In this first huge part, we developed the basic knowledge that allows us to move on and raise the level.

In the next chapter, we will learn how to use the Megascans Library, and we will set the basics to start creating our environment.

Part 2: Environment Creation Techniques

In this part, you will learn several techniques to create an environment directly inside Unreal Engine 5. In the first chapter of this part, you will explore the Megascans Library and learn how to use the Quixel Bridge plugin to import photorealistic assets directly inside the Engine. You will move on by learning everything about Landscape and terrain creation. Starting from the definition of Landscape, you will learn how to modify the Landscape surface with sculpting tools, how to place foliage assets with the Foliage tool, and how to create a Landscape material that allows you to paint different materials on the Landscape surface and procedurally place foliage assets on your terrain. The last chapter of this part will be a demonstration of how you can create a massive environment directly inside the Engine using all the different plugins that Unreal Engine 5 provides to us. In this chapter, you will learn how to use the Landmass plugin to procedurally modify your landscape surface, how to use the Water tools to add dynamic water to your environment, and you will also learn about the foundational concept of the Procedural Generation Content Framework.

This part has the following chapters:

- *Chapter 8, Utilizing the Megascans Library*
- *Chapter 9, Mastering Landscape and Terrain*
- *Chapter 10, Creating Diverse Environments with Plugins*

8

Utilizing the Megascans Library

In this chapter we will learn how to use the Megascans Library with the Quixel Bridge plugin. We will discover all the different types of assets that you can find inside the Megascans Library and how to use them. We will also understand the importance of blocking.

We will cover the following topics in this chapter:

- Discovering the Megascans Library
- Using the Quixel Bridge plugin
- Discovering different types of assets
- Blocking out your idea
- Exercise: Create a simple environment spot using Megascans Library

At the end of this chapter, you will be able to create your first environment spot by using all the different types of assets that Megascans Library provides to us.

Technical Requirements

In this chapter we will learn to use the Megascans Library. You only need the Engine installed on your workstation.

Discovering the Megascans Library

In this section we will learn how to use the assets that we can find inside the **Megascans Library**.

The **Megascans Library** is a huge online library created by **Quixel**. Inside it you can find both textures and 3D models. The most relevant characteristic of the Megascans Library's assets is that all 3d models and textures are **scanned assets.** That means that all the assets that you can find in the library are generated from photos of real objects. This technique ensures a very high level of detail and a real-life fidelity barely impossible to achieve with standard modelling pipeline (Unless you have a lot of time!).

Scanned assets are not new in the computer graphics industry but they have been used most of the time for pre-visualization purposes because of their huge number of polygons and broken topology. Quixel's assets are extremely well optimized and reworked to be used in any computer graphics pipeline, including real-time rendering.

All these characteristics make **Megascan Library** the perfect choice to create a photorealistic environment inside Unreal Engine 5.

Megascan Library was born as a standalone online library where you could buy assets to use in your own project (not necessarily inside Unreal Engine). After Epic Games acquired Quixel, the **Megascan Library** became free to use for all the Unreal Engine's users.

The possibility to use for free this amount of assets that cover such a several number of natural biomes, represents a one-of-a-kind resource both to create realistic and complex environments inside Unreal Engine 5 and to move first steps in the environment creation pipeline.

> NOTE:
> All the assets inside the Megascan Library are free to use only inside Unreal Engine. If you want to use its assets outside the Engine, you should subscribe to a license. You can find more information at this link: `https://quixel.com/pricing`

Thanks to the partnership between Epic Games and Quixel, using the **Megascan Library** inside the Engine is ridiculously simple. In the next section we will learn how to import assets from the **Megascan Library** to our project.

Using the Quixel Bridge plugin

In this section we will learn how to use the **Quixel Bridge plugin** that allows us to import any kind of assets you can find in the Megascans Library directly inside the Engine.

Since the **Quixel Bridge plugin** allows us to add assets to our level, we can find it inside the **place actor** panel:

Figure 8.1 – The Quixel Bridge plugin inside the place actor panel

If you can't see it inside the **place actor** panel, you should check if the plugin is enabled inside the **Plugins windows** (you can open the Plugins window from the **Edit menu**).

Figure 8.2 – The Quixel Bridge plugin inside the Plugins window

Once you click on the **Quixel Bridge** command, a new window opens.

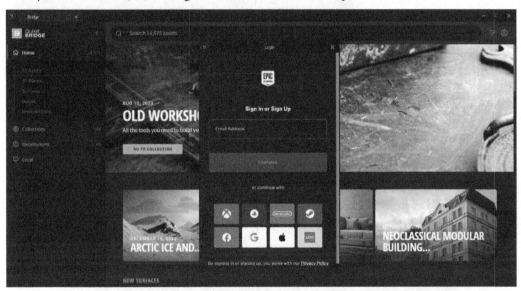

Figure 8.3 – The Quixel Bridge Plugin with the sign-in dialogue box

The first time you launch the plugin, you should log in with your Epic Games account or with the same account you used to launch the project. We are now ready to starting add assets to our level.

Adding asset to the project

To add asset to your project you have two different methods:

1. *Drag and drop* an asset from the Megascans Library to the Level Viewport:

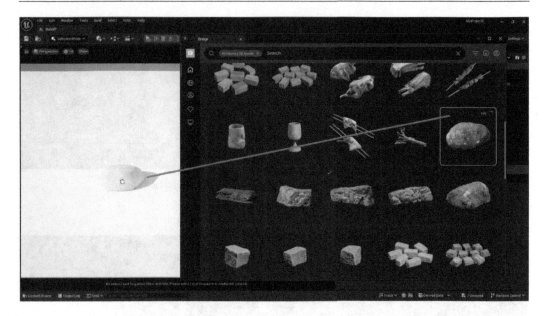

Figure 8.4 – Drag and drop an asset from the Quixel Bridge plugin to the Level Viewport

The first time you grab an asset from the library, it will take the time to download it to your local library BUT you can already see a draft version of the asset (basically the asset without the final material assigned) in the Level Viewport.

If you have already downloaded the asset you are trying to drag and drop in your level, the action will be instantaneous.

2. Download an asset with the icon on the top right of the asset thumbnail and then add the asset to the project with the dedicated command.

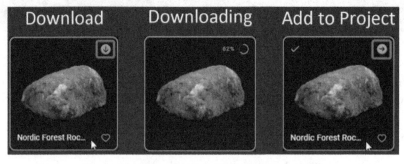

Figure 8.5 – Three steps to add an asset manually.

Both commands will download the 3D model and all the textures assigned to it on your local drive and then it will import everything inside the Engine. You can choose the destination folder for downloaded assets inside the Quixel Bridge's Preferences panel. You need to change the **Library Path**

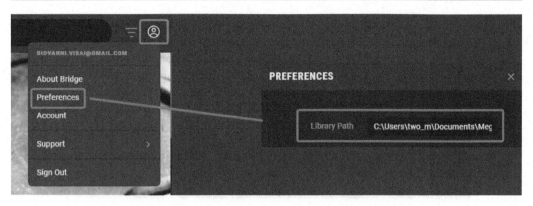

Figure 8.6 – Library Path option inside the Quixel Bridge's Preferences panel

Any asset you have downloaded will remain on your local drive and you won't need to download it again (also if you decide to use the same asset on a different project).

The fact that all the assets are kept on your local drive speeds up the workflow, but Megascans' assets use to be very heavy and the **Library folder** will became huge very fast. A good habit is to place the **Library folder** on a secondary capacious hard drive. Deleting the library folder's content will not delete assets inside your project.

When you select an asset in the Quixel Bridge plugin, a panel with the asset's details appears on the right.

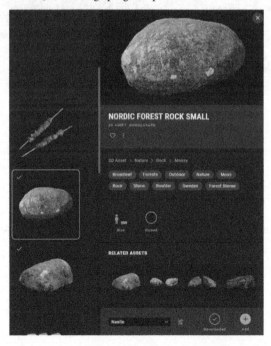

Figure 8.7 – Asset's details panel inside the Quixel Bridge plugin

In this panel you can see a bigger preview of the asset and some general useful information like the tags assigned to the asset to easily find it inside the Library; a graphic representation of its size in comparison with a human being and if the asset is closed (like a stone) or opened (like a cliff that you can use only in one side because the back part is opened); a couple of similar asset you should use together with yours.

But the most important commands are in the bottom part of the panel.

Figure 8.8 – Assets option inside the Quixel Bridge Plugin.

On the right, you can **Download** the asset (in our case we have already download it) and you can **Add** the asset to your project. The drop-down menu on the left allows us to decide which version of the asset we want to download.

Figure 8.9 – the menu that allows us to choose which version of the asset we want to download

If you change the version, you need to **download** and **add** the asset again. The asset versions differ for polycount and textures resolution. The Nanite version consists in an asset with dedicated polycount that comes with Nanite already enabled. To achieve the best quality, the right (but not most optimized) version is the high-quality asset.

If you click on the settings icon near the version drop-down menu, you can change some options about material creation.

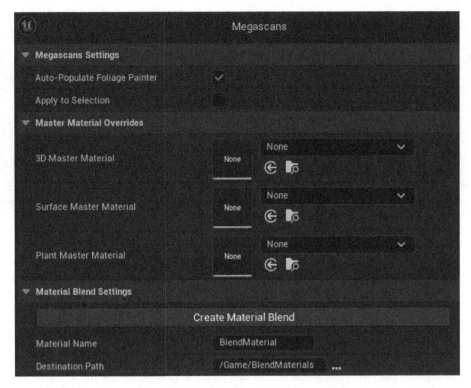

Figure 8.10 – Material creation options

These options are quite advanced. Inside this panel you can change the master material that Quixel Bridge will use to create the material assigned to your 3D asset. The default material that the plugin creates for you is perfect and works very well.

The first time you add a new asset to your project, the Engine will create a couple of folders to keep organized all the assets coming from the Quixel Bridge plugin.

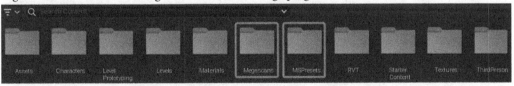

Figure 8.11 – Quixel bridge folders inside the Content Browser

Let's take a look inside these folders:

- **Megascans Folder**: Inside this folder are stored all the assets we have imported from Quixel Bridge plugin. The assets are divided by type (we will explore all the different asset types in the next section of this chapter) and type's folder are divided per asset name.

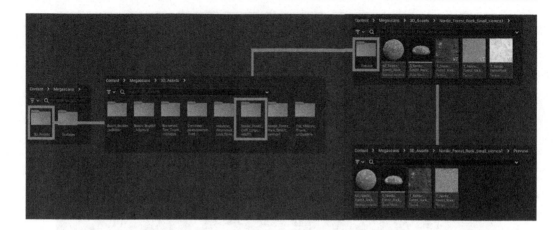

Figure 8.12 – Megascans assets's folder structure

In each asset folder we can find the asset itself, but also the Material Instance assigned to it and the textures used by the Material Instance.

The preview folder contains the asset and its material used to preview the asset in Viewport during download. This folder and all the assets inside it are created only if you drag and drop an asset directly in the Level Viewport from the Quixel Bridge plugin window.

- **MSPresets Folder**: In this folder we can find all the **Master Materials** and **Material Function** used by the Material Instances assigned to the asset we have imported. The first time you import an asset in a new project, the Quixel Bridge will also import all this stuff.

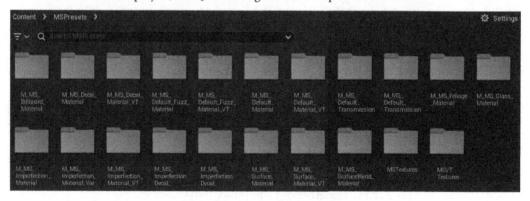

Figure 8.13 – MSPresets folder's content

Now that we know how to import 3D models from the Megascans Library using the Quixel Bridge plugin, we can go on and discover all the different type of assets we can find inside the Megascans Library.

Discovering different types of assets

In this section we will explore all the different type of assets that we can find inside the Quixel Bridge plugin. The import process is the same as we have just learnt for 3D models.

On the left side of the Quixel Bridge plugin we can find the categories in which the library is organized. Any category has subcategories to make it easier to find what we are looking for.

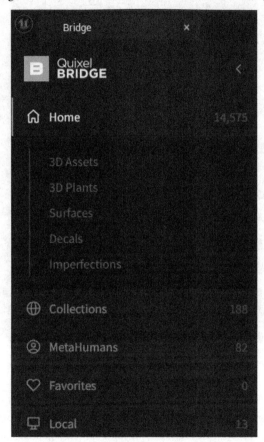

Figure 8.14 – Quixel Bridge plugin's assets categories

Let's take a look to each category:

- **3D Assets**: Inside this category are stored all the static mesh you can find inside the plugin. Any 3D asset comes with its material with a dedicated set of textures. 3D asset's textures are not tileable textures and work only with the asset they have been created for. In any case, you can modify the aspect of your 3D Model by changing values inside the assigner material instance. Inside it, there are many values, many of which are similar to those we created in our master material in *Chapter 5*.

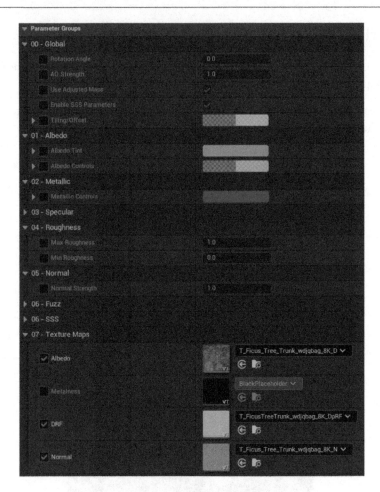

Figure 8.15 – Megascans 3D Asset's Material Instance

- **3d Plants**: In this category we can find 3D assets representing plants, grass, bushes, leaves, and trees. These are the assets that are usually used with foliage systems. We will learn more about foliage in *Chapter 9*. As we saw in *Chapter 7*, Foliage assets are not one hundred per cent compatible with Nanite. For this reason, you can't find the Nanite version of these assets.

- **Surfaces**: Inside this category we can find **scanned textures** (That means that all the textures that compose the final material are generated from photos **Scanned textures** ensure a very high-quality textures pack, especially at high resolution. Resolution changes according to the download option you choose inside the drop-down menu that we have already seen for other asset types. **Highest quality** option will import 8k textures. **Low Quality** will import a 1k textures set. **Medium Quality** and **Hight Quality** are respectively 2k textures and 4k textures. **Hight quality** textures are usually enough. **Highest quality** preset is perfect for close-up shots or, in general, for cinematic purposes.

Imported surfaces are collected into the **Surfaces subfolder** inside the **Megascans folder**.

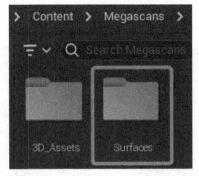

Figure 8.16 – Quixel Bridge's surfaces folder.

- Inside this folder, **surfaces** are organized by name in different folders.

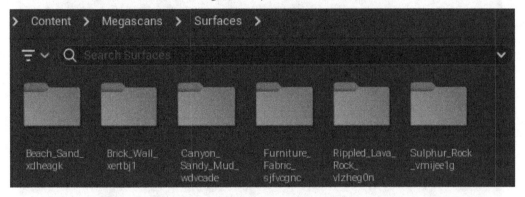

Figure 8.17 – Different surface folders

- Inside each surface folder, we can find textures and the dedicated Material Instance.

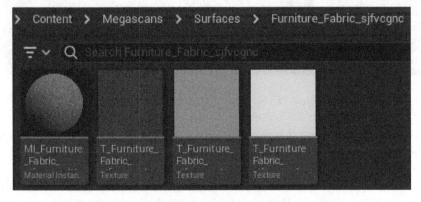

Figure 8.18 – Megascans surface folder's content

- Surface's textures are tileable textures. That means you can use them on barely any 3D model inside your project. Tou can change all the attributes inside the material instance that looks very similar to the one we have created in chapter 5.

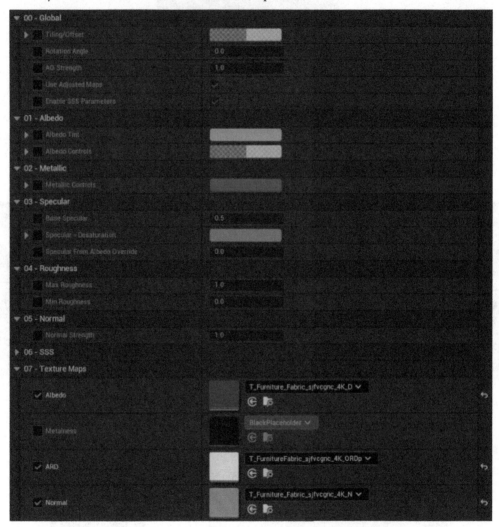

Figure 8.19 – Megascan surface's material instance

- **Decals**: **Decals** are assets that work like a masked material. We mention them in *Chapter 5* when we were talking about different material's domain. They consist in alphed textures that can be placed over other objects to add details like cracks, leaks, graffiti or everything you need to make more realistic your scene. When you import a Decal from the Quixel Bridge plugin, It will be collected into the **Decals subfolder** inside the **Megascans folder**.

- The difference between a standard masked material and **decals** is that a decal works independently from the material assigned to the object and can be placed, moved, rotated and scaled as a standard 3D assets. It works like a projected texture that can be placed whenever you want.

Figure 8.20 – Three decals examples

- Decals look like materials inside the Content Browser BUT If you drag and drop decal material in the Viewport, a volume will appear. The volume is the area where the decal material can be projected. In other words, you will see the decal on every object inside the volume.

Figure 8.21 – Decals volume and how it works.

The purple arrow indicates the direction of the projection.

As we mention in *Chapter 5*, Decals consist of materials that have as material domain the **Deferred Decals** option. That means two things:

- You can change decal material attributes inside the **Material Instance** assigned to the decal asset. This allows us to modify the original decal to obtain the result we want in our scene. If you double-click on the material inside the decal's details panel, the material instance editor will be shown.

Figure 8.22 – Decal Material inside the details panel

- You can create a decal from scratch using the material editor. To do that, you can simply duplicate the Material Instance coming from the Quixel Birdge's decal and change the assigned textures with yours.

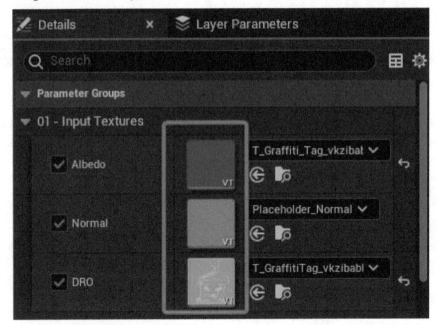

Figure 8.23 – Texture that you can change inside the decal material instance.

- Or you can create new **Master Material**. The process is very similar to the process we learned in *Chapter 5* but you need to change the **material domain** from **Surface** to **Deferred Decal** and the blend mode from **Opaque** to **Translucent**. Remember that you need an **opacity mask**.

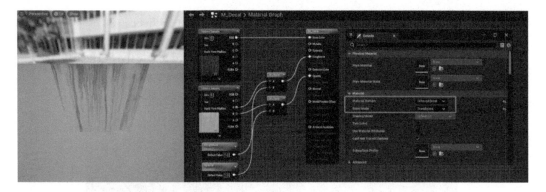

Figure 8.24 – A very simple example on how to create a Deferred Decal Master Material

- If you want to overlap two different decals on the same surface, you need to decide the order in which the decals will be rendered. To do that you can change the **Sort Order** value inside the Details panel.

Figure 8.25 – Sort order value inside the details panel.

- A higher number means priority in render. So, the decal you want to be visible on top must have the higher number.

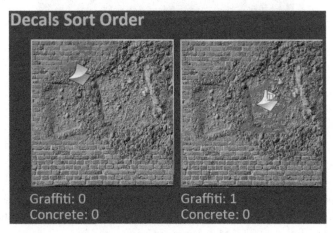

Figure 8.26 – Example on how Decals Sort value works.

- **Imperfections**: In this category we can find very useful textures that can be used in addition inside our material to create levels of dirt on our surfaces. When you download an imperfection texture a material instance is created. Imperfection is collected inside the **Surface folder**.

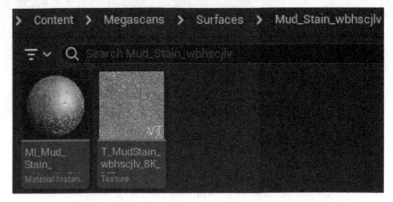

Figure 8.27 – Imperfection material instance and its texture.

In addition to these assets, inside the Quixel Bridge plugin we can also find:

- **Collection**: Here you can find all the assets organized in collections that group assets (of all types) per genre, biomes, or environment. For example, inside the environment category you can find all the assets (3D models, Surfaces, and everything you need) to create an Abandoned Factory environment.

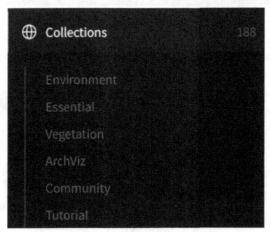

Figure 8.28 – Collections category

- **Metahuman**: This category is dedicated to the digital humans that you can create with Metahuman Plugin. Inside this category you can find hundreds of presets or import **Metahumans** that you have created with the external **Metahumans Creator plugin**.

Figure 8.29 – Metahuman category inside the Quixel Bridge plugin.

Digital humans are not a topic of this book but if you want to learn more about Metahuman you can browse to this link: `https://www.unrealengine.com/en-US/metahuman` and try the **Metahuman Creator Plugin** here: `https://metahuman.unrealengine.com/`

- **Favorites**: In this category are collected all the assets that you have saved as favorite inside the Quixel Bridge plugin. You can add an asset to this category by clicking on the heart icon in the down-left side of asset's thumbnail.

Figure 8.30 – Add to favorites option.

- **Local**: In this category you can find all the assets you have already downloaded. The assets are divided in the same category the Megascans Library is divided.

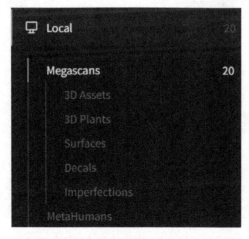

Figure 8.31 – Local category's sub-categories

The Megascans Library is one of the richest assets libraries that you can use for free, and the quality of its assets is very high. Having a similar resource available for free is something amazing and unthinkable some years ago. The only contraindication is the size of the assets. 4k textures are heavy on your hard drive and each asset brings to your project at least three textures. It is very easy to enlarge your project and reach 100gb of project size faster.

Now that we have learnt which assets we can find inside the Megascans Library and how we can import them inside our project, it's time to try to use them to create something inside the Engine.

Blocking out your idea

In this section we will talk about blocking. We will learn what blocking is, why it is so important and why Meganscans Library can be very useful also in blocking step.

One of the most important steps during the environment creation workflow is the **Blocking** phase. Blocking out a scene means creating a very draft version of our environment with very simple shapes to understand the general composition of our scene.

Figure 8.32 – An example on how to block out a scene

The incredibly usage's easiness of Quixel Bridge plugin allows us to increase the quality of our block out also if we are not going to render our final shot inside Unreal Engine 5. This is a simple but very important concept to be understood. Unreal Engine 5 is a complex and massive software. Mastering every possibility that it gives to us is an extremely hard goal to achieve. But some of its features are thought to be very accessible and to speed up our workflow in a smarter and cheaper way; also, if we are not using the Engine to achieve the final output. Quixel Bridge plugin is one of these features and allows us to represent in a faster and realistic way an idea, a concept or to block out our environment to show our idea to colleagues or clients.

Exercise: Create a simple environment spot using Megascans Library

Before going on to the next chapter and learning everything about Landscape and its potential, it's time to apply all the techniques we have learnt in the past chapters. Using Quixel Bridge plugin is the best way to create your first attempt of environment inside Unreal Engine 5.

In less than 30 minutes it is possible to create something like these:

Figure 8.33 – Very quick environment blocked out with Megascans
Library's assets. No light tweaking or effects.

And with a little bit more work on shading and lighting you can easily obtain something like this:

Figure 8.34 – Another example on how you can do with Megascans Library's assets.

Both examples are screenshots taken from the Unreal Engine 5 Viewport. Everything is created using Quixel Bridge plugin0s assets except for the water material in the canyon image that is a custom material. The first image has been composed by using the **Japanese Tropical Jungle** collection and some foliage assets from **Tropical Vegetation** collection. The canyon image has been created by using the **Canyons of Yuta** collection.

Now it is your turn. Try to reproduce one of the two examples above or create something new.

Some advice to start:

- Using a limited number of assets makes the work easier. Choose a collection and try to use the assets included in it.

- Find reference images! You are trying to reproduce something real. The best way to do that is copy a real place.

- Blocking out your scene with sample objects helps to create a better composition.

- Defining a subject in your scene will help you to compose a good frame and create an environment around it.

- Start from bigger assets and then move on by adding smaller assets to add details to your scene.

- Duplicate, scale, and rotate assets is a good strategy to create variation in your environment. You don't need hundreds of assets to create something good.

- Last but not least, take your time. It is normal if you get stuck or if you are not satisfied at the first attempt.

Environment creation is a complex task that requires experience to be mastered, but you know everything you need to start creating your scene in Unreal Engine 5.

Summary

In this chapter we have discovered the Megascans Library and its incredible amount of realistic 3d models and textures. We learnt what the Quixel Bridge plugin is and how easy is using it to import assets in your project. We explored all the different types of assets we can find inside the Megascans Library and we learnt how to create a simple decal's material. In the end of the chapter, we talked about blocking and its importance, and you try to create your first simple environment.

We are now ready to push up again the level and dive into the Landscape topic. In the next chapter we will explore everything about Landscape creation, Foliage and Landscape material.

Mastering Landscape and Terrain

In this chapter, we will learn everything we need to know about the Landscape system in Unreal Engine 5. We will understand what a Landscape is and how to use it to create a massive environment with sculpting tools and heightmaps. We will also learn how to use foliage tools to populate our environment with foliage assets and we will learn how to create a Landscape Material.

We will cover the following topics in this chapter:

- Creating your first Landscape
- Modifying your Landscape with Sculpt tools
- Unlocking heightmaps' power
- Discovering the Foliage mode
- Creating a Landscape Material

At the end of this chapter, you will know how to create a massive environment by using Landscape tools and Foliage tools. You will also know how to create a Landscape Material, which will allow you to paint texture on your Landscape and procedurally place Foliage actors.

Technical requirements

In this chapter, we will explore the Landscape system. To easily follow the chapter, you need Unreal Engine 5 installed on your workstation with the Quixel Bridge plugin enabled in your project.

Creating your first Landscape

In this section, we will learn how to create a Landscape and we will explore all the options we have in the Landscape creation panel.

The Landscape system in Unreal Engine 5 is a group of tools and options that allows us to create massive natural external environments in a fast and intuitive way. As we will discover in the following pages, the Landscape system allows us to create a huge ground that can be manually sculpted with several sculpting tools or generated from a texture (heightmap). In the same way, we can create mountains, hills, deserts, canyons, or massive fields and place Foliage actors on them (we will talk about Foliage tools in the *Discovering the Foliage mode* section of this chapter) to make them more realistic and vivid.

To create a new Landscape, you need to enter **Landscape** mode. As we saw in *Chapter 2*, to change mode, you can use the drop-down menu in the main toolbar. You can also use the *SHIFT + 2* keyboard shortcut to enter **Landscape** mode.

Once you have entered **Landscape** mode, you should see something like this:

Figure 9.1 – This is what we should see when we enter Landscape
mode without Landscape already placed inside the Level

> **Note**
>
> To make the Landscape more visible and everything clearer, I have created a dedicated Level called **Landscape** and added to it a basic light set by using the **Environment Light Mixer** tool that we learned about in *Chapter 6*.

Inside the Level Viewport, a preview (in terms of size) of our Landscape has appeared, and on the left side, we can see the **Landscape** mode panel with all its settings.

The **Landscape** mode menu is divided into three different panels. The first time we create a Landscape, we can interact only with the **Manage** panel and its **New** options.

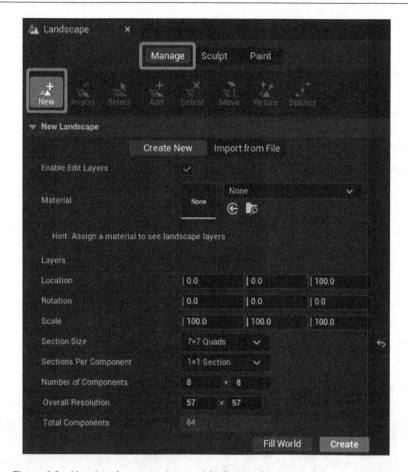

Figure 9.2 – New Landscape options inside the Landscape mode's manage panel

This **New** option panel gives us two different ways to create a Landscape divided into two different tabs:

- The **Create New** tab allows us to create a Landscape from scratch in terms of size and resolution by changing values manually
- The **Import from File** tab allows us to create a Landscape starting from a heightmap (we will talk about this in the *Unlocking heightmaps' power* section of this chapter).

Let's take a look at all the options inside the **Create New** panel:

- **Enable Edit Layers**: If this box is checked, your Landscape will support layer editing. We will learn more about that in the *Creating painting layers* section of this chapter.
- **Material**: Here, we can assign a Material to our Landscape. We can also leave this field empty and assign a Material later. We will learn how to create a Landscape Material in the *Creating a Landscape Material* section of this chapter.

- **Location**, **Rotation**, and **Scale**: These are the standard transformation values. It's a good habit to leave them as the default.

- **Section Size**: This is the first value that defines the Landscape size and resolution. **Section Size** defines the number of quads a component is composed of (see *Figure 9.3*).

- **Sections Per Component**: This value defines the number of sections there are inside a component. 1x1 means that each component contains one section. 2x2 means that each component is composed of 2x2 sections (4 sections in total) (see *Figure 9.3*).

- **Number of Components**: This value defines the total number of components that your Landscape is composed of. 8x8 will generate a square Landscape composed of 64 components in total (see *Figure 9.3*).

- **Overall Resolution**: This value defines the total number of quads that will compose your Landscape. The overall resolution is calculated in this way: *(Section size unit * Number of components) + 1*. Considering a **Section Size** value of 7x7 and a number of components of 8x8, the simple expression looks like this: *(7*8) + 1= 57*.

- **Total Components**: This value is not modifiable and simply announces the total number of components, according to the values set in the other options.

- **Fill World**: This command will adjust all the settings we have just learned about to create a Landscape that's as big as possible.

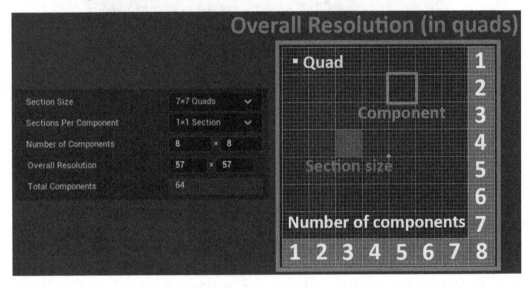

Figure 9.3 – Explanatory screenshot on how a Landscape is built

We can leave all the Landscape creation values as their default and click on **Create** to create our first Landscape.

> **Note**
> Considering that a Landscape is used to create massive natural environments, knowing its real size could be very useful. To calculate the Landscape size in meters, you need to apply a very simple expression: *1px is equal to 1 meter*. So, an overall resolution of *505*505* means a Landscape size of *505 meters * 505 meters*.

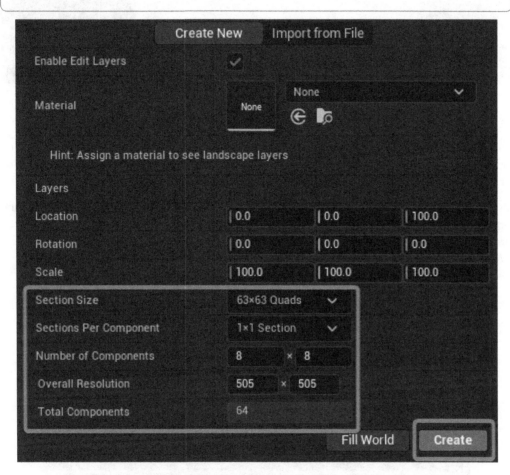

Figure 9.4 – Default Landscape creation values and the Create command

Once we have created our first Landscape, we can find it inside the Level Viewport and, obviously, also inside the Outliner. The **Landscape** mode has now automatically switched to the **Sculpt** panel:

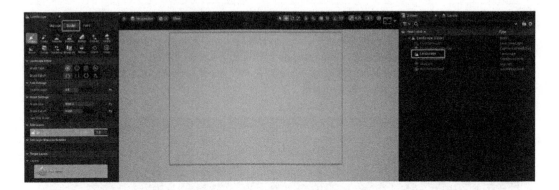

Figure 9.5 – This is how the Engine should look once we have created our first Landscape

Landscape can be moved, rotated, or scaled exactly like other actors in the Level Viewport, *but* to do that we need to come back to the **Selection** mode by using the drop-down menu in the main toolbar or by pressing the *SHIFT + 1* keyboard shortcut.

By selecting the Landscape inside the Level Viewport or the **Outliner** panel, we can find several options inside the **Details** panel. The most relevant, for now, is the Material option where we can assign a Material to our Landscape. We will talk about **Landscape Material** in the *Creating a Landscape Material* section of this chapter.

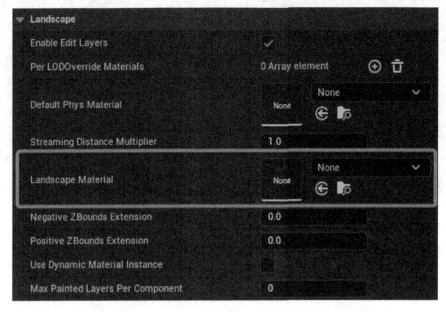

Figure 9.6 – Landscape Material option in the Details panel

In the **Details** panel, we can also find the **Virtual Textures** option that we saw in *Chapter 7*.

Now that we know how to create a Landscape and manage its size, we can go on and discover how to use Sculpt tools.

Modifying your Landscape with Sculpt tools

One of the main characteristics of a Landscape is that we can modify its shape directly inside the Engine to create diverse environments.

Sculpting tools are interactive tools. That means that you can use them directly on your Landscape inside the Level Viewport and see the result of your work in real time.

This is possible because when you use sculpting tools, you are painting a grayscale texture that the Engine uses to modify the Landscape. This texture is called a **heightmap** and works in the same way we learned about for a Roughness texture or a Metalness texture. White is equal to 1 and black is equal to 0 (zero). So, all the white pixels inside the heightmap will raise the Landscape shape. We will talk about it in the *Unlocking heightmaps' power* section of this chapter.

To sculpt and modify our Landscape, we can use all the tools inside the **Landscape** mode's **Sculpt** panel.

Figure 9.7 – Sculpt panel in Landscape mode

In the first part of the panel, we can choose the tool we want to use to modify our Landscape. In addition to the basic **Sculpt** tool, we can find several other tools that allow us to simulate natural effects on the ground in terms of shape details. Most of the tools work like a brush. We can modify the characteristics of the brush in the **Landscape Editor**, **Tool Settings**, and **Brush Settings** categories of the panel.

In the next sub-sections, we will learn how the different tools inside the **Sculpt** panel work and how to manage their options. To make the learning process less tedious, alongside individual explanations of tools like the **Sculpt** tool, you'll encounter sections where similar tools are grouped together (**Erosion**, **Hydro**, and **Noise**) for quicker comprehension. We'll focus solely on the most beneficial tools.

Let's get started.

The Sculpt tool

If you select **Sculpt** inside the **Landscape** mode's **Sculpt** panel and move the mouse on the Landscape inside the Level Viewport, you will see a brush shape appear (*Figure 9.8*). By left-clicking, you can activate the tool that will affect the Landscape according to the brush shape. The **Sculpt** tool will raise the Landscape. If you hold the *LMB*, the tool will continue its work until you release the *LMB*. If you want to create a hole instead of raising the Landscape, you can press and hold *SHIFT* when you perform the command (*SHIFT+ LMB*).

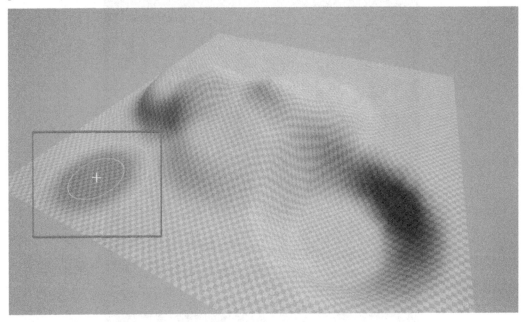

Figure 9.8 – The Sculpt tool can raise the Landscape or create holes in the Landscape

Under the **Landscape Editor** category, we can manage the brush shape that the **Sculpt** tool will use to modify our Landscape. By changing **Brush Type**, we can change the shape of our brush. We have four different options.

Figure 9.9 – Landscape mode's Brush Type options

Each **Brush Type** option has different settings to be modified in order to obtain the correct effect:

- **1**: This is the default brush. It works like a Photoshop brush with a falloff that manages its intensity. We can change the way the brush decreases its falloff power by changing the **Brush Falloff** setting. With this **Brush Type** option selected, we also have its brush settings, which you can see in the following screenshot:

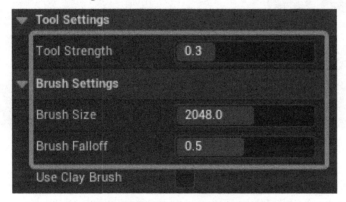

Figure 9.10 – Landscape mode's Brush Settings

  - **Tool Strength** defines the intensity of the brush. The higher the value, the higher the power of Landscape rises.

  - **Brush Size** allows us to change the size of our brush. The higher the value, the greater the area of influence of the brush.

  - **Brush Falloff** allows us to change the curve of the brush's intensity decreasing. It works like a Spot Light's Inner Cone Angle and Outer Cone Angle, which we looked at in *Chapter 6*.

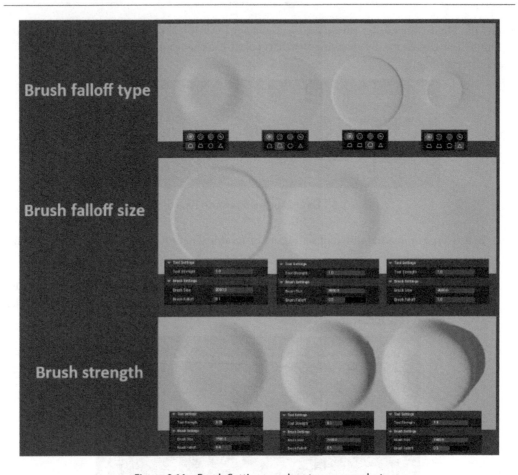

Figure 9.11 – Brush Settings explanatory screenshot

- **2**: The **Alpha brush** allows us to use an Alpha texture to change the way our brush modifies the Landscape. A white texture means maximum sculpt intensity; a black texture means no sculpt at all.

Figure 9.12 – An example of how the Alpha brush works

This brush also has its own settings, as you can see in the following screenshot:

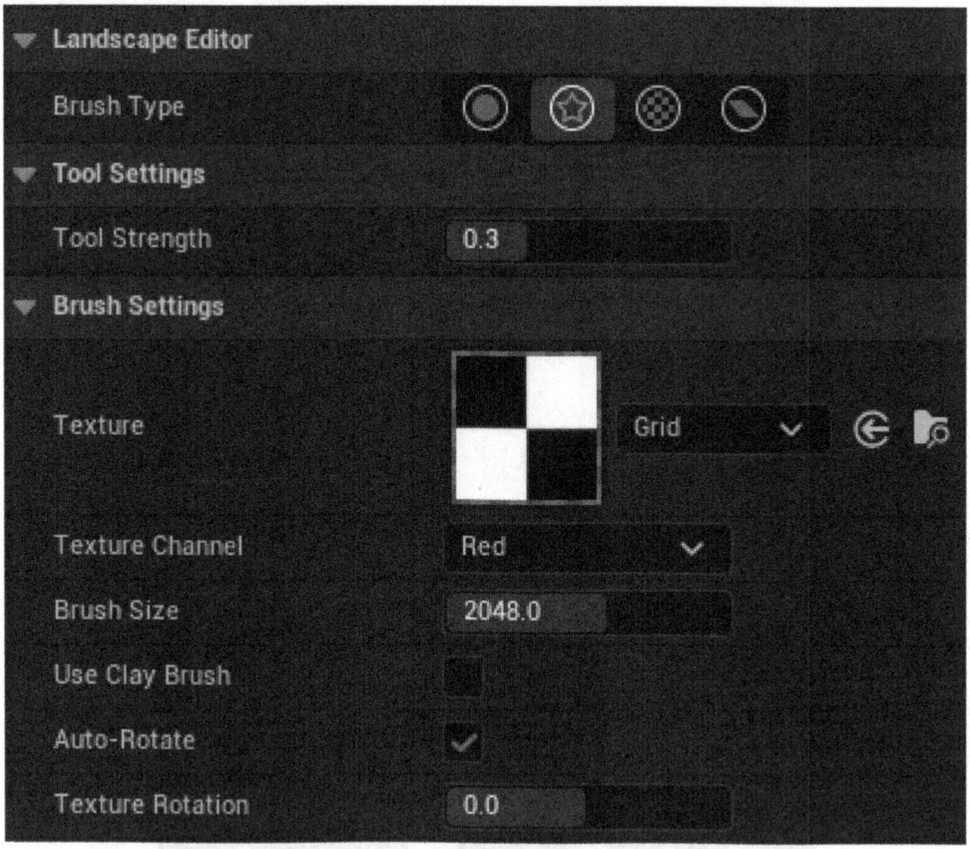

Figure 9.13 – Second brush type with its options

Some of the options are the same as we have already learned about for the default brush, so I will not repeat them. Let's take a look at the dedicated options:

- **Texture**: Here, we can change the **alpha texture** the brush will use. It is important to use a grayscale texture because it will be considered as an alpha channel, inside which the white values are positive (rise up action) and the black values are negative (rise down action).

- **Texture Channel**: Here, you can decide which uploaded texture channel the brush will use.

- **Auto-Rotate**: If enabled, the alpha texture will automatically rotate to follow the direction of your mouse. If disabled, the alpha texture will always be rotated by 0 degrees without following the mouse rotation.

- **Texture Rotation**: Here, you can change the rotation of your alpha texture. This value becomes useful if the **Auto-Rotate** option is disabled.

- **3**: The **Pattern brush** is very similar to the Alpha brush but the texture we assign is considered a pattern texture instead of an alpha texture. That means that the brush's shape doesn't change but works more like a tracing job.

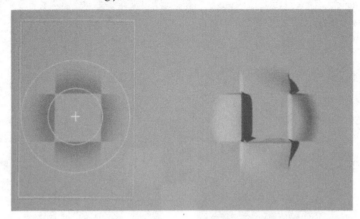

Figure 9.14 – Pattern brush example

This brush also has its own settings, as you can see in the following screenshot:

Figure 9.15 – Pattern brush options

Some of the options are the same as we have already learned about for the default brush and the Alpha brush, so I am not going to repeat them. Let's take a look at the dedicated options:

- **Texture Scale**: If this value is set to 1, the textures will have the same size as the Landscape. In other words, if you sculpt the entire Landscape surface, you will obtain the shape drawn inside your texture.

- **Texture Rotation**, **Texture Pan U**, and **Texture Pan V**: These values allow us to rotate and move our texture.

- **4**: The **Component brush** allows us to raise a single component of our Landscape.

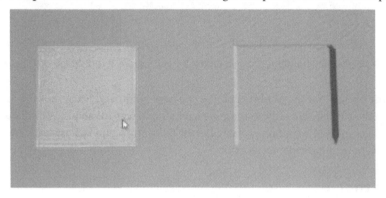

Figure 9.16 – An example of how the Component brush works

This brush also has its own settings, as you can see in the following screenshot:

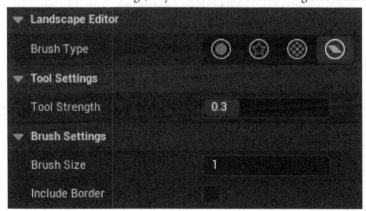

Figure 9.17 – Component brush's options

With these settings, we can do the following:

- **Brush Size**: This value allows us to change the number of Landscape components raised by the brush

- **Include Border**: If this value is enabled, when you are working on an edgy component, the Landscape's external edge will also be raised

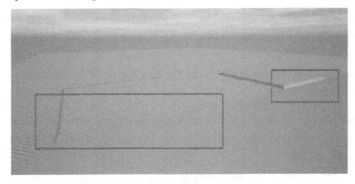

Figure 9.18 – Include Border is enabled on the left red square; it is disabled on the right one

These were the options for the **Sculpt** tool. We can now go on and learn more about other tools. Some of the options will be the same as those we have already learned about. We will not repeat every command. If you can't find an option explained in the following sections, it is because we have already learned about it in the *The Sculpt tool* section.

The Erase tool

The **Erase** tool allows us to delete the **Sculpt** brushwork. It works in the same way the **Sculpt** tool works, with the same options. It is not like an undo command, so you can use it to create effects that you can't create with the **Sculpt** tool's raising effect. For instance, with the **Erase** tool we can perform a rising down action on our Landscape. We will go on and learn about the **Smooth** tool.

The Smooth tool

The **Smooth** tool allows us to adjust the **Sculpt** tool's work by decreasing its influence on the Landscape.

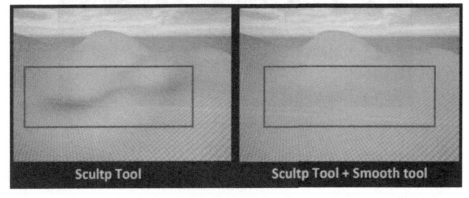

Figure 9.19 – An example of how the Smooth tool works

Let's take a look at its dedicated options:

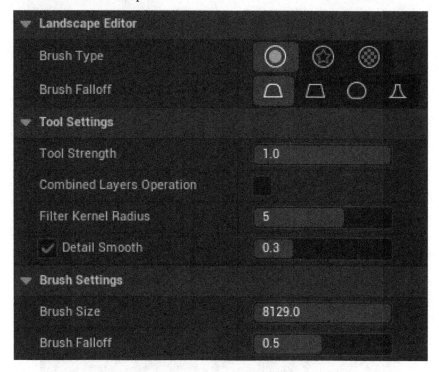

Figure 9.20 – Smooth tool options

- **Combined Layers Operation**: If this option is enabled, the **Smooth** tool can work on multiple Landscape layers (we will talk about Landscape layers in the *Landscape layers* section of this chapter).

- **Filter Kernel Radius**: This value allows us to change the Level of influence (in terms of details) of the **Smooth** tool. The higher the value, the greater the minimum size a detail needs to have to be smoothed.

- **Detail Smooth**: The higher this value, the greater the number of details that will be removed.

We can now go on and learn about the **Flatten** tool.

The Flatten tool

The **Flatten** tool allows us to flatten parts of a Landscape we have raised with the **Sculpt** tool. It is perfect for creating plateaus or highlands.

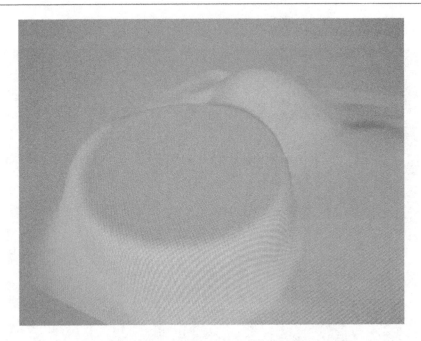

Figure 9.21 – An example of how to use the Flatten tool

Let's take a look at the dedicated options:

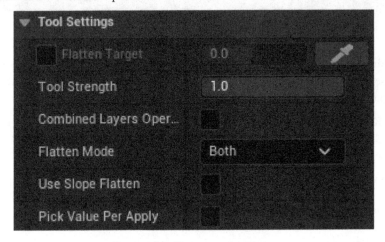

Figure 9.22 – Flatten tool settings

- **Flatten Target**: This option allows us to pick a point in the Landscape that will be used as a height target for the **Flatten** effect.

- **Flatten Mode**: This drop-down menu allows us to choose the way the **Flatten** tool works. See *Figure 9.23* to understand the difference between the available options.

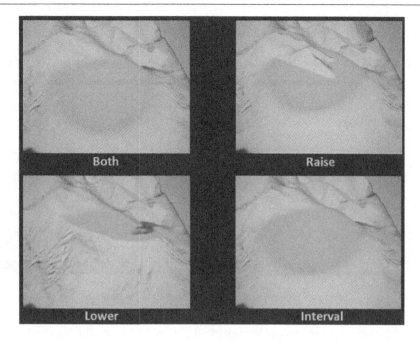

Figure 9.23 – Explanatory screenshot of different Flatten options

- **Use Slope Flatten**: If this option is enabled, the **Flatten** tool will work considering the angle of the clicked Landscape point.

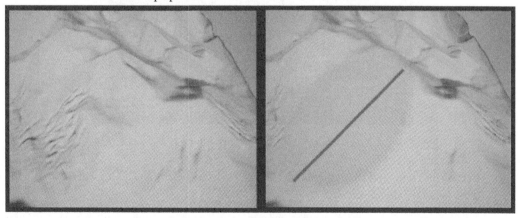

Figure 9.24 – Use Slope Flatten example

- **Pick Value Per Apply**: If this option is enabled, the flatten tool picks new values to flatten toward when dragging around, instead of using only the first value it picked.

We can now go on and learn about the **Ramp** tool.

The Ramp tool

The **Ramp** tool allows us to raise the Landscape between two points picked on the Landscape surface:

Figure 9.25 – An example of how the Ramp tool works

To create a new ramp, you have to move the two points on the Landscape and then press *Enter* on the keyboard. The way the **Ramp** tool will raise the Landscape is defined in **Tool Settings**:

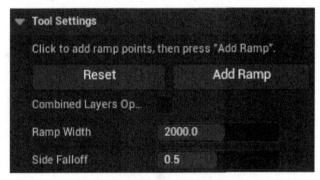

Figure 9.26 – Ramp Tool Settings

- **Reset**: This command resets the tool by deleting the two ramp points. This will not delete the ramp you have already created.

- **Add Ramp**: This command creates the ramp. It performs the same action as pressing *Enter* on the keyboard.

- **Ramp Width**: This value allows us to change the top width of the ramp. In other words, the higher the value, the larger the ramp.

- **Side Falloff**: This value allows us to change the falloff power of the ramp's side.

We can now go on and learn about natural erosion tools.

The Erosion, Hydro, and Noise tools

This group of tools allows us to add natural effects to our Landscape. We are going to learn about them together because they have the same objective, and they can be used together to obtain realistic results.

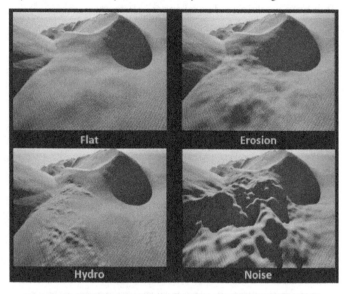

Figure 9.27 – Explanatory screenshot of erosion tools

The settings are very simple. They allow us to change the intensity and the scale of erosion tools.

You can test them out by trying to create a Landscape from scratch. It's very important to familiarize yourself with Landscape tools to be able to create any kind of environment in a very fast way or be able to modify an existing Landscape to achieve the effect you need. Try to create something like this:

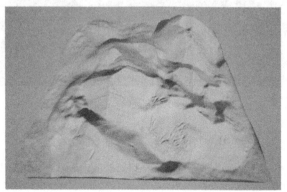

Figure 9.28 – Landscape created by using Sculpt tools

We can now go on and take a look at the **Select** tool.

The Select tool

The **Select** tool allows us to select a Landscape part that is not to be affected by other tool actions. The **Select** tool works in the same way as other **Sculpt** tools we have already seen, but when you left-click on the Landscape, it draws a mask instead of raising the surface.

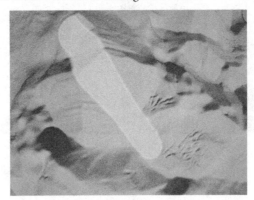

Figure 9.29 – How the Select tool action looks on a Landscape

After we create a selection, any **Sculpt** tool we want to use will affect the Landscape parts outside of the white selection.

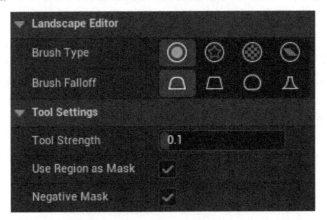

Figure 9.30 – Select tool options

With the tool's settings, we can do the following:

- **Use Region as Mask**: This option is enabled by default and it allows the **Select** tool to affect other **Sculpt** tools.

- **Negative Mask**: This option is enabled by default, and it allows us to paint the Landscape portions we want to exclude. Disabling it allows us to paint the parts we want to be affected by the **Sculpt** tools.

The **Select** tool is very useful to add detail to our Landscape or to apply modifications without changing other Landscape parts.

In this section, we have learned how to sculpt our Landscape with several tools that allow us to create massive ground with a naturalistic effect. We didn't explore all the available tools, only the ones that are useful in a creative process. We will learn about some more tools that we can find inside the **Sculpt** panel in *Chapter 10*.

Before going on and talking about heightmaps, we need to learn something about Landscape layers.

Landscape layers

Scrolling down the **Sculpt** panel, we can find the **Edit Layers** option, which allows us to divide our sculpting work into different layers. Layer work is very simple. The top layer will allow you to sculpt on the other layer. The **Alpha** value allows us to change the visibility of the layer and the way the layers are mixed.

Figure 9.31 – Edit Layers options

To add a layer, right-click on the existing layer and select **Create**:

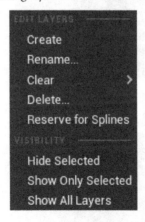

Figure 9.32 – Layer options menu

For each layer you have created, you can do the following:

- **Rename**: This command allows you to change the layer name.
- **Clear**: This command allows you to delete everything inside this layer (**All**) or a sculpting job portion. (**Sculpt**).

- **Delete**: This command allows you to delete the selected layer.

- **Reserve for Splines**: This command allows us to reserve this layer to be used with splines. We will learn more about this in *Chapter 10*.

- **VISIBILITY** options: In this category, we can change the visibility option of our layer. We can hide the layer or show it back.

Using layers is very useful for creating different Levels of sculpting and obtaining specific effects. Layers can also be used to try out new effects without losing sculpting work. We will use layers in *Chapter 10*.

Now that we have learned how to use the **Sculpt** tools to create diverse Landscapes, we can go on and discover how to generate a Landscape from a **heightmap**.

Unlocking heightmaps' power

One of the most powerful options in the Landscape creation process is the possibility to generate a Landscape from a heightmap. As we've already seen, a heightmap is a grayscale texture that defines the height. A purely white-colored pixel means the maximum height value and pure black means the opposite. In the case of a Landscape, a heightmap defines the Level of height the Landscape will be raised to in a pixel.

Figure 9.33 – An example of how a heightmap works

To generate a Landscape using a heightmap, we need to select the **Import from File** option in the **Landscape** mode's **New** panel.

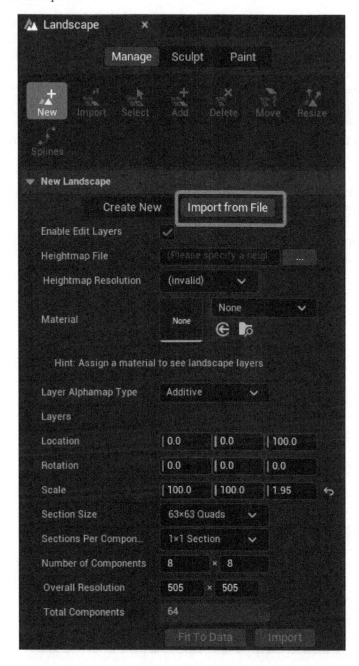

Figure 9.34 – Import from File tab in the Landscape mode's New panel

Most of the options that we can find inside the **Import from File** tab are the same as we have already seen inside the **Create New** tab. Let's look at the options dedicated to heightmap importing:

- **Heightmap File**: Here is where we need to upload our heightmap. To upload a new texture, we need to click on the **three-point** button on the right (*Figure 9.35*). The heightmap has to be a 16-bit grayscale texture. If it doesn't match with these characteristics, the Engine will tell you with an orange warning icon.

Figure 9.35 – Warning icon and three-point button related to the Heightmap File option

Once we have imported our heightmap, the Landscape's size settings change according to the heightmap resolution. It's very important to create the heightmap in the correct resolution because the overall resolution of the texture determines the size of our Landscape. In my case, I've created a heightmap texture that has a resolution of *505 pixels x 505 pixels*. This will generate a Landscape as big as *505 meters x 505 meters* square.

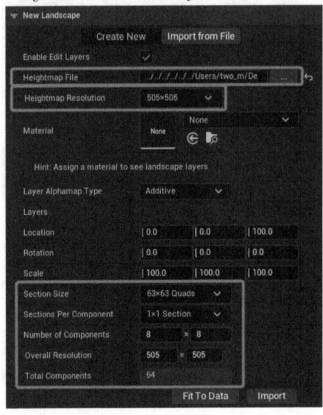

Figure 9.36 – The Import from File tab looks like this once you add a 505*505 pixel heightmap

If we want to create a Landscape that is as big as our heightmap, we need to leave all the values that the Engine has set once we have added the heightmap. If we change once between **Section Size**, **Sections Per Component**, **Number of Components**, or **Overall Resolution**, the Landscape size will change. That means that our heightmap will not be as big as the Landscape anymore. The result will be a heightmap that will not cover all of the Landscape's surface:

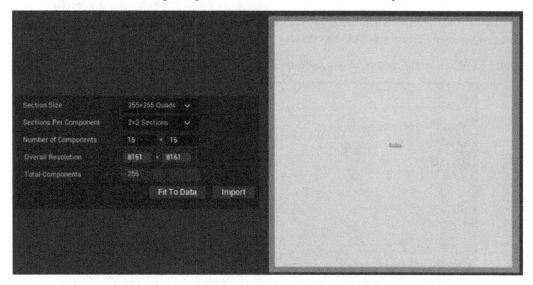

Figure 9.37 – An example of what happens if we set a different
Landscape size with a heightmap with another resolution

> **Note**
>
> Epic Games provides a very useful table in the Unreal Engine documentation that allows us to understand the correct Landscape size settings we need to use according to a specific heightmap resolution. You can find it at this link: `https://docs.unrealengine.com/4.27/en-US/BuildingWorlds/Landscape/TechnicalGuide/`

- **Fit Data**: If we have changed the Landscape size settings, this command will reset all the values to make them fit with the heightmap resolution.

- **Import**: This command will generate a Landscape using the heightmap you have uploaded.

Using heightmaps is very useful because it allows us to create very realistic Landscape in a fast way by using 2D textures. You can create a heightmap in several pieces of external software. Considering that it is a 2D texture, we can use any 2D drawing software (such as Photoshop) to create our heightmap. Otherwise, there is dedicated software that allows us to create a heightmap to be used in Unreal Engine 5. The most famous are **Gaea** from **QuadSpinner** (`https://quadspinner.com/`) and **World Machine** from **World Machine Software, LLC** (`https://www.world-machine.com/`). The difference between this software and common 2D drawing software is that Gaea and World Machine allow us to see the result in a very realistic three-dimensional representation and they have dedicated tools for generating naturalistic effects such as mountains and rivers. Both have a free version that allows you to try them out.

You can also find heightmaps online that are downloadable for free. The following examples (*Figure 9.39* and *Figure 9.40*) have been generated with heightmaps created by Motion Forge Pictures. You can download them for free at this link: `https://www.motionforgepictures.com/`.

With a good heightmap, it is very easy and super-fast to create something like this:

Figure 9.38 – Landscape generated from a heightmap with 8k resolution

Or, you could create something like this:

Figure 9.39 – Landscape generated from a heightmap with 4k resolution

The last thing we need to learn about heightmaps is how to define the real height of our Landscape. In other words, how to define the maximum (pure white) and the minimum (pure black) values in terms of height.

Unreal Engine 5 calculates the Landscape's height with values between -256 and +256 (+ 255.992 to be clear). That value is multiplied by the **Z scale** value in the **Transformation** option in the **Import from File** tab. As we know, Unreal Engine 5 works in centimeters, so the height value's limit is to be considered as -256 cm to +256 cm. By default, the **Z scale** value is set to 100. That means that the default height value has a range between -256 meters and +256 meters. In other words, a pure-white pixel will raise the Landscape to achieve 256 meters of height. Pure Black pixels will generate a hole 256 meters deep.

So, how can we create a mountain 4,000 meters high? To do that, we need to convert the height range to our custom height. Since the range is 512 units (-256 to 0 plus 0 to +256), the ratio is 1/512 or 0.001953125.

Multiplying our custom height to this ratio will give us the number to set inside the **Z scale** value. Remember that Unreal Engine 5 works in centimeters, so the first thing we need to do is to convert 4,000 meters into 400,000 centimeters:

$400,000 \times 0.001953125 = 781.25$

781.25 is the value to set in **Z scale** to obtain a Landscape that considers a height range between -200,000 cm and +200,000 cm.

Figure 9.40 – A Landscape generated from a heightmap with a
height range between -200,000 and +200,000

> **Note**
>
> The value we set in **Z scale** considers a range of values that starts from a negative value (-256 by default). That means that the black parts of your heightmaps don't represent the sea Level that is supposed to be 0 (zero). If you want to set the height from the 0 (zero) Level, you need to double the custom height value.

Once you generate a Landscape using a heightmap, all the **Sculpt** tools we have seen in this chapter still work in the same way to allow you to modify the result that you have obtained with the heightmap.

Now that we have learned how to create a Landscape and how to modify it with **Sculpt** tools, we can go on and discover the **Foliage** mode.

Understanding and working with the Foliage mode

In this section, we will learn what the **Foliage** mode is and how to use it. The **Foliage** mode is an Unreal Engine 5 mode that includes tools to place foliage assets on Landscapes, but also on Static Meshes. By using a brush tool, very similar to the brush that we can find in **Landscape** mode, we can place assets randomly on our surfaces. **Foliage** mode is very useful for placing repeatable assets such as trees, bushes, grass, or debris to make our environment rich in detail.

We can enable **Foliage** mode by changing the Viewport mode. To change mode, you can use the drop-down menu in the main toolbar. You can also use the *SHIFT + 3* keyboard shortcut to enter **Foliage** mode. The first time you enter **Foliage** mode, the dedicated panel looks like this:

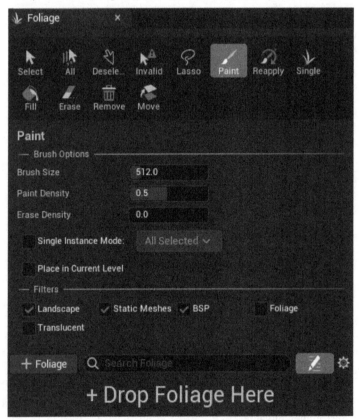

Figure 9.41 – Foliage mode options panel

In the first part of the panel, we can find the different tools the **Foliage** mode has. The middle part of the panel is dedicated to the tool settings and the last part is where we can add the assets to be placed on surfaces. By default, the **Foliage** mode is set to use the **Paint** tool. In the next sub-sections, we are going to explore the different tools the **Foliage** mode provides.

The Paint tool

The **Paint** tool is the core **Foliage** mode tool. It is the tool that allows us to place assets on our Landscape by using a brush as if we were drawing. To place assets on the Landscape, we need to *drag and drop* an asset from the **Content Browser** to the **Foliage** mode's **Paint** panel. You can drag and drop an asset on the + **Drop Foliage Here** text. Alternatively, we can click on the + **Foliage** button.

Figure 9.42 – Foliage assets panel inside the Foliage Mode's Paint tool

The **Foliage** mode's **Paint** tool works with **Static Mesh Foliage** assets. **Static Mesh Foliage** assets are assets that contain a Static Mesh and all the settings to be used by **Foliage** tools. Starting from Unreal Engine 5, we can use a Static Mesh Actor without converting it to a Static Mesh Foliage asset. But, by using the + **Foliage** button, you will be able to add only **Static Mesh Foliage** assets. To create a **Static Mesh Foliage** asset, *right-click* in the **Content Browser** and select **Static Mesh Foliage Actor** inside the **Foliage** category.

If you double-click the *LMB* on the **Static Mesh Foliage Actor** you have just created, the **Static Mesh Foliage Actor** editor will open.

You can add the Static Mesh Actor you want to use in the **Mesh** option.

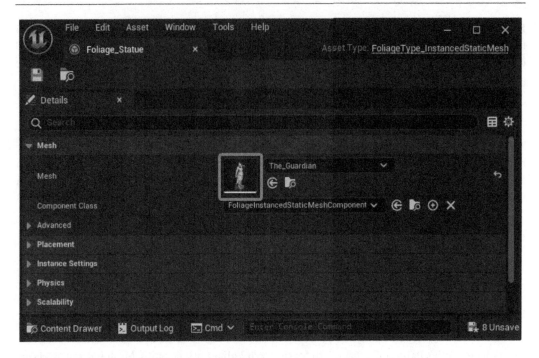

Figure 9.43 – Adding a Static Mesh inside the Static Mesh Foliage Actor

We don't need to explore all the options because we can change everything we need directly inside the **Paint** tool. So, once you have assigned your Static Mesh in the **Mesh** option, save and close the **Static Mesh Foliage actor** editor. Then, *drag and drop* the new **Static Mesh Foliage actor** inside the **Paint** tool or add it using the **+Foliage** button in the **Paint** tool panel.

Figure 9.44 – The asset added to the Paint tool looks like this

Now, if you move the cursor on the Landscape, you can see the brush, but if you try to left-click, nothing happens. The reason is that we need to activate the foliage asset. To do that, we need to check the box that appears every time you pass the cursor over the asset thumbnail.

Figure 9.45 – Use this checkbox to activate the foliage asset

Now it should work. If you left-click on your Landscape, the **Paint** tool will place your asset according to the brush settings.

Figure 9.46 – How the Paint tool works with default parameters

The Foliage actor thumbnail is also very important because it tells us the number of Foliage actor instances in the scene. You can check it with the number on the bottom-right side of the Foliage actor thumbnail (see *Figure 9.46*).

We can change **Brush Options** in the dedicated area of the **Paint** tool panel.

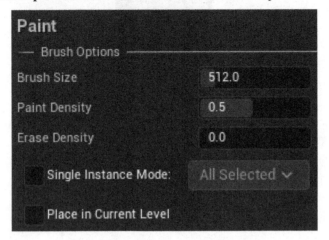

Figure 9.47 – Paint tool Brush Options

With these settings, we can do the following:

- **Brush Size**: This value defines the size of the brush. The larger the brush is, the larger the area will be where the assets will be placed.

- **Paint Density**: This value defines the density at which the assets will be placed with the brush. The higher the value, the higher the number of assets placed inside the area defined by **Brush Size**.

- **Erase Density**: If you press and hold *SHIFT* on the keyboard when you are using the **Paint** tool, it will delete foliage assets. The **Erase Density** value defines the value of assets to delete in terms of density inside the area defined by **Brush Size**.

- **Single Instance Mode**: If this option is checked, the brush will place one asset per click at the point of the landscape surface at which you are performing the command.

- **Place in Current Level**: If you are working with multiple Levels, this option allows you to place the foliage assets in the level set as current (we learned what that means in *Chapter 3*).

Before learning how to change the placement of assets, inside the **Filters** section, we can choose on which surface types of the **Paint** tool we can place assets.

Figure 9.48 – Filters section inside the Paint tool's panel

We already know what Landscapes and Static Meshes are. If these boxes are checked, it means that the **Paint** tool can work both on Landscapes and Static Meshes. BSP geometries are basic meshes such as cubes or pyramids that can be modified directly in the Engine. You will never use this option (by default, it is checked – you can leave it checked). If you check the **Foliage** box, the **Paint** tool will be allowed to place foliage assets on other foliage assets. By default, it is disabled, and I suggest you leave it disabled. It can cause some tedious overlapping problems.

Now that we know how the **Paint** tool works, we can take a look at how to change the way the Static Mesh will be placed.

Changing the placing options

If you click on a foliage asset inside the **Paint** tool, a list of settings appears under it:

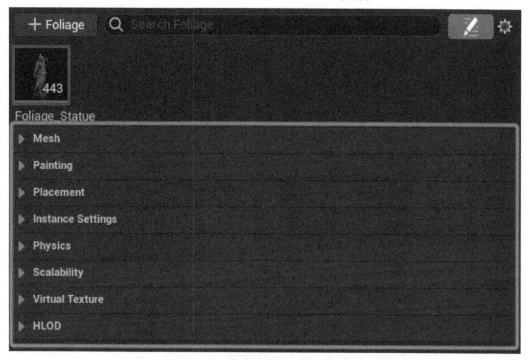

Figure 9.49 – Foliage actor's placing options inside the Paint tool panel

There are a lot of options here. We are going to learn about only the most useful.

As always, options are divided into categories:

- **Mesh**: Here, you can change the Static Mesh referred to **Foliage actor**. If you change the Static Mesh here, the placed asset will be updated.

Figure 9.50 – Mesh option inside the Mesh category

- **Painting**: In this category, we can change the quantity of assets that will be placed.

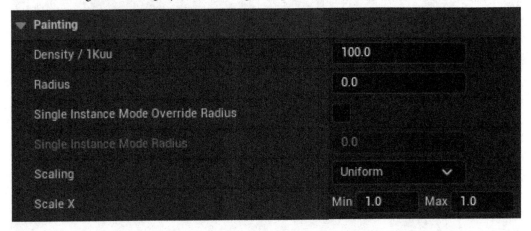

Figure 9.51 – Painting category's options

- **Density**: This value defines the number of assets that will be placed in terms of density. The value considers an area 1,000*1,000 units large.

- **Radius**: This value defines the minimum distance between any placed asset. By default, it is set to 0, which means that the asset can generate overlapping events.

- **Single Instance Mode Override Radius**: This value defines the minimum distance that can be between assets placed with the **Single Instance** mode option enabled.

- **Scaling** and **Scale X**: With the **Scaling** drop-down menu, we can change the way the asset changes its scale. It can be **Uniform**, **Free**, or **Locked on Axe Couple**. In any case, we can change the scale value range that the **Paint** tool will use in placing actions by changing the **Scale** value. These commands allow us to randomize the scale of our assets.

Figure 9.52 – Foliage actor placed with a scale range of 0.2 to 1

- **Placement**: In this category, we can change the way the **foliage actor** will be placed.

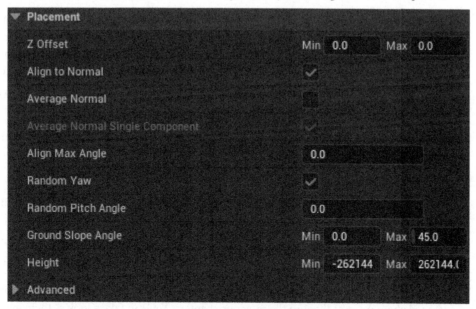

Figure 9.53 – Placement category's options

- **Z Offset**: This range of values allows us to randomize the Z positions of our Foliage actor. The offset is calculated from the painted surface, which means that a value range between 0 (zero) and 1,000 will place some assets 1,000 units above the Landscape.

- **Align to Normal**: If this option is enabled, the Foliage actor will be placed to be aligned with the destination surface's tangent normal, which means that the asset will be rotated according to the surface's slope.

Figure 9.54 – Align to normal explanatory screenshot

- **Average Normal**: If this option is enabled, the Foliage actor will be placed considering a surface's tangent normal average value. The average value is calculated considering the portion of the surface included inside the brush's radius. If the **Average normal single component** option is enabled, the **Average Normal** option will be applied to the single instance mode.

- **Align Max Angle**: This option allows us to define a maximum rotation angle that the **Paint** tool can apply to the Foliage actor when the **Average Normal** option is enabled.

- **Random Yaw**: If this option is enabled, the Foliage actor will be placed with a random yaw value.

- **Randow Pitch Angle**: This value allows us to define a random pitch angle value.

- **Ground Slope Angle**: This option allows us to define a range of slope values the **Paint** tool will work in between.

- **Height**: This option allows us to define the range height value the **Paint** tool will work in between. By default, it is set with the values we decided during the Landscape creation process.

Inside other categories, we can find more options that allow us to manage more Static Mesh settings. We have learned about most of them in the previous chapters. You can take a look at them and try out various setting combinations.

The **Paint** tool can obviously work with multiple Foliage actors. Each Foliage actor can have different settings. Any time we use the **Paint** tool, the brush will place only the Foliage actors marked as enabled with the checkbox on their thumbnail.

We can now go on and discover other **Foliage** mode tools. We are going to go faster now because the following tools are utilities to be used to improve the **Paint** tool's workflow.

The Select, All, Delete, Invalid, and Lasso tools

The first five tools in the **Foliage** mode panel are selection tools.

Figure 9.55 – Selection tools inside the Foliage mode panel

These tools don't have dedicated options:

- The **Select** tool allows us to select a single foliage actor instance placed in our Level Viewport. Once you have selected a single instance, you can transform it into a single asset.

Figure 9.56 – Select tool explanatory screenshot

- The **All** tool allows us to select all the Foliage actor instances. This can be useful if you need to delete all your Foliage actors with one action.

- The **Deselect** tool allows us to deselect everything.

- The **Invalid** tool will select any invalid foliage instance for you (if present). Invalid foliage instances are all assets placed off the ground. It is a good habit to check foliage instances with the **Invalid** tool. If everything looks great to you but the **Invalid** tool detects some foliage instances as invalid, you can tweak the threshold *invalid* state, via the `foliage.OffGroundThreshold` console command. *5* is the default value, which is a sensitive value.

- The **Lasso** select tool allows us to create an area selection. With foliage instances selected, we can perform different actions by using the tools we are going to learn about in the next section.

The Remove and Move tools

When you have selected one or more, or all, foliage instances, you can remove them by clicking on the **Remove** tool icon. This action will delete all the selected foliage instances. The action is reversible with the undo command (*CTRL + Z*). The **Move** tool allows us to move the selected foliage instances to the current Level (we learned what the current Level is in *Chapter 3*). This tool is very useful for moving part of our foliage work from a Level to the current one.

Figure 9.57 – Remove and Move tool icons in the Foliage mode panel

There are a couple more tools we can use inside the **Foliage** mode panel. We will learn about them in the next section.

The Reapply, Single, Fill, and Erase tools

These last four tools allow us to manage our placed foliage instances and use the brush in different ways.

Figure 9.58 – The Reapply, Single, Fill, and Erase tool icons in the Foliage mode panel

We can start from the simplest one:

- The **Erase** tool works in the same way as the **Paint** tool does, but it will delete all the foliage instances inside the brush radius instead of adding new ones. The **Erase** tool performs the same action that holding *SHIFT* while using the **Paint** tool does.

- The **Fill** tool allows us to fill a surface with active foliage actors. The foliage instances will be placed on the Static Mesh using the options set inside the foliage actor options panel.

Figure 9.59 – Fill tool example screenshot

- The **Single** tool allows us to place one foliage instance per click. It works the same as the **Paint** tool with the **Single Instance Mode** option enabled.
- The most useful tool in this section is the **Reapply** tool. This tool allows us to re-pose foliage instances with different settings. It works like the **Paint** tool, but it will change the pose of existing foliage instances (with a new posing option set inside the foliage actor option panel) instead of posing new ones.

In this section, we have learned everything we need to know about **Foliage** mode. For the purpose of learning, we have used the statue Static Mesh we imported in *Chapter 4*. It is obvious that the **Foliage** tool works better with natural assets such as grass, bushes, trees, and rocks, and also that little assets are very important to improve the realism and details of our scene, such as debris. Using the **Foliage** mode and its tools can improve the creation workflow, helping you to add a huge number of assets in a very fast way. The randomization options will help us to place different assets in a more realistic way, avoiding replications.

Figure 9.60 – An example of using Foliage mode with Megascans assets

When you use **Foliage** mode, you position hundreds, maybe thousands, of assets in your scene. This can be very expensive for performance. To avoid the frame rate dropping or a poor performance experience, you can use low poly assets with the **Paint** tool. This choice will not impact too much on the final quality of the scene because the Foliage tool is used to create quantity and not to add hero assets to your scene.

We have one more thing to learn about Landscape and terrain generation. In the next section, we will talk about Landscape Materials and how we can paint texture directly onto our Landscape.

Creating a Landscape Material

In this practical section, we will learn how to create a **Landscape Material**. The Material creation process is the same as we learned about in *Chapter 5*. To easily follow this section, it is very important to understand all the steps we have learned about to create a surface Master Material. In this section, we will refer to different nodes we have already learned about in *Chapter 5* without re-explaining them.

Before we start creating our first Landscape Material, we need to know that Unreal Engine 5 has specific nodes inside the Material Editor dedicated to Landscapes. To find them, you simply need to search for them by typing landscape in the right-click menu inside the Material Editor Viewport.

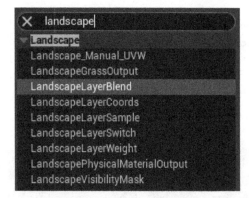

Figure 9.61 – All the nodes dedicated to Landscapes inside the Material Editor

We are not going to learn how to use all of them, but you need to know that all these nodes will work only with a Landscape surface. In the following sections, we will use some of these nodes to create a Landscape Material that will allow us to paint different materials directly on our Landscape inside the Level Viewport and to procedurally place Foliage actors. We will also learn how to apply different Materials according to the slope value of our Landscape surface.

Setting the Level

First, we need to set up our Level to make this section easier to follow. Follow these steps:

1. Create a new empty Level. Save it and call it Landscape.

2. Create a natural lighting set with the Environment Light Mixer (as we have already seen in *Chapter 6*) and save the Level.

3. Create a simple Landscape using the settings shown in *Figure 9.63*.

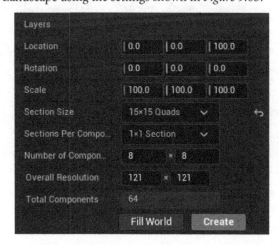

Figure 9.62 – Landscape creation settings for this section

4. Once the Landscape has been created, go back to selection mode by clicking *SHIFT+1*. In the **Content Browser**, create a new folder inside the **Materials** folder (if you don't have one yet, create one) and rename it Landscape. Inside this new folder, create a new Material and rename it M_Landscape. Finally, create a Material Instance from this new material and rename it MI_Landscape.

5. Select **Landscape** in the Outliner. In the **Details** panel, look for **Landscape Material**. Assign the **MI_Landscape** Material Instance to the Landscape.

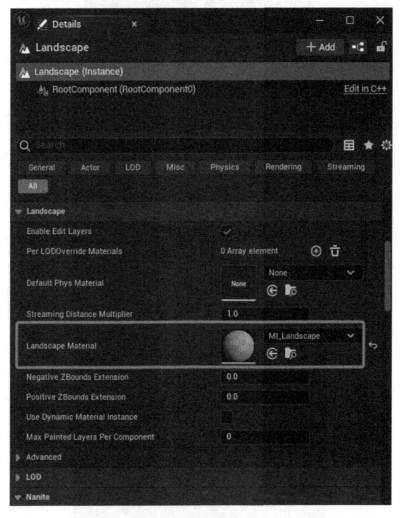

Figure 9.63 – Landscape Material option in the Landscape's Details panel

The Landscape should now look black with a shiny effect.

Perfect! We are now ready to start creating our Landscape Material.

Creating painting layers

The first thing we need to do is create the different layers we want to be able to paint on our Landscape. Double-click on the *LMB* on **M_Landscape** to open the Material Editor. Follow these steps:

1. Different layers mean having different values of the same Material attribute. We need to be able to create multiple Material attributes (meaning more than one base color, more than one roughness, and so on that can work contemporarily but separately) inside a single Master Material. To do that, we need to check the **Use Material Attributes** option inside the Material Domain's **Details** panel. This option collapses the Material Domain node into a one-input node.

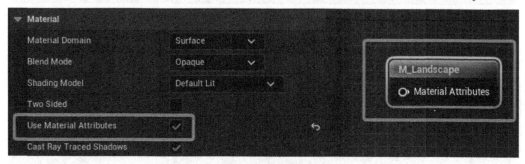

Figure 9.64 – Use Material Attributes option enabled

2. Create three **Constant 3-Vector** and change their colors. We need a green constant, a red constant, and a blue constant. These will be our three Landscape layers.

3. Create a **Landscape Layer Blend** node. This node allows us to assign our colors to different painting layers.

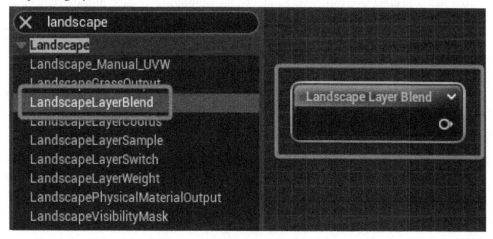

Figure 9.65 – Landscape Layer Blend node

By default, the **Landscape Layer Blend** node has no layers. To add a new layer, select the **Landscape Layer Blend** node and click on the + icon near the **Layers** option in the node's **Details** panel.

Figure 9.66 – Adding layers to the Landscape Layer Blend node

For each layer you have added, you have some options. The first option is **Layer Name**. We can rename the first layer to Grass.

Figure 9.67 – Landscape Layer Blend's layer options

The second is **Blend Type**. With this drop-down menu, we can choose the way this layer will be blended with other layers when we paint it on the Landscape. We have three different options:

- **LB Weight Blend**: This option allows us to paint each layer independently from others and without worrying about layer order

- **LB Alpha Blend**: This option allows us to paint in detail and define an order using alpha

- **LB Height Blend**: This works in the same way as **LB Weight Blend**, but it allows you to add detail in the transition between layers

We can leave it as **LB Weight Blend** for now.

4. We have created three different colors, so we need three different layers. We can call the other two layers Rocks and Snow. Finally, connect the green **Constant 3-vector** to the **Layer Grass** input; the red **Constant 3-vector** to the **Layer Rocks** input, and the blue **Constant 3-vector** to the **Layer Snow** input. You should have something like this:

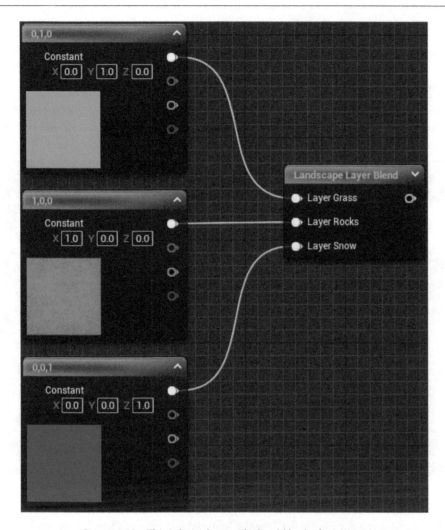

Figure 9.68 – This is how the graph should look after step 4

5. Now we need to connect the **Landscape Layer Blend** output to the Material Domain. If you try to directly connect it, the Engine will alert you to a compilation error. The reason is we need to convert our **Landscape Layer Blend** node's output into a **Material Attributes** output. To do that, we need to add a **SetMaterialAttributes** node to our Material graph.

Figure 9.69 – SetMaterialAttributes node

The **SetMaterialAttributes** node allows us to add the Material attributes we want to our Master Material. For now, we only have **Base Color**. To add a new attribute, you need to click on the plus icon near the **Array element** option in the node's **Details** panel (see *Figure 9.70*). **Base Color** is set by default.

6. Once you have created it, connect the **Landscape Layer Blend** output to the **SetMaterialAttributes Base Color** input and the **SetMaterialAttributes** output to the **Material Domain** input. If you have done everything in the right way, your Material graph should look like this:

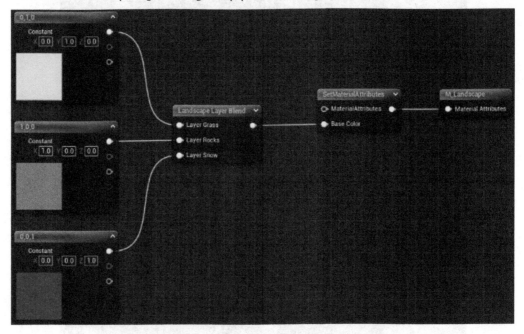

Figure 9.70 – This is how the graph should look after step 5

7. Apply and save your Material. Close the Material Editor, enter **Landscape** mode, and open the **Paint** tab.

Figure 9.71 – Landscape mode's Paint tab

The last thing we need to do to be able to paint our layers on the Landscape is to assign **Layer Info** to our painting layers. **Layer info** is an actor saved in the content that tells the Engine the way it needs to interpret the painting layer. We need one **Layer Info** for each painting layer we have set inside the Master Material. In the **Landscape** mode's **Paint** tab, under the **Layers** category, we can find the layers we have just created with the Landscape Material. To add **Layer Info**, we need to click on the plus icon on the right side of the painting layer.

Figure 9.72 – Adding Layer Info

We have two different **Layer Info** options:

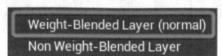

Figure 9.73 – Layer Info types

The first one allows us to blend the layer we are painting with other painting layers. The second one allows us to paint a layer without blending it with others. This option is used to create advanced effects. We can create **Weight-Blended Layer** info. The Engine will ask you where to save the **Layer Info**. Select the folder you want and click on **Save**.

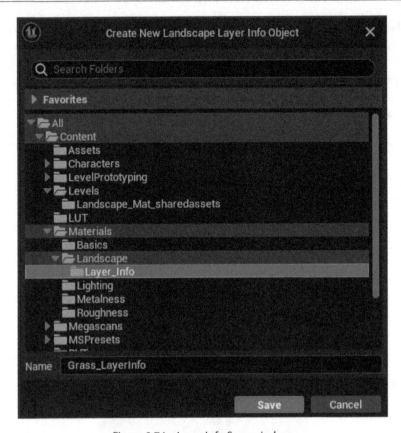

Figure 9.74 – Layer Info Save window

8.   Perform the same action for each layer.

Perfect! Now you can paint the selected layer to your Landscape. The brush options are the same as we have learned about in previous sections.

Figure 9.75 – Landscape painted with Material layers

We have some different tools in the **Landscape** mode's **Paint** tab. All of them are very simple variations of the main **Paint** tool.

Figure 9.76 – Paint tab tools

At this point in the book, you can try them out by yourself except for the **Blueprint** tool. We will learn about that in *Chapter 10*.

Now that we know how we can create layers inside the Master Material that allow us to paint colors directly on the Landscape, in the next section, we will learn how to use textures instead of colors.

Adding textures

In this section, we will learn how to use textures inside our Landscape Materials. First, we need some textures. We can download them from the Megascans Library. You can use any kind of texture. To easily follow this section, I suggest you download a grass ground surface, a rocks ground surface, and a snow ground surface. We will use the following materials:

Figure 9.77 – Preview of Materials that will be used in this section

The first thing we can do is to drag and drop the three **Base Color** textures inside our Master Material and try to substitute them for the **Constant 3-vector.** After you have done that, save and apply your Material and check what has happened in the Level Viewport. The Landscape should look something like this:

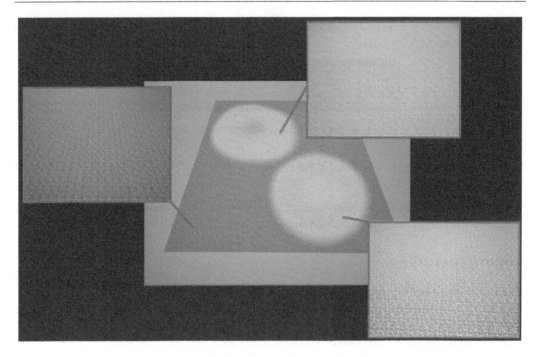

Figure 9.78 – The Viewport result at this point

Our Landscape Material is working but it doesn't look so good. Our three different materials have a clear repetition problem. We need to manage the tiling of our textures according to the Landscape size. To do that, follow these steps:

1. Inside the Material Editor, search for the **LandscapeLayerCoords** node.

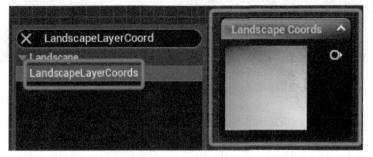

Figure 9.79 – LandscapeLayerCoords node

The **LandscapeLayerCoords** node works like the **Texture Coordinates** node we saw in *Chapter 5*. Its function is to tell the Material Domain that we are using **Landscape Coordinates** after it.

2. Talking about coordinates, we need to connect the **Landscape Layer Coord** output to the **UVs** input of each texture. The Material Editor node graph should now look like this:

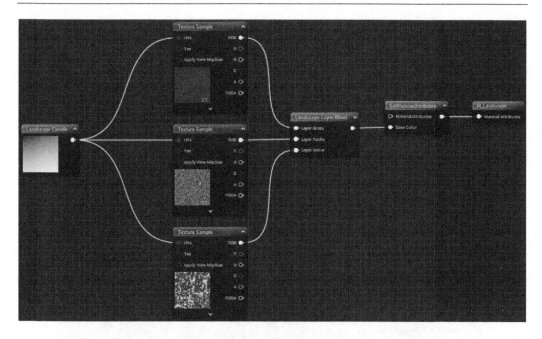

Figure 9.80 – Material Editor node graph with Landscape Layer Coords node

3. Inside the **LandscapeLayerCoords Details** panel, we need to set **Mapping Scale** to what we want to use to place our texture on the Landscape. We can find the correct value inside the **Landscape Details** panel, under the **Information** category.

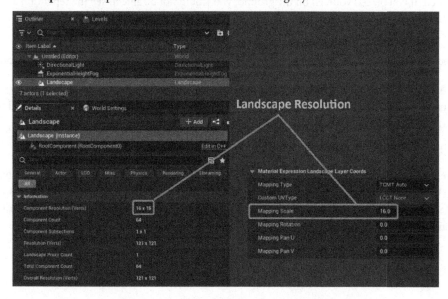

Figure 9.81 – The Component Resolution value is the value we need to
set for the LandscapeLayerCoords Mapping Scale value

4. We can now save and apply our Landscape Material and let's check what has happened inside the Viewport.

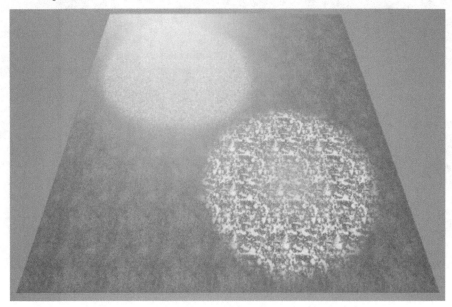

Figure 9.82 – Landscape painting layers with correct resolution

The repetition is still visible, but you need to think about the way a Landscape will usually be used. If you placed yourself on the ground, you would not be able to see the repetition anymore. By the way, you can play around a little bit with the **Mapping Scale** value.

We can also add other PBR textures to our Material to make the result more realistic. A roughness map and normal map will be more than enough. To add them, we need to perform two actions:

1. Add the inputs we need in the **SetMaterialAttributes** node. As we saw before, we can add a new input in the node's **Details** panel. We need the **Roughness** input and the **Normal** input.

2. We need to duplicate **Landscape Layer Blend** twice – once for the **Roughness** texture and once for the **Normal** texture.

Now we can connect our **Roughness** texture to the first new **Landscape Layer Blend** and the **Normal** texture to the second one. Finally, we need to connect the **Roughness Landscape Layer Blend** to the **SetMaterialAttributes Roughness** input and repeat the same action for the Normal texture. The result should look like this:

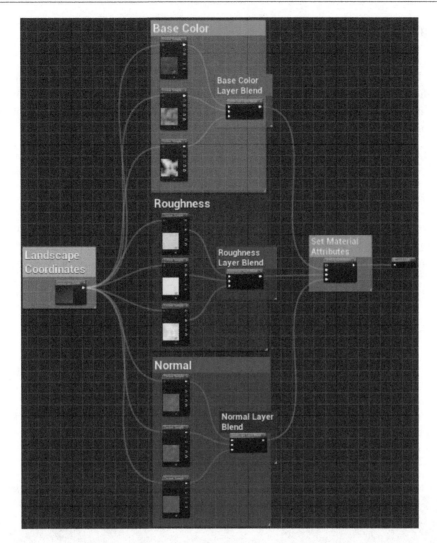

Figure 9.83 – Material Editor node graph with multiple textures

Remember to connect all the textures' **UV** inputs to the **Landscape Layer Coord** output to ensure correct texture placement on the Landscape.

Adding multiple textures to our Landscape Material could be expensive in terms of performance. Be wary of using very high-resolution textures in your Landscape Material. Remember that the Landscape will be the ground of your scene and it will probably be covered by other assets that will make it barely visible.

Perfect! We are almost done! We are now ready to learn how to procedurally spawn foliage assets with our Landscape Material.

Adding Landscape grass

As we saw before, in the *Discovering the Foliage mode* section, we can place assets on our Landscape by using a brush. That brush places assets without caring about the type of texture that is assigned in that specific Landscape portion. In this section, we will learn how to procedurally place foliage assets when we are painting a texture layer on the Landscape. In other words, we will learn how to paint textures together with procedural foliage assets.

To do that, we need some foliage assets. As always, we can easily find them in the Megascans Library. We need some grass, some rocks, and something to spawn where we decide to paint the snow material.

Adding spawned foliage is very simple. We can start with grass. Follow these steps:

1. Open your Landscape Material and create a **LandscapeGrassOutput** node. The **LandscapeGrassOutput** node works like an alternative Material Domain. Once you have created it, it looks like this:

Figure 9.84 – Landscape Grass input node

We don't need to link it to the Material Domain. By default, it has one input, called **Grass**. We are trying to add grass foliage, so we can leave it that way. By the way, you can change the input name inside the node's **Details** panel.

2. Inside the node's **Details** panel, we need to add the Foliage actor we want to spawn.

Figure 9.85 – Landscape Grass Output's Grass Type field

The **Grass Type** option needs a **Landscape Grass Type** object. A **Landscape Grass Type** object is very similar to a Foliage actor, which we learned how to create in the *Discovering the Foliage mode* section, but is built to be used with the **LandscapeGrassOutput** node.

3. Create a **Landscape Grass Type** object by clicking the *RMB* in the **Content Browser** and clicking on **Landscape Grass Type** under the **Foliage** category. Rename it LG_Grass.

Figure 9.86 – Landscape Grass Type creation command

4. Double-click on it and open the **Landscape Grass Type** editor.

5. Now we need to add the Static Mesh Actor we want to spawn when we paint the Grass Material. To do that, click on the + icon near the **Grass Varieties** option to add a new array.

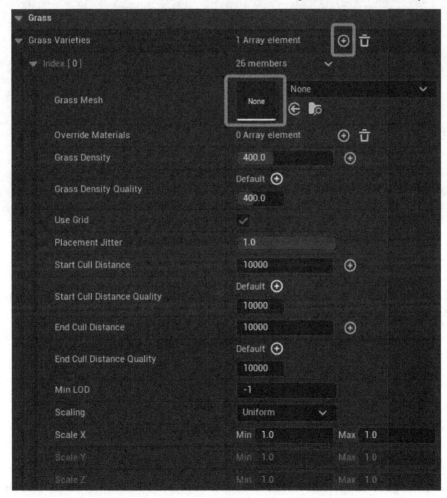

Figure 9.87 – Adding Static Mesh Actor to our Grass Material

6. Drag and drop your Grass Static Mesh into the **Grass Mesh** field. You can add all the Static Meshes you want and change the spawning option for each of them to create a random, more realistic effect. This is my setup:

Figure 9.88 – Landscape Grass Type set with four different Static
Meshes and different settings for each of them

7. Inside the **Landscape Grass Output Details** panel, assign the new **LG_Grass** as the Landscape **Grass Type**.

Figure 9.89 – Landscape Grass Type assigned to the Landscape Grass output node

8. The last thing we need to do is to tell the **Landscape Grass Output** which painting layers have to spawn grass Foliage actors. To do that, we need to create a **Landscape Layer Sample** node.

Figure 9.90 – Landscape Layer Sample node

This node works as a reference to one of the layers we have created with the **Landscape Layer Blend**. The reference works through the layer name. So, it is very important to call the Landscape layer sample with the correct Landscape layer name.

Figure 9.91 – The Landscape layer sample must have the same name as the destination layer

9. Finally, connect the Landscape layer sample's output to the **Landscape Grass Output**'s **Grass** input. Apply and save your Landscape Material. Now, if you try to paint the **Grass** layer on your Landscape, this action will also spawn assets on the surface. Going through the same process for all the layers you want to be able to spawn assets for will allow you to procedurally paint different kinds of assets on your Landscape.

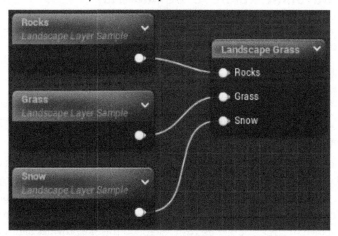

Figure 9.92 – Landscape Grass Output node with three different Landscape layer samples

You can now create something like this with literally one click:

Figure 9.93 – Assets placed with painting layers

Perfect! We are done! We are now able to create a Material that allows us to paint textures directly on our Landscape and procedurally place assets according to the layer we have decided to paint.

We have one more thing to learn about Landscape Materials and that is the possibility to automatically paint our Landscape according to its slope value.

Creating an automatic Landscape Material

In this last demonstration section, we will learn how to automatically assign painting layers to our Landscape according to its slope.

To do that, try to follow these steps:

1. Create a new Level (you can also use the same Level we created for the previous section).

2. Create a new Material, rename it M_AutoLandscape, and create a Material Instance. Rename the new material instance MI_AutoLandscape.

3. Create a new Landscape. We can use the same setting we used before (you can also use the same Landscape we have created before). Or, you can create a new Landscape using a heightmap. I am going to use a heightmap from Motion Forge Picture – the one named *Rugged Terrain with Rivers Height Map*, which you can find for free at this link: https://www. motionforgepictures.com/height-maps/. This site provides high-quality heightmaps for free with CCO licensing. You can use any of them. If you want to use a heightmap, before clicking on **Import**, remember to set a **Z scale** value of 500.

4. Assign the new Material Instance to the Landscape as we saw before.

5. Open the Material Editor by double-clicking on the new Material.

6. Create three **Constants 3-vector** and change their colors to white, brown, and green. During the Material creation process. It's always a good habit to use **Constants** instead of more expensive textures.

7. Create three **MakeMaterialAttributes** nodes. This node allows us to have the same input a Material Domain has but with an output.

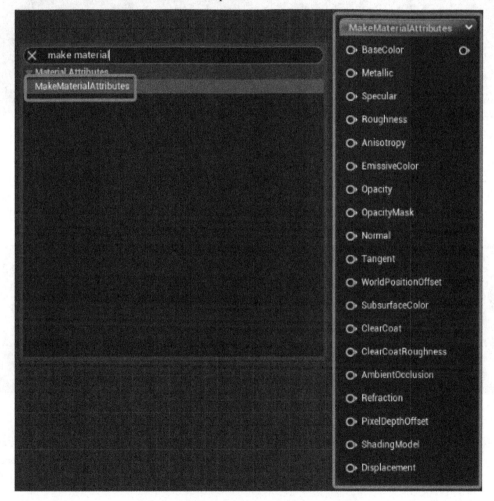

Figure 9.94 – MakeMaterialAttributes node

8. Connect the three **Constants 3-vector** to the **Base Color** input of the **MakeMaterialAttributes** node – one constant for each attribute node.

Figure 9.95 – How to connect constants to MakeMaterialAttributes nodes

9. We need to blend the three Materials together. We want the green Material (grass) and the brown Material (rocks) to be blended according to the slope value. The white Material (snow) will be blended by the height. We can start with green and brown materials. Create a **MatLayerBlend_Standard** function.

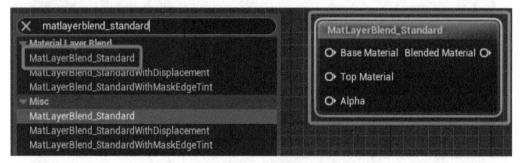

Figure 9.96 – MatLayerBLend_Standard function node.

10. The **MatLayerBlend_Standard** function allows us to blend two different Materials with an alpha mask. We can connect the brown Material's **MakeMaterialAttributes** output to the **Base Material** input and the green Material's **MakeMaterialAttributes** output to the **Top Material** input.

11. We need to blend these two Materials according to the surface slope value. To do that, we need to add a **SlopeMask** function.

Figure 9.97 – SlopeMask function node

Let's take a look at the function input:

- **SlopAngle**: Here, we can decide which angle the function uses to calculate the surface slope. We want the slope to be calculated considering the Z axis. To do that, we can simply add a **Constant 3-vector** with a value equal to one in the blue channel.

- **FalloffPower**: This is the falloff intensity that will be used to blend the two Materials. We can promote it to a parameter and set it to 5.

- **CheapContrast**: This value is useful to change the falloff effect. We can promote it to a parameter.

1. We can now connect the **SlopeMask** node's output to the **MatLayerBlend_Standard** node's **Alpha** input.

2. Create a **Landscape Layer Blend** node. Add a new layer and rename it `Auto`.

3. Connect the **MatLayerBlend_Standard** output to the **Landscape Layer Blend** node's **Auto** input.

4. Connect the **Landscape Layer Blend** node's output to the Material Domain input. The graph node should look like this:

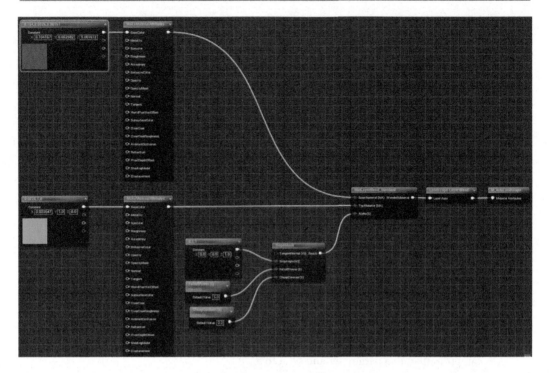

Figure 9.98 – Blending two Materials with SlopeMask

Your Landscape should look like this:

Figure 9.99 – Landscape with automatic Material step 1

5. Inside the Material Instance, you can play with the **Falloff Power** and **Cheap Contrast** values to obtain the result you want.

6. Now it is time to add snow (blue Material) to our Landscape. Above a specific height, we want the automatic Material to start to place the snow Material. To do that, we need to add the **SmoothStep** function.

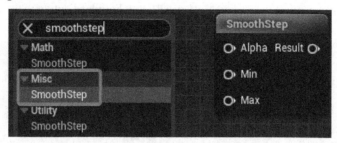

Figure 9.100 – SmoothStep function node

7. Let's take a look at its input:

- **Alpha**: Here, we can decide the criteria the function will use to blend the two Materials. We said that we want to apply snow according to the height of the Landscape point in the world. To do that, we can create a **World Position** node and connect its **Z** output to the **SmoothStep** node's **Alpha** input.

- **Min** and **Max**: These two inputs allow us to define the value range within which the Alpha will work. In other words, the starting height value from which the Landscape starts to be covered by the snow Material. We can promote them to parameters.

The **SlopeMask** graph node should look like this:

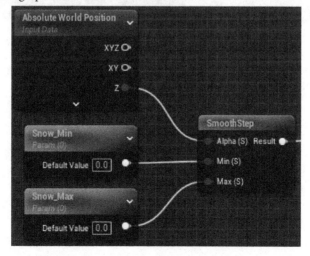

Figure 9.101 – SmoothStep node setup

8. The last thing we need to do is to blend the snow Material with the other two. To do that, we can use the same **MatLayerBLend_Standard** function we used before. We need to connect the **SmoothStep** output to the **MatLayerBLend_Standard** node's **Alpha** input, the snow Material to the **Base Material** input, and the result of the blending of the green and the brown Material to the **Top Material** input.

9. Finally, we can connect the second **MatLayerBLend_Standard** output to the **Landscape Layer Blend** node's **Auto** input. The final node graph should look like this:

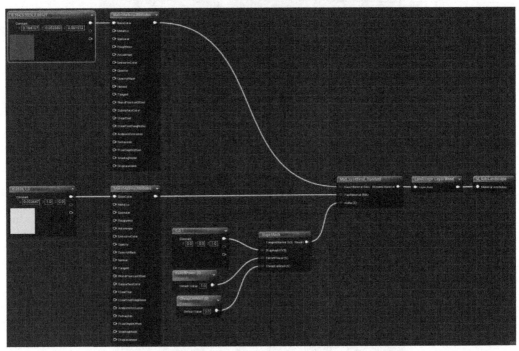

Figure 9.102 – Automaterial final node graph

Your **Landscape** should look like this:

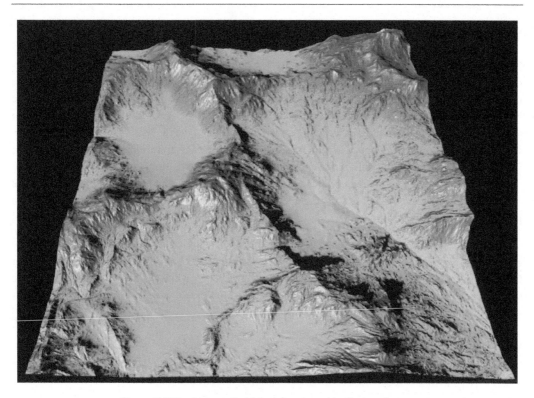

Figure 9.103 – Automatic Material assigned to the Landscape

Perfect! We are done! Now, if you want, you can substitute color with realistic Materials by adding textures to each **MakeMaterialAttributes** node. As we saw in *Chapter 5*, you can also create a Material Function for each Material and use them in the Material Editor to make the **Landscape** Master Material more sorted.

> **Note**
>
> The **Landscape** Auto Material works interactively. If you are not using a heightmap but are sculpting the Landscape with the **Sculpt** tools, the placed Material will change according to the slope Level of your sculpting action and the height of your Landscape's surface point.

In this last section, we learned how to create a **Landscape** Auto Material that automatically assigns different Materials in different Landscape portions according to the Landscape's surface variations. This technique is very useful to speed up the creation process for massive environments. The **Landscape** Auto Material, along with the sculpting tools, painting layers, and procedural foliage, are the perfect kit to generate huge, realistic natural environments in an incredibly short time.

Summary

In this long but game-changing chapter, we have learned everything we need to know about terrain creation with Landscapes. In the first section, we learned what a Landscape is and how to create a new one considering a real-life size. In the next section, we explored all the different **Sculpt** tools the Engine provides to create diverse terrain surfaces. We went on and learned how to use a heightmap to automatically generate terrain from a texture with a high Level of detail. Thanks to the **Foliage** mode, we learned how to place Foliage actors using a brush that allows us to randomly place assets on the Landscape's surface. Finally, we learned different techniques for creating a Landscape Material that allows us to paint different textures on the Landscape directly inside the Level Viewport. This allows us to procedurally place Foliage actors through the Material and allows us to procedurally paint the Landscape's surface according to its slope and height variation.

Our journey comes ever closer to the end. The next chapter will be a hands-on chapter on what we can create using the Engine's plugins, such as **Landmass**, the **Water** tool, and the **Procedural Content Generation framework**. After that, in *Chapters 11*, *12*, and *13*, we will learn how to set up a cinematic shot, improve its quality with effects, and render out the final video.

10

Creating Diverse Environments with Plugins

In this demonstrative chapter, we will create a new level to cover, from scratch, the workflow we can use to create an environment from draft using the diverse plugins that Unreal Engine provides us with to modify the landscape and place actors procedurally. We will create a new **Landscape** material and discover some very useful new nodes, and we will learn how to activate and use the **Landmass** plugin to modify landscape shape and painting. We will also learn how to activate and use the **Water** plugin to add a water system to our environment and how to pose assets procedurally with the new **Procedural Content Generation** (**PCG**) system.

In this chapter, we will cover the following topics:

- Setting the level to work procedurally
- Modifying the landscape with the Landmass plugin
- Exploring the Water plugin
- Creating your first PCG Framework
- Exercise – Create an island environment

At the end of this chapter, we will be able to create a Landscape scenario from the draft by using Landmass tools and we will be able to modify the morphology of the landscape by adding rivers and lakes. We will also be able to create a simple graph inside the new PCG system to procedurally pose assets on our landscape.

Technical requirements

In this chapter, we will create an environment from scratch by using various plugins that you can find directly inside the Unreal Engine. To easily follow the chapter, you need at least the 5.3 version of the Engine installed on your workstation.

Setting the level to work procedurally

In this section, we will create a landscape and its material to be able to work procedurally in the following sections. The Landmass plugin, Water plugin, and PCG Framework allow us to change our environment creation workflow by introducing specific techniques to generate diverse environments without using the standard brushes and tools we learned about in *Chapter 9*.

To be able to use all the tools we are going to learn about in this chapter, we need to create a simple landscape setup to make our workflow smoother.

The first thing we need to do is to create a landscape. We can use the default **Landscape** creation values.

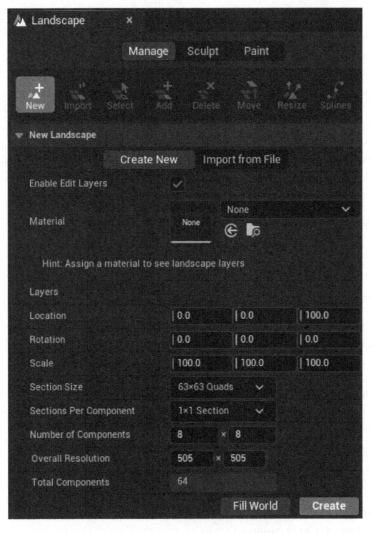

Figure 10.1 – Landscape settings

Next, we need to create a Landscape material. We want to create something different from what we learned during *Chapter 9* – something more optimized and suitable to be used with the **Landmass** tool.

To create our new Landscape material, try to follow these steps:

1. Create a new material and rename it M_Sample_Landscape.

2. Create a Material Instance from the new material and rename it MI_Sample_Landscape. Assign it to the landscape.

3. Double-click the **left mouse button (LMB)** on M_Sample_Landscape to enter **Material Editor**.

4. As we saw in *Chapter 9*, enable the **Use Material Attributes** option inside the **Material** domain's **Details** panel.

5. We want to blend a **Grass** material with a **Dirt** material. As always, we can use textures from the Megascans Library or Marketplace's free asset packs. We need **Base Color**, **Roughness**, and **Normal Map**. I'm going to use the materials shown in *Figure 10.2*:

Figure 10.2 – Materials we are going to use in this chapter

6. Create one **SetMaterialAttributes** node for the **Grass** material and one for the **Dirt** material.

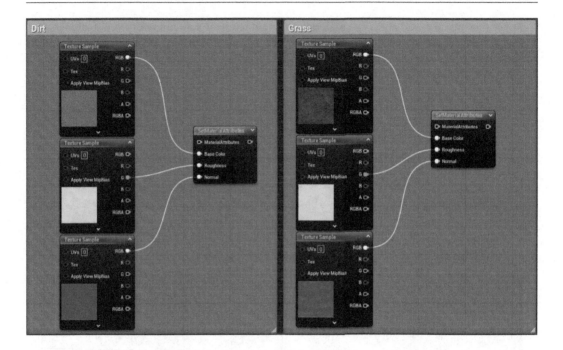

Figure 10.3 – SetMaterialAttributes nodes with textures linked to them

7. Now, we need to blend these two materials. To do that, we can use a **BlendMaterialAttributes** node (the same one we saw in *Chapter 9*). We can connect the **Dirt** material to the **BlendMaterialAttributes A** input, and we can connect the **Grass** material to the **BlendMaterialAttributes B** input.

8. Create **Landscape Layer Sample** and rename it Grass. This will be our painting layer. Connect its output to the **BlendMaterialAttributes Alpha** input. You can also connect the **BlendMaterialAttributes** output to the **Material Domain** input. The graph should look like this:

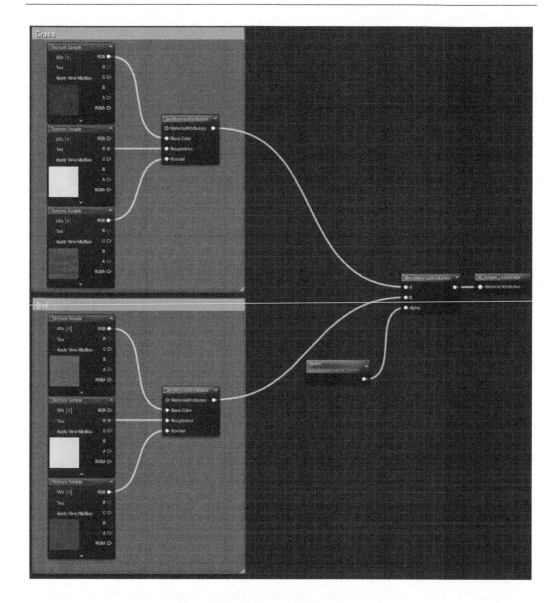

Figure 10.4 – Node graph state after step 8

9. Apply and save your material.

10. In the **Landscape** mode, inside the **Paint** panel, you should now see the **Grass** layer we have just created. If you can't see it, try to assign another casual material to **Landscape** and then re-assign the correct one. This workaround should fix the issue.

11. As we saw in *Chapter 9*, we need to create **Layer_Info** for each layer we have in our **Landscape** material. But this time, we want a **Non Weight-Blended Layer** info because we want to have control over how layers blend themselves together.

Figure 10.5 – Adding a Non Weight-Blended Layer info

We are now able to paint some **Grass** material on our landscape. If you press and hold *Shift* and click *LMB*, you can paint the **Dirt** material. Your landscape should now look like this:

Figure 10.6 – Landscape filled with Grass material and with a portion painted with Dirt material

12. As we can see in *Figure 10.6*, the materials look very bad, and the tiling is very visible. We already saw in *Chapter 9* how to fix this problem but now we want to adopt another way. There is a node called **TextureVariation** that can help us.

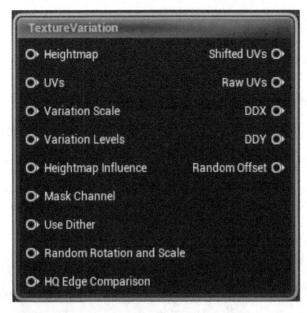

Figure 10.7 – TextureVariation node

The **TextureVariation** node shifts the texture many times and randomly on the UVs (so in a 2D space) to avoid repetitions. All its inputs help us decide which kind of shifting we want to apply. The outputs define what we want to shift. For now, we don't need any custom input.

13. Connect the **TextureVariation**'s **Shifted UVs** output to the **UVs** input of each texture we have in the graph. We need to create two different **TextureVariation** nodes, one for the **Grass** material and one for the **Dirt** material.

14. Apply and save the material and check what has happened in the Level Viewport.

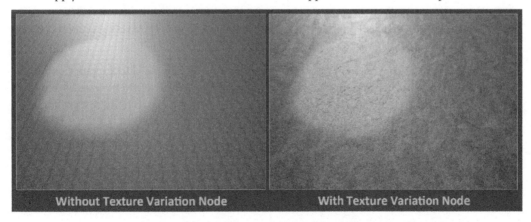

Figure 10.8 – How material looks different without and with the TextureVariation node

The **TextureVariation** node is quick to use and super effective. It works on UVs, so it is not so expensive in terms of performance. But when we use the UVs in this strange mode to shift textures randomly to avoid repetitions, the standard way the Engine uses to calculate texture streaming can't be the best one.

The Engine uses different texture resolutions according to the texture's distance from the camera. A bigger high-res texture with a starting resolution of 4096x4096 pixels will be scaled to 2048x2048 pixels and again to 1024x1024, 512x512, 256x256, 128x128, 64x64, 16x16, and 8x8 pixels.

This method can create some problems when we shift UVs to generate texture variation in terms of quality because the Engine could use different resolutions to blend the shifted textures together. To avoid this situation, we need to change the **MipValueMode** option inside the **Details** panel of **Material Expression Texture Sample** to **Derivative (explicit derivative to compute mip level)**.

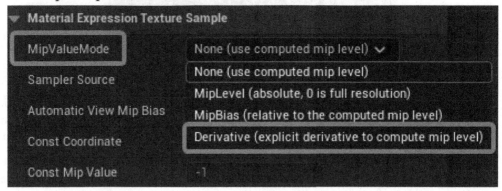

Figure 10.9 – MipValueMode inside the Texture Sample's Details panel

This option will allow the Engine to consider the actual size of the texture. Once we have enabled it, the **Texture Sample** node acquires two new inputs: **DDX(UVs)** and **DDY(UVs)** (see *Figure 10.10*).

15. Connect the **TextureVariation**'s **DDX** output to the **Texture Sample**'s **DDX** input. Connect the **TextureVariation**'s **DDY** output to the **Texture Sample**'s **DDY** input. Do these actions for each texture you have in the Material Editor Viewport. Connections between the **TextureVariation** node and the **Texture Sample** node should look like this:

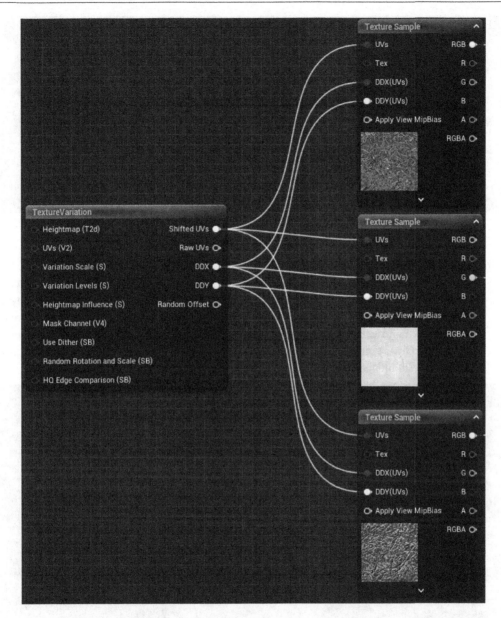

Figure 10.10 – Connections between the TextureVariation node and Texture Sample node

Note

Remember that you can use the **Named Reroute Declaration** node (we saw them in *Chapter 5*) to organize your master material. You can create a **Reroute** node for both the **Grass** and **Dirt** material and reorder your node graph (see *Figure 10.11*).

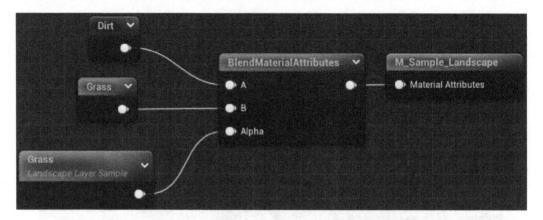

Figure 10.11 – Landscape material's node graph with reroute nodes

16. Now it's time to add procedural **Grass**. The way is the same as we learned in *Chapter 9*. We can summarize the process of creating a new **Landscape Grass Type** asset and adding to it the grass static meshes you want to procedurally spawn. First, create a **Landscape Grass Output** node inside the Material Editor and assign to it the **Grass Landscape Foliage Type**. Second, create a new **Landscape Layer Sample**, rename it Grass, and connect it to the **Grass** input of **Landscape Grass Output**. You can check the entire process in *Chapter 9*. The Material Editor node graph should look like this:

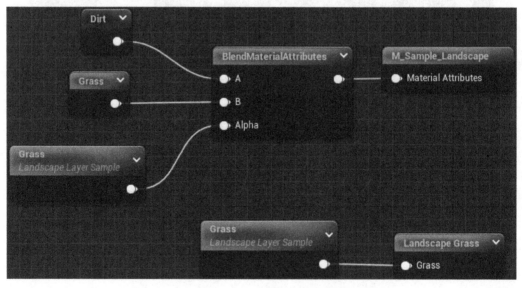

Figure 10.12 – Landscape material's node graph

Your landscape should now look like this:

Figure 10.13 – Landscape with procedural grass

Perfect! Now, we have a landscape and a landscape material perfectly set to start creating diverse environments with the **Landmass** plugin.

Modifying the landscape with the Landmass plugin

In this section, we will learn what the **Landmass** plugin is and how to use it to modify our landscape.

Landmass is a precompiled plugin that allows us to use custom brushes inside the **Landscape** mode's **Sculpt** panel to procedurally modify our landscape surface and create more complex grounds in a faster way.

Landmass is disabled by default. To enable it, open the **Plugins** window and search for Landmass. The Engine will ask you to restart.

Figure 10.14 – Landmass plugin activation inside the Plugin window

Once we have enabled the **Landmass** plugin, we can enter the **Landscape** mode to use the **Landmass custom brushes**.

To add a new **Landmass** custom brush, select the **Blueprint** tool inside the **Landscape** mode's **Sculpt** tab and add a new **CustomBrush_Landmass** in the **Blueprint Brush** option.

Figure 10.15 – Adding a Landmass custom brush

To definitively add the new brush, click on the landscape inside the Level Viewport. This *pyramid* should appear on your landscape surface.

Figure 10.16 – This is how the custom brush appears the first time you add it

You can select your new custom brush under the **Edit Layer Blueprint Brushes** category inside the **Blueprint** tool options panel. It is called **Landscape_CustomBrush_Landmass_CustomBrush**:

Figure 10.17 – Landmass_CustomBrush inside the Landscape mode's Sculpt panel

But what is **CustomBrush**? It works like a standard sculpting tool but it uses a *spline* (an editable line) to define the area of its influence and it is procedural. The spline defines the surface-raising action's edge on our Landscape. By default, on the spline, the raising power has the minimum power. That power increases according to the distance from the spline and decreases again when it reaches another segment of the spline (see *Figure 10.18*).

In other words, the center point inside an area defined by the spline has the maximum raising power (see *Figure 10.19*). We can move around the spline and its influence will affect the Landscape of the new **CustomBrush**'s position. We can select any single point of the spline and move it independently from others.

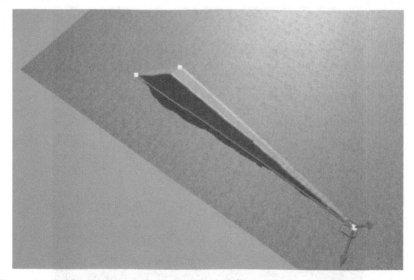

Figure 10.18 – If you move a spline point, the Landscape shape will interactively change

To add a new spline point (to create a diverse shape), drag an existent point by clicking *LMB* on it while holding down *Alt*. You can easily create something like this:

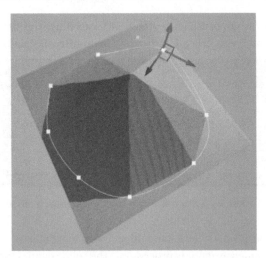

Figure 10.19 – An example of how Landmass CustomBrush works

We can now try to create a natural depression in the center of our Landscape that we will use to place a lake in the next session. To do that, try to follow these steps:

1. The first thing we need is to make flatter the action of our custom brush. If we select the custom brush under the **Edit Layer Blueprint Brushes** category inside the **Blueprint** tool options panel, a lot of options appear inside the **Details** panel. The one we need is called **Cap Shape**.

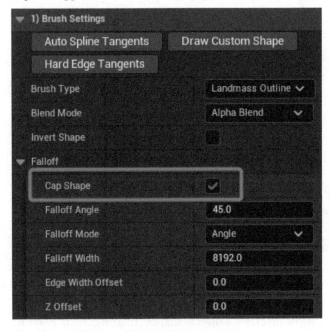

Figure 10.20 – Cap Shape option inside the custom brush's Details panel

This option allows us to cap the raising action on the Landscape. The result is something like this:

Figure 10.21 – Landscape with the custom brush's Cap Shape option enabled

2. To create the terrain depression we need, you can simply move down the spline to dig the Landscape. Under the **Cap Shape** option inside the **Details** panel, we can find all the settings we need to modify the final effect:

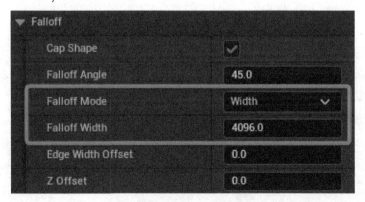

Figure 10.22 – Falloff options inside the Details panel

-   **Falloff Mode**: This option allows us to decide which criteria we want to use to modify the falloff. By default, it is set to **Angle**, which allows you to choose the angle value to generate the falloff effect. The **Width** choice is more effective and allows us to consider the width instead of an angle.

- **Falloff Width**: This value works only if we have selected the **Width** option and allows us to define the falloff value.

- **Z Offset**: This value allows us to apply an offset to the brush action on the Z axis.

By playing with the values, you can simply obtain something like this:

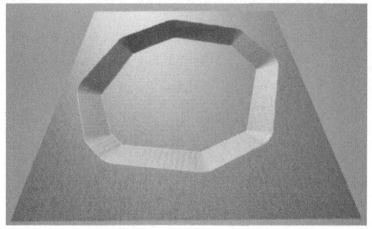

Figure 10.23 – Result at the end of step 2

3. Now, we have a raw and very geometrical shape. It is far from being realistic and credible but it is a good starting point to start adding details. We can try to make the ground less flat and generate some imperfections. To do that, we can use a **Displacement** effect. Inside the custom brush's **Details** Panel, we can search for Displacement inside the search type field.

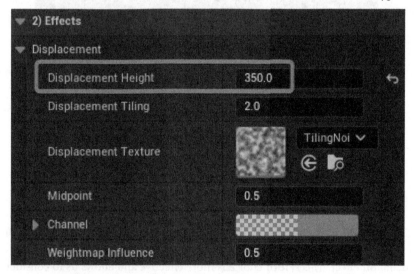

Figure 10.24 – Displacement options inside the Details Panel

By changing the **Displacement Height** value, we can increase the effect that **Displacement Texture** has on our custom brush. With the **Displacement Tiling** value, we can decide the times the texture will be repeated.

Figure 10.25 – Displacement effect

As you can see in *Figure 10.25*, the **Displacement Texture** affects only the part of the landscape inside the custom brush. That's normal because we have assigned the **Displacement** effect to our custom brush.

4. We can add more details and variations to the Landscape's parts not affected by the custom brush by duplicating this one. To duplicate the custom brush, select it inside the **Landscape** mode's **Sculpt** panel. Now that you have the custom brush selected, inside the Level Viewport, press and hold *Alt* while moving the custom brush. You can also duplicate custom brushes infinite times to create the desired effect. You can modify all the options we have already seen for each custom brush. I have duplicated it four times to obtain this effect:

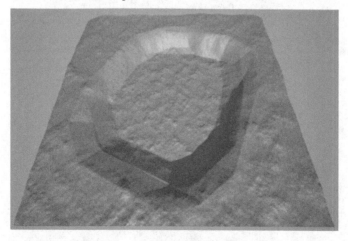

Figure 10.26 – Adding new custom brushes to make variations

5. Now it's time to start using our **Landscape** material along with the custom brushes to generate material variations in a procedural way. In other words, we want to change materials according to the custom brush's spline. First, we want to assign the **Grass** material to our first custom brush (the one we use to create the terrain depression – you should find it inside the **Outliner** tab as **Landscape_CustomBrush_Landmass_CustomBrush**). In other words, we want to allow the custom brush to paint the **Grass** material in its influence area.

To do that, search for `Paint Layers` inside the **Detail** panel's search type field. Press the + icon to add a new **Paint** layer. You need to give the layer the same name we used inside the **Landscape** material. Rename it `Grass`.

Figure 10.27 – Adding a Paint layer to our custom brush

If we expand the **Grass** layer with the arrow on the left side of the name, we can find the **Paint Layer**'s options.

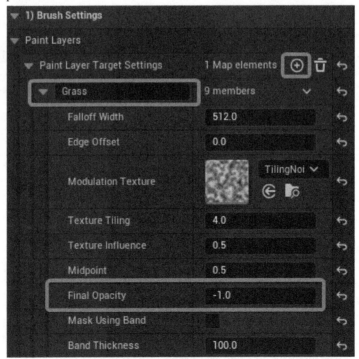

Figure 10.28 – Paint Layer's options

In order to see the **Dirt** material, we need to invert the effect of the **Paint Layer** by setting the **Final Opacity** value to -1.0. You should now see something like this:

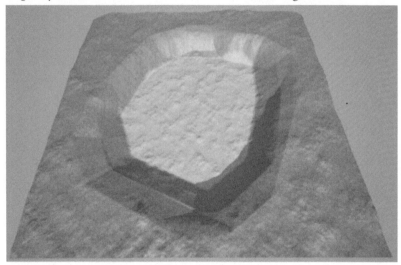

Figure 10.29 – Paint Layer result

6. What we want to achieve is to paint the most sloping parts with the **Dirt** material. To do that, we need to check the **Mask Using Band** option (see *Figure 10.28*). This option allows us to use the custom brush's spline as a rail to be followed by the **Paint Layer**.

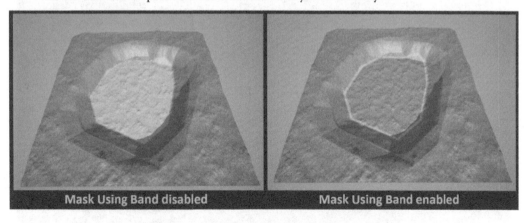

Figure 10.30 – Mask Using Band comparison image

7. To increase the thickness of the final effect, we can use the **Falloff Width** and **Edge Offset** values. **Falloff Width** increases the thickness; **Edge Offset** allows us to paint the material starting with an offset from the spline. Try to play with the values to obtain something like this:

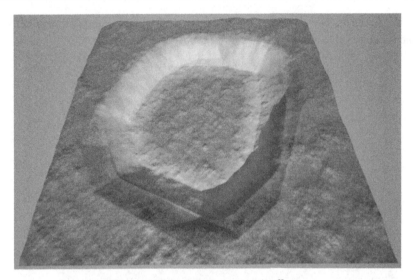

Figure 10.31 – Paint Layer result effect

We have now the steepest part painted with the **Dirt** material. To obtain the same result we can see in *Figure 10.31*, we can use these settings:

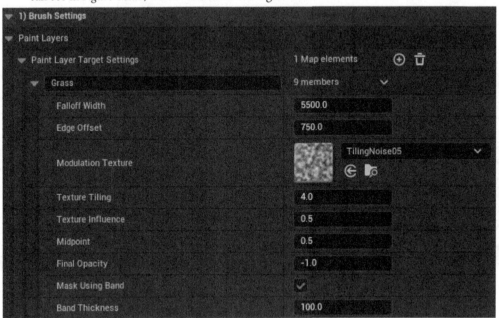

Figure 10.32 – The settings I used to obtain the result in Figure 10.31

In addition, you can also change **Modulation Texture** to obtain a different painting effect. It works like a mask.

8.   The last thing we want to add to our Landscape is a path. We can paint it with the painting tools we have already seen in *Chapter 9* or try to use custom brushes. To create a procedural path, we simply need to apply everything we have just learned in this section. To make everything more ordered, we can create a new sculpting layer and rename it `Path`.

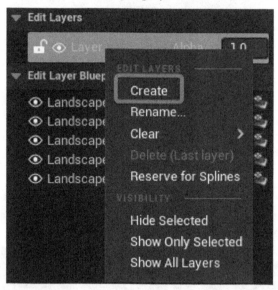

Figure 10.33 – Creating a new layer

We can add a **CustomBrush_Landmass** brush to this layer:

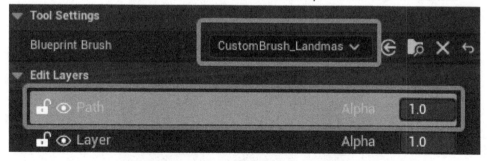

Figure 10.34 – New Path layer with CustomBrush_Landmass assigned

9.   Modify the custom brush's spline to obtain a line that you want to use as a rail of your path.

Figure 10.35 – Spline we want to use to create a path

10. Now, we need to tell the custom brush that we want to raise the Landscape only alongside the custom brush's spline. To do that, we need to change the **Brush Type** option inside the custom brush's **Details** panel to **Spline Mesh**.

Figure 10.36 – Brush type option

The result should look like this:

Figure 10.37 – The custom brush effect with the Spline Mesh option enabled

11. Now, by modifying all the settings we learned in this section, you can obtain a more natural effect. Remember that you can assign the **Grass** paint layer to this custom brush to automatically paint the **Dirt** material on the path (as we did in *Step 5*). The result should look like this:

Figure 10.38 – The final aspect of our Path layer

Perfect! We have done it! We have just created a custom brush system that allows us to procedurally sculpt our Landscape and create paths with auto material. We are now ready to learn how to add water to our scene.

Exploring the Water plugin

In this section, we will learn how to use the **Water** plugin to add a procedural water system to our scene.

The **Water** plugin is a group of tools that allows us to easily add water bodies such as lakes, rivers, and oceans to our scene. All the water bodies come with a customizable material, a realistic physic system, and a post-process volume that simulates the underwater lighting and atmosphere that allows us to create any kind of water scenario we need.

To be able to use the **Water** plugin, we need to enable it inside the **Plugins** window:

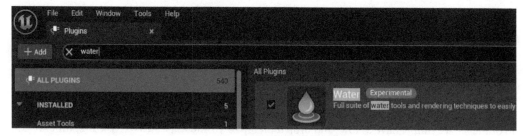

Figure 10.39 – Enabling the Water plugin

Water tools are actors that we can find inside the **Place Actors** panel. Click on the **Place Actors** panel icon and type `water` to see all the **Water** tools actors.

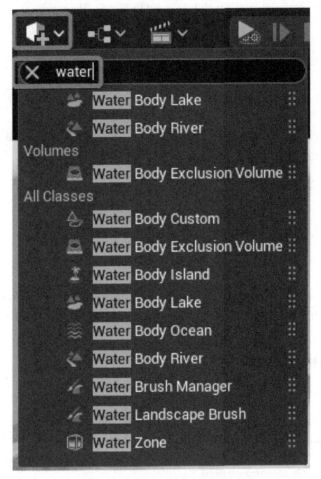

Figure 10.40 – Water tools actors inside the Place Actors panel

As you can see, the **Water** plugin provides a lot of different actors. We are going to use some of them. We want to learn how to use **Water Body Lake**, **Water Body River**, and **Water Body Ocean**. In the next sections, we'll learn more about these actors and then we will use them to improve our scene.

Using the Water Body Lake actor

In this section, we will learn how to use the **Water Body Lake** actor. To add a **Water Body Lake** actor to our level, we simply have to drag and drop it on top of a Landscape surface. The first time we add a **Water Body Lake** actor to our Landscape, it should look like this:

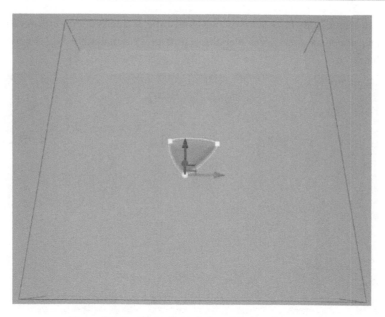

Figure 10.41 – Water Body Lake added to the scene

It works like **CustomBrush_Landmass**. We can modify its shape by modifying the spline and its points. We can move the **Water Body Lake** actor around the Landscape and it will update its influence on the surface.

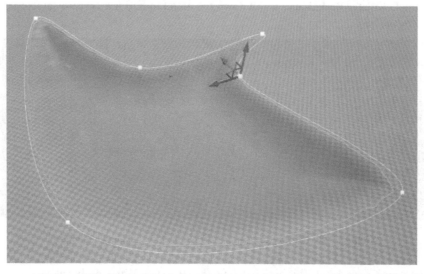

Figure 10.42 – Water Body Lake with more points and a modified shape

It already comes with customizable material and a complete physics system that simulates waves.

When we place a **Water Body Lake** actor on our Landscape, it creates an underwater shape by pulling down the surface under the water level. It applies a post-process material when you move the camera under the water level.

Figure 10.43 – Water Body Lake's underwater view

If you think that we didn't change any values or options, it looks incredible.

We can change the way the **Water Body Lake** actor changes the Landscape's surface inside the **Details** panel of **Water Body Lake**. Scroll down the menu to find the **Terrain** category, which has the following options:

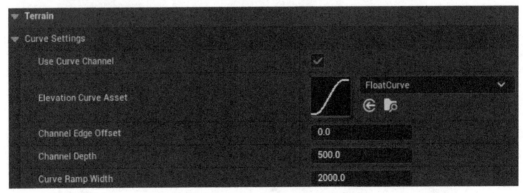

Figure 10.44 – Terrain options inside Water Body Lake's Details panel

- **Elevation Curve Asset**: This option defines the curve that **Water Body Lake** uses to pull down the Landscape under the water level. You can choose from several presets.

- **Channel Depth**: We can change the lake's depth by modifying this value.

- **Curve Ramp Width**: If we want to change the stepping level of the underwater border, we can change this value.

- **Channel Edge Offset**: This value allows us to change the distance between the spline and the sloping initial point.

The second **Water** tool we want to learn about is the **Water Body River** actor.

Using the Water Body River actor

We can add a **Water Body River** actor by dragging and dropping it on our Landscape. It works like the **Path** custom brush we created in the previous sections. **Water Body River** modifies the Landscape and adds water alongside a spline. We can move the river all around the Landscape's surface, modify the spline's points, and move the spline points to create different shapes.

If we click the **right mouse button (RMB)** on a spline's point, we have a couple of interesting options:

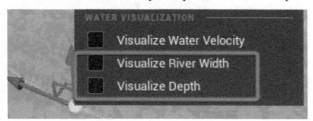

Figure 10.45 – RMB spline point's options

Visualize River Width will show a new handle that can be used to modify the width of our river directly in the Viewport.

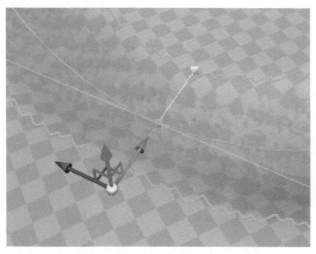

Figure 10.46 – Handle for modifying River Width

Visualize Depth will show a new handle that allows us to change the river's depth directly inside the Level Viewport.

Figure 10.47 – Handle for modifying River Depth

If you place the initial or the final spline point of **Water Body River** on the edge of **Water Body Lake**, the two actors will be automatically joined.

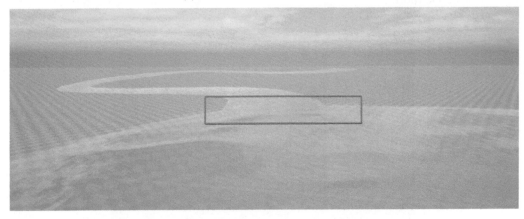

Figure 10.48 – River joined with a lake

Finally, if you move a **Water Body River** spline point on the Z axis, the river will follow the Landscape raising.

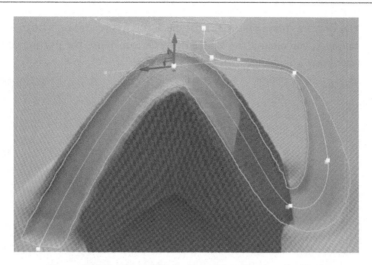

Figure 10.49 – River with a spline point raised to the Z axis

If you want more options, all the **Water Body Lake** settings we have already learned about also work for **Water Body River**.

We can now move on and learn how to use **Water Body Ocean**.

Using the Water Body Ocean actor

The last **Water** actor we want to learn about is the **Water Body Ocean** actor. As the name says, it allows us to add an ocean to our scene. It is very simple to use. As always, we need to drag and drop it from the **Place Actors** panel.

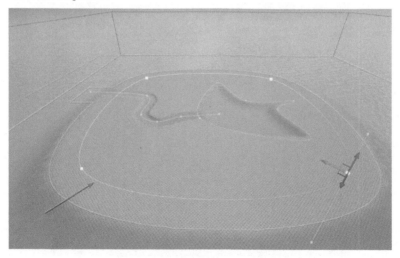

Figure 10.50 – Adding Water Body Ocean

Water Body Ocean draws a spline on the Landscape and starts rendering a huge water body from the edge of that spline. If you change the **Water Body Ocean** spline, the portion of the Landscape affected by the water body will change.

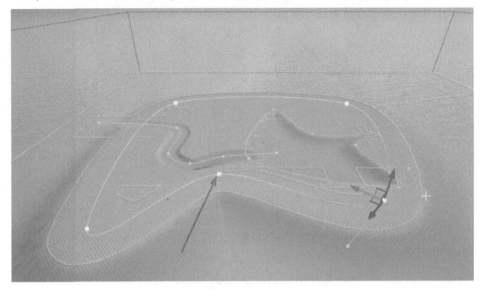

Figure 10.51 – Changing the Water Body Ocean spline

Perfect! We now know everything we need to add some water bodies to our scene. Come back to our level (the level in which we have created our Landscape and all the different custom brushes) and try to add a lake in the middle of our Landscape.

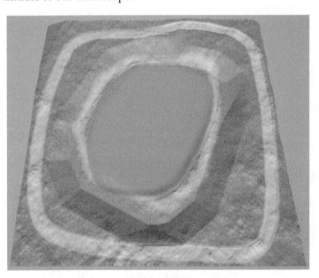

Figure 10.52 – Adding a lake to the main scene

If you move the camera under the water level, you can see that the Landscape is painted with the **Grass** material.

Figure 10.53 – How the lake looks underwater

Exactly as we saw for the custom brushes, we can tell the **Water Body Lake** spline to paint a specific layer. Underwater probably means a **Mud** material. We can add a new layer to our **Landscape** material and tell **Water Body Lake** to paint it on the Landscape.

The workflow is the same as we have already applied for the **Grass** and **Dirt** materials. You can try to add the **Mud** layer to the **Landscape** material graph yourself. Anyway, you can check the final **Material Editor** graph in *Figure 10.54*.

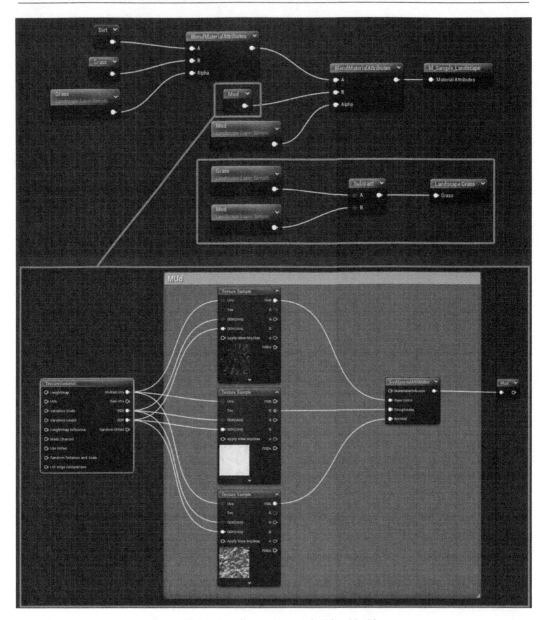

Figure 10.54 – Landscape material with a Mud layer

Next, we need to tell **Water Body Lake** that it has to paint our new **Mud** material. To do that, while we are in the selection mode, select **Water Body Lake** inside the **Outliner**, and inside the **Details** panel of **Water Body Lake**, search for `weight`.

We need to add an array to **Layer Weightmap Settings** and call it Mud (or the same name you used for the **Mud** layer inside the Material Editor):

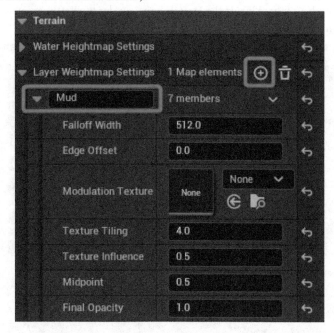

Figure 10.55 – Adding a Mud layer to Water Body Lake

Now, the lake should look like this:

Figure 10.56 – Lake with a Mud layer painted on the landscape

If the lake doesn't look like what we can see in *Figure 10.56*, it is because **Landscape_WaterBrushManager** doesn't support **Weightmap** by default. You only need to select **Landscape_WaterBrushManager** inside the **Outliner** tab and then, inside the **Details** panel, under the **Settings** category, flag the **Affect Weightmap** option. Now it should work.

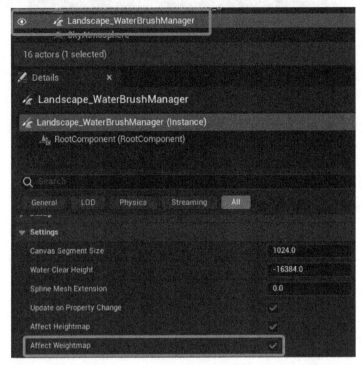

Figure 10.57 – The Affect Weightmap option

We have one more thing to learn about **Water** tools before taking a quick look at the PCG Framework. We need to learn how to modify the water's color.

Changing the water's color

The **Water** bodies have assigned a Material Instance that allows us to change several water settings, including the color. We can find the material inside the **Details** panel of each **Water Body** actor we have placed in our level under the **Rendering** category.

Figure 10.58 – Water material inside the Details panel

Before modifying it, it is a good habit to duplicate it and assign the new Material Instance to **Water Body Lake**. In this way, you will not change the Engine's water lake material and, consequently, the material for all the lakes you will create in the future.

To change the water's color, enter the Material Instance Editor by double-clicking on our new Material Instance and searching for Absorption in the search type field.

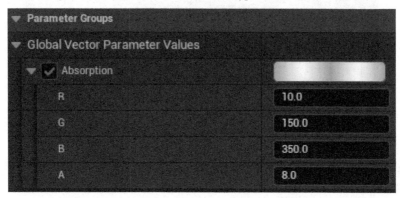

Figure 10.59 – Absorption settings inside the Material Instance editor

A clean water's color is defined by the quantity of light the water can absorb. The **Absorption** value simulates that in terms of color and quantity. The **Red (R)**, **Green (G)**, and **Blue (B)** channels define the color, and the **Alpha (A)** channel defines the quantity of absorption. The **A** channel works like a multiplier. So, if you want a result closer to the color you need, you will need to set a higher value.

The default water material looks great but it is too cartoonish for our goal. We want something more like this:

Figure 10.60 – Water Body Lake with tuned material

We have now a more realistic water color. To obtain the same result we can see in *Figure 10.60*, we can use these settings:

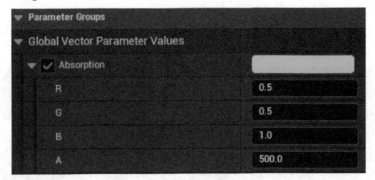

Figure 10.61 – The values I used inside the Material Instance

Perfect! We have done it! Now, we know about the **Landmass** and **Water** plugin fundamentals to create diverse environments procedurally. We have one more bonus section in this chapter that will introduce you to the power of PCG.

Introducing the Procedural Content Generation Framework

Epic Games introduced the **Procedural Content Generation Framework** (**PCG**) with Unreal Engine, version 5.2. It is a brand-new, node-based system that allows us to generate an environment procedurally. Epic Games overviews the PCG potential by distributing a sample project called **Electric Dreams**, a massive forest environment created using the PCG along with the Megascans library's assets. You can download it for free on the Unreal Engine Marketplace. You can find it at this link: `https://www.unrealengine.com/marketplace/en-US/product/electric-dreams-env?sessionInvalidated=true`.

Figure 10.62 – Electric Dreams sample project page

You can see the official presentation at this link: `https://www.youtube.com/watch?v=dYk-7byKHSRw`.

PCG should have a dedicated book because of its number of options, nodes, and all its possibilities. It can also be helpful at a low level to speed up some of the steps we have already learned in this chapter and in *Chapter 9*.

In this section, we will introduce the fundamental concepts of procedural asset placing with PCG to make our scene more live. This is going to be a demonstrative section divided into steps.

Step 1 – Creating our first PCG graph

First, we need to enable the PCG plugin. As always, we can do that inside the **Plugins** window. We need to enable **Procedural Content Generation Framework (PCG)** and **Procedural Content Generation Framework (PCG) Geometry Script Interop**. The Engine will need to be restarted to enable the PCG plugin.

Figure 10.63 – Enabling the PCG plugin

Once we have restarted the Engine, we can create the new **PCG Graph**. To create a new **PCG Graph**, click on the *RMB* inside **Content Browser** and select **PCG Graph** inside the **PCG** category. Rename it `PCG_Main`.

Figure 10.64 – Creating a new PCG graph

Place the new **PCG Graph** in the Level Viewport. This action will create a **PCG** volume in the level. It looks like a yellow empty volume.

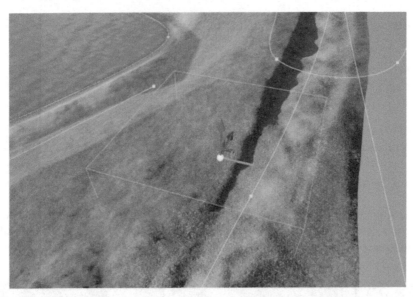

Figure 10.65 – How a PCG volume looks inside the Level Viewport

Everything we will set inside **PCG Graph** will happen inside **PCG Volume**.

If you double-click on the **PCG** graph we have just created, the **PCG Graph Editor** opens. It looks like a Material Editor.

Figure 10.66 – The PCG Graph Editor

The PCG works on a node-based system. On the left, we can find all the nodes we can add to our graph. On the right, we can find the **Details** panel that changes its content according to the selected node. In the center, we can find the **Editor** Viewport where we can build our graph.

We can add nodes in the same way we learned in *Chapter 5* for the Material Editor, by right-clicking inside the **Editor** Viewport and searching for the node name.

We are now ready to build our first graph. Try to follow these steps:

1. First, we need to tell the PCG which surface we want to use to spawn assets. To do that, expand the **Input** node with the *arrow* icon. Create a **Surface Sampler** node and connect its **Surface** input to the **Input** node's **Landscape** output.

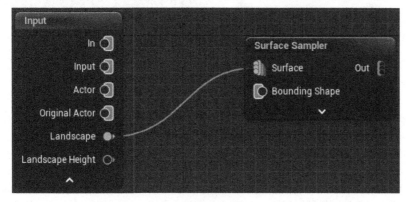

Figure 10.67 – How the PCG node graph should look

With this action, we are telling **PCG Volume** that it has to use the **Landscape** surface as the ground to place procedural assets.

2. Before adding static meshes to be spawned, we can check whether the PCG is correctly working by entering the **Debug mode**. To do that, on the Main toolbar, select **PCG_Main** in the drop-down menu. Then, select the **Surface Sampler** node and press *D* (which means "debug"). A *light blue circle* should appear in the node's top-left corner. The light blue circle on the node means that we will see the result of that node inside the **Level Viewport**.

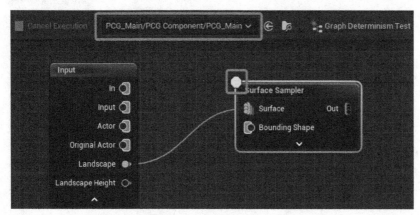

Figure 10.68 – Activating the Debug mode

3.   Save your graph and take a look at the **Level** Viewport. You should see **PCG Volume** populated by several *gray-scaled cubes*.

Figure 10.69 – PCG Debug mode inside the Level Viewport

The Debug mode is a very useful way to check that everything is going well without stressing the GPU with hundreds of assets. It is also a fast way to understand how the PCG works.

If you try to move around **PCG Volume**, you will see that all the cubes inside it will change their placement according to the landscape surface. If you try to change the **PCG Volume** scale inside the **Details** panel, the cube number will change to fill the new scale. If you set **PCG Volume** to *infinite*, it will affect the whole landscape. To set **PCG Volume** to *infinite*, we need to check the **Unbounded** option inside the **Surface Sampler** node's **Details** panel.

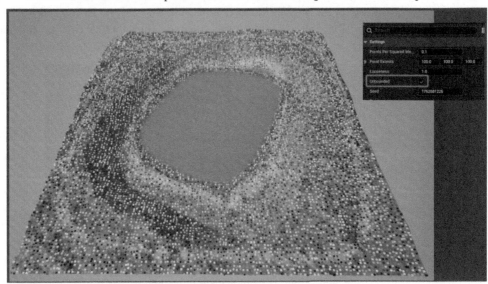

Figure 10.70 – Setting Surface Sampler to Unbounded

4. We can now come back into **PCG Graph Editor** and add some variations on our cube placement. To do that, we can create a **Transform Points** node and connect its input to the **Surface Sampler** output. Inside the **Transform Point**'s **Details** panel, we can change the **Rotation Max**, **Scale Min**, and **Scale Max** values to add some randomness to the cube placement.

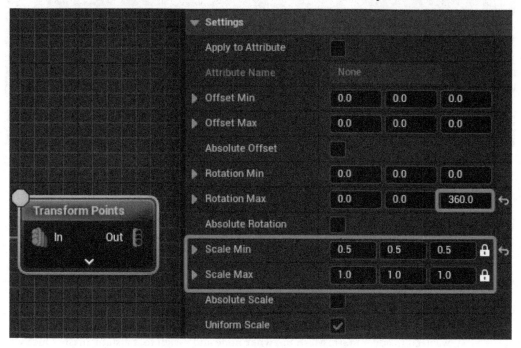

Figure 10.71 – Changing the Transform Points node's settings

This action will affect the placement of all the assets that we will place with **PCG Volume**. To check this, select the **Transform Points** node and press *D* to activate the debug visualization on it. Save and check what happened inside the **Level** Viewport.

Figure 10.72 – The result of adding a Transform Points node

Now, each of our cubes has a random scale and rotation according to the values we set inside the **Transform Points** node. Maybe we have too many cubes. We can change the density inside the **Surface Sampler** node by modifying the **Points Per Squared Meter** value.

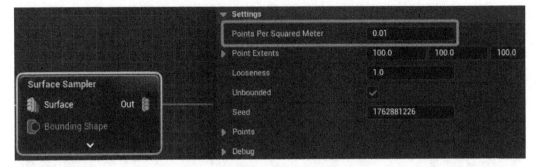

Figure 10.73 – Changing the density

The cubes that we can see when the Debug mode is enabled simulate the placement and the transformation that our static meshes will have once we assign them to the PCG Graph.

Now, it is time to place some trees on our landscape.

Step 2 – Placing trees

To place static meshes with **PCG Volume**, try to follow these steps:

1. First, we need to add a **Static Mesh Spawner** node and assign to it a static mesh. Once you have created the node, connect it to the **Transform Points** node so our trees will follow the **Transform Points** randomness information. Inside the **Static Mesh Spawner**'s **Details** panel, we can add several static meshes to be spawned. You can add them by adding an array with the + icon on the **Mesh Entries** option.

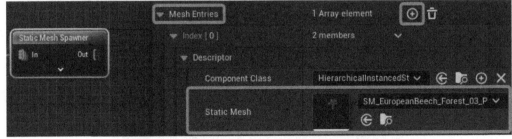

Figure 10.74 – Adding static mesh to the Static Mesh Spawner node

2. Select the **Transform Points** node and press *D* to disable the Debug mode.

3. Save and check the result inside the **Level** Viewport:

Figure 10.75 – Trees spawned on the landscape

4. The first thing we can see is that we also have trees inside our lake. We can tell **PCG Volume** to exclude **Water Body Lake** from its influence. To do that, we need a **Get Spline Data (Self)** node. This node allows us to consider a spline placed in our level to perform actions inside the PCG node graph.

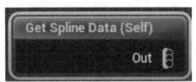

Figure 10.76 – Get Spline Data node

5. Now, we need to tell the node which *spline data* it has to consider. To do that, we need to change the **Actor Filter** option inside the node's **Details** panel to **All Word Actors**. Then we can change the **Actor Selection** option to **By Class**. This action will allow us to select the class actor that we want to consider. All the assets inside the level that are part of this specific class will be considered by the **Get Spline Data** node. In our case, we need to select **WaterBodyLake**.

Figure 10.77 – Selecting the WaterBodyLake spline inside the Get Spline Data node

6. Next, we need a **Spline Sampler** node to tell how the **Water Body Lake** spline has to be used. We want to exclude the area covered by the water – that is, the area inside the **Water Body Lake** spline. So, we need to set the **Dimension** option inside the **Spline Sampler's Details** panel to **On Interior**.

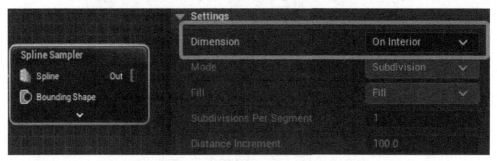

Figure 10.78 – Dimension option inside the node's Details panel

Connect the **Spline** input of **Spline Sampler** to the **Get Spline Data (Water Body Lake)** output and go on to the next step. Remember to also set **Spline Sampler** as **Unbounded** inside its **Details** panel (as we did for **Surface Sampler** – *Figure 10.70*).

7. Now we need to tell the spline that we want to use its area as a **Landscape** surface selection. So, we need to project the spline area on the **Landscape** surface. To do that, we need a **Projection** node. Once you have created it, connect the **Spline Sampler** output to the **Projection** input and the **Projection Target** input of **Projection** to the **Input** node's **Landscape** output. The node graph should look like this:

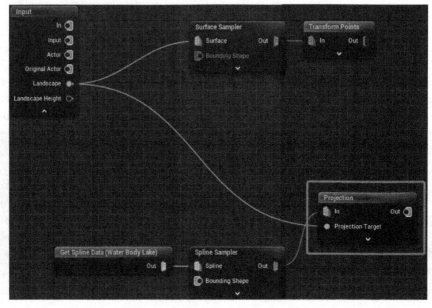

Figure 10.79 – How the node graph should look after step 7

8. To finally exclude trees from the lake, we need to add a **Difference** node. Once you have created it, inside its **Details** panel, set the **Density Function** option to **Binary** so it will consider only the two inputs we need (the **Landscape** surface and the **Water Body Lake** spline). Connect the **Source** input to **Transform Points** and the **Difference** input to the **Projection** output. To see the trees inside the **Level Viewport**, we can connect the **Difference** output to the **Static Mesh Spawner** input. The final graph should look like this:

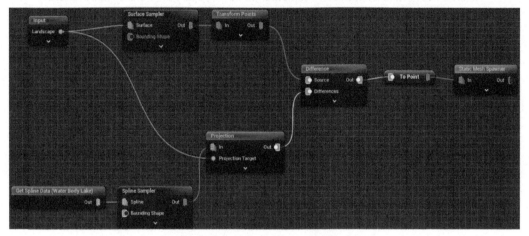

Figure 10.80 – Graph result after step 8

9. Save the graph and take a look at the **Level** Viewport:

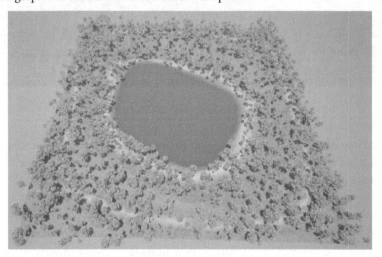

Figure 10.81 – Result inside the Level Viewport

Perfect! Now, the trees are automatically excluded from the lake's area. Now, we need to do one more thing: exclude the path.

Step 3 – Excluding the path from the PCG action

The last thing we need to change inside our PCG Graph is the fact that trees are also placed on the path. We are going to use a different method from the one we learned with the lake. Try to follow these steps:

1. To exclude the path area, we can use the painting layer we have created inside the **Landscape** material. We need to tell the PCG Graph that we want to apply the **Density** value (**Density** equal to **0** means no spawned asset) only on **Grass Paint Layer**. To do that, we can use a **Multiply** node.

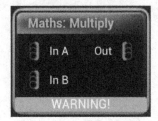

Figure 10.82 – Multiply node

We can connect both the **In A** and **In B** input to the **Difference** node's output because the **Multiply** node allows us to create custom multiplication between several different data. We can change the **Multiply** factors directly inside the node's **Details** panel.

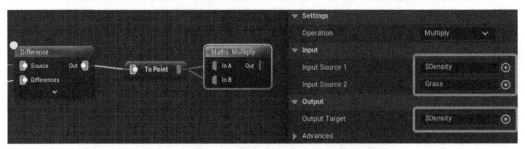

Figure 10.83 – Multiply node's Details panel

2. We need to modify **Input Source 1**, **Input Source 2**, and **Output Target** (see *Figure 10.83*). We can select an input preset by clicking on the + icons or typing the name of the input. As you can see in *Figure 10.83*, we need to multiply **Density** (you can add it to the **Input Source 1** with the + icon) per **Grass** (you can simply type it inside the **Input Source 2**'s type field – it needs to be the same name we used for the **Landscape** painting layers) to obtain a new **Density** (you can add it with the + icon) value as result.

3. Last but not least, we want the possibility to manage the resulting density. To do that, we can add a **Density Filter** node. Inside it, we can manage the resulting **Density** value.

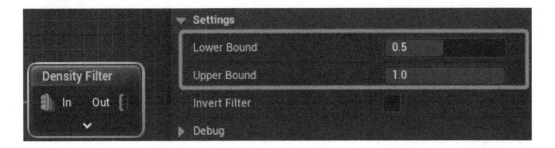

Figure 10.84 – Density Filter's options

The final graph should look like this:

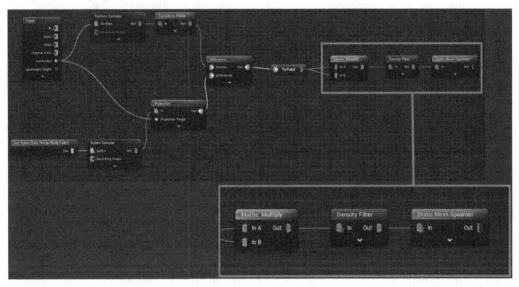

Figure 10.85 – PCG final graph

4.   Save and close the PCG Graph Editor.

We have done it! Now, your PCG Graph allows you to procedurally populate your environment with trees considering the lake and the path. It works procedurally in real time so if you try to change the size of the lake or the shape of the path, the trees will be replaced procedurally according to the new morphology of the landscape.

Obviously, the PCG Graph can be more and more complex to allow you to place a group of assets that consider different variables such as painting layers, splines, water bodies, and everything you need to create a procedural system.

In this section, we have overviewed the fundamentals of the PCG system but, by duplicating the nodes inside our graph, we can create something more complex that allows us to procedurally place not only trees but also rocks and grass.

If you want to learn more about the PCG system, you can take a look at this Epic Games showcase that explains different techniques: `https://www.youtube.com/watch?v=6JUfisUhm68`.

Perfect! You are now ready to try to create a new environment from a draft by using all the techniques we have learned in this chapter.

Exercise – Create an island environment

In this section, you have to create a new environment by using the **Landmass** and **Water** tools and PCG.

The goal is to create an environment with the following characteristics:

- A volcanic island
- A river
- A beach on one side and a cliff on the other
- Procedural foliage (using PCG to place it)

Trying to create this environment will help you to consolidate all the skills we have developed during this chapter.

Summary

In this chapter, we have learned how simple it can be to create diverse environments by using Unreal Engine 5's plugins. We started by creating an **Auto Landscape** material that could allow us to automatically paint different materials on the **Landscape** surface. We went on to introduce the **Landmass** plugin. Thanks to its custom brushes, we learned how to sculpt a landscape with a spline and how to assign different paint layers to create variations such as paths.

Next, we started adding water to our scene. After we introduced the **Water Body Lake**, **Water Body River**, and **Water Body Ocean** actors, we added a lake to our scene, and we learned how to modify the **Water** material. Last but not least, in the last section, we explored the fundamentals of the Procedural Content Generation Framework by creating a simple but useful PCG Graph.

At the end of this chapter, we closed the environment creation part and, with it, the second part of the book. We are now ready to improve our Look Development skills and discover all the tools that Unreal Engine 5 provides us with to increase the cinematic aspect of our scene. In the next chapter, we will learn how to compose a cinematic shot with **Cine Camera Actor** and **Level Sequence**.

Part 3:
Cinematic Fundamentals
and Rendering

In this final part, you will learn how to cinematically improve your environment by using the Cinematic tool inside Unreal Engine 5. First, you will learn how to compose a cinematic shot by exploring framing fundamentals and discovering how to use the Cine Camera Actor and how to animate it inside Sequencer. Then, you will move on by learning how to artistically improve your frame with a postprocess volume. You will also learn about the basic concept of Niagara by creating a sample atmospheric effect. In the last chapter, you will learn how to export a high-resolution sequence with the rendering tool provided to us by Unreal Engine 5.

This part has the following chapters:

- *Chapter 11, Crafting Cinematic Shots with Cameras and Sequencer*

- *Chapter 12, Enhancing Scenes with Post-Processing and Niagara*

- *Chapter 13, Rendering and Exporting Cinematic Shots*

11
Crafting Cinematic Shots with Cameras and a Sequencer

Starting from this chapter, we will enter the final part of our book. After we have learned everything about the environment creation process, it is now time to learn how to represent it in a more cinematographic way. In this chapter, we will learn how to create and set up a **Cine Camera Actor** and how to create a **Level Sequence**. We will use a **Sequencer** inside Unreal Engine 5 to animate a shot. We will also learn how to create a simple Blueprint to add a camera shake effect to our camera and how to combine multiple shots.

We will cover the following topics in this chapter:

- Creating a Cine Camera Actor and exploring its settings
- Discovering the Sequencer
- Animating the Cine Camera Actor
- Creating a **Camera Shake Blueprint**
- Combining multiple shots

By the end of this chapter, we will be able to use a Cine Camera Actor, compose a frame, animate a camera into the Sequencer, and edit complex cinematic shots directly inside the Unreal Engine.

Technical requirements

In this chapter, we will use the Megascans Abandoned Apartment project that we used in *Chapter 6*. To easily follow the chapter, you should have it opened on your workstation.

Creating a Cine Camera Actor and exploring its settings

Until now in this book, we have created everything through the technical eyes of the Engine's default camera; and that was the correct thing to do because we were studying all the different techniques we need to craft environments. But now, it's time to valorize our work by seeing it through the eyes of a Cine Camera Actor and understand how to use it to frame a portion of our environment.

A Cine Camera Actor is a digitalization of a real-life camera that simulates all the different settings and physical characteristics that a real-life camera has.

We can create a Cine Camera Actor in a couple of different ways:

- We can find **Cine Camera Actor** inside the **Place Actor** panel under the **Cinematic** category.

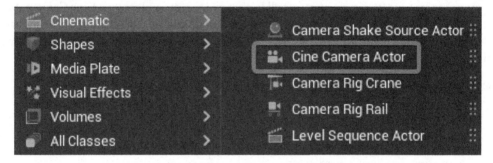

Figure 11.1 – Cine Camera Actor inside the Place Actor Panel

By clicking on the **Cine Camera Actor** entry, the Engine will add the Cine Camera Actor at a random position in the world. You can also drag and drop the Cine Camera Actor in the position you want the camera to be created.

- Another way to create a Cine Camera Actor is to use the **Create Camera Here** command inside the Level Viewport's sandwich menu icon.

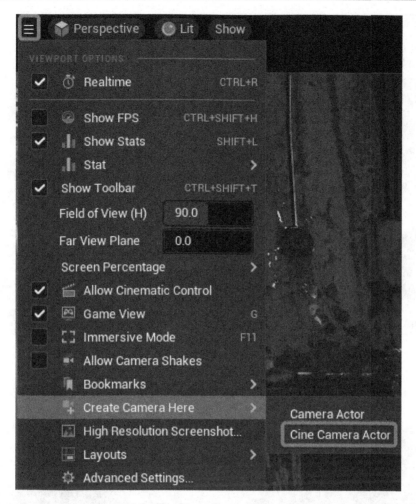

Figure 11.2 – The Create Camera Here command

This command will create a Cine Camera Actor in the same position as the Engine's default camera at the moment you have performed the command.

A Cine Camera Actor looks like this inside the Level Viewport:

Figure 11.3 – The Cine Camera Actor inside the Level Viewport

If you select **Cine Camera Actor**, the Engine will show you a preview of what the Cine Camera Actor is seeing.

Figure 11.4 – Camera preview inside the Level Viewport

We can move the Cine Camera Actor in the exact same way we can move all the actors we have learned about in the previous chapters. If you try to move or rotate the Cine Camera Actor, the **camera preview** will change in real time.

Figure 11.5 – Camera preview changes according to the new Cine Camera Actor's position

> **Note**
>
> When you use the **Create Camera Here** command, you can choose between **Cine Camera Actor** and **Camera Actor** (*Figure 11.2*). Take care to use the **Cine Camera Actor** option instead of the **Camera Actor** option. The second one has different options, and it is more appropriate for technical stuff than a Cine Camera Actor, which is built to be used to craft cinematic shots.

The Level Viewport's camera preview is useful for checking what our Cine Camera Actor is seeing but is far from being a good tool for framing. To make the Level Viewport show what the Cinema Camera Actor is seeing, we can enter the **Pilot Cine Camera Actor** mode. To do that, we have to click on the **Viewport Mode** menu in the top left side of the Level Viewport and select which **CinemaCameraActor** we want to see through.

Figure 11.6 – PLACED CAMERAS inside the Viewport Mode menu

If you have more than one Cine Camera Actor in your Level, you will find all the cameras ordered inside the **Viewport Mode** menu under the **PLACED CAMERAS** category.

Once you have done this, the **Pilot Actor: CineCameraActor** banner appears on the top-left side of the Level Viewport.

Figure 11.7 – The Pilot Actor banner

That means that we are piloting the Cine Camera Actor that we have selected. By default, the Engine allows you to pilot the camera without seeing through its eyes. That means that we are still using the Engine's default camera to see the Level but our movement in the Viewport will move the Cine Camera Actor we are piloting.

To see through the Cine Camera Actor we are piloting, we have to click on the camera icon inside the **Pilot Actor** banner.

Figure 11.8 – Enter the camera view

By enabling this command, you should now see through the eyes of the Cine Camera Actor while you are piloting it. The Level Viewport should look like what we can see in *Figure 11.9*, with two black boxes on both sides of the Viewport.

Figure 11.9 – The Level Viewport when we see through a camera

To exit the piloting mode, we need to click on the triangle icon inside the **Pilot Actor** banner.

Figure 11.10 – Exit the Pilot Actor mode

> **Note**
> Remember that if you are in the **Pilot Actor** mode but the camera icon is disabled (so it is not blue), you are still piloting the camera and changing its position. This action could make you lose the camera position you are working on. So, a good habit to get into is to always use the **Pilot Actor** mode with the camera icon enabled (blue) to be sure to see through the camera while you are moving it and exit the **Pilot Camera** mode every time you need to do something different from moving your camera. This will ensure you do not lose the camera position.

There is one more important thing to learn before we start to explore all of the camera's settings. Inside the **Viewport Mode** menu (the same where we can find all the Camera Cinema Actors placed on Level), we can activate **Cinematic Viewport**.

Figure 11.11 – Enable Cinematic Viewport

By using **Cinematic Viewport**, we can improve the cameras and cinematic works. The Cinematic Viewport has two main differences from the default Viewport. The first is that when the **Cinematic Viewport** option is enabled, what we see inside the Level Viewport will consider the sensor size of the camera (we will learn more about this in a couple of pages). In other words, the Viewport will show us only what the camera can see in the same proportion we will have with the rendered images.

Figure 11.12 – Cinematic Viewport enabled

Second, at the bottom side of the Level Viewport, we will be able to see the playback options and some more interesting notions. Now, we can't see anything instead of a message because we don't have yet a Sequencer in our scene. We will learn more about the Sequencer during the *Discovering the Sequencer* section in this chapter.

Perfect! Now that we know how to place a Cine Camera Actor and visualize the Viewport through its eyes, we can move on and explore the camera settings.

Exploring the Cine Camera Actor settings

In this section, we will explore the most useful Cine Camera Actor settings.

As for all the types of actors we have already learned about, we can find all the Cine Camera Actor's settings inside the **Details** panel.

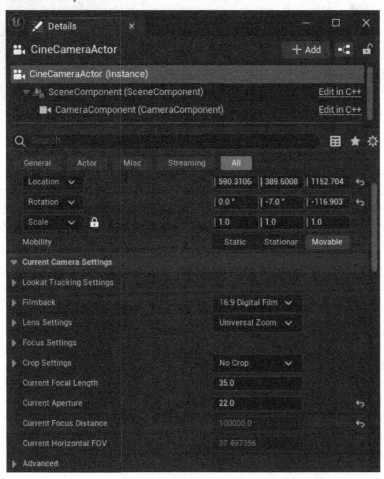

Figure 11.13 – Camera settings inside the Detail panels

Inside the **Details** panel, we can find a variety of settings divided into several categories. We will focus on the options that allow us to reproduce real-life cameras. You can find all of these settings under the **Current Camera Settings** category.

For a learning process purpose, we are going to explore the settings in a different order from the one in which they are listed inside the **Details** panel. The first thing we need to talk about is the **Filmback** option.

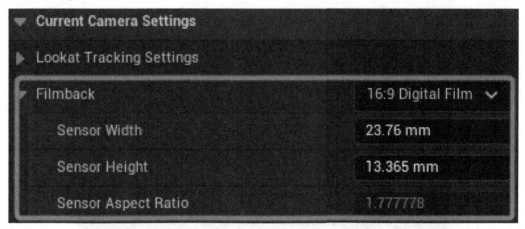

Figure 11.14 – The Filmback options

Filmback identifies the sensor of the camera. If you change it, the shape of the final frame will change. You can browse between different presets inside the drop-down menu or set a custom sensor size with the **Sensor Width** and **Sensor Height** values. When you switch from a **Filmback** preset to another, the **Sensor Width** and **Sensor Height** values will change automatically to show you the actual size of the sensor.

Figure 11.15 – Different Filmback settings

There are two very important things we need to understand about the Cine Camera Actor's **Filmback** setting:

- When we change the size of the camera's sensor, we are physically changing the surface of the light hit inside the camera to record the frame. That means that the bigger or smaller black parts around the frame in the Level Viewport are not overlayed black boxes.

- According to the previous point, changing the sensor size means changing any correlated aspect of the camera. If we change the sensor size, we are also changing the way the lens of the camera interprets the scene. The three examples in *Figure 11.16* have been taken with a 35 mm lens mounted on the camera (we will learn how to change that in a minute). The same lens but different sensor size will generate three totally different effects.

Assuming these two points, the first thing we need to do when we decide to compose a new frame is to choose the sensor size. It's like choosing the camera model we want to use to shoot our movie. We can choose from the presets or create a custom one. For instance, we can search on the web for the size of a RED camera and input the values into the Filmback option to simulate the real-life camera settings. We are going to use an ultrawide custom value (*Figure 11.17*).

Figure 11.16 – Sensor Width set to 54 mm, and Sensor Height set to 23 mm

Once we have chosen the camera model by changing the **Filmback** settings, we can move on and choose the lens we want to mount on our Cine Camera Actor. To do that, we need to explore the **Lens Settings** options.

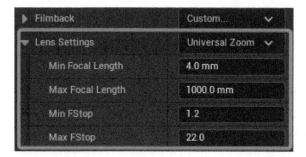

Figure 11.17 – The Lens Settings options

As always, we can choose to use a lens preset by selecting one inside the drop-down menu. If you change the mounted lens, the frame that you see inside the Level Viewport will change.

Figure 11.18 – Different lens presets

By default, the **Lens Settings** option is set to **Universal Zoom** and, unless you specifically want to use one of the present presets for some reason, it is the set you should use. It works like a real-life zoom lens but it's virtually infinite, which means that you can use it to simulate any kind of lens present in the preset list and real life. To do so, we have four different values. **Min Focal Length** and **Max Focal Length** define the minimum and maximum **focal length** values you can use.

Focal length is a fundamental concept in photography and optics that refers to the distance between the lens of a camera and the image sensor or film when the lens is focused at infinity. It is usually measured in millimeters. The focal length of a lens determines how much of the scene will be captured in the final image and influences the magnification and perspective.

In simpler terms, a shorter focal length (18 mm) captures a wider scene, making objects appear smaller and fitting more into the frame. On the other hand, a longer focal length (200 mm) zooms in on a smaller portion of the scene, making objects appear larger and closer together.

In summary, focal length is a key factor in shaping how your photos will look, influencing both the field of view and the apparent size of objects in your images.

The other two values are **Min Fstop** and **Max Fstop**. These settings allow us to define the minimum and the maximum **aperture** value that our lens can reach.

Aperture is an important concept in photography that refers to the opening in a camera lens through which light passes to enter the camera. It's like the pupil of your eye, controlling the amount of light that reaches the camera's sensor or film. Aperture is measured in **f-stops**.

One important thing to keep in mind is that if you change those values, what you are seeing inside the Level Viewport doesn't change. The reason for this is that we are changing the general lens specifications and not the focal length or the aperture we want to use. To decide which focal length we want to use, we have to scroll a little bit down in the **Details** panel and search for **Current Focal Length**.

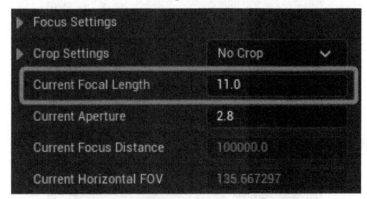

Figure 11.19 – The Current Focal Length value

Current Focal Length defines the focal length we want to use to shoot our scene. In other words, this value defines the lens we want to use. For instance, if you are working with a director who tells you to use an 85 mm lens, the only thing you need to do is to set the **Current Focal Length** value to 85. The value limit is defined by the **Min Focal Length** and **Max Focal Length** values we have just learned about.

Figure 11.20 – Camera Current Focal Length set to 85 mm

As we can see in *Figure 11.21*, we have a problem with the focus point. We have a couple of options to adjust the Cine Camera Actor's focus, and we can find them under the **Focus Settings** category inside the Cinema Camera Actor's **Details** panel.

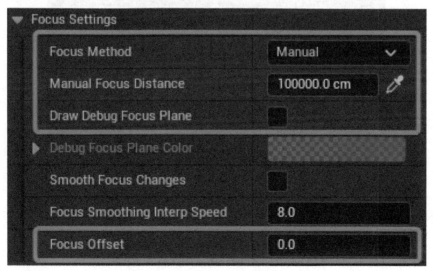

Figure 11.21 – Focus Settings

Let's take a look at what we can do with **Focus Settings**:

- **Focus Method**: This drop-down menu allows us to choose the focus method we want to use for the selected camera. By default, it is set to **Manual**, which allows us to have full control of our focus settings. We are not interested in any other options because we want to have the ability to manage our focus in the way we want.

- **Manual Focal Distance**: This value allows us to define the focus point of the camera. Everything at a distance from the camera defined by the **Manual Focal Distance** value will always be in focus. Starting from the point defined by the **Manual Focal Distance** value, everything will gradually go out of focus.

- **Draw Debug Focus Plane**: This very useful option, if enabled, will show us the focus point defined by the **Manual Focal Distance** value by drawing a purple plane inside the Level Viewport.

Figure 11.22 – Draw Debug Focus Plane enabled inside the Level Viewport

- **Focus Offset**: This value allows us to shift the focus point defined by the **Manual Focal Distance** value in the space.

Perfect! We have already learned how to set our camera in terms of parameters and how to change its lens and focus point. However, we still don't know how to choose how out of focus the out-of-focus part of our frame should be. To manage this, we need to change the **Current Aperture** value. We can find it under the **Current Focal Length** value we have just learned about.

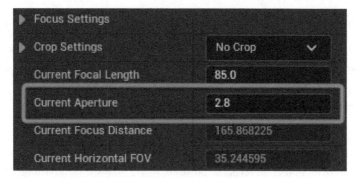

Figure 11.23 – The Current Aperture setting

The **Current Aperture** value allows us to change the quantity of light that can enter the lens. In Unreal Engine, a variation of this value means a focus variation. So, the lower the **Current Aperture** value, the higher the out-of-focus strength. Take a look at the environment part behind the spheres in *Figure 11.25*:

Figure 11.24 – Different Current Aperture values comparison

Great! These are the settings we need to know to set our Cine Camera Actor to simulate a real-life camera.

We are now ready to discover how to animate our camera. To do that, we need to know more about what a Sequencer is and how to use it.

Discovering the Sequencer

In this section, we will learn what a Sequencer is and how to use it to animate simple objects. To understand what a Level Sequence, is we need to define what an animation is. Animating means changing the status of an object, in terms of position, rotation, scale, or anything else, over time.

To be able to modify something over time, we need a **Timeline**. Inside Unreal Engine 5, we don't have a fixed **Timeline** as we can find inside an editing software such as Adobe Premier or Blackmagic DaVinci Resolve, or inside a 3D animation software such as Autodesk Maya. Inside Unreal Engine 5, **Timeline**s are assets that we can create several times. These **Timeline** assets are called Level Sequence.

To create a Level Sequence, we can use different methods:

- Inside the main toolbar, we can click on the ciak icon and select **Add Level Sequence**.

Figure 11.25 – Add Level Sequence command inside the Main Tool Bar

This action will open the **Save Asset As** window to allow us to save the new Level Sequence. A good habit to get into is to create a dedicated folder for all the Level Sequences we will create in our project and call it Cinematics.

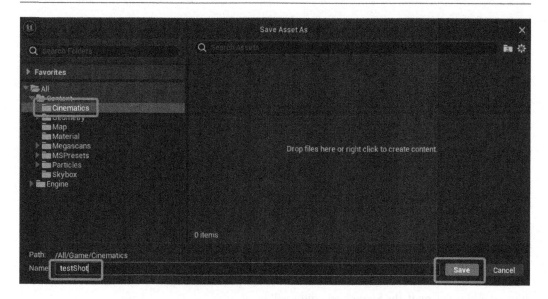

Figure 11.26 – The Save Asset As window for the Level Sequence

Click on the **Save** button to create your Level Sequence.

- Another way to create a new Level Sequence is by right-clicking inside the **Content Browser** and under the **Cinematics** category, select **Level Sequence**.

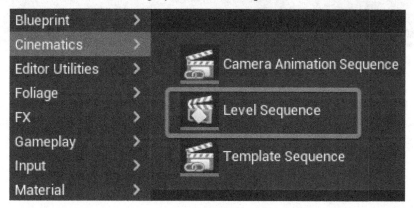

Figure 11.27 – Creating a Level Sequence from the RMB menu inside the Content Browser

Both methods will create an actor in the **Content Browser** that looks like this:

Figure 11.28 – Level Sequence actor

If you double-click on it, the **Sequencer** editor will open.

Figure 11.29 – The Sequencer editor

Opening the **Sequencer** editor will also change what we can see in the Viewport (only if we have **Cinematic Viewport** enabled as we saw during the *Creating a Cine Camera Actor and exploring its settings* section in this chapter).

Figure 11.30 – Playback options

Perfect! We can start to explore what we can do inside the **Sequencer** editor. The top part of the **Sequencer** editor is occupied by a toolbar.

Figure 11.31 – The Sequencer editor's toolbar

The following part will be an overview of what we can find inside the **Sequencer** editor's toolbar:

- The first group of tools allows us to save (the floppy disk icon) our Level Sequence (this command will also create a screenshot of the Viewport to be used as a thumbnail of the Level Sequence inside the **Content Browser**). The folder icon with the magnifying glass allows us to select the Level Sequence we are modifying inside the **Content Browser**; the camera icon allows us to directly create a Cine Camer Actor inside our Level Sequence (we will learn how to add our Cine Camera Actor to the Level Sequence during the next section). Finally, the ciak icon will open the rendering window (we will learn everything about rendering in *Chapter 13*).

- The second group contains several options divided into three different menus. If we click on the wrench icon, we have access to the **Actions** menu. Here, we can find some general options such as the **Save As** option, **Import** and **Export** options, and some animation transformation options, such as the **Trim** option and the **Stretch** option. We don't need to know more about that for now. The next icon hides the View Options menu (eye icon). Inside this menu, we can find general visibility options to customize what we want to see inside our Sequencer. The gear icon gives you access to the **Playback** options.

- The third group brings together all the options we need to manage keyframes. The first tool (the rhombus icon) allows us to change the keyframe type (we will learn more about this topic in the next section). The second one (the rhombus icon with a key inside) enables or disables the autokey function. This function, if enabled, will automatically add keyframes on each action you perform. Finally, the horseshoe icon enables and disables snaps inside the **Timeline**.

- The four icons of the **Sequencer** toolbar allow us to change the **Timeline framerate**. The **Timeline** frame rate allows us to set how many frames we need to cover one second of animation. Its unit is **frame per second (FPS)**.

- The last icon opens the Curve Editor, which manages animation curves.

Moving down, we have the **Timeline** on the right side. On the left side is the space where we can add assets to our Level Sequence to be animated. On the bottom of the **Sequencer** window, we have the playback command on the left and a gray bar on the right, which allows us to zoom in or zoom out on the **Timeline**.

Figure 11.32 – The Sequencer sections

Great! We are now ready to learn how to animate an object using the Sequencer.

First, we need to add an object to our Level Sequence. To do that, drag and drop an asset from the **Outliner** panel, which is on the left side of the **Sequencer** editor:

Figure 11.33 – Adding a cube to the Sequencer

We can also add an object to the Sequencer by using the + **Track** button (*Figure 11.35*). If you click on the + **Track** button, you can choose from several actors dedicated to the Sequencer or choose the **Actor to Sequencer** option, which allows us to add all the assets we can find inside the **Outliner** panel. If you have one or more objects selected the **Add "asset name"** option will add the selected objects.

Figure 11.34 – + Track menu inside the Sequencer editor

Nice! All we need to do now is animate our cube! As we can see in *Figure 11.35*, under the **Cube** line inside the **Sequencer** window we can find a **Transform** line. While the **Transform** line is selected, press *Enter* on the keyboard. A keyframe should appear.

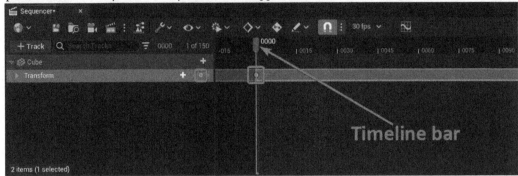

Figure 11.35 – Adding a keyframe

We can also add a keyframe by clicking on the keyframe icon on the right side of the **Transform** line (*Figure 11.37*).

The keyframe will always be placed at the time defined by the **Timeline** bar position (*Figure 11.37*).

The keyframe we have just placed will be the starting position of our cube animation. Now, move forward to the **Timeline** bar, then move the cube and place another keyframe. It is very important to do these actions in the following order:

1. Move the **Timeline** bar.
2. Move the cube.
3. Place a keyframe.

If we don't follow this order and move the cube first, when you move the **Timeline** bar, the cube will return to the initial frame position. This happens because the initial frame is the only frame the cube has in the **Timeline** so it must keep the position saved on that initial keyframe.

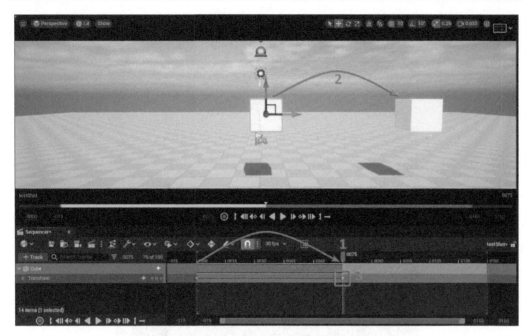

Figure 11.36 – Three steps to correctly animate the cube

If you have done everything in the correct way, by moving the **Timeline** bar, you should see the cube move inside the Level Viewport.

You can also play the animation by using the playback tool, which you can find at the bottom-left side of the **Sequencer** window and the bottom side of the Level Viewport (if you have **Cinematic Viewport** enabled).

Figure 11.37 – Playback tools

Now, try to add a keyframe in the middle of the two keyframes we have just created to make the cube go up. The animation will automatically change thanks to the Engine's interpolation work.

Figure 11.38 – Adding another keyframe to the cube's movement

By adding a keyframe to the **Transform** line, we are adding a keyframe to all the basic **Cube** transformations such as **Location**, **Rotation**, and **Scale**. If you explode the **Transform** line by clicking on the left-side arrow, you can find all the transformations. Again, you can explode any single transformation to show the three axes.

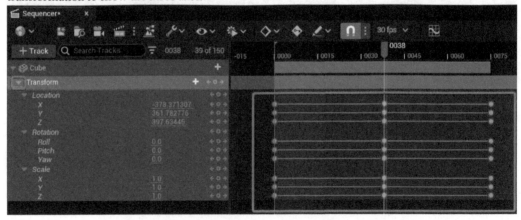

Figure 11.39 – Exploded view of the Transform keyframes

By selecting a single transformation such as **Location**, you can add a keyframe only to the Location axis (**X**, **Y**, or **Z**). By selecting a single **Location** axis (such as **X**), you will add a keyframe only to that axis.

Now, the cube should move by following the curve that the Engine has drawn inside the Level Viewport (*Figure 11.40*). That curve shows us how the keyframes we have placed inside the Sequencer will change the cube's status (in our case, the position inside the world).

If we play the animation, we should notify that the cube's movement speeds up as far as it is from a keyframe and slows down when it reaches a new keyframe. This effect that changes the velocity of our cube's animation is called **ease in** and **ease out** and it is determined by the types of keyframes we set inside the Sequencer. Different keyframe types mean different curves are drawn in the Level Viewport, hence different speed movements.

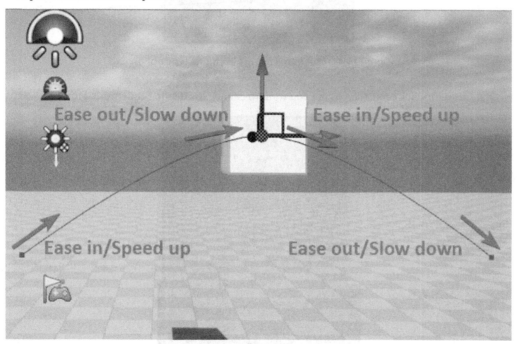

Figure 11.40 – Ease in and ease out explanation image

To change the keyframe type, we can use the keyframe option menu inside the **Sequencer** toolbar.

Figure 11.41 – Keyframe menu's keyframe type options

Or, you can right-click on the keyframe you want to change inside the Sequencer's **Timeline**.

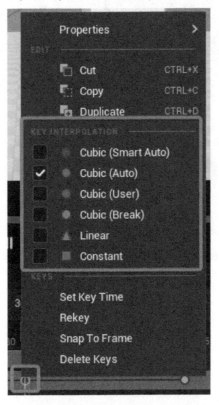

Figure 11.42 – Keyframe options inside the Sequencer's Timeline

When you change the keyframe type from the toolbar's menu, you are changing the default keyframe type that the Engine uses. When you use the *RMB* keyframe option menu inside the Sequencer's **Timeline**, you are changing only the selected keyframe. Once you change the keyframe type, the keyframe icon inside the Sequencer's **Timeline** will change accordingly.

We have several different types of keyframes we can use (*Figure 11.44*). We are interested in the following:

- **Cubic (Auto)**: This is the default keyframe type. It creates a keyframe that generates a curve (*Figure 11.40* and *Figure 11.41*). That means that the animation between two or more keyframes will always be defined by a curve that has an ease in and an ease out effect.

- **Linear**: If we want an animation that always maintains the same velocity, we need to use a **Linear** keyframe type. The animation between **Linear** keyframes will always generate a line instead of a curve. This will prevent the ease in and ease out effect generation.

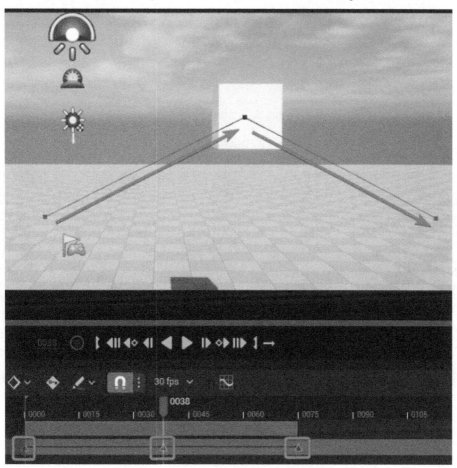

Figure 11.43 – A Linear keyframe example image

- **Constant**: This keyframe type allows us to preserve the animated object status until the next keyframe. This means that the cube will preserve the first keyframe position until the second one. When the **Timeline** bar reaches the second keyframe, the cube will instantly change its position.

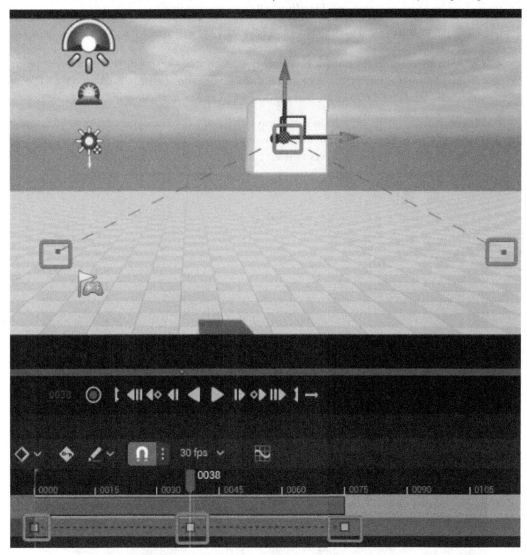

Figure 11.44 – A Constant keyframe example image

We can combine different keyframe types to obtain several animation results.

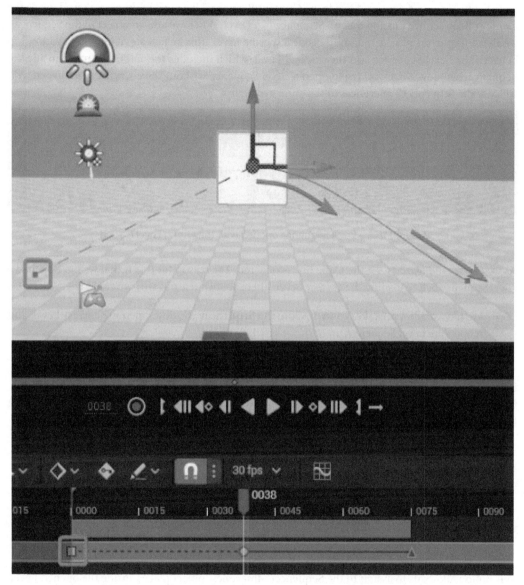

Figure 11.45 – Multiple keyframe types on the same animation curve

There is one more important thing that we need to know about the Sequencer and Level Sequences. Level Sequence is an actor saved inside the **Content Browser**. Like most of the actors saved inside the **Content Browser**, we can add a Level Sequence to a Level. When we add an object to the Sequencer, we are adding actors placed and saved inside a specific Level. This fact creates a univocal relationship between the Level Sequence and the original Level, which includes the actors animated inside the **Sequencer** window. So, if you try to open a Level Sequence without the correct Level opened, you will lose the Sequencer's references to the animated actors.

Figure 11.46 – Level Sequence opened with the wrong Level loaded

As we can see in *Figure 11.49*, the **Cube** line is now red. The reason for this is that we have opened a Level Sequence before loading the correct Level. There are two reasons why we could have done this:

- We have made a mistake. To fix it, close the **Sequencer** window, open the correct Level, and reopen the Level Sequence.

- We want to use the animation inside the Level Sequence with actors placed in another Level.

If we find ourselves in the second situation, we can fix the actor's wrong reference error (in our case, **Cube**), by right-clicking on the red line inside the **Sequencer** window (*Figure 11.48*) and selecting the **Assign Actor** option.

Figure 11.47 – The Assign Actor option inside the Sequencer

This option allows us to assign to the Sequencer's line a new object placed inside the opened Level. The object will inherit all of the keyframes existing inside the Sequencer. This action could be very useful when we want to migrate our Level Sequence to another project, or we want to create a copy of the Level Sequence to create some tests in another Level.

Perfect! Now we know how to animate an object inside the Sequencer. It's quite simple, so we can move on and start animating our Cine Camera Actor.

Animating the Cine Camera Actor

In this section, we will learn how to animate a Cine Camer Actor to create dynamic shots inside your environment. This is going to be a practical section. We are going to use the Megascans Abandoned Apartment project to make it easier for everyone to follow all the steps. We already used it in *Chapter 6*. You can also use the environment you should have created at the end of *Chapter 8* or the end of *Chapter 10*.

To animate a Cine Camera Actor, we don't have to use any different techniques we learned about during the *Discovering the Sequencer* section.

Try to replicate all the following steps (divided into sections) to create your first environment shot.

Placing the Cine Camera Actor

First, we need to create a Cine Camera Actor and a Level Sequence. Try to follow the following steps:

1. Create a Cine Camera Actor and rename it C_shot01.

2. Create a Level Sequence and rename it Scene01.

   The idea behind this naming convention is to create a Level Sequence that will include multiple shots. For this reason, the Level Sequence has the name of the scene, and the camera has the name of the shot.

3. Enable **Cinematic Viewport** (if you don't remember how to do this, you can check the *Creating a Cine Camera Actor and exploring its settings* section of this chapter).

4. Add the Cine Camera Actor to the Level Sequence we have just created. The Level Sequence should look like this:

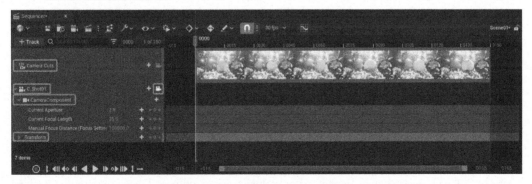

Figure 11.48 – Sequencer with a Cine Camera Actor inside

As we can see in *Figure 11.48*, a Cine Camera Actor will enter the Sequencer with more than just the **Transform** line. Under the **C_Shot01** line, we also have a line called **CameraComponent**, which allows us to animate the camera's options we learned about during the *Creating a Cine Camera Actor and exploring its settings* section. By default, we can animate **Current Aperture**, **Current Focal Length**, and **Manual Focal Distance**. Obviously, the **Transform** line is present and allows us to animate the movement of our camera.

The camera icon on the **C_Shot01** line's right side allows us to enable or disable the **Pivot Actor** option, which we saw during the *Creating a Cine Camera Actor and exploring its settings* section.

Finally, adding a Cine Camera Actor to our Sequencer will automatically create Camera Cuts. Camera Cuts is the recording of what the camera is seeing inside the Level Viewport. We will learn more about this during the *Combining multiple shots* section of this chapter.

5. Choose the **Timeline frame rate**. As we saw before, we can change it with the second tool from the right inside the **Sequencer** toolbar. It is very important to set the frame rate before starting any kind of animation to avoid synchronization problems. The frame rate defines how many frames we need to cover one second of animation. If we change it later, the animation length will progressively change.

Figure 11.49 – Frame rate settings

We can leave it at 30 fps.

> **Note**
>
> Choosing the correct frame rate is very important. A different frame rate means a different animation speed. In other words, a lower FPS value means a lower number of frames needed to cover one second inside the **Timeline**. If we need a lower number of images to cover one second of animation, we will need less time to cover one second of animation. So, our animation will be shorter in terms of total time. On the other side, a higher FPS value will make our animation slower. In other words, with a higher FPS value, we can create a slow-motion effect.

Perfect! We are now ready to compose the starting point of our shot.

Framing the start and end points of the shot

There are different ways to build a dynamic shot to show our environment. One of the simplest is trying to compose the starting frame and then the ending frame without taking care of the intermediate frames. Having a good initial point, an idea of duration and a well-framed final shot is a more than good starting point for crafting a nice environment shot.

But how we can create a good frame? What are the rules that we need to follow to craft a balanced shot? We are going to overview them in the next section.

Exploring framing fundamentals for an environment shot

In this section, we will overview the fundamentals of framing with an eye-to-environment shot.

The composition of a good frame passes through two different main aspects: first, the choice of the correct lens to give our shot the correct depth of field by changing the focus point and the placement of the camera, considering the position of our subject or subjects.

Talking about the lens, there are three main shot types: **wide shot**, **medium shot**, and **close up shot**. Their names refer to the size of the subject within the frame. In other words, how close the camera is to the subject.

Figure 11.50 – Different types of shots in the same environment

Each of these different types of shots is usually referred to as a class of lenses that are commonly adopted for that specific shot type. This is only a convention, not a rule, but knowing it is a good starting point.

When we are planning to compose a wide shot, we can use a lens with a **Focal Length** value between 20 mm to 40 mm. This will allow us to see a huge object through the camera's eyes. For a medium shot, we can use a lens with a **Focal Length** value between 35 mm to 85 mm (with a value nearer to 85 mm used when we want the background to be out of focus). Finally, a lens with a **Focal Length** value starting from 80 mm can be a good lens for a close-up shot. In the case of a close-up shot, it depends a lot on the size of the subjects. A human face is a different size from an insect that is larger than a group of skin pores that should probably need a lens with a 300 mm focal length value to be shot.

Regarding the composition issue, there are a lot of different rules that we can follow to help us in the framing phase. The most famous is the **rule of thirds**. The rule of thirds is a fundamental guideline in cinematography and photography that helps in creating visually balanced and aesthetically pleasing compositions. The frame is divided into a grid of nine equal parts by two horizontal and two vertical lines, creating four intersecting points. We can summarize the rule of thirds in the following points:

- Imagine your frame divided into a 3 x 3 grid with two horizontal lines and two vertical lines.

- Position important elements, such as the main subject or focal points, at or near the intersections of these lines. This placement draws the viewer's attention and adds visual interest.

- Compose your shot so that significant elements align with the gridlines. For example, a horizon might align with one of the horizontal lines, creating balance in the composition.

- **Avoid centered compositions**: Refrain from placing your main subject directly in the center of the frame. Offsetting the subject using the rule of thirds adds dynamism and interest to the composition.

Figure 11.51 – Rule of thirds composition example

Perfect! We are now ready to compose our starting point.

Unreal Engine gives us a couple of tools that help us in frame composition. With **Cinematic Viewport** enabled, we can access the cinematics tool by clicking on the grid icon in the top-right corner of the Level Viewport.

Figure 11.52 – The cinematics tool icon

The menu looks like this:

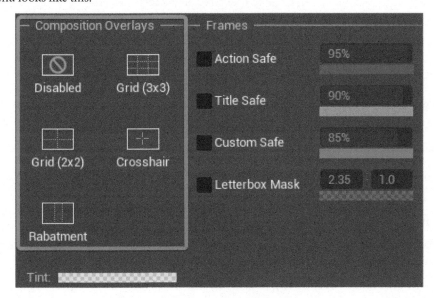

Figure 11.53 – Cinematic tools

Inside this window, we can enable or disable some helpful overlays that we can use as a guide to compose our frame. By default, it is set to **Disabled**. The most commonly used setting is **Grid (3x3)**, which shows a guide to follow the rule of thirds.

Figure 11.54 – Grid 3x3 enabled on the Level Viewport

Great! Now we know everything we need to compose our starting frame.

Composing the first frame

To compose the first frame of our dynamic shot, we can apply all the notions we have learned during the previous sections. We want to create a shot that, starting from a detail, will reveal our environment.

To do that, we need to create a starting close-up shot. Try to follow the following steps:

1. Change the **Current Focal Length** value to 85 mm.
2. Place the camera on the ground and orient it to face the big hole in the wall.
3. Find a subject and compose the frame using the **Grid 3x3** overlay.
4. Play with the **Manual Focus Distance** and the **Current Aperture** values to set the focus point on your subject and make the background out of focus.
5. When you are satisfied, set a keyframe on all the settings you have changed.

Figure 11.55 – Starting frame example

To reproduce the same frame, check the position of the camera and all its settings in *Figure 11.55*.

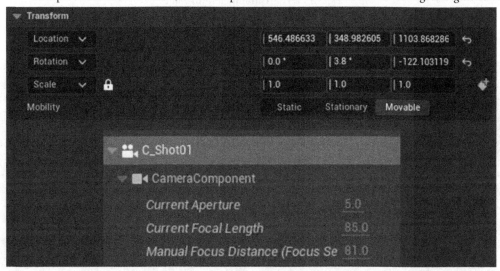

Figure 11.56 – The Cine Camera Actor settings to obtain the frame in Figure 11.54

Perfect! We can now move on and compose the final frame of our dynamic shot.

Composing the last frame

Now, we need to compose a frame that reveals our environment. We will need to change the focal length and the focus point along with the camera position.

To compose the last frame, try to follow the following steps:

1.   Move the **Timeline** bar forward in the **Timeline**. The last keyframe's position determines the duration of our camera's movement. The **Timeline** length is determined by the grey numbers at the bottom of the **Timeline**. The temporal unit is determined by the frame rate we chose before.

Figure 11.57 – **Timeline** length value

If we want to change the playback time, we need to use the green and red vertical lines we can find inside the **Sequencer Timeline**.

Figure 11.58 – Playback range starting and ending bar

By moving the green and red bars, you can change the playback starting and ending points. You can also type the frame number on the bottom side of the Level Viewport (*Figure 10.58*) to set the start and the end manually.

2. Set the **Current Aperture** value to 22 and place a keyframe. This will help us to see everything at focus to create the composition phase sample.

3. Move the Cine Camera Actor backward and find a good frame that shows the environment. When you are satisfied, place a keyframe on the **Transform** line.

Figure 11.59 – Final frame

4. To reproduce the same frame, check the position of the camera and all its settings in *Figure 11.60*. We are using a custom sensor with a **Weight** value equal to 54 mm and a **Height** value equal to 23 mm.

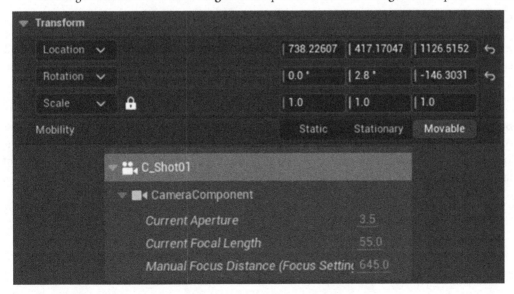

Figure 11.60 – The Cine Camera Actor settings to obtain the frame in Figure 11.59

5. We can now play the animation to check the result. The Engine will interpolate the intermediate frames for you to create the camera movement.

6. Finally, we can move the ending frame's keyframes forward to slow down the movement.

Perfect! We have just created our first dynamic shot by animating our Cine Camera Actor. Now, you can create all the shots you want to enhance your environment. The techniques we have learned in this chapter are also helpful in creating shots with characters and moving objects. The process can always be the same:

1. Choose the correct lens.

2. Compose the starting frame.

3. Compose the ending frame.

4. Check the interpolation work made by the Engine.

5. Modify, if necessary, the intermediate frames.

Another simple rule that can be helpful when you start crafting shoots is to try to create a good frame on every keyframe you place in the **Timeline**. What I mean is that if you decide to add a corrective keyframe in the middle of your camera movement animation, be sure that this corrective keyframe generates a well-composed frame.

Perfect! We have a couple of things to learn about camera movements. In the next section, we are going to learn how to create a camera shake effect.

Creating a Camera Shake Blueprint

In this section, we will learn how to create and add a camera shake effect to our Cine Camera Actor. A camera shake is an effect that gives natural movement to our Cine Camera Actor's animation. In other words, with a camera shake effect, we can simulate a hand-held camera to create a more adrenaline effect or give the camera animation the movement of a man walking, without manually placing keyframes.

Before creating a camera shake effect, we need to craft a new shot. We can use the same Megascans Abandoned Apartment project. We are not going to create it step by step because the workflow is the same as one we have already learned about. Try to create it by yourself. We need a forward movement that passes through the corridor we have inside our environment. I leave the starting frame and ending frame there just for reference.

Figure 11.61 – The starting frame and ending frame of the new shot

Ok! We are now ready to create our camera shake effect! To do that, we need to create a Camera Shake Blueprint. Don't worry about that. We are not going to learn coding stuff. If you follow the next steps, we can create a Camera Shake Blueprint in less than five minutes:

1. Right-click inside the **Content Browser** and select **Blueprint Class**.

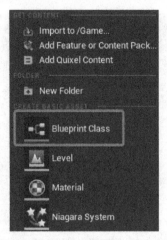

Figure 11.62 – Creating Blueprint Class

This action will open the **Pick Parent Class** window.

2. Inside the **Pick Parent Class** window, explode the **ALL CLASSES** line and search for camera shake by using the type search field. Select the **CameraShakeBase** option and click on **Select** to create the new **Camera Shake Blueprint**.

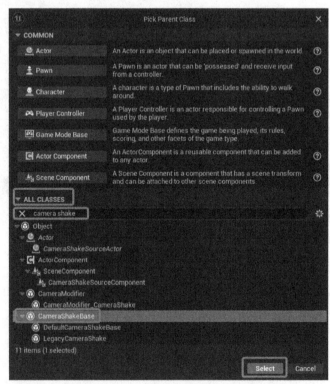

Figure 11.63 – Create a new Camera Shake Blueprint

3.   Rename the new Camera Shake Blueprint as BP_CameraShake_v01.

Figure 11.64 – Camera Shake Blueprint inside the Content Browser

Perfect! We have just created our first Blueprint! Now, we need to add our new BP_CameraShake_ v01 Blueprint to our camera inside the Sequencer. To do that, try to follow the following steps:

1.   Open the Level Sequence with the Cine Camera Actor on which you want to apply the **Camera Shake** effect.

2.   Inside the **Sequencer** window, click on the + icon on the right side of the **Cine Camera Actor** line (in my case, this is the **C_Shot02** line) (*Figure 11.67*).

3.   Inside the appeared menu, enter the **Camera Shake** category and select the **BP_CameraShake_v01** we have just created (*Figure 11.67*).

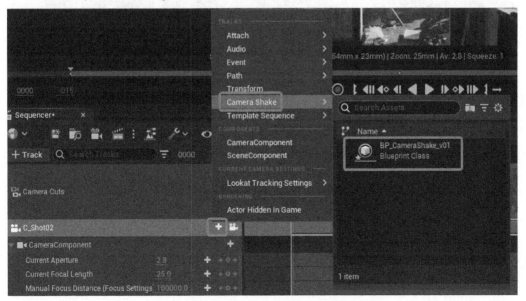

Figure 11.65 – Adding a Camera Shake Blueprint to the Cine Camera Actor inside the Sequencer

The Sequencer should look now like this:

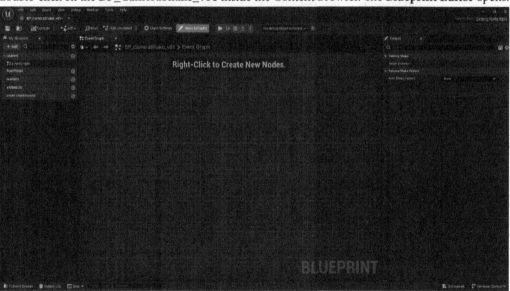

Figure 11.66 – Sequencer with the Camera Shake Blueprint added to the Cine Camera Actor

Now, if we try to move the **Timeline** bar or play our camera's animation, we can't notice any changes in our camera movement. The reason for this is that we need to set **BP_CameraShake_v01**. To do that, double-click on the **BP_CameraShake_v01** inside the Content Browser. The **Blueprint Editor** opens.

Figure 11.67 – The Blueprint Editor

For some strange reason, if you close the Blueprint Editor and then try to reopen **BP_CameraShake_v01**, it will look different:

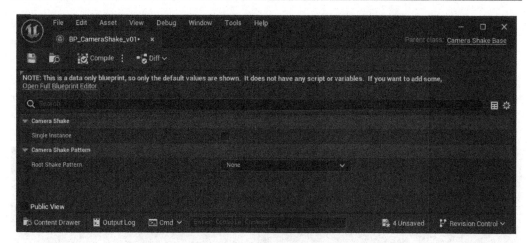

Figure 11.68 – The Blueprint Editor compact version

I am not sure if this is a bug or an intentional thing but, anyway, we can use the one that we can see in *Figure 11.70*.

To change the **BP_CameraShake_v01** settings, try to follow the following steps:

1. Change the **Root Shake Pattern** option from **None** to **Perlin Noise Camera Shake Pattern**.

Figure 11.69 – Changing Root Shake Pattern

With this drop-down menu, we can change the algorithm we want to use to generate our camera shake effect. Each of them has different options and values to change. **Perlin Noise Camera Shake Pattern** works well most of the time.

2. Explode the **Timing** line and set the **Duration** value to 0. This means that the camera shake will apply to the entire length of the **Timeline**. For instance, if you want to create a camera shake that lasts one second, you need to set the **Duration** value to 1 (*Figure 11.72*).

3. Explode the **Rotation** line and set the **Rotation Amplitude Multiplier** value to 1 and the **Rotation Frequency Multiplier** value to 10 (*Figure 11.72*). **Rotation Amplitude Multiplier** is the size of the rotation movement applied to the camera. **Rotation Frequency Multiplier** is the frequency with which **Rotation Amplitude Multiplier** will be applied.

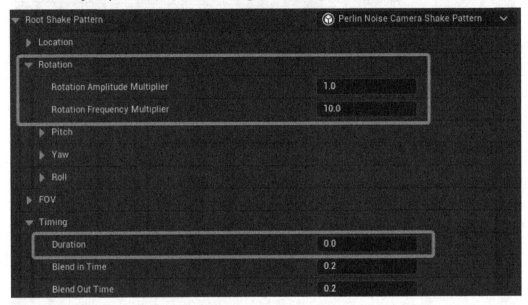

Figure 11.70 – Changing the Camera Shake Blueprint settings

4. Try to play the camera animation to test the **Camera Shake** effect.

Perfect! Your camera should now have a camera shake effect. What we have done is added a generic rotation movement to our camera. You can now create several camera shake effects by changing the **Rotation** values, but also any single **Rotation** transformation (**Pitch**, **Yaw**, and **Roll** in *Figure 11.72*). You can do the same for a **Location** transformation.

We can add more than one **Camera Shake** effect to our camera. The fact that a camera shake effect is a Blueprint actor allows us to migrate our camera shake effects to other projects. This means that you can make your camera shake effects library to be shared through projects.

Perfect! We are almost done with Sequencer and Level Sequences. We have one more thing to learn. In the next section, we will discover how to combine multiple shots.

Combining multiple shots

In this section, we will learn how to combine multiple shots to create a more complex edit directly inside Unreal Engine 5. There are two different methods to do this:

- Add multiple cameras to the Sequencer
- Create a Sequencer with multiple Level Sequences inside

You can add infinite Cine Camera Actors inside your Sequencer using the same process we have already learned about. Drag and drop the new camera inside the Sequencer, and that's it.

Figure 11.71 – Multiple cameras inside the Sequencer

Once you have more than one camera inside the Sequencer, you can animate them to obtain the camera movement you need. Both of the cameras we can see inside the Sequencer in *Figure 11.72* start their animation at frame 0. This means that if we play the Sequencer, both cameras start their movement contemporary. So, we need to switch the camera we are looking through during the animation playback. To do that, we need to use Camera Cuts, the Engine added when we added the first Cine Camera Actor to our Sequencer.

Figure 11.72 – Camera Cuts inside the Sequencer

Camera Cuts works like a recorder for the Cine Camera Actors we have added to our Sequencer. To look at what Camera Cuts has recorded, we need to enable the Lock Viewport to Camera Cuts option by clicking on the camera icon on the right side of the **Camera Cuts** line.

Figure 11.73 – Enabling the Lock Viewport to Camera Cuts option

When we have the Lock Viewport to Camera Cuts option enabled, we can't move the camera inside the Level Viewport because the Level Viewport is set to show us the Camera Cuts record.

If we have more than one camera inside our Sequencer, we can decide which camera Camera Cuts need to record and which part of their movement.

To record a new camera inside Camera Cuts, try to follow the following steps:

1. Create a Level Sequence with more than one Cine Camera Actor inside (*Figure 11.72*). In this example, we are going to use C_Shot01, which we created during the *Placing the Cine Camera Actor* section, and C_Shot02, which we created during the *Creating a Camera Shake Blueprint* section.

> **Note**
>
> You can copy and paste cameras from one Level Sequence to another without losing animation keyframes. This is very useful for testing a variation of the camera animation in another Level Sequence or adding a new existing and already animated camera inside another Level Sequence.

2. With the + icon near the camera icon, on the right side of **Camera Cuts**, we can choose the Cine Camera Actor inside the Sequencer that we want to record inside Camera Cuts.

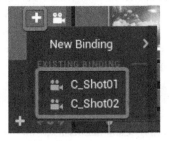

Figure 11.74 – Selecting the Cine Camera Actor to record

3. Select the Cine Camera Actor you want to record. By default, Camera Cuts shows us the first Cine Camera Actor we have imported inside the Sequencer. So, try to select a different Cine Camera Actor. The result will be a different **Camera Cuts** preview inside the **Timeline**. Camera Cuts now shows the newly selected camera inside the Level Viewport.

Camera Cuts starts to record the selected camera from the **Timeline** bar's actual position and ends the record on the frame we have set as the ending frame (the frame with the red line inside the **Timeline**). According to that, we can record multiple cameras inside Camera Cuts to create an edit to be shown directly inside the Level Viewport. To do that, try to follow the following steps:

1. Place the **Timeline** bar at 0 and record the starting camera.

2. Place the **Timeline** bar on the frame you want to start recording the second camera.

3. Select the second Cine Camera Actor to record.

4. Move the **Timeline** bar forward again and record the first camera again to create another cut.

5. The Camera Cuts should look like this:

Figure 11.75 – Camera Cuts with multiple Cine Camera Actors

Perfect! Now we know how to add multiple cameras inside a Sequencer to create an edit with **Camera Cuts**. This is very important because when we render out our Level Sequence, the Rendering process will consider everything we can see inside Camera Cuts. We will learn more about rendering in *Chapter 13*.

> **Note**
>
> Camera Cuts considers the keyframe position of the Cine Camera Actor we want to record. This means that if we start recording a Cine Camera Actor after its last keyframe in the **Timeline**, Camera Cuts will record the static final position of the selected Cine Camera Actor. To avoid this issue, we can move all the keyframes of the Cine Camera Actor we want to record forward in the **Timeline**. This action will make the Cine Camera Actor start its animation in a different frame to frame 0.

Perfect! We have only one more thing to learn before closing this chapter. We have just learned how to add multiple Cine Camera Actors to our **Sequencer** and how to record them inside Camera Cuts. But as we have already said, we can also add multiple **Level Sequences** inside a **Sequencer**.

To do that, try to follow the following steps:

1. Create a new Level Sequence and rename it Master_Sequence.

2. With the **+ Track** button, add a **Shot Track** item to the Sequencer.

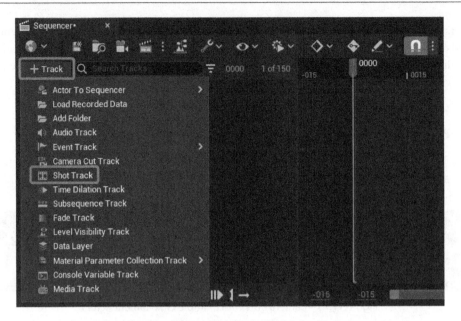

Figure 11.76 – Adding a Shot Track item to the Sequencer

3.   Assign one of your Level Sequences to **Shot Track** by clicking on the + icon on the right side of the **Shot Track** line.

Figure 11.77 – Adding a Level Sequence to Shot Track

This action will add all the selected Level Sequence's content to the new `Master_Sequence` as a single item. It should look like a video track that we usually find inside editing software.

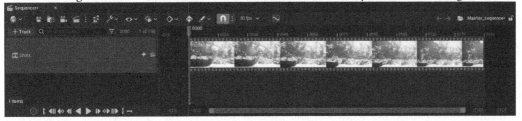

Figure 11.78 – Sequencer with a Level Sequence added to Shot Track

The Level Sequence we have just added is editable, like a video file. So, you can move it backward or forward inside the **Timeline** or cut it to use only a portion of it.

Figure 11.79 – Modified Level Sequence inside the Sequencer

4. Add another Level Sequence to `Master_Sequence` by clicking again on the + icon and selecting another Level Sequence.

Figure 11.80 - Adding an additional shot

The new Level Sequence will be added starting from the **Timeline** bar position.

5. The Sequencer is now an editing software's **Timeline**. The upper shot has always precedence over the other ones. We can move all the different shots around and cut them to create the edit we want.

6. Click on the upper **Shots** line's camera icon to see the whole edit inside the Level Viewport.

> **Note**
>
> For learning purposes, we have called our Level Sequence with the Scene name. If you are planning to use the Master_Sequence technique, you should call your Level Sequence with the Shot name.

Perfect! We have done it! We can now create multiple shots and combine them in a single Level Sequence to create an edit directly inside the Engine.

Cinematic tools such as the Sequencer and Cine Camera Actor are incredibly powerful tools that allow us to craft stunning camera movements in a fast and easy way. The goal of this book is to learn how to create an environment to be used inside a cinematic shot but thanks to the potential of the **Cinematic** tools, you should be able to create short movies directly inside the Engine. For more details on filmmaking in Unreal Engine, you can check out *Virtual Filmmaking with Unreal Engine 5* by Hussin Khan, available at `https://www.packtpub.com/product/virtual-filmmaking-with-unreal-engine-5/9781801813808`.

Summary

With this dense notions chapter, we have left behind all the techniques involved in creating an environment and have entered the final phase of our workflow: the output phase. In this chapter, we first learned what a Cine Camera Actor is and how to use it by exploring all of its parameters. We moved on to introducing the Level Sequence actor and how to edit it with the Sequencer editor. After exploring the animation fundamentals, we learned how to animate a Cine Camera Actor to create camera movements. After that, we summarized the framing principles needed to compose an environment shot in the best way possible. In order to do so, we explored the Viewport overlays that the Engine provides to us as the 3 x 3 overlay that helps us to follow the rule of thirds. We moved on by learning how to create a camera shake effect and we finished by explaining how to combine multiple cameras and shots.

Now, we can see the end of our journey. At this point of the book, with only two chapters left, we should be able to create an environment by using all of the tools the Engine provides to us by managing materials, lighting, and Landscape. Crafting cinematic shots is a fundamental skill needed to approach the next chapter, where we will learn how to improve the look of our scene with post-process volume and Niagara.

12

Enhancing Scenes with Post-Processing and Niagara

In this chapter, we will learn what a Post Process Volume is and how to use it to improve the visual quality of our scenes in terms of both rendering quality and creative effects. We will also learn what a Color Lookup Table is, what the process is to create a new Color Lookup Table, and how to use it inside the Post Process Volume. We will also introduce the fundamentals of the Niagara particle system by creating a simple dust effect to be added to our Level.

In this chapter, we will cover the following main topics:

- Discovering the **Post Process Volume** (**PPV**)
- Exploring PPV settings
- Creating a Color Lookup Table
- Introducing Niagara

At the end of this chapter, we will be able to color-correct our scene using Post Process Volume and add some camera effects. We will know how to create a Color Lookup Table to be used to color-correct our frame. We will also be able to use Niagara to create some simple atmospheric effects.

Technical requirements

In this chapter, we will use the *Megascans Abandoned Apartment* project we used in *Chapter 6* and *Chapter 11*. To easily follow the chapter, you should have it opened on your workstation.

Discovering the Post Process Volume

In this section, we will learn what a Post Process Volume is and how to use it. A **Post Process Volume** (from here on, **PPV**) is a volume that can be used to add post-processing effects to our scene. When we talk about post-processing effects, we are talking about everything regardless of **color correction** and image effects. With a PPV placed inside the Level, we can simply modify the result in terms of what we are seeing inside the Level Viewport.

The PPV also includes a lot of different parameters to improve different rendering features such as Reflection samples or global illumination bounces. We will talk about them in *Chapter 13*. In this chapter, we are going to cover the parameters that allow us to artistically improve our frame.

Considering that we are talking about color correction, we need to talk about color space in Unreal Engine 5 and color space management in general before starting to explore what we can do with a PPV. This is going to be a very simple explanation about the color space problem just to let you know how to face some color problems that you might face during the workflow.

Color space refers to a specific organization of colors, defined by a mathematical model. It encompasses the range and representation of colors within a digital environment, ensuring consistency and accuracy across various devices and software. Proper **color space management** is crucial in **Computer-Generated Imagery** (**CGI**) to achieve accurate and consistent color reproduction across different platforms and devices.

Adopting a color space means using a defined range of colors. When we use a tool or software that uses a specific color space, the challenge is maintaining consistent and accurate colors across different devices, such as computers, cameras, and printers. Imagine you take a photo on your camera, edit it on a computer, and then print it. If these devices use different color settings or *languages* (color spaces), the colors in the final print might not match what you saw on your computer.

Managing color spaces ensures that colors look consistent and accurate from device to device, preventing unexpected variations in how images appear.

There are different color spaces considered as standard in the industry. Unreal Engine 5 works with **sRGB/REC709**. Ninety-nine percent of the time, our output device will be our screen. So, the simplest thing we can do to reduce the color space problem is to set our monitor to work with the same color space that Unreal Engine 5 uses.

The following points can help you with monitor calibration:

- Set the monitor color space to **sRGB/REC709**
- Use a high contrast ratio such as **2000:1** or higher
- Use a peak luminance equal to **100** nits (candelas/m²)
- Set the **Black** level to **0.05** nits or less

Most of the monitors that we use daily in our CGI work have a built-in calibration tool that allows us to set a specific color range to use and change some settings to improve the color fidelity.

All these settings are not mandatory but recommended, especially if you are using Unreal Engine 5 in a production workflow and your output will be worked by a post-production house (that works with colors!).

Anyway, you can easily follow the chapter without a calibrated monitor but it is always important to understand how the tool we are using interprets colors.

Perfect! We are now ready to learn everything about PPVs.

Creating and understanding a PPV

To create a PPV, open the **Place Actors** panel and search for **Post Process Volume** under the **Visual Effects** category.

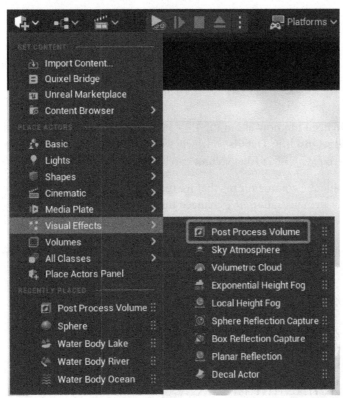

Figure 12.1 – Post Process Volume inside the Place Actors panel

You can also find the **Post Process Volume** option under the **Volumes** category inside the **Place Actors** panel.

The PPV looks like this inside the Level Viewport:

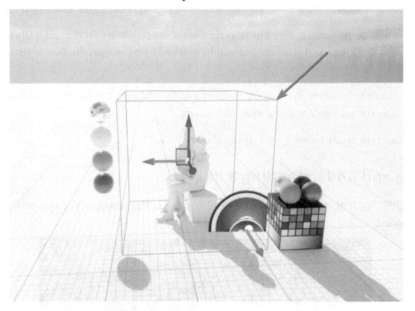

Figure 12.2 – PPV placed inside the Level Viewport

The first thing we need to know about the PPV is how it works. Considering its volume nature, everything we will set inside its **Details** panel will work only inside the volume that we can see in the Level Viewport (see *Figure 12.2*). That volume can be scaled and moved around the Level.

Working only inside the volume means that we need to move inside it with the camera to see the PPV effect. Just for demonstration, I've changed the **Temperature** value (we will see it next during the *Exploring PPV settings* section). We can see the result of moving the camera inside the volume in *Figure 12.3*.

Figure 12.3 – An example of how a PPV works

Why does the PPV work in this way? Because we can have more than one PPV in our Level and create different effects at different points of the Level. Remember that Unreal Engine 5 was created to make video games. For instance, with a PPV, you can change the overall color of a single room, a portion of a room, or a forest.

But what if we want the PPV to affect the whole Level? We have already seen that in *Chapter 6*. We can set the PPV to work infinitely inside the Level by enabling **Infinite Extent (Unbound)** under the **Post Process Volume Settings** category inside the PPV's **Details** panel.

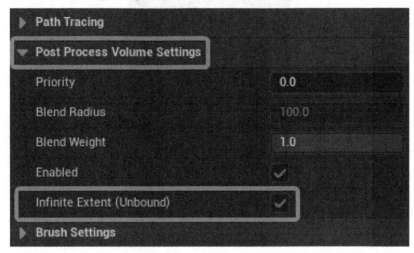

Figure 12.4 – Infinite Extent (Unbound) enabled

With this option enabled, any settings we will change inside the PPV will affect the whole Level in all its points. We can leave this option enabled for the rest of this chapter to easily understand how any settings work.

Perfect! We are now ready to explore **Post Process Volume Settings** inside the **Details** panel.

Exploring Post Process Volume Settings

In this section, we will explore several settings that we can find inside the PPV's **Details** panel. We are not going to cover all the settings – only the ones that are more useful for cinematic works.

Considering that the PPV is an actor placed in the Level Viewport, the first thing we can find is the **Transform** tab that allows us to change the location, rotation, and scale of our PPV.

As we have set our PPV to be infinite, the **Transform** options will affect the PPV shape in the Level Viewport but the PPV will affect the whole Level until we disable **Infinite Extent (Unbound)**. Once we disable that option, the PPV will consider the shape defined by the **Transform** tab again.

Scrolling down, we have the **Lens** category.

Figure 12.5 – The Lens category inside the Details panel

Inside the **Lens** category, we can find several effects that we can add to our Level. These effects are usually applied to artistically improve the aspect of our final image.

Let's take a look at what we can do:

- **Mobile Depth of Field**: In this category, we can find parameters to set a depth of field effect that will work online on a mobile platform. I personally never use this. It can be useful in some specific cases only when you are working on a mobile platform project. We are learning how to create a cinematic environment so we don't need it.

- **Bloom**: This is a visual effect that simulates the perception of intense light, creating a glow or halo around bright areas in an image or scene. The **Bloom** effect enhances the luminance and intensity of light sources, giving them a soft, radiant appearance.

    In practical terms, when a light source in an image exceeds a certain threshold of brightness, **Bloom** is applied to simulate the way our eyes perceive and react to intense light. **Bloom** is commonly utilized to enhance scenes with bright highlights, such as sunlight, artificial lighting, or other intense light sources, adding a touch of realism and esthetic appeal to the overall visual experience.

Figure 12.6 – Bloom effect example

We have some parameters that we can use to enhance the **Bloom** effect:

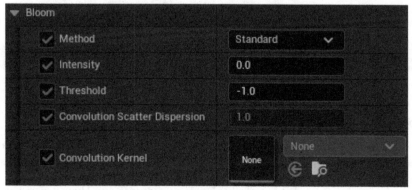

Figure 12.7 – Bloom settings

- **Method**: We have two options here. We are going to use the **Standard** option, but you can also try out **Convolution**.

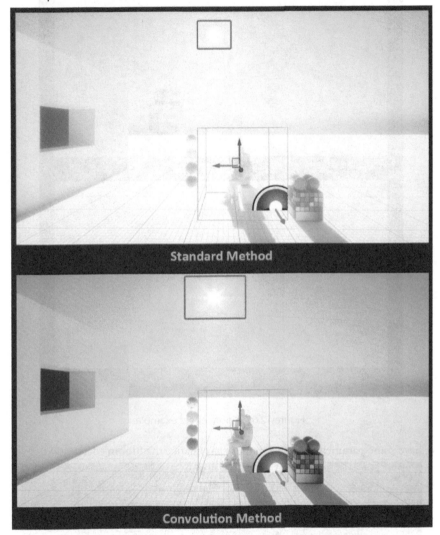

Figure 12.8 – Difference between the Bloom methods

- **Intensity**: This value defines how much **Bloom** we want in our scene.

- **Threshold**: This value defines the minimum brightness value at which **Bloom** starts having an effect. By default, it is set to **-1**, which means that **Bloom** will affect all the pixels equally.

- **Exposure**: We have already learned what **Exposure Control** is and how it works in *Chapter 6*. We will come back to this in a couple of pages when we talk about **Camera** options.

- **Chromatic Aberration**: This refers to a common optical phenomenon that occurs when a lens fails to focus all colors of light to the same point. This results in color fringing or distortion around the edges of objects in an image.

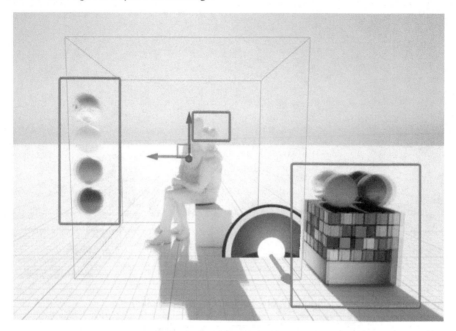

Figure 12.9 – Chromatic aberration example

Chromatic aberration is caused by the fact that different colors of light have slightly different wavelengths, and as they pass through a lens, they are refracted by varying amounts. Inside Unreal Engine, we can simulate the **Chromatic Aberration** effect by modifying the values under the **Chromatic Aberration** category:

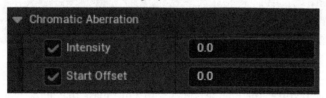

Figure 12.10 – Chromatic Aberration settings

- **Intensity**: This value is the amount of the **Chromatic Aberration** effect. For instance, in *Figure 12.9*, it is set to 5.

- **Start Offset**: This value allows us to set an offset for the **Chromatic Aberration** starting point. If we leave it at **0.0** (zero), the effect will start on the edge of every object and light. The higher the value, the further the effect.

- **Dirt Mask**: This option allows us to add an overlay mask on the camera to create some creative effect.

Figure 12.11 – Sample Dirt Mask applied

We have some options to modify the aspect of **Dirt Mask**:

Figure 12.12 – Dirt Mask settings

- **Dirt Mask Texture**: The Engine comes with a dirt mask that allows you to check what the effect does. With **Dirt Mask Texture**, we can change the mask we want to use. We can use any kind of texture but the effect works better with a gray-scale image.

- **Dirt Mask Intensity**: This value allows us to set the strength of the **Dirt Mask** effect on our screen.

- **Dirt Mask Tint**: Here, we can change the **Dirt Mask** color.

  Dirt Mask is linked to the camera so the texture will always follow the camera movement.

- **Camera**: To correctly talk about the parameters inside the **Camera** category, we need to go back to the **Exposure** controls. The PPV's **Camera** settings will work only with the PPV **Exposure** category **Metering Mode** setting set to **Manual** and a starting **Exposure Compensation** value set to **0.0** (zero). The **Exposure** category settings should be set like this:

Figure 12.13 – Exposure control settings inside the PPV's Details panel

Now, the Level Viewport should look totally black.

We can now use the **Camera** options. Let's take a look at what we can do with them:

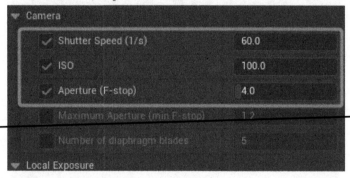

Figure 12.14 – Camera settings

The parameters we can find inside the **Camera** category simulate some characteristics of a real-world camera:

- **Shutter Speed (1/s)**: This regulates the duration of light exposure, influencing factors such as motion blur, freeze-frame effects, and overall image brightness. In a real-life camera, *shutter* refers to a mechanical or electronic device that controls the duration of time during which light is allowed to reach the camera's sensor or film. If we try to decrease this value, the Level Viewport will progressively become brighter.

- **ISO**: This measures the sensitivity of our camera's sensor to light. A low **ISO** setting is suitable for well-lit conditions, while a high **ISO** setting is used in low-light situations. Adjusting the ISO setting allows us to achieve proper exposure in different conditions. So, if we try to increase the ISO value, the Level Viewport will progressively become brighter.

- **Aperture (F-stop)**: This defines the quantity of light that can reach the camera sensor. We have already talked about this in *Chapter 11*.

The only issue about using these parameters is that they influence the way **Cine Camera Actor** works. If you place a Cine Camera Actor in your Level and start to pilot it, you will see that the exposure is different from what we have set inside the PPV.

Figure 12.15 – Frame differences with and without Cine Camera Actor piloting

This happens because now the Cine Camera Actor's **Current Aperture** value (which we learned about in *Chapter 11*) works exactly the same as a real-life aperture works. The Cine Camera Actor I used to take the screenshot for *Figure 12.15* has **Current Aperture** set to 7. If we try to decrease it, the Level Viewport will progressively become brighter.

To summarize, If we decide to use the **Camera** settings inside the PPV's **Camera** category to get access to a more realistic virtualization of a real-life camera, we need to remember that the Cine Camera Actor's **Current Aperture** setting will work more realistically.

- **Local Exposure**: In this category, we have a bunch of new settings that come with Unreal Engine 5 that allow us to control the final aspect of the scene in a deeper way. In synthesis, **Local Exposure** divides the luminance of the scene into two different levels: a base layer and a detail layer to let us have more control over the final frame.

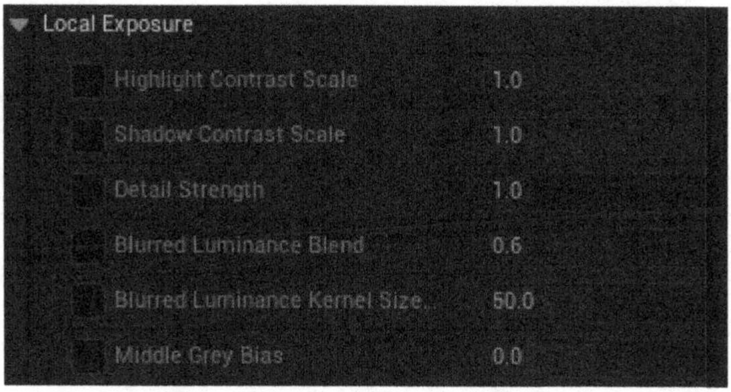

Local Exposure
Highlight Contrast Scale 1.0
Shadow Contrast Scale 1.0
Detail Strength 1.0
Blurred Luminance Blend 0.6
Blurred Luminance Kernel Size... 50.0
Middle Grey Bias 0.0

Figure 12.16 – Local Exposure settings

Let's take a look at what these settings do:

- **Highlight Contrast Scale**: This value controls the contrast of the highlight point in the scene. That means that it will act on the brighter parts of the frame. If you want to make the bright parts of the scene darker, you need to set a low value.

Highlight Contrast Scale: 1
Highlight Contrast Scale: 0.2

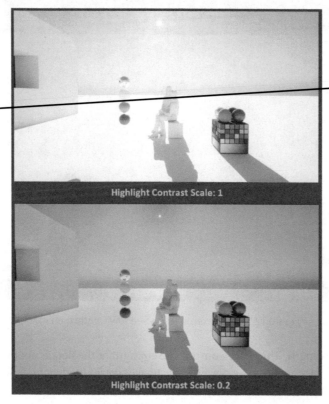

Figure 12.17 – An example of a Highlight Contrast Scale image

- **Shadow Contrast Scale**: This value controls the shadow's contrast. If we want a darker shadow, we need to use a higher value.

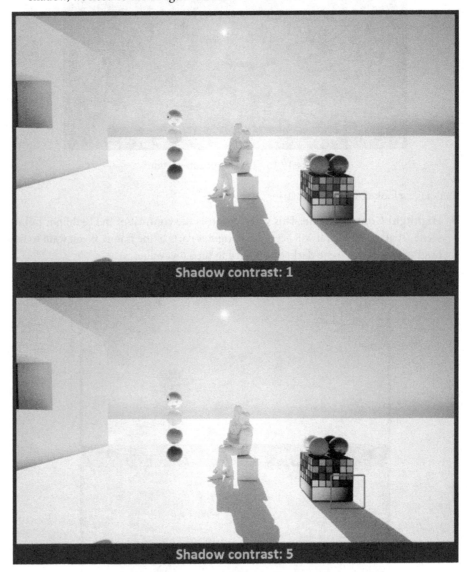

Figure 12.18 – An example of a Shadow Contrast image

- **Detail Strength**: This value controls the strength of the details applied to the scene. By changing this parameter, we can make the image's details brighter or darker. See *Figure 12.19* to understand what that means.

Figure 12.19 – An example of a Detail Strength image

- **Blurred Luminance Blend** and **Blurred Luminance Kernel Size Percent**: These values help to balance the brighter parts of the frame a little bit more. Try them out to check how they can help you.

- **Middle Grey Bias**: This value allows us to choose what **Local Exposure** considers **middle gray** (the tone that is perceptually halfway between black and white). Here, **0** is equal to no adjustment, -1 is twice the darker value, -2 is four times the darker value, 1 is twice the brighter value, and 2 is four times the brighter value.

- **Lens Flares**: A lens flare is a visual phenomenon that occurs in photography or filmmaking when bright light, such as sunlight, enters the camera lens directly or at an angle. This can result in streaks or circles of light appearing in the image.

Figure 12.20 – An example of a Lens Flare image

While it's generally considered an optical flaw, some photographers and filmmakers intentionally use lens flare for artistic or stylistic purposes to create a sense of atmosphere or mood in their work. For this reason, the Engine provides us with some settings to create the desired **Lens Flares** effect.

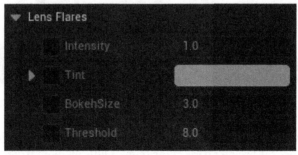

Figure 12.21 – Lens Flares most common settings

Let's take a look at the **Lens Flares** settings:

- **Intensity**: This value defines the quantity of lens flares we want to see in our frame.

- **Tint**: With this value, we can change the overlay color of the **Lens Flares** effect.

- **BokehSize**: This value defines the size of the in-camera artifact that **Lens Flares** creates.

- **Threshold**: This parameter defines the minimum brightness value at which **Lens Flares** happens. That means that if you want a low-intensity light to generate a **Lens Flares** effect, the threshold value should be very low.

- **Image Effects**: This option allows us to add a **Vignette** effect to our frame. The **Vignette** effect generates a black mask with decreasing intensity starting from the frame border.

Figure 12.22 – An image demonstrating the Vignette effect

Figure 12.22 shows the **Vignette** mask with a very high value to clearly show the result. A good value to use is usually between 0.2 and 0.4.

Figure 12.23 – Image Effects Vignette setting

- **Depth of Field**: These options work like the **Depth of Field** settings we saw in *Chapter 11*. The main difference is that these are independent of the camera, and they work according to the PPV's bound options.

Figure 12.24 – An example of a Depth of Field image with custom settings

Instead of the **Draw Debug Focus Plane** option that we have inside the Cine Camera Actor's **Details** panel, we can check the focus point's position by activating the **Depth of Field Layers Show** option. To do that, click on the **Show** menu on the top-left side of the Level Viewport, and under the **Visualize** category, select **Depth of Field Layers**.

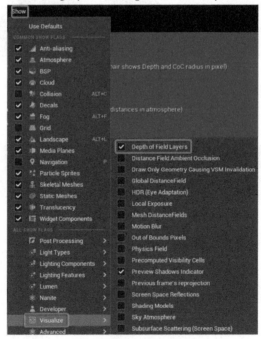

Figure 12.25 – Depth of Field Layers option

Once we have activated it, the Level Viewport should look like this:

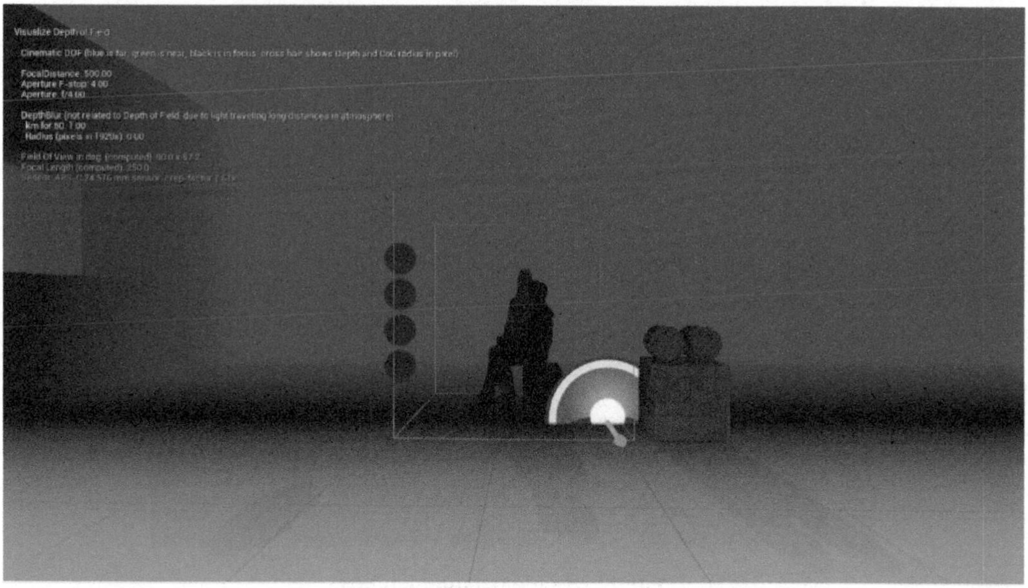

Figure 12.26 – Depth of Field Layers option enabled

The black parts of the image are in focus, the green parts of the image are the foreground part of the frame, and the blue parts of the image are progressively out of focus.

Depth of Field is the last effect we can find under the **Lens** category. You can use all these effects to give your scene a specific mood and improve it in terms of visuals.

Exploring the Color Grading parameters

We can now move on to the next category and explore what we can do with the **Color Grading** parameters.

Figure 12.27 – Color Grading options

As the name says, inside the **Color Grading** category, we can find several parameters that allow us to color-correct our frame.

We can divide the category into three different groups. First, we have the **Temperature** options that allow us to modify the overall color temperature of our frame. Then we have the **Global**, **Shadows**, **Midtones**, and **Highlights** parameters, which allow us to color-correct different chromatic components of our frame. Finally, **Misc** groups some interesting settings including the possibility to add a Color **Lookup Table** (**LUT**) to our PPV.

Inside the **Temperature** category, we can find a couple of useful parameters.

Figure 12.28 – Temperature settings

Let's take a look at what we can do with these parameters:

- **Temperature Type**: With this drop-down menu, we can change the type of temperature we want to use to modify our frame. We have two options:

  - **White Balance**: This method allows us to change the *white point* of our frame. In other words, we can change the white color value to another color.

  - **Color Temperature**: This method works like the **Color Temperature** option we learned about for Light Actors in *Chapter 6*. If we use this option, the PPV will overlay a specific color to the frame's colors.

  We can use both methods. I usually find myself more comfortable with the **White Balance** method.

- **Temp**: This value allows us to choose the **Temperature** value we want to apply to our frame. Temperature is measured in Kelvin. By default, it is set to **6500**, which is equal to white. If we are using the **White Balance** option, the lower the **Temp** value, the colder the overall tint of the frame (blueish effect). The higher the **Temp** value, the warmer the overall tint of the frame (reddish effect). If we want to use **Color Temperature**, it works in reverse.

- **Tint**: This value works in the same way that the **Temp** value works but it considers a color instead of a Kelvin value.

Figure 12.29 – Temperature comparison image

- **Global**, **Shadows**, **Midtones**, and **Highlights**: All the parameters that we can find inside this category work exactly as any color grading tool works. The categories refer to what we want to modify. **Global** affects all the color components of the frame, **Shadows** affects only shadows, **Midtones** affects only the frame's midtones, and **Highlights** affects only the brighter parts of the frame.

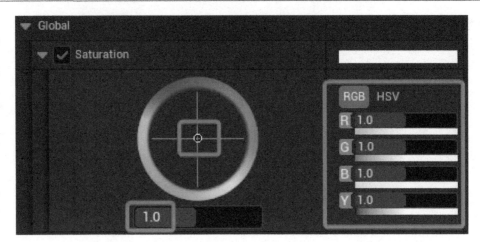

Figure 12.30 – Color grading wheel inside Saturation option

Inside each of these categories, we can find the same parameters (the ones we can see in *Figure 12.27*). We are going to see the **Global | Saturation** panel that can be transposed to the others.

The value on the bottom side of the panel allows us to increase or decrease **Saturation**. The *color wheel* allows us to interactively change the saturation of our frame by modifying colors. To do that, we can move the *central cursor* of the color wheel to the color we want. We can do the same by using the color parameters on the right side of the panel.

There are two more categories dedicated to artistic and creative purposes that we can explore inside the PPV's **Details** panel: **Film** and **Film Grain**.

We can start with the **Film** category. Inside this category, we can find five additional values that can help us manage the color grading of our scene.

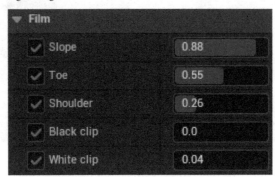

Figure 12.31 – Film category's settings

- **Slope**: With this value, we can change the brightness (in terms of colors) of the scene. The higher the **Slope** value, the darker the scene. The lower the **Slope** value, the brighter the frame.

- **Toe**: With this value, we can manage the darker color of our scene. The higher the value of **Toe**, the darker the darkest part of the frame. The lower the **Toe** value, the brighter the darkest part of the frame.

- **Shoulder**: This works in the same way that **Toe** works but with brighter colors.

- **Black clip**: This value allows us to set a black value of our frame that is not pure black.

- **White clip**: This value allows us to set a white value of our frame that is not pure white.

The last category we want to explore is the **Film Grain** category. With the parameters we can find under this category, we can add and modify a Grain effect to our frame. A **grain effect** is like a noise effect that can help to make the frame less digital. Inside the **Film Grain** category, we have a lot of different parameters. We are going to explain only the parameters highlighted by the red boxes inside *Figure 12.32*. The others are derivations of these two:

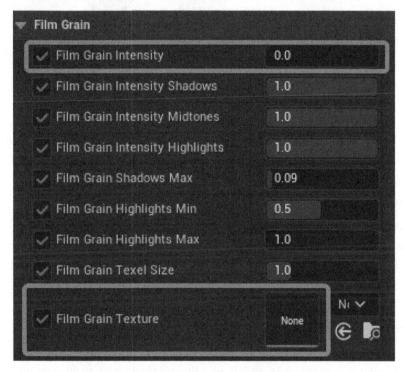

Figure 12.32 – The Film Grain category's parameters

- **Film Grain Intensity**: With this value, we can define the amount of grain to apply to our frame.

Figure 12.33 – The frame with Film Grain enabled

- **Film Grain Texture**: Here, we can add a **Film Grain** texture to use on our frame. We can import an existing **Film Grain** file or create a brand new one using a 2D painting software tool such as Photoshop.

- All the other parameters are useful to color-correct the **Film Grain** effect. You can try them by yourself and find out the ideal **Film Grain** effect for your project.

Perfect! We have just learned how to visually improve our frame by adding visual effects and color-correcting it with the PPV. There is one more very useful option inside the PPV that we need to know to unlock all the possibilities the Engine gives us to manage the color grading of our frame. We need to talk about the Color **Lookup Table** (from here on, **LUT**).

Creating a Color LUT

All the PPV's **Color Grading** tools we have learned about so far are great and they can help us greatly improve our frame in terms of visual appearance. But what if we want to take advantage of the use of external software to color-correct our frame? I'm not talking about a post-production pipeline on the final export (we will talk about exporting in *Chapter 13*) but about applying a color grading done with external software directly inside Unreal Engine.

We can do something like that by using the PPV's **Color Grading LUT** option.

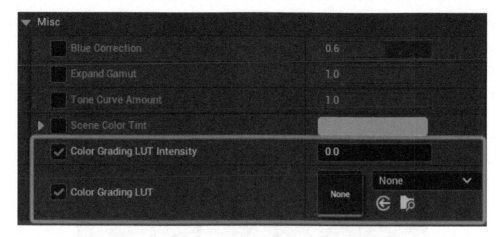

Figure 12.34 – LUT parameters inside the PPV's Details panel

A **Color LUT** is like a magic filter for your photos or videos. Imagine you have a set of special glasses that make all the colors in the world look a little different – warmer, cooler, or more vibrant. A LUT works in a similar way. It's a pre-made set of instructions that tells our PPV how to adjust the colors in our frame to give it a certain style or mood.

In a more technical way, a LUT is a predefined mathematical formula or set of data that is used to transform the colors in an image or video from one color space to another. In simpler terms, a LUT acts as a guide for adjusting and mapping colors to achieve a specific desired look or style.

As we can see in *Figure 12.34*, **Post Process Volume** provides us with two LUT options:

- **Color Grading LUT**: This is where we need to plug our LUT
- **Color Grading LUT Intensity**: This is the amount of the effect provided by the LUT that we want to apply to our frame

Now that we know what a LUT is, we need to learn how to create a new one to be imported inside the Engine and used with the PPV. To do that, we need a couple of things:

- Adobe Photoshop (or any other 2D graphic software).
- A **neutral LUT** as a starting point. We can download one by browsing this link: `https://docs.unrealengine.com/4.27/Images/RenderingAndGraphics/PostProcessEffects/UsingLUTs/RGBTable16x1.png`.

  The image looks like this:

Figure 12.35 – Neutral LUT

Perfect! Open the Level in which you want to use the LUT we are going to create, open Adobe Photoshop (or any other 2D graphic software), and try to follow these steps:

1. Click **Copy image** to copy the neutral LUT image from the previous link:

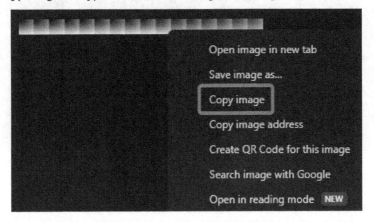

Figure 12.36 – Copying the LUT image

2. Open Photoshop, create a new document by clicking *Ctrl + O*, and select **Clipboard** to create a new document with the same size as the neutral LUT we have just copied.

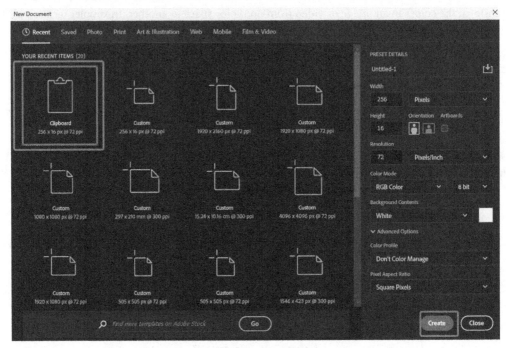

Figure 12.37 – Importing the LUT image to Photoshop

3. Paste the copied image inside the new Photoshop document.

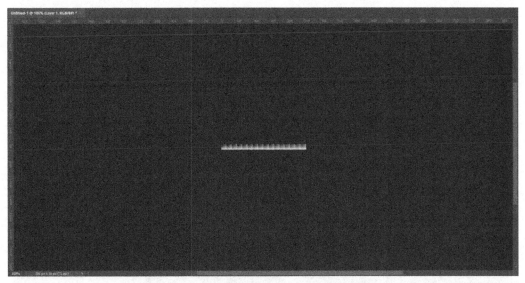

Figure 12.38 – The neutral LUT image inside Photoshop

4. Now, we need to import into Photoshop a reference image of our Level to be able to work on it in terms of color grading. To do this, we can use the **High Resolution Screenshot…** command inside the Level Viewport's *sandwich menu*.

Figure 12.39 – The High Resolution Screenshot command

This command allows us to take a screenshot of the Viewport. Clicking on the command opens a new window with some settings:

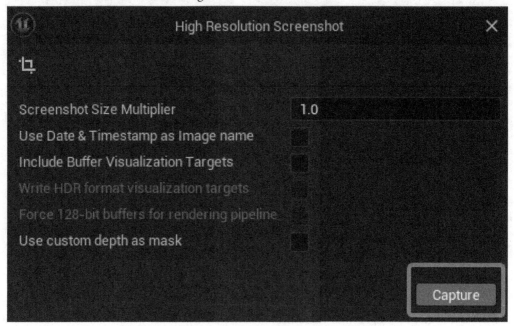

Figure 12.40 – High Resolution Screenshot options window

We can leave everything as default and click on **Capture**. The screenshot will be saved inside the `WindowsEditor` folder, which you can access by browsing to your project folder, entering the `Saved` folder, and searching for the `Screenshot` folder.

5. Create a new Photoshop document with the screenshot inside.

6. Now, we are ready to color-correct our image. Apply all the color corrections you want to your image before going to the next step (*Figure 12.42*). Use a non-destructive workflow inside Photoshop by adding adjustment layers. You can add adjustment layers by using the icon under the **Layers** panel, as *Figure 12.41* shows.

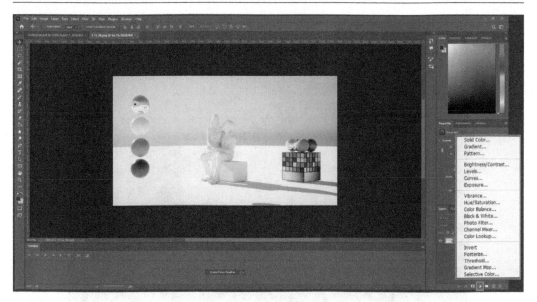

Figure 12.41 – Adjustment layers inside Photoshop

This is how I color-corrected my screenshot:

Figure 12.42 – The screenshot color corrected inside Photoshop

7. The last thing we need to do inside Photoshop is assign the adjustment layers we have used to color-correct our screenshot to the neutral LUT. To do that, you simply need to drag and drop them from the Screenshot document to the neutral LUT document.

Figure 12.43 – Adding adjustment layers to the neutral LUT

8. Save your color-corrected LUT image as a PNG file.

Figure 12.44 – Comparison between the neutral LUT and the color-corrected one

Creating a Color LUT

9. Perfect! We have just created our first Color LUT. Now, import it inside the Engine. It should look like this inside the **Content Browser**:

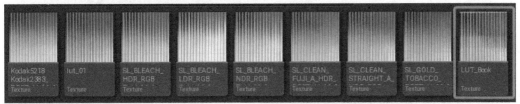

Figure 12.45 – Color-corrected LUT image imported inside the Engine

10. Before assigning our LUT to the PPV to test the result, we need to tell the Engine that it needs to consider the image we have just imported as a *Color LUT* image. To do that, double-click on it to open the **Image Editor** window. Inside this, we need to perform two actions:

    • Change **Mip Gen Settings** to **NoMipMaps**. This will exclude any kind of texture optimization.

    • Change the **Texture Group** setting to **ColorLookupTable**. This is the command that tells the Engine to consider our texture as a LUT.

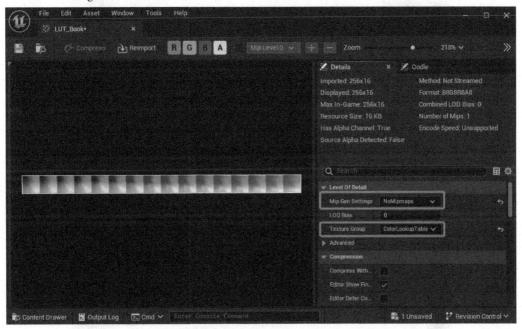

Figure 12.46 – Setting the image as a ColorLookupTable image

11. Great! We can now assign our new LUT to the PPV's **Color Grading LUT** option.

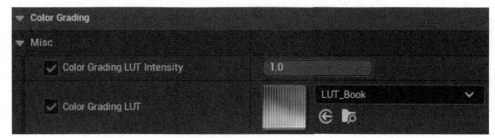

Figure 12.47 – LUT image assigned to the PPV

12. Now, the Level Viewport should look like the screenshot you have modified inside Adobe Photoshop.

Figure 12.48 – Comparison image showing the screenshot color corrected in Photoshop
(top) and the same frame inside the Engine (bottom) with the LUT assigned to the PPV

Color LUTs are very useful to increase the visual quality of your scene. The workflow we have just learned is the best way to take control of the effect we want to obtain by using a LUT.

We can also work more freely by creating LUTs using screenshots from movies we like and trying to apply them to our frame inside the Engine or we can also use LUT files from other software such as, for example, Blackmagic's DaVinci Resolve.

In any case, using LUTs is not mandatory because you can reproduce most of the effects with the PPV's **Color Grading** tools, but it can significantly speed up the workflow if you feel more comfortable using another color grading software.

Alright! We are now ready to jump into the FX world by introducing the Niagara Particle System.

Introducing Niagara

In this section, we will learn how to create our first Niagara effect. Before that, we need to know what Niagara is and why it is important to know how to approach it.

Unreal Engine's **Niagara** is a robust and versatile Particle System that empowers game developers and designers to create dynamic and visually stunning effects in their projects. It is a comprehensive tool within the Unreal Engine game development environment that specializes in handling particle simulations, allowing for the creation of intricate and realistic visual elements.

In other words, Unreal Engine's Niagara is a powerful tool for creating captivating and dynamic particle effects. With Niagara, we can create anything from simple smoke to crowd simulation.

Considering the number of possibilities and its complexity and the fact that VFXs are not the main topic of this book, this section and the next one are going to be demonstrative sections in which we are going to see what we can do with Niagara and how it can help us in developing the final aspect of our environment. For this reason, we will not go through any command we can find inside the Niagara Editor (we will see it in a minute) and any aspects of the Niagara effects creation process.

Now that we understand what it is, we can start to create our first Niagara effect. We will start with a sample atmospheric dust effect to familiarize ourselves with the Niagara Editor and learn how it works

Adding dust to our scene with Niagara

In this section, we will create a sample dust effect by going through some of Niagara's fundamental concepts. Niagara is a very complex topic to cover; for this reason, we are going to approach it step by step to make the workflow easier to follow.

Before starting, we need to download a texture to use to create the dust effect. You can find a dust texture downloadable for free here: `https://www.freeiconspng.com/img/35075`.

Figure 12.49 – Dust texture

This will be the texture we will use to give the particles a dust aspect. Download and import it into your project. The project we are using is the *Megascans Abandoned Apartment* we have already used in *Chapter 6* and *Chapter 11*.

Perfect! We can start to create our first dust effect. The first thing we need to do is to create a new Niagara system. To do that, click the **right mouse button** (*RMB*) inside the **Content Browser** and select **Niagara System**.

Figure 12.50 – Creating a Niagara system

Once you have clicked on the **Niagara System** command, the **Pick a starting point for your system** window opens. Inside this window, we can choose which kind of Niagara system we want to create, not in terms of effect type but in terms of the starting point. In other words, we can choose whether we want to start from scratch or from a preset.

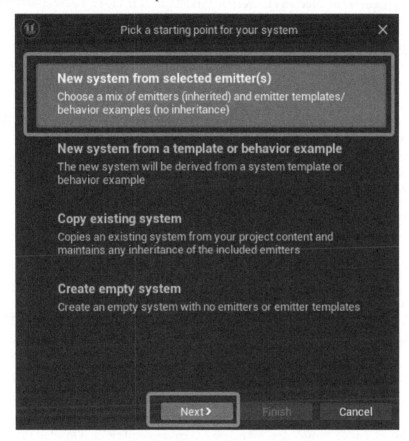

Figure 12.51 – Choosing the Niagara system starting point

Let's look at the options in reverse order:

- **Create empty system**: This allows us to start from scratch. We will find nothing inside our system, and we will need to create everything from scratch. This is the most advanced option.

- **Copy existing system**: This allows us to start from a Niagara system we have already created. This option is very useful if we want to create a variation of an existing effect or if we want to create something more complex that has some of the parameters another system has.

- **New system from a template or behavior example**: This allows us to pick a Niagara system template as a starting point. Niagara system templates are complex systems with a lot of parameters such as explosions.

- **New system from selected emitter(s)**: This allows us to create a new system by using an existing emitter.

An **emitter** is a fundamental component in a Niagara system responsible for generating and controlling particle effects. An emitter defines how particles are created, their initial properties, and their behavior over time. Think of it as the source or origin of a particular visual effect within the Niagara Particle System.

A Niagara system can have multiple emitters inside it to create diverse effects. We can add different components to each emitter that will help us to change the way the emitter works. These components work like the nodes we learned about in *Chapter 5* for material creation, and they are called **modules**. Each module has several parameters to be modified in order to obtain the desired effect.

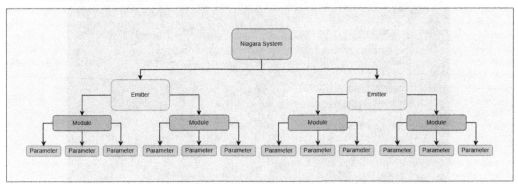

Figure 12.52 – Niagara system components

The best thing we can do, considering our purpose to create a dust effect, is to select the **New system from selected emitter(s)** option and click on **Next>** (see *Figure 12.51*).

Next, we need to choose the emitter we want to use to create our Niagara system. There are a lot of different emitters that can help us create different effects. To create a dust effect, we can select the **Hanging Particulates** emitter preset.

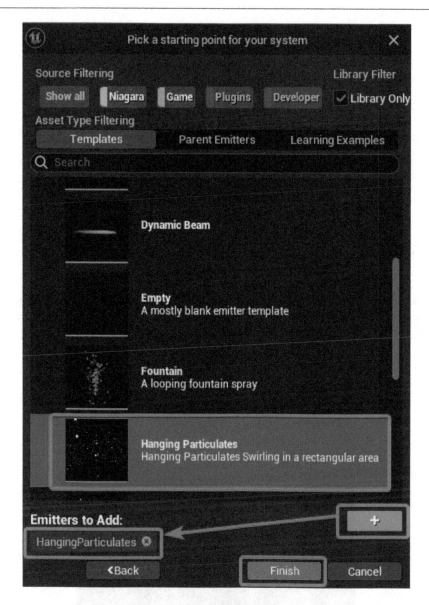

Figure 12.53 – Adding the Hanging Particulates emitter

Once we have selected the **Hanging Particulates** emitter, we have to add it to our Niagara system by clicking on the + button. It works in this way because, as we saw before, we can have more than one emitter in our Niagara system. Finally, click on the **Finish** button to create your first Niagara system.

Perfect! Now you should have your Niagara system created inside the **Content Browser**. Rename it NS_Dust_1.

Figure 12.54 – Niagara System thumbnail

Perfect! Before we start modifying our new Niagara system, we need to create a material with the Dust texture we have just downloaded. To do that, try to follow these steps:

1. Click the *RMB* on the Dust texture file inside the **Content Browser** and select **Create Material**. This command will automatically create a new *Master Material* with the dust texture connected to the **Base Color** input of **Material Domain**. Rename it M_Dust.

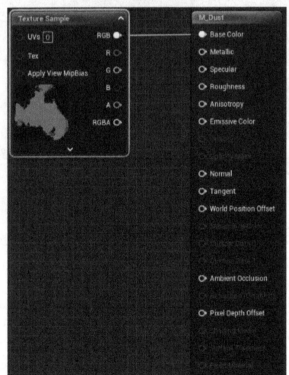

Figure 12.55 – Dust material inside the Material Editor

2. We need to change the **Blend Mode** of **Material** from **Opaque** to **Translucent** (we learned how to do that in *Chapter 5*) and connect the dust texture's **A** (alpha) output to the **Material Domain**'s **Opacity** input.

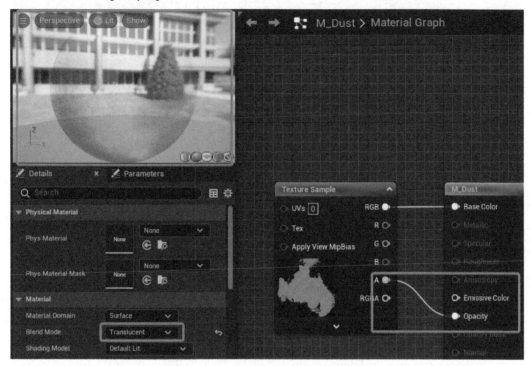

Figure 12.56 – Changing Blend Mode and connecting the A channel to the Opacity input

3. Apply and save our material.

Great! We are now ready to enter the Niagara Editor and change some parameters to create our **Dust** effect.

Double-click on the NS_Dust_1 Niagara system and try to follow these steps:

1. Double-clicking on the NS_Dust_1 Niagara system will open the Niagara Editor.

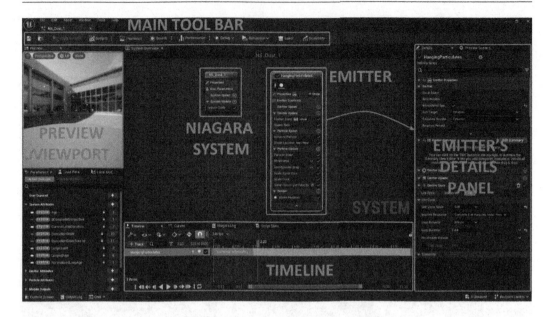

Figure 12.57 – Niagara Editor overview image

The **Niagara Editor** allows us to manage all aspects of our Niagara system. It is organized like other editors we have already seen. At the top, we can find the main toolbar. This provides us with basic commands such as **Save** and **Compile** that work in the same way as the Material Editor we saw in *Chapter 5*.

In the center part of the Editor, we can find all the elements that compose the Niagara system. If we select one of them, we can change settings inside the **Details** panel on the right-hand side of the Niagara Editor.

At the bottom of the Niagara Editor, there is the **Timeline** section, which allows us to play the particle animation.

On the left-hand side, we can find the **Preview** viewport, which shows us a preview of how the particle effect will look.

2. Now, we need to assign our dust material to our particles. To do that, select **Sprite Renderer** inside the emitter and assign our M_Dust material to the **Material** option inside the emitter's **Details** panel.

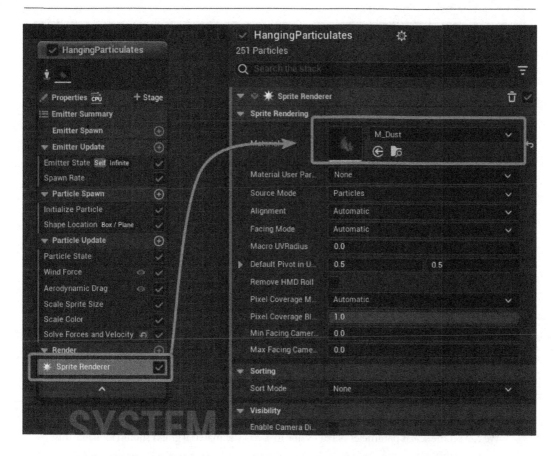

Figure 12.58 – Assigning dust material to the Sprite Renderer module

All the different settings we can select inside the emitter are *modules*. Each of them has different *parameters* inside the **Details** panel (see *Figure 12.47*).

3. Save our Niagara system with the *floppy disk* icon inside the main toolbar (it is the first icon in *Figure 12.57*).

4. Close the Niagara Editor and drag and drop your NS_Dust_1 Niagara system into the Level Viewport. Wait a second for Unreal Engine to compile some shaders and then the dust particles should start to appear.

Figure 12.59 – Dust particles inside the Level Viewport

As we can see in *Figure 12.59*, dust particles are not so visible. There are a couple of things that we can do to improve their visibility.

5.   First, open the **Dust** material and multiply the dust texture's **A** channel with a scalar parameter (we have already learned how to do that in *Chapter 5*). This action helps us to make the texture less transparent. We can set the scalar parameter default value to 1.5. The material graph should look like this:

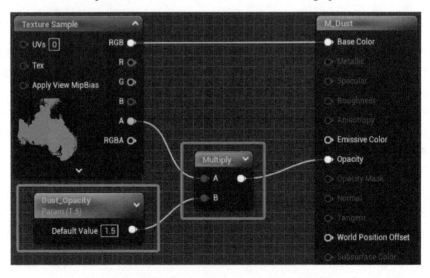

Figure 12.60 – Adding a parameter to control the dust opacity

6. Second, we can improve the number of particles inside the Niagara system. To do that, enter the Niagara Editor and select **Spawn Rate** inside the emitter. We can set the **SpawnRate** value to 300.

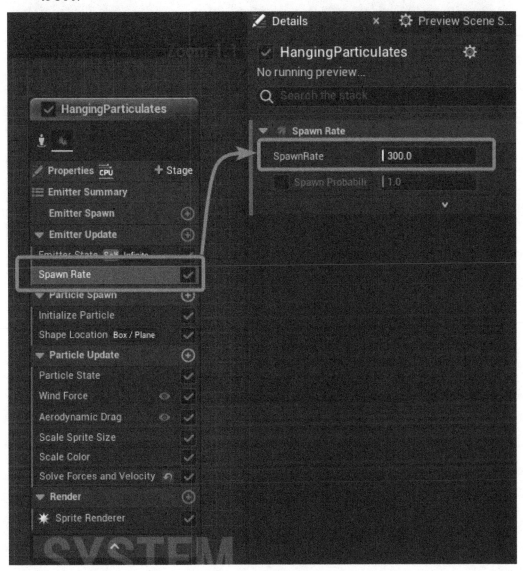

Figure 12.61 – Increasing the particle spawn rate

7. Save our Niagara system and look at what happened inside the Level Viewport.

Figure 12.62 – Dust particles inside the Level Viewport

8. Now, we want to change the size of our particles. They look too big. To do that, enter the Niagara Editor and select the **Initialize Particle** module inside the emitter. Search for the **Sprite Size Mode** option. It should already be set to **Random Uniform**. If not, change it. This option allows us to set a range of scale values in which the particle can be spawned. We can set the **Uniform Sprite Size Min** value to 0.5 and the **Uniform Sprite Size Max** value to 1.0.

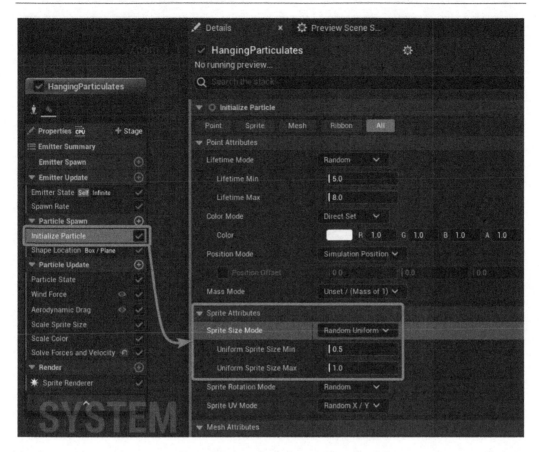

Figure 12.63 – Changing Sprite Size Mode and its values

Great! The dust effect is starting to look good. We have a couple more settings we can change to improve the result.

9. Particles are spawned inside a virtual shape. **Spawn Rate** considers the size of that shape. In other words, if we have a bigger spawner shape, there will be more distance between the particles themselves. Inside the emitter, there is a module that allows us to manage the type and the size of the spawner shape. So, select **Shape Location** inside the emitter.

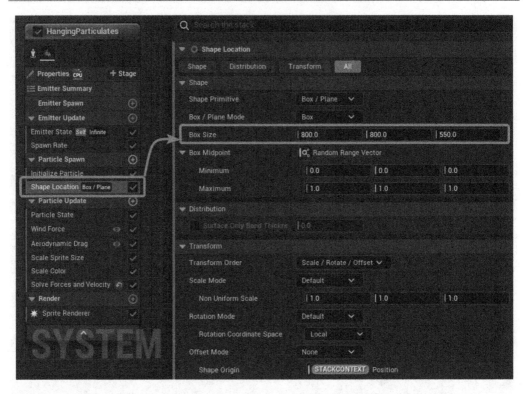

Figure 12.64 – Shape Location settings inside the emitter's Details panel

We can double the values we have by default, as we can see in *Figure 12.64*

10. We now probably need to increase again the **Spawn Rate** value we modified during *step 6*. We can now set it to 1500.

11. The last thing we need to do is to change the speed of the particle's movement. The **HangingParticulates** emitter we are using comes with a **Wind Force** module that gives the particles the typical turbulence movement. If we try to set its **Wind Speed Scale** parameter to 10, we should see our particle move very fast inside the Level Viewport.

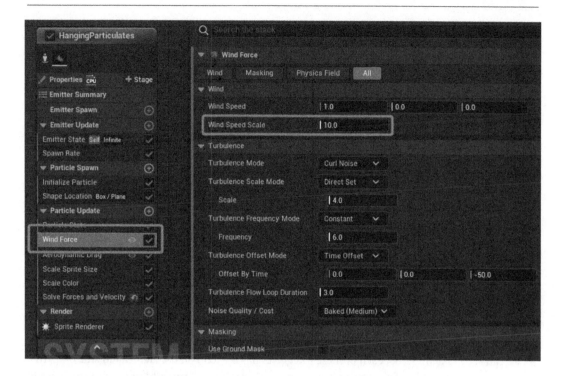

Figure 12.65 – Changing the Wind Speed Scale parameter

We probably don't need this in our Level, but this parameter can help us if we want to create a windy environment.

Perfect! We have just created our first particle effect using Niagara. The effect we have just created is very simple but also very common and useful in a lot of different kinds of environments. This demonstration could be a good starting point to start studying Niagara and improve the quality of your effects inside Unreal Engine.

Before closing this chapter and in preparation for the last chapter (!), you need to learn how to add new modules to the emitter to enable you to explore, in depth, the Niagara system by yourself (if you need to).

The emitter is divided into categories:

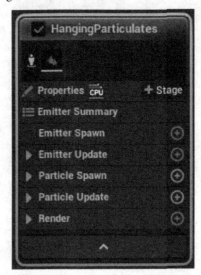

Figure 12.66 – Emitter's categories

As we can see in *Figure 12.66*, each of these categories has a + icon on the right-hand side of it. That + icon allows us to add different modules to each category in order to add different properties to our particles.

Let's take a look at what these categories allow us to do:

- **Emitter Spawn**: In this category, we can add modules to control the creation and emission of particles. Each module inside this category determines how particles are generated over time and influences the overall behavior of the particle emitter.

  For instance, here, we can add modules such as the following:

  - **Initial Location**: This module allows us to control where particles are initially placed in the simulated environment. This can include settings for spawning particles at specific locations, such as a point, a volume, or a shape.

  - **Initial Velocity**: This module allows us to control the initial speed and direction of particles upon creation. This determines how particles move from their spawn point.

  - **Initial Size**: This module allows us to control the size of particles when they are first spawned. This can be a fixed value or vary based on specified conditions.

  - **Initial Color** This module allows us to control the initial color of particles. This is crucial for establishing the appearance of particles as soon as they are created.

  - **Initial Rotation** This module allows us to control how particles are oriented when they are spawned. This can include random rotation or specific alignment based on defined angles.

- **Initial Mass and Rotation Rate**: These modules allow us to control the mass and rotation rate. These properties influence how particles behave in response to external forces and their own rotational motion.

- **Spawn Rate and Burst Settings**: These modules allow us to control the rate at which particles are emitted per second and can include burst settings for emitting particles in groups at specific intervals.

- **Lifetime and Decay**: This module allows us to control settings related to particle lifetime and decay. These properties define how long each particle lives and how it behaves as it reaches the end of its lifespan.

- **Emitter Update**: In this category, we can add modules to control the ongoing behavior and evolution of particles emitted by a specific emitter. The **Emitter Update** properties control how particles change and interact over time, shaping the overall appearance and dynamics of the particle effect.

For instance, here, we can add modules such as the following:

- **Velocity and Movement**: This module allows us to control the velocity and movement of particles. This encompasses settings such as initial velocity, acceleration, and drag, determining how particles move through the simulated environment.

- **Rotation and Orientation**: This module allows us to control the rotation and orientation of particles. This allows for dynamic changes in the orientation of each particle, influencing how they spin, rotate, or align themselves over their lifetime.

- **Size and Scale**: This module allows us to control the size and scale of particles. This includes parameters such as initial size, size over life, and size scaling, allowing for changes in particle size as they evolve.

- **Color and Opacity**: This module allows us to control the color and opacity of particles. These settings determine the initial color, color over life, and opacity over life, affecting the visual appearance of particles as they progress through their life cycle.

- **Collision and Interaction**: This module allows us to control particle collision and interaction with the environment. This may involve specifying how particles respond when colliding with surfaces or other particles.

- **Material Parameters**: This module allows us to control the dynamic adjustment of material parameters over time. This can include altering textures, emissive properties, or other material characteristics.

- **Dynamic Parameters**: This module allows us to control dynamic parameters that enable adjustments based on various factors, such as the distance to a specific point in the scene or the velocity of particles.

- **Particle Spawn**: In this category, we can add modules to control the creation and initial characteristics of individual particles emitted by an emitter. These settings define how particles are spawned, their initial appearance, and various attributes at the moment of creation.

  For instance, here, we can add modules such as those we listed for the **Emitter Spawn** category, with the difference that they will relate to any individual particle.

- **Particle Update**: In this category, we can add modules to control the ongoing behavior and evolution of individual particles over their lifetime. The **Particle Update** settings control how particles change and interact after their initial creation, shaping the overall appearance and dynamics of the particle effect.

  For instance, here, we can add modules such as those we listed for the **Emitter Update** category, with the difference that they will be related to any individual particle.

Great! We have finished! Now, we know how to add modules to the different emitter categories. You can now try to experiment with the Niagara system and emitters to create a more complex dust effect or a totally new effect starting from an empty emitter.

Summary

With this chapter, we have entered the final phase of the environment creation workflow that will conclude at the end of *Chapter 13*: the post-processing and rendering phase. We started by learning what a PPV is and how it works. We moved on by learning more about color spaces and color workflows to ensure color consistency through different devices.

Next, we explored all the PPV's parameters that can help us to artistically improve our frame. We learned what the **Bloom** effect is, how to manage **Chromatic Aberration**, how to add a Dirt Mask to our frame, and how to use physical **Camera** settings. We also learned about **Local Exposure** and how to use it to improve our frame, how to add **Lens Flares** and **Vignette** effects, how to change the frame **Temperature** settings to create diverse lighting mood, how to color-correct our frame, and how to change the film properties and add some grain to our frame.

In the following section, we learned what a Color LUT is and how we can create one to be used inside our PPV to change the overall aspect of our frame. Finally, we introduced the Niagara Particle System by creating a dust effect.

The amount of knowledge we have developed during these 12 intensive chapters is awesome. Take your time to refine your environment or to create a new one and compose your shot because, in the next and final chapter, we will learn how to export the final video to present your environment.

13

Rendering and Exporting Cinematic Shots

We have finally arrived at the ending chapter of this book. After discovering everything about creating a realistic environment inside Unreal Engine 5 and how to compose a cinematic shot, we are now ready to learn how to export image sequences and render out a high-resolution video.

In this chapter, we will learn the fundamental concepts of real-time rendering. We will move on and learn how to prepare a Level Sequence for the rendering phase; we will also learn what the **Movie Render Queue** plugin is and how to set it to improve the final quality of the exported video.

We will cover the following topics in this chapter:

- Fundamentals of real-time rendering
- Setting the Level Sequence
- Discovering the **Movie Render Queue** plugin
- Setting up a render
- Exporting the final shot

By the end of this chapter, we will be able to set a render with the **Movie Render Queue** plugin to export our cinematic shots.

Technical requirements

In this chapter, we will use the **Megascans Abandoned Apartment** project we have already used during *Chapter 6* and *Chapter 11*. To easily follow the chapter, you should have it opened on your workstation.

Fundamentals of real-time rendering

Before starting the process that will allow us to export a high-definition video of the shot we have created inside Unreal Engine 5, we need to understand how the rendering process works inside the Engine.

First, we need to define what real-time rendering is and what are the differences with offline rendering.

Real-time rendering is a process in computer graphics where images or animations are generated and displayed in real time, meaning the rendering happens quickly enough to provide an interactive experience. For this reason, it is commonly used in video games. We have tasted what we have just said during the entire book: everything we perform inside the Engine's Level Viewport is rendered in real time to show us what we are doing; everything happens in a quality that can be considered equal to the final one.

On the other side, **offline rendering** refers to the generation of images or animations over a longer period, often requiring significant computational resources. This method is commonly used in the production of films, animations, and high-quality visual effects where the emphasis is on achieving the highest possible image quality, even if it takes a considerable amount of time. Offline rendering excludes any interaction possibility and forces us to work with a draft version in terms of visual quality.

The choice between real-time rendering and offline rendering depends on the specific requirements of the project, with real-time rendering offering interactivity and efficiency, while offline rendering prioritizes maximum image quality and realism, even at the cost of longer processing times.

At the end of the day, the quality we can achieve with real-time rendering is not on the same level as the quality we can achieve with offline rendering. But the advantages we can acquire with a real-time rendering pipeline in terms of time efficiency and interactivity are convincing a lot of studios (that typically haven't worked in the video game industry) to change their pipeline in favor of a real-time pipeline with Unreal Engine 5.

One of the most important things we want to understand with this chapter and, in general, with this book is the fact that Unreal Engine 5 and, in general, real-time technologies could be an incredible improvement in any kind of digital pipeline (also outside the video games field) without losing that much quality.

Defining that, in this chapter, we are going to learn how to export a video using Unreal Engine 5 and real-time technologies. That means that we are going to perform work that offline rendering usually does, trying to get advantages from the real-time technology we are using.

Perfect! Now that we know what real-time rendering means, we can move on and start to set our Level Sequence.

Setting the Level Sequence

In this section, we will learn how to set the Level Sequence to be rendered. The first thing we need to know is the fact that when we render something with Unreal Engine 5, we are rendering the content of a **Level Sequence**.

In fact, we are rendering what we have recorded inside **Camera Cuts**. So, the first thing we need to be sure of is to have **Camera Cuts** set in our Level Sequence with all the Cine Camera Actors we want to export inside it:

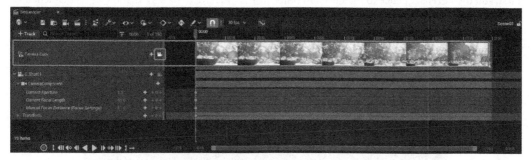

Figure 13.1 – Camera Cuts inside the Level Sequence

We also have to be sure to have the **Lock Viewport to Camera Cuts** option enabled by selecting the *camera* icon on the **Camera Cuts** line's right side (see *Figure 13.1*).

The second thing we need to know is the fact that the Engine will render all the frames included between the Timeline's *Green Line* and the Timeline's *Red Line*. You can change their positions also by changing the green and red frame values in the bottom part of the Level Viewport (see *Figure 13.2*):

> **Note**
>
> Remember that we can see the green and red frame values only if we have the Cinematic Viewport enabled, as we have already learned in *Chapter 11*.

Figure 13.2 – Starting and ending frame values

There are two more things we need to do before starting the rendering process.

First, add the Level Sequence to the Level. In other words, we have to be sure that the Level Sequence we want to render has been placed inside the Level Viewport (so that we can find it inside the **Outliner** tab).

Second, we need to flag the **Auto Play** option inside the Level Sequence's **Details** panel:

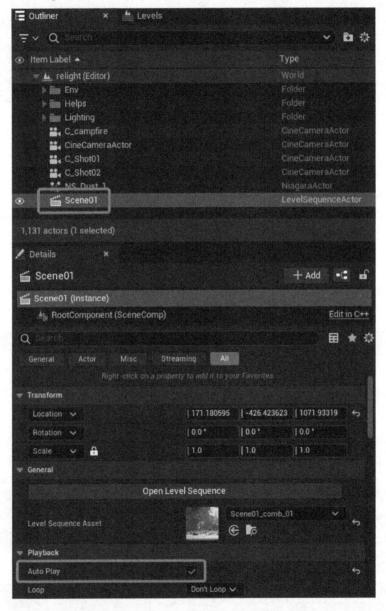

Figure 13.3 – Auto Play option inside the Level Sequence's Details panel

This option ensures that the Level Sequence will be played when the Level will be loaded. In other words, when the game starts, the Engine will load the Level we want to play because the proprieties of all the assets, including the Level Sequence, are saved inside the Level. And if it finds a Level Sequence with the **Auto Play** option enabled, it will play the **Camera Cut** saved in it. So, this option is created for a gaming purpose but enabling it will also avoid issues in the rendering phase.

Perfect! We are now ready to activate the **Movie Render Queue** plugin and explore its settings.

Discovering the Movie Render Queue plugin

Across the last Unreal Engine 4 versions and the first Unreal Engine 5 release, Epic Games has introduced **Movie Render Queue**, a new built-in plugin that allows us to manage in a more "offline way" our rendering setup. The **Movie Render Queue** plugin has been created to encourage users to use Unreal Engine 5 in cinematic productions outside the gaming industry.

Movie Render Queue is a plugin, so we need to activate it inside the **All Plugins** window (as we have already done a lot of time during this book). As always, the Engine will ask us to restart:

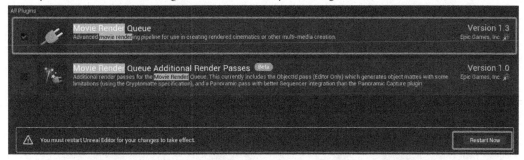

Figure 13.4 – Enabling the Movie Render Queue plugin inside the All Plugins window

Once we have reloaded the Engine, we can open the **Movie Render Queue** plugin in two ways:

- Inside the **Window** menu, under the **Cinematics** category, we can find the **Movie Render Queue** option:

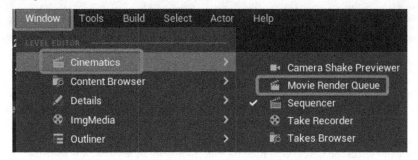

Figure 13.5 – Movie Render Queue option inside the Window menu

- Inside **Sequencer**, near the toolbar's *Ciak* icon (we have seen it in *Chapter 11*), the *three-point* menu allows us to choose which render method we want to use. If we select the **Movie Render Queue** option, the *Ciak* menu will open the **Movie Render Queue** plugin:

Figure 13.6 – Enabling the Movie Render Queue plugin inside the Level Sequence

There are no differences using the two methods apart from the fact that if we launch the **Movie Render Queue** plugin from the **Sequencer**, the Level Sequence opened in the **Sequencer** will be automatically added to the **Movie Render Queue** plugin. We will learn what that means in a minute.

Great! We can now open the **Movie Render Queue** plugin. To easily follow the explanation, open it using the **Window** menu:

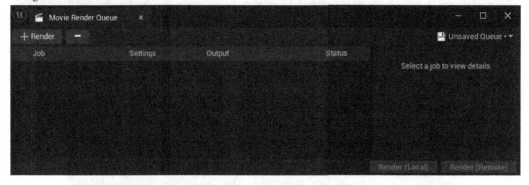

Figure 13.7 – Movie Render Queue window

The first time we open the **Movie Render Queue** window, it is empty. The only thing we can do is to click on the **+ Render** button. This action allows us to choose the Level Sequence that we want to add to the render queue.

So, click on it and select the Level Sequence you want to render. In my case, it is the Scene01 Level Sequence Level Sequence:

Figure 13.8 – Adding a Level Sequence to the render queue

Once you have selected the Level Sequence you want to render, the **Movie Render Queue** window should look like this:

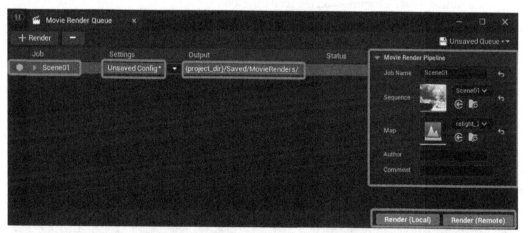

Figure 13.9 – Movie Render Queue with one Level Sequence in queue

If we decide to launch the plugin from inside the **Sequencer** (see *Figure 13.6*), the **Movie Render Queue** window will look like what we see in *Figure 13.9*. So, you will not need to add the Level Sequence again inside the **Movie Render Queue** window.

As we can see in *Figure 13.9*, a line dedicated to our Level Sequence appears inside **Movie Render Queue**'s **Job** panel. The line is divided into the following:

- **Job**: This is the name of the Level Sequence.

- **Settings**: Here is where we will able to change the render settings. We will explore them in the *Setting up a render* section later in this chapter.

- **Output**: This is a link to the `Output` folder. This is only a link; we can't change the destination folder here.

- **Status**: This line segment defines the render status. Now, it is empty because we have not rendered the Level Sequence yet.

On the right side of the **Movie Render Queue** window, we have the **Movie Render Pipeline** panel. It is visible only if you have a job selected in the **Job** panel on the left side. Inside the **Movie Render Pipeline** tab, we see the following options:

- **Job Name**: Change the name the Engine will give to the rendering job.

- **Sequence**: Check which Level Sequence is referred to in the rendering job. If we need to, we can change it.

- **Map**: Check to which Level the Level Sequence refers. If we need to, we can change it.

- **Author**: Give the author's name to the rendering job.

- **Comment**: Leave a comment on the rendering job.

As the plugin name says, we can create a queue of rendering jobs by adding multiple Level Sequences to the **Job** panel. Each rendering job could have different settings and destination folders and could refer to different Levels inside the project:

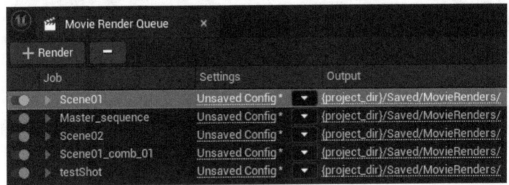

Figure 13.10 – Movie Render Queue with multiple rendering jobs

Perfect! We are now ready to learn how to change render settings.

Setting up a render

In this section, we will learn how to set a render to obtain the highest quality. This is going to be a very technical section in which we will explain some rendering concepts and define a balanced rendering setting.

We will not go through all the possible settings; we will learn only the most useful. This section is very important to understand how to valorize our shot with a high-quality render.

The first thing we need to do is to open the **Render Settings** window. To do that, click on the **Unsaved Config*** link under the **Settings** segment of the render job's line you want to change:

Figure 13.11 – Opening the Render Settings window

The **Render Settings** window looks like this:

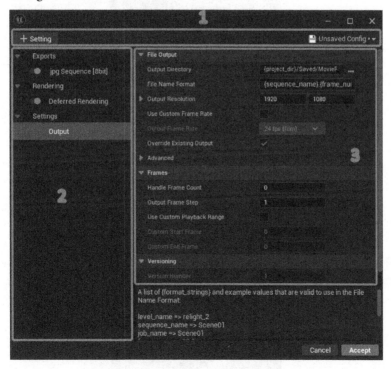

Figure 13.12 – Movie Render Queue render settings

Once we open the **Render Settings** window, it shows us the **Output** option (number **3** in *Figure 13.12*). We will come back to this later.

Let's take a look at what the **Render Settings** window provides to us:

- On the top side of the window, we have the *toolbar* (number **1** in *Figure 13.12*). Here, we can add settings to our render settings using the **+ Setting** button. We can save the setting config as a preset by clicking on **Unsaved Config*** on the toolbar's right side. We will save it at the end of the rendering configuration process.

- On the left side, we have the *settings tab* (number **2** in *Figure 13.12*) where we can find all the settings we have added by clicking on the **+ Setting** button.

- On the right side (number **3** in *Figure 13.12*), we can find the option about the setting we have selected in the settings tab.

OK. To clearly understand the rendering workflow, we should start from the draft by deleting everything we can find by default inside the settings tab. To do that, select all the settings and press *Delete* on the keyboard. Note that the **Output** setting can't be deleted.

Once we have deleted everything, we can start adding settings. To do that, click on the **+ Setting** button:

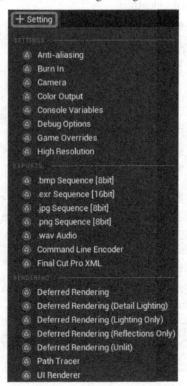

Figure 13.13 – Settings we can add to our render settings' config

The settings we can add to our render job are divided into three categories (see *Figure 13.13*):

- **SETTINGS**: In this category, we can find all the settings that allow us to manage the render quality.

- **EXPORTS**: In this category, we can find all the file types supported by the **Movie Render Queue** plugin.

- **RENDERING**: In this category, we can find all the different rendering processes we can add to our rendering job. For instance, **Deferred Rendering (Unlit)** allows us to render the Level Sequence in Unlit mode (the view mode we saw during *Chapter 2*).

From here on, we are going to describe the workflow to create a balanced render setting. We are going to cover it in section steps to make it easier to follow.

Choosing a rendering method

The first thing we need to do is to add a rendering type. The option we need to generate a render that represents what we can see inside our Level Viewport is **Deferred Rendering**:

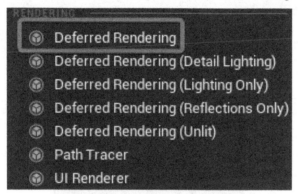

Figure 13.14 – Rendering settings

Deferred rendering is a rendering technique used in computer graphics to efficiently handle complex lighting and shading in scenes. Instead of immediately calculating lighting during the initial rendering pass, information about the scene is stored in a set of buffers called the G-Buffer.

The **G-Buffer** contains data such as position, normal, base color, roughness, and other material properties for each pixel. After the G-Buffer is created, a separate pass is used to calculate lighting. This is called **deferred shading**. In this pass, lighting calculations are performed per pixel using the information stored in the G-Buffer. This decouples the shading calculations from the number of lights in the scene, resulting in better performance.

The other deferred rendering options utilize the same technique to generate what we can see in the Level Viewport with specific view modes enabled.

Finally, we have another two options. **UI Renderer** has been created to help us render user interface elements. It is useful in gaming projects or in any kind of project that has interactive elements such as a *Viewport* icon that can be clicked to activate any kind of event. No use at all for us.

The last one is **Path Tracer**. **Path tracing** is a more advanced way of rendering scenes in Unreal Engine. It's like simulating how light would naturally behave in the real world, resulting in more lifelike and visually appealing graphics. Path tracing is part of broader ray-tracing capabilities (we talked about it in *Chapter 6*) introduced in Unreal Engine 5. It works more like an offline render process. It takes time to process one single frame, but we can achieve more fidelity images in terms of lighting using it. This does not mean in any way that with **Deferred Rendering** we can't achieve high-quality rendering. It is a different way to do the same thing with different technologies.

In this section, we want to explore how to achieve stunning rendering, taking advantage of the **Deferred Rendering** real-time capability. Anyway, you can try to make a render with **Path Tracer** by simulating it inside the Level Viewport. To do that, we need to enable some options inside the **Project Settings** window. **Path Tracer** works only with the **Support Hardware Raytracing** and **Path Tracing** options enabled plus **DefaultRHI** set to **Directx12** (as we already learned in *Chapter 6* when we talked about Lumen).

Now, we simply have to change the Level Viewport's view mode to **Path Tracing**:

Figure 13.15 – Activating Path Tracing view mode

Once we have activated the **Path Tracing** view mode, the Engine starts to process the frame with **Path Tracer**. It will take more or less time according to the power of your graphics card. A *progress bar* on the bottom side of the Level Viewport helps us understand how much longer the process will be:

Figure 13.16 – Path tracing process

Note that if you move the camera position inside the Level Viewport, the process will start all over again because changing the camera position means changing the frame.

> **Note**
>
> To use **Path Tracing**, you need to enable some options inside the **Project Settings** window. **Path Tracer** works only with the **Support Hardware Raytracing** and **Path Tracing** options enabled plus **DefaultRHI** set to **Directx12** (as we already learned in *Chapter 6* when we talked about Lumen).

If you want to learn more about **Path Tracer**, you can read more about it at this link: https://docs.unrealengine.com/5.3/en-US/path-tracer-in-unreal-engine/

Great! We can now select **Deferred Rendering**. The setting will be added to the **Settings** panel. By selecting it, we can check all the options dedicated to it in the right panel:

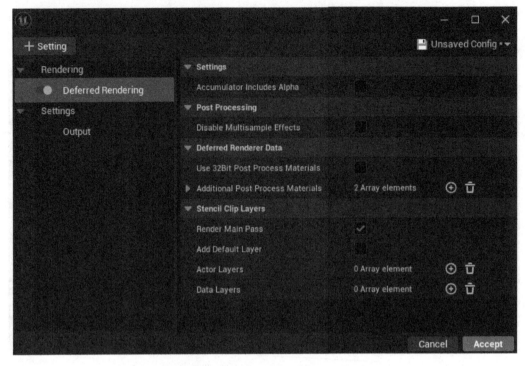

Figure 13.17 – Deferred Rendering options

We can leave the options by default.

We can now move on and choose an export file type.

Choosing an export file type

Now, it is time to choose in which format in terms of file type we want to export our shot. As we have already seen, we have a dedicated **EXPORTS** category inside the **+ Settings** menu:

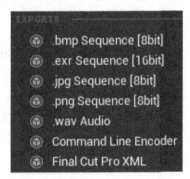

Figure 13.18 – File types that can be used

Let's take a look at what options the Engine provides to us:

- **.bmp Sequence [8bit]**: The .bmp format is very quick to be written on disk but generates large file sizes due to its uncompressed nature.

- **.exr Sequence [16bit]**: A high-dynamic range format developed by Industrial Light & Magic and used in video compositing. This is the VFX industry standard format thanks to its color range capability. The .exr file format usually works at 32 bits; Unreal Engine can generate *only* 16-bit EXRs. This file format will generate a huge file size but is totally lossless in terms of quality. We have two options for **EXR** (as seen in *Figure 13.19*):

Figure 13.19 – EXR format options

  - **Compression**: It allows us to choose the EXR compression algorithm we want to use. We can use the default one.

  - **Multilayer**: If this option is enabled, we can store multilayer images inside a single EXR frame. This is the way a high-end post-production studio works.

- **.jpg Sequence [8bit]**: The .jpg format generates a small file size, but it is lossy in terms of quality. It is perfect for generating fast rendering previews.

- **.png Sequence [8bit]**: The .png format generates a larger file size but ensures higher quality. It can also include an alpha channel on each frame:

Figure 13.20 – PNG format options

- **.wav Audio**: This setting allows us to export audio if there are any audio tracks in our Level Sequence.

- **Command Line Encoder**: This setting allows us to refer to an external software or tool that is used to encode or compress rendered frames into a final video format. The *Command Line* part indicates that this process is performed through commands entered in a **command-line interface** (CLI), which is a text-based interface for interacting with the computer.

To use this setting, we need to change some options inside the **Project Settings** window. This is just to let you know that this thing is possible. We don't need to know more about it than that.

- **Final Cut Pro XML**: This file acts as a bridge between Unreal Engine and video editing software. Final Cut Pro XML files are designed to be understood by Final Cut Pro software. By using this file, you can easily import your rendered video project into Final Cut Pro for further editing, adding effects, or combining it with other footage. This setting is usually added in addition to another file format.

Having defined all the different options the **Movie Render Queue** plugin provides to us, in 90 percent of cases, .png will be the best choice; if we are planning to make a lot of post-production outside the Engine, .exr should be the file format to select.

The *Sequence* word inside the file type's name means that the Engine will export an image sequence. In other words, the Engine will not export a video file but an image for each frame.

> **Note**
>
> To allow .png and .exr file formats to include an alpha channel, we need to enable this support inside the **Project Settings** window. Search for **Enable alpha channel support in post processing (experimental)** and set it to **Linear color space only**. You will need to restart the Engine.

Figure 13.21 – Enabling alpha channel support

Remember that we can always add more than one setting to allow us, in this case, to export the same Level Sequence in multiple formats.

Perfect! We can select **PNG** and go on.

Adding render settings

We can finally start to add quality settings to improve our render. We have a lot of different settings under the **SETTINGS** category:

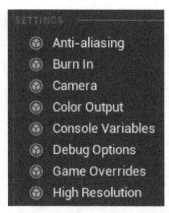

Figure 13.22 – Render settings that can be added

Let's take a look at the most useful options:

- **Anti-aliasing**: Anti-aliasing is a technique used in computer graphics to reduce visual artifacts and make images appear smoother, especially when dealing with diagonal lines and edges. In digital graphics, images are created using a grid of pixels. When a line or edge doesn't align perfectly with this grid, the Engine has to decide which pixels to color, leading to a jagged appearance.

  Anti-aliasing works by adding additional shades of color along the edges to smooth out the jagged appearance. Instead of having a sharp transition from one color to another, there's a gradual blending, creating a smoother visual effect:

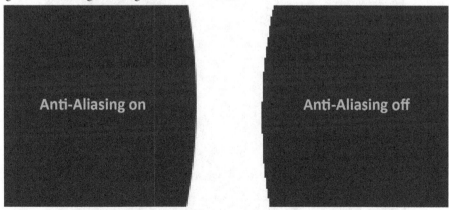

Figure 13.23 – Anti-aliasing explanation screenshot

The aliasing problem increases when we have dynamic scenes with a huge amount of motion blur.

Unreal Engine 5 applies anti-aliasing by default according to what we have set inside the **Project Settings** window. There are different anti-aliasing algorithms. By default, the Engine is set to use **Temporal Super-Resolution (TSR)**, which is the most evolved:

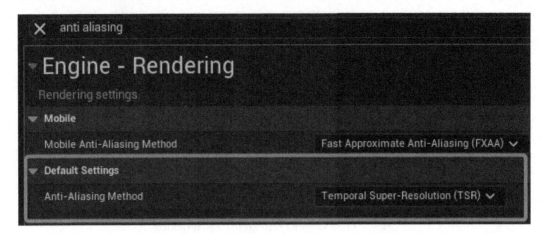

Figure 13.24 – Anti-aliasing option inside the Project Settings window

Exploring the differences between different anti-aliasing algorithms is not the purpose of this section but it could be important to know which one is used by default.

Inside the **Rendering Settings** window, we can improve the way the Engine uses the anti-aliasing technique to increase the final quality of our output. We can add it to our **Settings** panel and start to explore which options we can change (as seen in *Figure 13.25*):

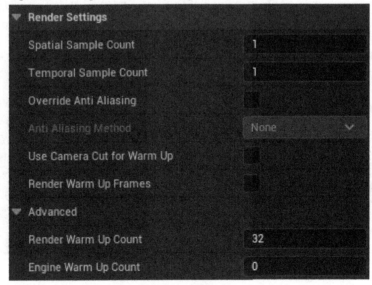

Figure 13.25 – Anti-aliasing options

- **Spatial Sample Count** and **Temporal Sample Count**: These values define how many times we want to apply (sample) the aliasing correction to each frame. They work in two different ways to face different aliasing problems.

- **Spatial sampling** works by rendering the same frame multiple times (a number of times equal to the sample count), each time jittering the camera a little bit. This technique works very well with scenes with a low number of dynamic elements.

- On the other hand, **temporal sampling** works together with the motion blur amount by closing the number of times equal to the sample count of the camera shutter. This works very well with dynamic scenes.

- **We can use them together to achieve the best result. Anyway, it is more convenient to add samples to** temporal sampling **considering that non-moving objects will receive anti-aliasing in the same way, and moving objects will be blurred, correcting the aliasing.**

- A good setting could be leaving at 1 the **Spatial Sample Count** value and raising the **Temporal Sample Count** value to a max value equal to 64. These settings are very helpful in very dynamic scenes with strong movements and curved lines involved in the composition. For this reason and considering our scene, we can set **Temporal Sample Count** to 16:

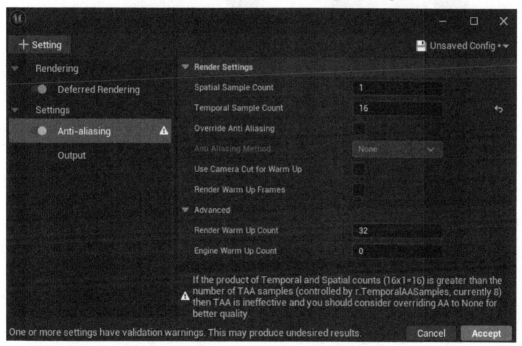

Figure 13.26 – Setting anti-aliasing samples

- Showing the difference between different anti-aliasing is not so easy with static frames. You can check a very helpful interactive slide on Unreal Engine 5's official documentation by browsing to this link: https://docs.unrealengine.com/5.3/en-US/cinematic-rendering-image-quality-settings-in-unreal-engine/#anti-aliasing

- You can see the static version in *Figure 13.27*:

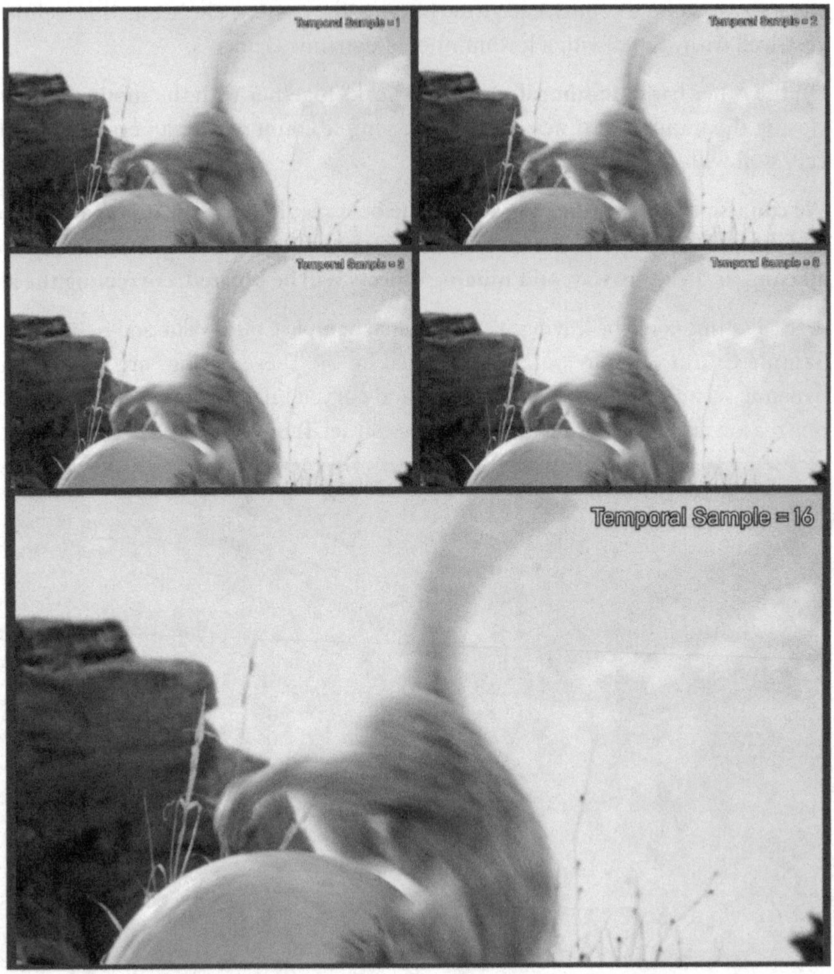

Figure 13.27 – Temporal sample examples from Epic Games' Unreal Engine documentation

- As we can see in *Figure 13.26*, a warning message has appeared. It says:

If the product of Temporal and Spatial counts (16X1=16) is greater than the number of TAA samples (controlled by r.TemporalAASamples, currently 8), then TAA is ineffective and you should consider overriding AA to none for better quality.

- In other words, the Engine is telling us that we are trying to set an anti-aliasing overall value that is higher than the one set by default according to the r.TemporalAASamples console variable. We have two possibilities to resolve this problem. The first is to change the default value, but this action could cause a worse Level Viewport experience in terms of performance, or we could check the **Override Anti Aliasing** option (*Figure 13.28*).

- **Render Warm Up Count** and **Engine Warm Up Count**: These values refer to the number of frames or iterations used for a warm-up phase before the actual rendering job starts. At this time, image effects such as auto-exposure or other screen effects can achieve a good starting point, avoiding issues in the first frames. We can set both to 32:

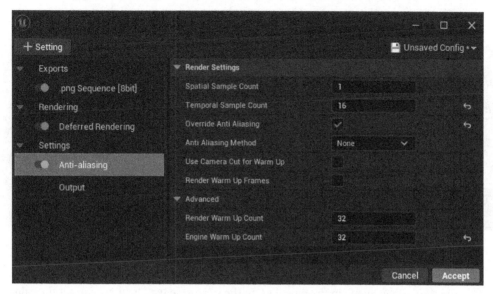

Figure 13.28 – Anti-aliasing options set

- **Burn In**: With this setting, we can write information directly on each frame. This is very useful for reviewing jobs or sharing activities:

Figure 13.29 – A frame with the Burn In setting enabled

- **Console Variables**: This is a very important setting because it allows us to push the quality of any single aspect of our scene using console variables. In other words, if we want to improve the shadow quality only during the rendering process, we can do it with the **Console Variables** setting. Don't worry about it; it is far away from being as complex as coding. We only need to know which parameters we want to improve during the rendering job and put them into the **Console Variables** panel:

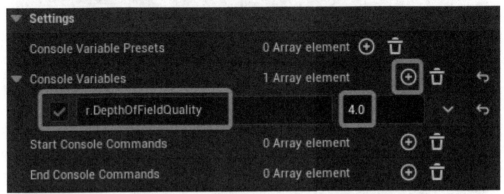

Figure 13.30 – An example of a console variable

To add a new console variable, we need to click on the plus (+) icon (see *Figure 13.30*) and write the variable name in the type files. In the right-side type field, we can set the value we want to use during the rendering job. If we try to type a letter inside the type field, the Engine helps us with a list of console variables using that letter in the name:

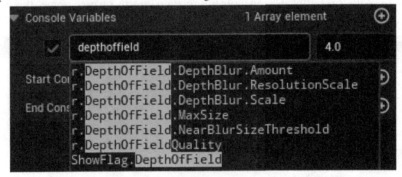

Figure 13.31 – An example of how to search the console variable we need

The are hundreds of console variables, and choosing which ones we want to use depends on what we are doing. For instance, if we are using hardware raytracing, there are a bunch of console variables dedicated to improving its quality. For this reason, we are going to list a group of console variables that could be useful in any case:

- `r.MotionBlurQuality`: This variable controls the quality of motion blur that helps dynamic scenes and movable elements. We can set it to 4.

- `r.DepthOfFieldQuality`: This variable improves the quality of **Depth of Field** (**DOF**). If we have a lot of focus changes and out-of-focus parts in our frame, this variable will help a lot. We can set it to 4.

- `r.BloomQuality`: This variable improves the **Bloom** effect quality. As we saw in *Chapter 12*, the **Bloom** effect can help to achieve a particular lighting effect in our scene. We can set it to 5.

- `r.ShadowQuality`: This variable helps us to push the shadow quality of our scene. Nothing more to say. We set it to 5.

- Last but not least, if we are using volumetric fog in our level, we can add these variables:

  - `r.VolumetricFog.GridSizeZ` set to 256

  - `r.VolumetricFog.GridPixelSize` set to 2

  - `r.VolumetricFog.TemporalReprojection` set to 1

- The console variables' option panel should look like this:

Figure 13.32 – Console variables' option panel filled with console variables

- **Game Overrides**: This is the last setting we need to ensure a high-quality render. Having game overrides in our rendering settings means telling the Engine that we want to use the best possible quality, ignoring all the gaming techniques to manage scalable quality. We only need to add it to the game settings without changing anything.

Great! We have done it! Your **Render Settings** panel should now look like this:

Figure 13.33 – Render Settings panel

We are now ready to set the **Output** preferences.

Setting the Output preferences

The last thing we need to do before launching our rendering job is to set the **Output** preferences:

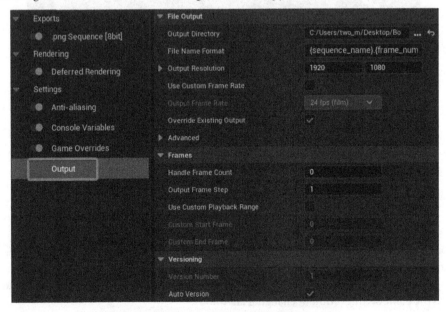

Figure 13.34 – Output preferences inside the Render Settings panel

Let's take a look at what we can manage inside the **Output** preferences. We are going to learn only the most relevant options:

- **Output Directory**: Here, we can choose the destination folder of our render.

- **File Name Format**: With this option, we can choose the naming convention of our frames. We can type anything we want in the type of field or use tokens that will automatically rename any frames with specific information. By default, it is set to `{sequence_name}.{frame_number}`, which means every frame will be renamed with the name of the Level Sequence we are exporting dot the frame number. In my case, the first frame will be `Scene01.001.png`.

  We can use any kind of naming convention, but using the `{frame_number}` token at the end of the name is very useful to allow us to easily manage the image sequence as a video. This is because the editing software will recognize the image sequence as a video thanks to the increasing frame number.

- **Output Resolution**: Here, we can set the final resolution of our render. By default, it is set to `1920x1080`. To change it, we can simply type the new resolution's values. We can try to render a 4k export. To do that, we can set the output resolution to `3840x2160`.

- **Use Custom Frame Rate**: If this option is enabled, the **Output Frame Rate** drop-down menu will allow us to set a custom frame rate to use during the rendering job. Using a custom frame rate doesn't mean using random values. As we already learned in *Chapter 11*, a frame rate that does not match the Level Sequence's original frame rate will create timing issues in the final render. This option has been thought to set a frame rate that can be used to generate a **slow-motion** effect.

  To create a slow-motion effect, we need at least double the number of frames per second. For instance, if we have an origin frame rate set to `30`, we can set the output frame rate to `60` or any value multiple of `30`.

  A good habit is to have **Use Custom Frame Rate** always enabled and set out Level Sequence's original frame rate. This action will force the Engine to use the frame rate we have set inside the **Output** preferences avoiding any kind of timing issue.

- **Override Existing Output**: If this option is enabled, the rendering job will override rendered frames with the same name in the destination folder.

- **Use Custom Playback Range**: If enabled, this option allows us to choose a custom frame range to render. For instance, if our sequence is 150 frames long, we can set **Custom Start Frame** to `50` and **Custom End Frame** to `120`. In this way, the rendering job will consider only frames between the 50th and the 120th frames.

Perfect! We are done! We have set out rendering settings to obtain a high-resolution output of our shot. Before starting the rendering job, we can save our rendering settings as a preset. To do that, we can click on the **Unsaved Config** button on the top-right side of the **Rendering Settings** window:

Figure 13.35 – Save as Preset option

A **Save Config Preset** window appears:

Figure 13.36 – Save Config Preset window

In this window, we can select the folder location of our render config preset and the name. I usually create a Rendering_preset folder inside my Cinematics folder. About the name, it is important to use a name that suggests to us what we will find inside the render config preset.

In our case, we are saving a render config that allows us to export a 4k .png image sequence with **Temporal Anti-Aliasing** set to 16. We can use a name such as 4k_PNG_TAA_16. We can click on **Save** to save the render config preset.

When we are done, we can click on the **Accept** button inside the **Render Settings** panel:

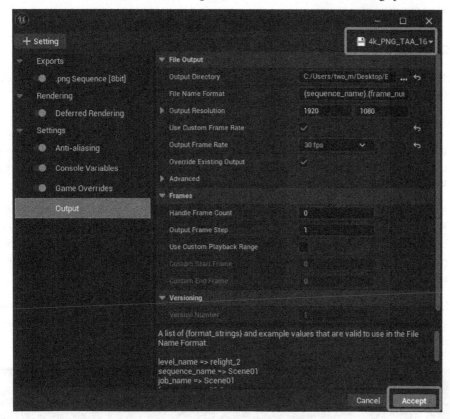

Figure 13.37 – Accepting rendering settings

Now, the **Movie Render Queue** plugin's **Job** panel should look like this:

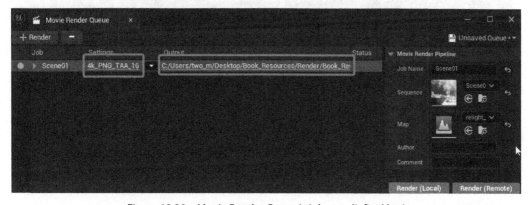

Figure 13.38 – Movie Render Queue's Job panel's final look

Great! We have just set our rendering job to generate a high-resolution output. We can now go on and finalize our exports.

Exporting the final shot

In this last section, we will learn how to effectively export our image sequence. We have already set everything we need. The only thing we need to do is to launch the rendering job.

To do that, we have two choices (see *Figure 13.38*):

- **Render (Local)**: This means that the rendering process occurs on the same machine where Unreal Engine is running. In other words, if you want to quickly start the rendering job, the **Render (Local)** button will launch the rendering job using local resources.

- **Render (Remote)**: This means that the rendering process can utilize remote rendering resources. Remote rendering is a practice very common in offline rendering pipelines when any frames usually take a lot of time to be rendered. In these cases, we can take advantage of the power of multiple machines to shorten the rendering time. The **Render (Remote)** button allows us to use (if available) the same techniques during Unreal Engine 5's rendering process.

Considering the nature of our scene, we can use the **Render (Local)** option. So, click on the button. The Engine will take a while, and then a **Movie Pipeline Render (Preview)** window will appear. The first time we launch the rendering job, the Engine will need to compile the shaders:

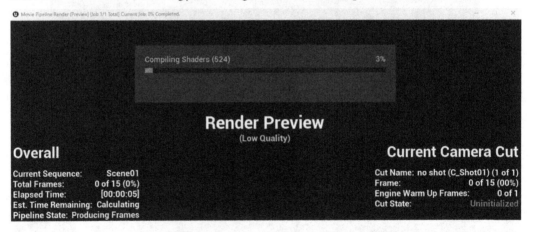

Figure 13.39 – Compiling shaders inside the Movie Pipeline Render (Preview) window

Once the process is ended, the rendering job begins. The **Movie Pipeline Render (Preview)** window will show a preview of the frame that is currently rendering:

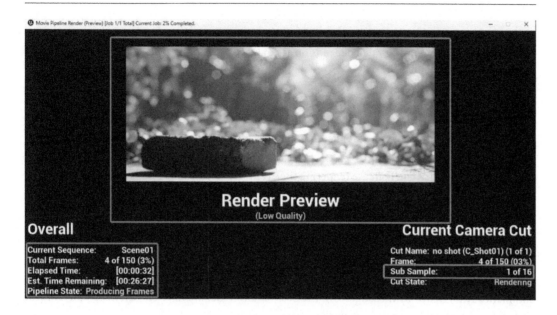

Figure 13.40 – Movie Pipeline Render (Preview) window

Let's take a look at what the **Movie Pipeline Render (Preview)** window shows us:

- **Render Preview**: This is a preview of what the rendering job is doing. This is only a preview, and it does not represent the final look of the output, but it could be very useful for spotting huge rendering problems.

- **Overall**: In this portion of the **Movie Pipeline Render (Preview)** window, we have general information about our rendering job. Here, we can find the name of the current sequence we are rendering, the **Total Frames** number, the elapsed time, and the estimated time remaining. The **Pipeline State** field tells us the rendering job phase.

- **Current Camera Cut**: In this portion of the **Movie Pipeline Render (Preview)** window, we can find information about the Level Sequence (specifically about the Camera Cut we are rendering).

  Cut Name tells us the name of the shot (if we have multiple Level Sequences inside the **Sequencer**) or the name of the camera recorded by the Camera Cut. In our case, we are rendering a single Level Sequence with a single camera inside. The **Frame** line indicates which frame the Engine is rendering. Finally, **Sub Sample** shows us the anti-aliasing samples. In our case, we have set 16 samples to **Temporal Sample Count** so that the **Movie Pipeline Render (Preview)** window shows us 16 samples for each frame.

> **Note**
>
> The **Est. Time Remaining** value depends on several factors: first of all, the graphics card power and memory capability. The rendering process is all about the graphics card on your workstation. CPU isn't involved in the process.
>
> In the second instance, the amount of rendering settings will impact the quality but also the rendering time. The **Anti-aliasing** setting is very heavy on performance, and very high sample values will increase a lot the time the Engine needs to export your frames. Console variables will also increase rendering time.
>
> Another option that can increase rendering time is the resolution. The settings we have learned will ensure a balance between a high level of detail and a short rendering time. Obviously, it depends a lot on your workstation specs and on your scene. Unfortunately, there isn't a magic recipe to create a rendering config that can suit any kind of project or that works with any kind of hardware specs.

Great! When the rendering process is over, the **Movie Pipeline Render (Preview)** window will automatically be closed by the Engine. In the destination folder we have chosen inside the **Output** preferences, we should have something like this:

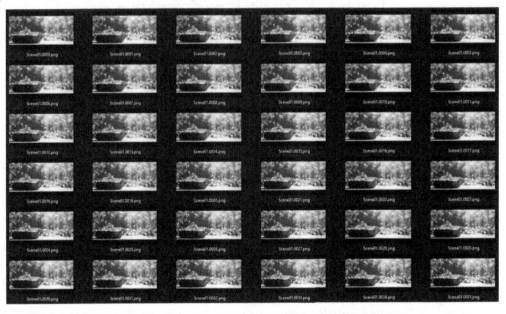

Figure 13.41 – An example of how the output folder should look

Before editing the Level Sequence into a video, we have one more thing to discuss. If you remember, to craft the shot in *Figure 13.41*, we used a custom camera sensor. It is 54mm x 23mm, which has a different aspect ratio from the standard 16:9, but we have set a 3460x2160 output resolution that follows the standard 16:9 ratio. The consequence of that is a final frame with a black letterbox:

Figure 13.42 – Frame Scene01.0001 with letterbox

This is not necessarily a problem, but maybe we want an output without a black letterbox. To do that, we simply need to convert the 4k resolution to our aspect ratio (that is different from 16:9). A simple way to do that is to use Photoshop or any other 2D graphics software. We can simply follow the next steps:

1. Create a new Photoshop document with a size equal to the Cine Camera Actor sensor size. Remember to set the document in millimeters:

Figure 13.43 – Creating a new Photoshop document in millimeters

2. Once you have created the document, click the **Image Size…** option under the **Image** menu:

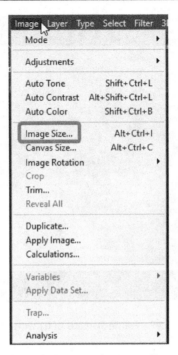

Figure 13.44 – Opening the Image Size panel

3. Inside the **Image Size** panel, lock the **Width** and **Weight** values with the *lock* icon, change **Millimeters** to **Pixels**, and set the **Width** value to 3840 (or with the resolution width you want to use). The **Height** value will be updated automatically:

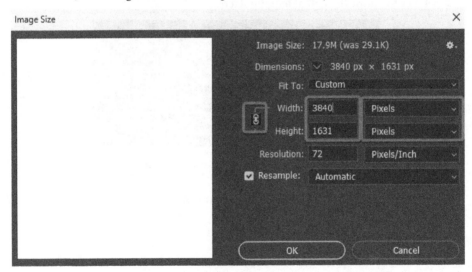

Figure 13.45 – Image Size panel

4.   The **Width** and **Height** values we now have inside the **Image Size** panel represent the resolution we need to use inside the Engine to avoid a black letterbox.

> **Note**
>
> If you want to preserve the height and the number of pixels, you can set the **Height** value to 2160 (for 4k resolution) and let Photoshop change the **Width** value for you.

We are now ready to edit our image sequence. You can do that with any video editing software. The only thing you have to take care of is to tell the editing software to consider your output frames as an image sequence and not as a single frame. For just such an instance, Adobe Premiere has a checkbox to flag inside the **Import** panel:

Figure 13.46 – Importing the Engine output as an image sequence in Adobe Premiere

Perfect! We have done it! We are now able to set high-detailed rendering in Unreal Engine 5 and generate a high-resolution output of our environment shot.

Summary

This was the final chapter of this book. During this incredible journey, we entered the Unreal Engine 5 environment creation world. Starting from the very beginning by installing the Engine on our workstations, we are now able to create stunning environments and craft cinematic shots. And we can do that entirely inside the Engine.

In this last chapter, we introduced the fundamental concepts of real-time rendering by confronting it with the standard offline rendering pipeline. After announcing the pros and cons of both technologies, we went on and started to set the Level Sequence to be rendered by the Engine.

After that, we learned what the **Movie Render Queue** plugin is and how to enable it. We moved on by exploring all the rendering settings the **Movie Render Queue** plugin provides to us, and we created a render config preset, balanced in terms of quality and rendering time, that allowed us to generate a high-resolution output.

After understanding the difference between **Render (Local)** and **Render (Remote)**, we finally exported our image sequence. Last but not least, we learned how to change the frame resolution to avoid a letterbox effect according to the Cine Camera Actor's sensor frame.

In hoping that you have found this book useful and interesting, I want to give you my last two cents. Unreal Engine 5 and, in general, real-time technologies are growing fast, and even more studios are converting their pipeline to a real-time rendering workflow (I'm talking about VFX and animation studios – game studios already use real-time technologies). That means only one thing: an increasing need for Unreal Engine artists.

We have started from the very beginning to make everyone able to approach Unreal Engine 5 in the easiest way possible and allow everyone to gain knowledge to build a convincing portfolio and open the door to a new career in the real-time world.

Index

www.packtpub.com

Subscribe to our online digital library for full access to over 7,000 books and videos, as well as industry leading tools to help you plan your personal development and advance your career. For more information, please visit our website.

Why subscribe?

- Spend less time learning and more time coding with practical eBooks and Videos from over 4,000 industry professionals

- Improve your learning with Skill Plans built especially for you

- Get a free eBook or video every month

- Fully searchable for easy access to vital information

- Copy and paste, print, and bookmark content

Did you know that Packt offers eBook versions of every book published, with PDF and ePub files available? You can upgrade to the eBook version at packtpub.com and as a print book customer, you are entitled to a discount on the eBook copy. Get in touch with us at customercare@packtpub.com for more details.

At www.packtpub.com, you can also read a collection of free technical articles, sign up for a range of free newsletters, and receive exclusive discounts and offers on Packt books and eBooks.

Other Books You May Enjoy

If you enjoyed this book, you may be interested in these other books by Packt:

Unreal Engine 5 Shaders and Effects Cookbook – Second Edition

Brais Brenlla Ramos

ISBN: 978-1-83763-308-1

- Leverage the capabilities of Lumen and Nanite to create breathtaking experiences
- Attain proficiency in the rendering pipeline of Unreal Engine to develop real-time graphics
- Utilize the physically based rendering pipeline to achieve photorealistic rendering across multiple scenes
- Explore the Material Editor to build complex materials and textures and achieve a high level of detail
- Optimize your materials to run seamlessly on multiple platforms
- Understand the various nodes and functions required to create impressive visual effects

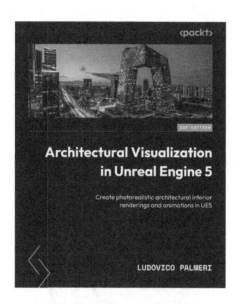

Architectural Visualization in Unreal Engine 5

Ludovico Palmeri

ISBN: 978-1-83763-976-2

- Import and organize assets and prepare a project structure
- Ensure a smooth architectural visualization workflow to quickly iterate your project
- Experiment with different types of lighting techniques to create photorealistic scenarios
- Create and tweak materials using the material editor, and apply them to models in the scene
- Use post-processing features to achieve cinematic-quality visuals
- Discover how to use blueprints to create interactive elements
- Build captivating animations with the sequencer tool
- Optimize your scene for smooth real-time performance

Packt is searching for authors like you

If you're interested in becoming an author for Packt, please visit `authors.packtpub.com` and apply today. We have worked with thousands of developers and tech professionals, just like you, to help them share their insight with the global tech community. You can make a general application, apply for a specific hot topic that we are recruiting an author for, or submit your own idea.

Hi!

I am Giovanni Visai author of *Cinematic Photoreal Environments in Unreal Engine 5*. I really hope you enjoyed reading this book and found it useful for increasing your productivity and efficiency using Unreal Engine.

It would really help me (and other potential readers!) if you could leave a review on Amazon sharing your thoughts on this book.

Go to the link below or scan the QR code to leave your review:

`https://packt.link/r/1803244119`

Your review will help me to understand what's worked well in this book, and what could be improved upon for future editions, so it really is appreciated.

Best Wishes,

Giovanni Visai

Download a free PDF copy of this book

Thanks for purchasing this book!

Do you like to read on the go but are unable to carry your print books everywhere?

Is your eBook purchase not compatible with the device of your choice?

Don't worry, now with every Packt book you get a DRM-free PDF version of that book at no cost.

Read anywhere, any place, on any device. Search, copy, and paste code from your favorite technical books directly into your application.

The perks don't stop there, you can get exclusive access to discounts, newsletters, and great free content in your inbox daily

Follow these simple steps to get the benefits:

1. Scan the QR code or visit the link below

https://packt.link/free-ebook/9781803244112

2. Submit your proof of purchase
3. That's it! We'll send your free PDF and other benefits to your email directly

Made in the USA
Coppell, TX
09 June 2024

33287447R00302